A·N·N·U·A·L EDITIONS

W9-BOL-793

American History Volume 1

Nineteenth Edition

Pre-Colonial Through Reconstruction

EDITOR

Robert James Maddox (Emeritus)

Pennsylvania State University
University Park

Robert James Maddox, distinguished historian and professor emeritus of American history at Pennsylvania State University, received a B.S. from Fairleigh Dickinson University in 1957, an M.S. from the University of Wisconsin in 1958, and a Ph.D. from Rutgers in 1964. He has written, reviewed, and lectured extensively, and is widely respected for his interpretations of presidential character and policy.

Contemporary Learning Series

2460 Kerper Blvd., Dubuque, IA 52001

Visit us on the Internet
http://www.mhcls.com

Credits

1. **The New Land**
   Unit photo—Courtesy of the Library of Congress.
2. **Revolutionary America**
   Unit photo—Library of Congress, Prints and Photographs Division
3. **National Consolidation and Expansion**
   Unit photo—Texas Energy Museum, Beaumont, TX
4. **The Civil War and Reconstruction**
   Unit photo—Courtesy of the Library of Congress.

Copyright

Cataloging in Publication Data
Main entry under title: Annual Editions: American History Vol. 1: Pre-Colonial Through Reconstruction. 19e.
1. United States —History—Periodicals. 2. United States—Historiography—Periodicals. 3. United States—Civilization—
Periodicals. I. 1. Maddox, Robert James, comp. II Title: American History, Vol. One: Pre-Colonial Through Reconstruction.
ISBN-13: 978–0–07–351600–4   ISBN-10: 0–07–351600-7   973'.05   ISSN 0733–3560

Nineteenth Edition

Cover image © Library of Congress, Prints and Photographs Division
Printed in the United States of America   1234567890QPDQPD9876   Printed on Recycled Paper

Editors/Advisory Board

Members of the Advisory Board are instrumental in the final selection of articles for each edition of ANNUAL EDITIONS. Their review of articles for content, level, currentness, and appropriateness provides critical direction to the editor and staff. We think that you will find their careful consideration well reflected in this volume.

Preface

In publishing ANNUAL EDITIONS we recognize the enormous role played by the magazines, newspapers, and journals of the public press in providing current, first-rate educational information in a broad spectrum of interest areas. Many of these articles are appropriate for students, researchers, and professionals seeking accurate, current material to help bridge the gap between principles and theories and the real world. These articles, however, become more useful for study when those of lasting value are carefully collected, organized, indexed, and reproduced in a low-cost format, which provides easy and permanent access when the material is needed. That is the role played by ANNUAL EDITIONS.

The most important lesson history teaches us, one scholar has written, is that there are no lessons in history. He was criticizing the tendency of some to claim that studying earlier times can produce a "usable past" to help us cope with present-day problems. Because all historical events are unique, according to this view, attempts to dredge guiding principles from earlier periods are not much different from reading tea leaves. Usually, it must be added, such efforts are made in service of some agenda whether explicitly stated or simply assumed. And, as often happens, individuals can draw entirely different "lessons" from the same event.

In a broader sense, however, studying history (aside from being fascinating in its own right) can provide us with valuable perspectives not available to those who are ignorant of the past. If there is any constant in history it is the inevitability of change. One article in this volume, for instance, deals with the Salem "witch trials" of the 1690s. How, the modern reader, might ask, could otherwise intelligent people have believed that evil spirits possess individuals causing them to bark like dogs or to assume different shapes? It is obvious that the people caught up in the situation were victims of some sort of mass hysteria. It was not so at the time, and at least most of those involved sincerely believed that their actions were appropriate to meet the perceived threat. One does not have to accept any particular set of assumptions in order to try to understand why people acted as they did in given situations.

Practically all of our beliefs about the "natural" order of things have undergone radical changes over the course of history and will continue to do so. Consider the role of women in society. Once referred to as the "weaker sex," women were assumed (at least by men) to be suited by nature to marry, maintain households, bear children, and to defer to their husbands on matters outside the home. Owing to their delicate natures and superior morality, the conventional wisdom held, they should be kept isolated from the rough-and-tumble world of politics or the sordid dealings of the marketplace. The most obvious symbol of that mindset was the question of suffrage. Women had to fight for decades (and often were vilified for their efforts) to achieve the most elementary benefit of citizenship: The right to vote. Although there is still a long way to go, women now hold high positions in government and business and serve as police officers, construction workers, and soldiers.

The list may be extended indefinitely to almost every group. Blacks were once considered (by whites) to be lazy, shiftless, and lacking intelligence. Those of Italian descent were seen to be emotional and prone to violence. Jews were said to be avaricious and untrustworthy in financial matters. Unfortunately many of these stereotypes still exist. Most people who lived during the time period, covered in this volume, would have been astounded had they been able to peer into the future and see the status members of such groups have attained.

A pitfall similar to the ransacking of history for "lessons" is the arrogance of "presentism." This is the practice, all too common, of judging the past by modern-day standards and beliefs. How easy it is to look at an earlier period and condemn or patronize people for their ignorance and prejudices. It is certain that two hundred years from now many of our own assumptions will seem equally wrong-headed or quaint. One does not have to accept such obvious evils as slavery, for instance, to seek to understand how individuals could have justified as "natural" such an abominable institution. The study of immigration patterns provides another case in point. Some of those today who view with such alarm the "threat" of immigration from Latin America and Asia might be surprised to find that their own European ancestors were similarly vilified during the 19th and early 20th Century.

Annual Editions: American History, Volume 1 is designed for non-specialized survey courses. We have attempted to present a fair sampling of articles that incorporate newer approaches to the study of history as well as more traditional ones. The sources from which these essays have been taken for the most part are intended for the general reader: they require no particular expertise to understand them and they avoid the dreadful jargon that permeates so much of modern academic writing.

This volume contains a number of features designed to aid students, researchers, and professionals. These include a *topic guide* for locating articles on specific subjects; the *table of contents abstracts* that summarize each essay, with key concepts in bold italics; and a comprehensive *index*. Articles are organized into four units, each preceded by an overview that provides a background for informed reading of the articles, emphasizes critical issues, and presents *Key Point questions*.

Every revision of *Annual Editions: American History, Volume 1* replaces about fifty percent of the previous articles with new ones. We try to update and improve the quality of the sections, and we would like to consider alternatives that we may have missed. If you find an article that you think merits inclusion in the next edition, please send it to us (or at least send us the citation, so that the editor can track it down for consideration). We welcome your comments about the readings in this volume, and a postage-paid reader response card is included in the back of the book for your convenience. Your suggestions will be carefully considered and greatly appreciated.

Robert James Maddox

Editor

To the Instructor

What Are Annual Editions?

Annual Editions are an exciting instructional tool—diverse and challenging. Published by *McGraw-Hill Contemporary Learning Series*, **Annual Editions** are a collection of the most interesting, informative, and important articles related to a particular subject area. Every article has been carefully chosen from a broad range of the public press including magazines, professional journals, and major newspapers. The latest information and research is supplemented by enduring articles, essays, and important basic documents.

Annual Editions bring topics into sharp focus for students—a focus that no textbook can match! The amount of material available in today's information-oriented society is staggering. With **Annual Editions**, the problem of how to sort through this mountain of material is solved. **Annual Editions** offer the *best* from the current press. Every article has been carefully reviewed by professional editors, an academic editor, and an **Annual Editions** Advisory Board. **Annual Editions** are updated annually, which guarantees that students are exposed to the latest ideas that are shaping the discipline.

How Can Annual Editions Be Used in the Classroom?

- For Supplementary Reading
- As a Basic Text
- As a Starting Point for Student Research
- For Independent Study
- For Extra Credit or Make-Up Work

This handy supplement provides a wealth of ideas for easily and inexpensively incorporating the best of the current press into your instructional program.

Ask your McGraw-Hill Sales Representative for a copy today!

ISBN 0-07-254844-4

Instructor's Resource Guide for American History volume 1

A comprehensive Instructor's Resource Guide is available for every **Annual Editions** title. A must for every teacher, this instructor's resource guide contains:

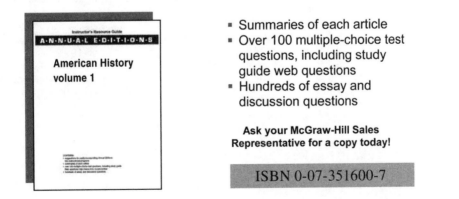

- Summaries of each article
- Over 100 multiple-choice test questions, including study guide web questions
- Hundreds of essay and discussion questions

Ask your McGraw-Hill Sales Representative for a copy today!

ISBN 0-07-351600-7

Additionally, the question bank in each Instructor's Resource Guide is also available online as an ASCII text file. To access these banks, contact your McGraw-Hill Sales Representative or refer to the title page of the *printed* Instructor's Resource Guide; there you will find a boxed paragraph explaining how to access the ASCII file for the book you are using. The steps are quite simple: enter our Internet address, **http://www.mhcls.com/irg**, then enter the unique 5-digit password that is provided at the beginning of the guide.

Contents

UNIT 1
The New Land

The concepts in bold italics are developed in the article. For further expansion, please refer to the Topic Guide and the Index.

UNIT 2
Revolutionary America

The concepts in bold italics are developed in the article. For further expansion, please refer to the Topic Guide and the Index.

UNIT 3
National Consolidation and Expansion

Unit Overview **90**

The concepts in bold italics are developed in the article. For further expansion, please refer to the Topic Guide and the Index.

The concepts in bold italics are developed in the article. For further expansion, please refer to the Topic Guide and the Index.

UNIT 4
The Civil War and Reconstruction

The concepts in bold italics are developed in the article. For further expansion, please refer to the Topic Guide and the Index.

The concepts in bold italics are developed in the article. For further expansion, please refer to the Topic Guide and the Index.

Topic Guide

This topic guide suggests how the selections in this book relate to the subjects covered in your course. You may want to use the topics listed on these pages to search the Web more easily.

On the following pages a number of Web sites have been gathered specifically for this book. They are arranged to reflect the units of this *Annual Edition*. You can link to these sites by going to the student online support site at *http://www.mhcls.com/online/.*

ALL THE ARTICLES THAT RELATE TO EACH TOPIC ARE LISTED BELOW THE BOLD-FACED TERM.

Internet References

The following internet sites have been carefully researched and selected to support the articles found in this reader. The easiest way to access these selected sites is to go to our student online support site at *http://www.mhcls.com/online/*.

AE: American History, Volume 1

The following sites were available at the time of publication. Visit our Web site—we update our student online support site regularly to reflect any changes.

General Sources

American Historical Association (AHA)
http://www.theaha.org

This site is an excellent source for data on just about any topic in American history. All affiliated societies and publications are noted, and AHA and its links provide material related to myriad fields of history.

American Studies Web
http://www.georgetown.edu/crossroads/asw/

Links to a wealth of Internet resources for research in American studies, from agriculture and rural development, to government, to race and ethnicity, are provided on this eclectic site.

Harvard's John F. Kennedy School of Government
http://www.ksg.harvard.edu

Starting from this home page, click on a huge variety of links to information about American history, politics, and government, including material related to debates of enduring issues.

History Net
http://www.thehistorynet.com/

Supported by the National Historical Society, this site provides information on a wide range of topics. The articles are of excellent quality, and the site has book reviews and even special interviews. It is also frequently updated.

Library of Congress
http://www.loc.gov

Examine this Web site to learn about the extensive resource tools, library services/resources, exhibitions, and databases available through the Library of Congress in many different subfields of government studies.

Smithsonian Institution
http://www.si.edu

This site provides access to the enormous resources of the Smithsonian, which holds some 140 million artifacts and specimens for "the increase and diffusion of knowledge." Learn about American social, cultural, economic, and political history from a variety of viewpoints here.

UNIT 1: The New Land

Early America
http://earlyamerica.com/earlyamerica/index.html

Explore the "amazing world of early America" through early media data at this site. Topics include Pages of the Past, Lives of Early Americans, Notable Women of Early America, Milestone Events, and many more.

1492: An Ongoing Voyage/Library of Congress
http://lcweb.loc.gov/exhibits/1492/

Displays examining the causes and effects of Columbus's voyages to the Americas can be accessed on this Web site. "An Ongoing Voyage" explores the rich mixture of societies coexisting in five areas of this hemisphere before European arrival. It then surveys the polyglot Mediterranean world at a dynamic turning point in its development.

The Mayflower Web Page
http://www.mayflowerhistory.com

The Mayflower Web Page represents thousands of hours of research, organization, and typing; it grows daily. Visitors include everyone from kindergarten students to history professors, from beginning genealogists to some of the most noted genealogists in the nation. The site is a merger of two fields: genealogy and history.

UNIT 2: Revolutionary America

The Early America Review
http://www.earlyamerica.com/review/

Explore the Web site of *The Early America Review*, an electronic journal of fact and opinion on the people, issues, and events of eighteenth-century America. The quarterly is of excellent quality.

House of Representatives
http://www.house.gov

This home page of the House of Representatives will lead to information about current and past House members and agendas, the legislative process, and so on.

National Center for Policy Analysis
http://www.public-policy.org/web.public-policy.org/index.php

Through this site, click onto links to read discussions of an array of topics that are of major interest in the study of American history, from regulatory policy and privatization to economy and income.

Supreme Court/Legal Information Institute
http://supct.law.cornell.edu/supct/index.html

Open this site for current and historical information about the Supreme Court. The archive contains a collection of nearly 600 of the most historical decisions of the Court.

U.S. Senate
http://www.senate.gov

The U.S. Senate home page will lead to information about current and past Senate members and agendas, legislative activities, committees, and so on.

The White House
http://www.whitehouse.gov/

Visit the home page of the White House for direct access to information about commonly requested federal services, the White House Briefing Room, and all of the presidents and vice presidents. The "Virtual Library" provides an opportunity to search White House documents,listen to speeches, and view photos.

The World of Benjamin Franklin
http://www.fi.edu/franklin/

Presented by the Franklin Institute Science Museum, "Benjamin Franklin: Glimpses of the Man" is an excellent multimedia site that lends insight into Revolutionary America.

www.mhcls.com/online/

UNIT 3: National Consolidation and Expansion

Consortium for Political and Social Research
http://www.icpsr.umich.edu

At this site, the inter-university Consortium for Political and Social Research offers materials in various categories of historical social, economic, and demographic data. Presented is a statistical overview of the United States beginning in the late eighteenth century.

Department of State
http://www.state.gov

View this site for an understanding into the workings of what has become a major U.S. executive branch department. Links explain what the Department does, what services it provides, what it says about U.S. interests around the world, and much more information.

Mystic Seaport
http://amistad.mysticseaport.org/

The complex Amistad case is explored in a clear and informative manner on this online educational site. It places the event in the context of the issues of the 1830s and 1840s.

Social Influence Website
http://www.workingpsychology.com/intro.html

The nature of persuasion, compliance, and propaganda is the focus of this Web site, with many practical examples and applications. Students of such topics as the roles of public opinion and media influence in policy making should find these discussions of interest.

University of Virginia Library
http://www.lib.virginia.edu/exhibits/lewis_clark/

Created by the University of Virginia Library, this site examines the famous Lewis and Clark exploration of the trans-Mississippi west.

Women in America
http://xroads.virginia.edu/~HYPER/DETOC/FEM/

Providing the views of women travelers from the British Isles, France, and Germany on the lives of American women, this valuable site covers the years between 1820 and 1842 and is informative, stimulating, and highly original.

Women of the West
http://www.wowmuseum.org/

The home page of the Women of the West Museum offers several interesting links that include stories, poems, educational resources, and exhibits.

UNIT 4: The Civil War and Reconstruction

The American Civil War
http://sunsite.utk.edu/civil-war/warweb.html

This site provides a wide-ranging list of data on the Civil War. Some examples of the data that are available are: army life, the British connection, diaries/letters/memos, maps, movies, museums, music, people, photographs, and poetry.

Anacostia Museum/Smithsonian Institution
http://www.si.edu/archives/historic/anacost.htm

This is the home page of the Center for African American History and Culture of the Smithsonian Institution, which is expected to become a major repository of information. Explore its many avenues.

Abraham Lincoln Online
http://www.netins.net/showcase/creative/lincoln.html

This is a well-organized, high-quality site that will lead to substantial material about Abraham Lincoln and his era.

Discussions among Lincoln scholars can be accessed in the Mailbag section.

Gilder Lehrman Institute of American History
http://www.digitalhistory.uh.edu/index.cfm?

Click on the links to various articles presented through this Web site to read outstanding, first-hand accounts of slavery in America through the period of Reconstruction.

Secession Era Editorials Project
http://history.furman.edu/~benson/docs/dsmenu.htm

Newspaper editorials of the 1800s regarding events leading up to secession are presented on this Furman University site. When complete, this distinctive project will offer additional features that include mapping, statistical tools, and text analysis.

We highly recommend that you review our Web site for expanded information and our other product lines. We are continually updating and adding links to our Web site in order to offer you the most usable and useful information that will support and expand the value of your Annual Editions. You can reach us at: *http://www.mhcls.com/annualeditions/*.

UNIT 1
The New Land

Unit Selections

Key Points to Consider

- What new evidence is there that American Indians may have come to the Western Hemisphere at a much earlier time than previously thought?

- Conventional wisdom has it that the Americas in 1491 were only sparsely populated by native peoples who led a simple existence. How does new research challenge this view? What implications does it have for contemporary environmental issues?

- Consider the trials of Ann Hibben and Anne Hutchinson in the 1630s. What were they accused of, and how does this shed light on the condition of women at the time?

- Discuss the constitution William Penn framed for the colony he wished to establish. What aspects of it were "progressive" for the time?

- How did prevailing attitudes and beliefs lead to the persecution of at least 150 people during the Salem Witch trials of 1692?

- Some historians have likened the treatment of American Indians to Hitler's destruction of European Jews during World War II. Is this valid? What are the similarities, and what are the differences?

Student Website

www.mhcls.com/online

Internet References

Further information regarding these websites may be found in this book's preface or online.

Early America
http://earlyamerica.com/earlyamerica/index.html

1492: An Ongoing Voyage/Library of Congress
http://lcweb.loc.gov/exhibits/1492/

The Mayflower Web Page
http://www.mayflowerhistory.com

When we use terms such as "the age of discovery" with regard to European exploration of the Western Hemisphere, we are really looking at only one side of a coin. Native peoples had been here for a long time and scarcely needed to be discovered. From their standpoint, the period might better be known as "the age of devastation." Expeditions mounted first by the Spanish, then the English and French, had profound and often disastrous effects on them. Partly this was due to military operations conducted by the invaders, some of whom deliberately slaughtered anyone who stood in the way of acquiring jewels and precious metals. Even more devastating were the communicable diseases the Europeans brought with them against which the native peoples had no immunity. The expansion of Europe came at the expense of millions of inhabitants of the so-called "New World."

At one time it was believed that those we call "native" Americans came from Asia tens of thousands of years ago across an ancient land bridge to Alaska. The article, "America's First Immigrants," shows that this view has been challenged by archaeologists who have found settlements dating from at least 1,000 years before this migration is supposed to have taken place. "1491" discusses population estimates and what is known about their societies, and suggests that they had a much larger impact on the environment than previously believed.

Although those who settled in what is now the United States never established powerful empires such as the Aztecs in Mexico or the Incas in Peru, some developed sophisticated social and economic organizations. "Mystery Tribe" describes one such group that flourished for 600 years in what is now the state of Utah. This civilization began to disintegrate about A.D. 1250 and within a century ceased to exist. Experts disagree as to the causes of this collapse.

The English arrived late in the process. Some of them were searching for precious metals and jewels as had their predecessors. Others came to settle permanently, either to escape religious persecution or merely to build new lives for themselves. "Rethinking Modern History" shows how the relatively new discipline of Historical Archaeology provides insights that can not be found in written records, particularly with regard to disenfranchised groups such as women and Afro-Americans. "Before New England" tells the story of the Popham settlement in what is now the State of Maine. Because it was abandoned after only a few years and therefore remained uncontaminated by later generations, this short-lived colony has provided historical archaelogists with many insights about the lives of ordinary people struggling to survive. "Instruments of Seduction: A Tale of Two Women" discusses the trials of two women in Boston during the 1630s. Their "crime" was to violate Puritan teachings about society, particularly with regard to the proper role of women.

"Penning a Legacy" is about William Penn's acquisition of a grant of land that would become Pennsylvania. Penn crafted a constitution that provided for religious freedom, voting rights,

and penal reform. He also hoped that the Native Americans already in the area would permit the new settlers to live among them "with your love and consent." "Blessed and Bedeviled: Tales of Remarkable Providences in Puritan New England" treats the notorious Salem "witch trials" of 1692. "Providences issued from God," Puritans believed, "and witchcraft from the devil, and they marked the tide of battle between the forces of Christ and the minions of Satan." The idea that witches walked among them was widely held.

The last selection in this unit is "Were American Indians the Victims of Genocide?" Its author presents an unsparing account of the atrocities committed against Indians, but denies that this should be compared with Adolf Hitler's genocide against European Jews. The difference lies in intent. Although some individuals may have thought that "the only good Indian was a dead one," neither the European governments nor the United States ever followed a policy of systematic extermination. Between 75 and 90 percent of Indian deaths were caused inadvertently by diseases whites carried with them.

America's First Immigrants

You were probably taught that the hemisphere's first people came from Siberia across a long-gone land bridge. Now a sea route looks increasingly likely, from Asia or even Europe.

Evan Hadingham

ABOUT FOUR MILES from the tiny cattle town of Florence, Texas, a narrow dirt road winds across parched limestone, through juniper, prickly pear and stunted oaks, and drops down to a creek. A lush parkland of shade trees offers welcome relief from the 100-degree heat of summer. Running beside the creek for almost half a mile is a swath of chipped, gray stone flakes and soil blackened by cooking fires—thousands of years of cooking fires. This blackened earth, covering 40 acres and almost six feet thick in places, marks a settlement dating back as far as the last ice age 13,000 years ago, when mammoths, giant sloths and saber-toothed cats roamed the North American wilderness.

Since archaeologists began working here systematically seven years ago, they have amassed an astonishing collection of early prehistoric artifacts—nearly half a million so far. Among these are large, stone spearheads skillfully flaked on both sides to give an elegant, leaf-shaped appearance. These projectiles, found by archaeologists throughout North America and as far south as Costa Rica, are known as Clovis points, and their makers, who lived roughly 12,500 to 13,500 years ago, are known as Clovis people, after the town in New Mexico near where the first such point was identified some seven decades ago.

A visit to the Gault site—named after the family who owned the land when the site was first investigated in 1929—along the cottonwood- and walnut-shaded creek in central Texas raises two monumental questions. The first, of course, is, Who were these people? The emerging answer is that they were not simple-minded big-game hunters as they have often been depicted. Rather, they led a less nomadic and more sophisticated life than previously believed.

The second question—Where did they come from?— lies at the center of one of archaeology's most contentious debates. The standard view holds that Clovis people were the first to enter the Americas, migrating from Siberia 13,500 years ago by a now-submerged land bridge across

the Bering Strait. This view has been challenged recently by a wide range of discoveries, including an astonishingly well-preserved site in South America predating the supposed migration by at least 1,000 years.

Researchers delving into the origins question have sought to make sense of archaeological finds far and wide, from Canada, California and Chile; from Siberia; and even, most controversially, from France and Spain. The possibility that the first people in the Americas came from Europe is the boldest proposal among a host of new ideas. According to University of Texas at Austin archaeologist Michael Collins, the chief excavator of the Gault site, "you couldn't have a more exciting time to be involved in the whole issue of the peopling of the Americas. You can't write a paper on it and get it published before it's out of date. Surprising new finds keep rocking the boat and launching fresh waves of debate."

IN 1932, AN AMERICAN ARCHAEOLOGIST IDENTIFIED DISTINCTIVE SPEARHEADS ASSOCIATED WITH MAMMOTH SKELETONS NEAR CLOVIS, NEW MEXICO. THE DISCOVERY SUPPORTED AN EMERGING REALIZATION THAT HUMANS LIVED WITH NOW-EXTINCT ICE AGE CREATURES IN NORTH AMERICA.

FOR PREHISTORIC PEOPLE, one of the chief attractions of the Gault site was a knobby outcrop of a creamy white rock called chert, which conceals a fine, gray, glasslike interior. If struck expertly with a stone or antler tool, the rock fractures in predictable ways, yielding a Clovis point. In the end, each spearhead has distinctive grooves, or "flutes," at the base of each face and was fastened to a wooden shaft with sinew and resin.

Ancient pollen and soil clues tell archaeologists that the climate in Clovis-era Texas was cooler, drier and more tolerable than today's summertime cauldron. Vast herds of mammoths, bison, horses and antelope ranged on the grasslands southeast of Gault, and deer and turkeys inhabited the plateau to the west. Along the creek, based on bones found at the site, Clovis hunters also preyed on frogs, birds, turtles and other small animals.

This abundance of food, coupled with the exceptional quality of the chert, drew people to Gault in large numbers. Unlike the majority of Clovis sites, which are mostly the remains of temporary camps, Gault appears to have been inhabited over long periods and thus contradicts the standard view that Clovis people were always highly mobile, nomadic hunters. Michael Collins says that of the vast quantity of artifacts found at the site, many are tool fragments, left behind by people who'd stuck around long enough to not only break their tools but also to salvage and rework them. The researchers also unearthed a seven by seven foot square of gravel—perhaps the floor of a house—and a possible well, both signs of more than a fleeting presence.

Another clue was concealed on a 13,000-year-old Clovis blade about the size of a dinner knife. Under a magnifying lens, the blade's edge is glossy, rounded and smooth. Marilyn Shoberg, a stone tool analyst on the Gault team who has experimented with replicas, says the blade's polish probably came from cutting grass. This grass could have been used for basketry, bedding, or thatching to make roofs for huts.

Among the most unusual and tantalizing finds at the Gault site are a hundred or so fragments of limestone covered with lightly scratched patterns. Some resemble nets or basketry, while a few could be simple outlines of plants or animals. Although only a dozen can be securely dated to Clovis times, these enigmatic rocks are among the very few surviving artworks from ice age America.

"What this site tells us is that Clovis folks were not specialized mammoth hunters constantly wandering over the landscape," says Collins. "They exploited a variety of animals, they had tools for gathering plants and working wood, stone and hide, and they stayed through the useful life of those tools. All these things are contrary to what you'd expect if they were highly nomadic, dedicated big-game hunters." Yet this unexpected complexity sheds only a feeble glimmer on the more contentious issue of where the Clovis people came from and how they got here.

IN THE OLD SCENARIO, still popular in classrooms and picture books, fur-clad hunters in the waning moments of the last ice age, when so much seawater was locked up in the polar ice caps that the sea level was as much as 300 feet lower than today, ventured across a land bridge from Siberia to Alaska. Then, pursuing big game, the hunters trekked south through present-day Canada. They passed down a narrow, 1,000-mile-long treeless corridor bounded by the towering walls of retreating ice sheets until they reached the Great Plains, which teemed with prey. The human population exploded, and the hunters soon drove into extinction some 35 genera of big animals (see box). All of these were supposedly dispatched by the Clovis point, a Stone Age weapon of mass destruction.

DIGGING AT THE GAULT SITE IN CENTRAL TEXAS, ACCORDING TO PROJECT DIRECTOR MICHAEL COLLINS, HAS ALMOST DOUBLED THE NUMBER OF CLOVIS ARTIFACTS EXCAVATED IN NORTH AMERICA. RESEARCHERS THERE HAVE ALSO UNCOVERED EVIDENCE OF ICE AGE ART.

For more than half a century, this plausible, "big-game" theory carried with it an appealing, heroic image. As James Adovasio of Mercyhurst College puts it in his book *The First Americans*, it was as if the ice sheets had parted "like the Red Sea for some Clovis Moses to lead his intrepid band of spear-toting, mammoth-slaying wayfarers to the south." But recent discoveries are indicating that almost everything about the theory could be wrong. For one thing, the latest studies show that the ice-free corridor didn't exist until around 12,000 years ago—too late to have served as the route for the very first people to come to America.

CLOVIS PEOPLE BURIED CACHES OF TOOLS. SOME STASHED POINTS WERE CRAFTED FROM EXOTIC STONE; OTHERS SEEM TOO BIG AND THIN TO HAVE FUNCTIONED AS WEAPONS. ONE CACHE WAS FOUND WITH A CHILD'S BONES, SUGGESTING THAT BURYING TOOLS COULD BE A RITUAL ACT.

Perhaps the strongest ammunition against the old scenario comes from Monte Verde, an archaeological site on a remote terrace, which is today some 40 miles from the Pacific in southern Chile. Here, about 14,500 years ago, a hunting-and-gathering band lived year-round beside a creek in a long, oval hide tent, partitioned with logs. Archaeologist Tom Dillehay of Vanderbilt University began probing Monte Verde in 1977, unearthing the surface of the ancient encampment, complete with wood, plants and even remains of food, all preserved under a layer of waterlogged peat. Dillehay recovered three human footprints, two chunks of uneaten mastodon meat and possibly even traces of herbal medicine (indicated by nonfood plants still used by healers in the Andes). The dating of these extraordinary finds, at least 1,000 years before the earliest Clovis sites in North America, aroused skepticism for two decades until, in 1997, a group of leading archaeologists inspected the site and vindicated Dille-hay's meticulous work.

No such triumph has emerged for any of the dozen or so sites in North America claimed to predate Clovis. But among the most intriguing is a rock overhang in Pennsylvania called Meadowcroft, where a 30-year campaign of excavation suggests that hunters may have reached the Northeast 3,000 or 4,000 years before the Clovis era.

SABER-TOOTHED CATS PROWLED NORTH AMERICA FOR MILLIONS OF YEARS. FOR SOME REASON, THEY DIED OUT ABOUT 13,000 YEARS AGO.

Meanwhile, genetics studies are pointing even more strongly to an early entry into the continent. By analyzing the mitochondrial DNA of living Native Americans, Douglas Wallace, a geneticist at the University of California at Irvine, and his colleagues have identified five distinct lineages that stretch back like family trees. Mitochondria are the cells' energy factories. Their DNA changes very little from one generation to the next, altered only by tiny variations that creep in at a steady and predictable rate. By counting the number of these variations in related lineages, Wallace's team can estimate their ages. When the team applied this technique to the DNA of Native Americans, they reached the stunning conclusion that there were at least four separate waves of prehistoric migration into the Americas, the earliest well over 20,000 years ago.

IF THE FIRST AMERICANS did arrive well before the oldest known Clovis settlements, how did they get here? The most radical theory for the peopling of the New World argues that Stone Age mariners journeyed from Europe around the southern fringes of the great ice sheets in the North Atlantic. Many archaeologists greet this idea with head-shaking scorn, but the proposition is getting harder to dismiss outright.

Dennis Stanford, a Clovis expert at the Smithsonian Institution's Department of Anthropology who delights in prodding his colleagues with unconventional thinking, was a longtime supporter of the land bridge scenario. Then, with the end of the cold war came the chance to visit archaeological sites and museums in Siberia—museums that should have been filled with tools that were predecessors of the Clovis point. "The result was a big disappointment," says Stanford. "What we found was nothing like we expected, and I was surprised that the technologies were so different." Instead of a single leaf-shaped Clovis spearhead, ice age Siberian hunters made projectiles that were bristling with rows of tiny razor-like blades embedded in wooden shafts. To Stanford, that meant no Siberian hunters armed with Clovis technology had walked to the Americas.

Meanwhile, Bruce Bradley, a prehistoric stone tool specialist at Britain's University of Exeter, had noticed a strong resemblance between Clovis points and weapons from ice age Europe. But the idea that the two cultures might be directly connected was heretical. "It certainly wasn't part of the scientific process at that point," Bradley says. "There was no possibility, forget it, don't even think about it." Bradley eventually pursued it to the storerooms of the Musée National de Préhistoire in Les Eyzies-de-Tayac in southwest France, where he pored through boxes of local prehistoric stone tools and waste flakes. "I was absolutely flabbergasted," he recalls. "If somebody had brought out a box of this stuff in the United States and set it down in front of me, I'd have said, 'Man, where did you get all that great Clovis stuff?'" But the material was the work of a culture called the Solutrean that thrived in southwest France and northern Spain during the coldest spell of the ice age, from around 24,000 to 19,000 years ago.

Thousands of years before their successors created the masterworks of Lascaux and Altamira, Solutrean-age artists began painting vivid murals in the depths of caves such as Cougnac and Cosquer. They made delicate, eyed sewing needles out of bone, enabling them to stitch tight-fitting skin garments to repel the cold. They devised the *atlatl*, or spear thrower, a hooked bone or wood handle that extends the reach of the hunter's arm to multiply throwing power. But their most distinctive creation was a stone spearhead shaped like a laurel leaf.

Apart from the absence of a fluted base, the Solutrean laurel leaf strongly resembles the Clovis point and was made using the same, highly skillful flaking technique. Both Clovis and Solutrean stone crafters practiced controlled overshot flaking, which involved trimming one edge by striking a flake off the opposite side, a virtuoso feat of handiwork rarely seen in other prehistoric cultures. To Bradley, "there had to be some sort of historic connection" between the Solutrean and Clovis peoples.

DENNIS STANFORD AND BRUCE BRADLEY SAY THAT SIMILARITIES BETWEEN CLOVIS AND SOLUTREAM FINDS ARE OVERWHELMING.

Critics of the theory point to a yawning gap between the two peoples: roughly 5,000 years divide the end of Solutrean culture and the emergence of Clovis. But Stanford and Bradley say that recent claims of pre-Clovis sites in the southeastern United States may bridge the time gap. In the mid-1990s at Cactus Hill, the remains of an ancient sand dune overlooking the Nottoway River on Virginia's coastal plain, project director Joseph McAvoy dug down a few inches beneath a Clovis layer and uncovered simple stone blades and projectile points associated with a hearth, radiocarbon dated to some 17,000 to 19,000 years ago. This startlingly early date has drawn skeptical fire, but the site's age was recently confirmed by an independent dating technique. Stanford and Bradley suggest that the early people at Cactus Hill were Clovis forerunners who had not yet developed the full-blown Clovis style. They are convinced that many more sites like Cactus Hill

Hunted to Extinction?

At the end of the last ice age, 35 genera of big animals, or "megafauna," went extinct in the Americas, including mammoths, mastodons, giant ground sloths, giant beavers, horses, short-faced bears and saber-toothed cats. Archaeologists have argued for decades that the arrival of hunters wielding Clovis spear points at around the same time was no coincidence. Clovis hunters pursued big game—their signature stone points are found with the bones of mammoths and mastodons at 14 kill sites in North America. Experiments carried out with replica spears thrust into the corpses of circus elephants indicate that the Clovis point could have penetrated a mammoth's hide. And computer simulations suggest that large, slow-breeding animals could have easily been wiped out by hunting as the human population expanded.

But humans might not be entirely to blame. The rapidly cycling climate at the end of the ice age may have changed the distribution of plants that the big herbivores grazed on, leading to a population crash among meat-eating predators too. New research on DNA fragments recovered from ice age bison bones suggests that some species were suffering a slow decline in diversity—probably caused by dwindling populations—long before any Clovis hunters showed up. Indigenous horses are now thought to have died out in Alaska about 500 years before the Clovis era. For mammoths and other beasts who did meet their demise during the Clovis times, many experts believe that a combination of factors—climate change plus pressure from human hunters—drove them into oblivion.

Amid all the debate, one point is clear: the Clovis hunter wasn't as macho as people once thought. Bones at the Gault site in central Texas reveal that the hunters there were feeding on less daunting prey—frogs, birds, turtles and antelope—as well as mammoth, mastodon and bison. As the late, renowned archaeologist Richard (Scotty) MacNeish is said to have remarked, "Each Clovis generation probably killed one mammoth, then spent the rest of their lives talking about it."

large skin-covered canoes, or *umiaks*, which enable them to catch seals, walrus and other sea mammals that abound along the frozen edges of the pack ice. When twilight arrives or storms threaten, the hunters pull their boats up on the ice and camp beneath them. Ronald Brower of the Inupiat Heritage Center in Barrow says, "There's nothing that would have prevented ... people from crossing the Atlantic into the Americas 19,000 years ago. It would be a perfectly normal situation from my perspective."

A different critique of the out-of-Europe theory dismisses the resemblance between Solutrean and Clovis points. Many archaeologists suggest that similarities between Clovis and Solutrean artifacts are coincidental, the result of what they call convergence. "These were people faced with similar problems," says Solutrean expert Lawrence Straus of the University of New Mexico. "And the problems involved hunting large- and medium-sized game with a similar, limited range of raw materials—stone, bone, ivory, antler, wood and sinew. They're going to come up with similar solutions."

More tellingly, in Straus' view, is that he can find little evidence of seafaring technology in the Solutrean sites he has dug in northern Spain. Although rising sea levels have drowned sites on the ice age coastline, Straus has investigated surviving inland cave sites no more than a couple of hours' walk from the beach. "There's no evidence of deep-sea fishing," says Straus, "no evidence of marine mammal hunting, and consequently no evidence, even indirect, for their possession of seaworthy boats."

And David Meltzer, an archaeologist at Southern Methodist University and a critic of the European-origins idea, is struck more by the differences between the Solutrean and Clovis cultures than their similarities—particularly the near-absence of art and personal ornaments from Clovis. Still, he says, the controversy is good for the field. "In the process of either killing or curing" the theory, "we will have learned a whole lot more about the archaeological record, and we'll all come out smarter than we went in."

BESIDES CROSSING THE LAND BRIDGE from Asia and traveling to ice age America from Europe by boat, a third possible entryway is a sea route down the west coast. Using maritime skills later perfected by the Inuit, prehistoric south Asians might have spread gradually around the northern rim of the Pacific in small skin-covered boats. They skirt the southern edge of the Bering land bridge and paddle down the coast of Alaska, dodging calving glaciers and icebergs as they pursue seals and other marine mammals. They keep going all the way to the beaches of Central and South America. They arrive at Monte Verde, inland from the Chilean coast, some 14,500 years ago. Each new generation claims fresh hunting grounds a few miles beyond the last, and in a matter of centuries these first immigrants have populated the entire west coast of the Americas. Soon the hunters start moving inland and, in the north, their descendants become the Clovis people.

will turn up on the East Coast. But the burning question is, Did these ice age Virginians invent the Clovis point all by themselves, or were they descendants of Solutreans who brought the point with them from Europe?

Many archaeologists ridicule the notion that people made an arduous, 3,000-mile journey during the bleakest period of the ice age, when the Atlantic would have been much colder and stormier than today. Stanford believes that traditional Inuit technology suggests otherwise; he has witnessed traditional seagoing skills among Inupiat communities in Barrow, Alaska. Inupiat hunters still build

CLOVIS PEOPLE MAY WELL HAVE REACHED NORTH AMERICA VIA SEA ROUTE. SEALS AND OTHER MARINE PREY MAY HAVE SUSTAINED THEM UNTIL THEY FOUND NEW WORLD HUNTING GROUNDS.

Many archaeologists now accept the west coast theory as a likely solution to the origin of the earliest Americans. On Prince of Wales Island in southeastern Alaska, inside the aptly named On Your Knees Cave, University of South Dakota paleontologist Timothy Heaton and University of Colorado at Boulder archaeologist E. James Dixon recovered an accumulation of animal bones from the last ice age. When mile-high ice sheets still straddled the interior of the continent 17,000 years ago, ringed seals, foxes and seabirds made their home on the island. "Humans could easily have survived there," Heaton says.

The ultimate evidence for the western sea route would be the discovery of pre-Clovis human remains on the coast. No such luck. Dixon and Heaton have found human jaw fragments and other remains in the On Your Knees Cave, but those date to about 11,000 years ago—too recent to establish the theory. And what may be the oldest-known human remains in North America—leg bones found on Santa Rosa Island, off the California coast—are from 13,000 years ago, the heart of the Clovis era. Still, those remains hint that by then people were plying the waters along the Pacific Coast.

IF THE TRAIL of the very earliest Americans remains elusive, so, too, does the origin of the Clovis point. "Although the technology needed to produce a Clovis point was found among other cultures during the ice age," says Ken Tankersley of Northern Kentucky University, "the actual point itself is unique to the Americas, suggesting that it was invented here in the New World." If so, the spearhead would be the first great American invention—the Stone Age equivalent of the Swiss Army Knife, a trademark tool that would be widely imitated. The demand for the weapon and the high-quality stone it required probably encouraged Clovis people to begin long-distance trading and social exchanges. The spearhead may also have delivered a new level of hunting proficiency and this, in turn, would have fueled a population spurt, giving Clovis people their lasting presence in the archaeological record.

Sheltering from the broiling heat under the cottonwoods at Gault, Michael Collins told me of his conviction that the Clovis people who flocked to the shady creek were not pioneers but had profited from a long line of forebears. "Clovis represents the end product of centuries, if not millennia, of learning how to live in North American environments," he said. "The Clovis culture is too widespread, is found in too many environments, and has too much evidence for diverse activities to be the leavings of people just coming into the country." Collins reminded me that his team has investigated less than 10 percent of the enormous site. And archaeologists have barely scratched the surface of a handful of other Gault-size, Clovis-era sites—Williamsburg, in Virginia, for instance, or Shoop, in Pennsylvania. "One thing you can be sure," he said, beaming, "there'll be great new discoveries just around the corner."

Evan Hadingham is the senior science editor of the PBS series NOVA and the author of books on prehistory. PBS will broadcast the NOVA program "America's Stone Age Explorers" November 9.

1491

*Before it became the New World, the Western Hemisphere was vastly more populous
and sophisticated than has been thought—an altogether more salubrious
place to live at the time than, say, Europe. New evidence of both the extent
of the population and its agricultural advancement leads to a remarkable conjecture:
the Amazon rain forest may be largely a human artifact*

BY CHARLES C. MANN

The plane took off in weather that was surprisingly cool for north-central Bolivia and flew east, toward the Brazilian border. In a few minutes the roads and houses disappeared, and the only evidence of human settlement was the cattle scattered over the savannah like jimmies on ice cream. Then they, too, disappeared. By that time the archaeologists had their cameras out and were clicking away in delight.

Below us was the Beni, a Bolivian province about the size of Illinois and Indiana put together, and nearly as flat. For almost half the year rain and snowmelt from the mountains to the south and west cover the land with an irregular, slowly moving skin of water that eventually ends up in the province's northern rivers, which are sub-subtributaries of the Amazon. The rest of the year the water dries up and the bright-green vastness turns into something that resembles a desert. This peculiar, remote, watery plain was what had drawn the researchers' attention, and not just because it was one of the few places on earth inhabited by people who might never have seen Westerners with cameras.

Clark Erickson and William Balée, the archaeologists, sat up front. Erickson is based at the University of Pennsylvania; he works in concert with a Bolivian archaeologist, whose seat in the plane I usurped that day. Balée is at Tulane University, in New Orleans. He is actually an anthropologist, but as native peoples have vanished, the distinction between anthropologists and archaeologists has blurred. The two men differ in build, temperament, and scholarly proclivity, but they pressed their faces to the windows with identical enthusiasm.

---

*Indians were here in
greater numbers than
previously thought, and
they imposed their will on
the landscape. Columbus
set foot in a hemisphere
thoroughly dominated
by humankind.*

Dappled across the grasslands below was an archipelago of forest islands, many of them startlingly round and hundreds of acres across. Each island rose ten or thirty or sixty feet above the floodplain, allowing trees to grow that would otherwise never survive the water. The forests were linked by raised berms, as straight as a rifle shot and up to three miles long. It is Erickson's belief that this entire landscape—30,000 square miles of forest mounds surrounded by raised fields and linked by causeways—was constructed by a complex, populous society more than 2,000 years ago. Balée, newer to the Beni, leaned toward this view but was not yet ready to commit himself.

Erickson and Balée belong to a cohort of scholars that has radically challenged conventional notions of what the Western Hemisphere was like before Columbus. When I went to high school, in the 1970s, I was taught that Indians came to the Americas across the Bering Strait about 12,000 years ago, that they lived for the most part in small, isolated groups, and that they had so little impact on their environment that even after millennia of habitation it remained mostly wilderness. My son picked up the same ideas at his schools. One way to summarize the views of people like Erickson and Balée would be to say that in their opinion this picture of Indian life is wrong in almost every aspect. Indians were here far longer than previously thought, these researchers believe, and in much greater numbers. And they were so successful at imposing their will on the landscape that in 1492 Columbus set foot in a hemisphere thoroughly dominated by humankind.

Given the charged relations between white societies and native peoples, inquiry into Indian culture and history is inevitably contentious. But the recent scholarship is especially controversial. To begin with, some researchers—many but not all from an older generation—deride the new theories as fantasies arising from an almost willful misinterpretation of data and a perverse kind of political correctness. "I have seen no evidence that large numbers of people ever lived in the Beni," says Betty J. Meggers, of the Smithsonian Institution. "Claiming otherwise is just wishful thinking." Similar criticisms apply to many of the new scholarly claims about Indians, according to Dean R. Snow, an anthropologist at Pennsylvania State University. The problem is that "you can make the meager evidence from the ethnohistorical record tell you anything you want," he says. "It's really easy to kid yourself."

More important are the implications of the new theories for today's ecological battles. Much of the environmental movements is animated, consciously or not, by what William Denevan, a geographer at the University of Wisconsin, calls, polemically, "the pristine myth"—the belief that the Americas in 1491 were an almost unmarked, even Edenic land, "untrammeled by man," in the words of the Wilderness Act of 1964, one of the nation's first and most important environmental laws. As the University of Wisconsin historian William Cronon has written, restoring this long-ago, putatively natural state is, in the view of environmentalists, a task that society is morally bound to undertake. Yet if the new view is correct and the work of humankind was pervasive, where does that leave efforts to restore nature?

The Beni is a case in point. In addition to building up the Beni mounds for houses and gardens, Erickson says, the Indians trapped fish in the seasonally flooded grassland. Indeed, he says, they fashioned dense zigzagging networks of earthen fish weirs between the causeways. To keep the habitat clear of unwanted trees and undergrowth, they regularly set huge areas on fire. Over the centuries the burning created an intricate ecosystem of fire-adapted plant species dependent on native pyrophilia. The current inhabitants of the Beni still burn, although now it is to maintain the savannah for cattle. When we flew over the ar-

eas, the dry season had just begun, but mile-long lines of flame were already on the march. In the charred areas behind the fires were the blackened spikes of trees—many of them one assumes, of the varieties that activists fight to save in other parts of Amazonia.

After we landed, I asked Balée, Should we let people keep burning the Beni? Or should we let the trees invade and create a verdant tropical forest in the grasslands, even if one had not existed here for millennia?

Balée laughed. "You're trying to trap me, aren't you?" he said.

LIKE A CLUB BETWEEN THE EYES

According to family lore, my great-grandmother's great-grandmother's great-grandfather was the first white person hanged in America. His name was John Billington. He came on the *Mayflower*, which anchored off the coast of Massachusetts on November 9, 1620. Billington was not a Puritan; within six months of arrival he also became the first white person in America to be tried for complaining about the police. "He is a knave," William Bradford, the colony's governor, wrote to Billington, "and so will live and die." What one historian called Billington's "troublesome career" ended in 1630, when he was hanged for murder. My family has always said the he was framed—but we *would* say that, wouldn't we?

A few years ago it occurred to me that my ancestor and everyone else in the colony had voluntarily enlisted in a venture that brought them to New England without food or shelter six weeks before winter. Half the 102 people on the *Mayflower* made it through to spring, which to me was amazing. How, I wondered, did they survive?

In his history of Plymouth Colony, Bradford provided the answer: by robbing Indian houses and graves. The *Mayflower* first hove to at Cape Cod. An armed company staggered out. Eventually it found a recently deserted Indian settlement. The newcomers—hungry, cold, sick—dug up graves and ransacked houses, looking for underground stashes of corn. "And sure it was God's good

providence that we found this corn," Bradford wrote, "for else we know not how we should have done." (He felt uneasy about the thievery, though.) When the colonists came to Plymouth, a month later, they set up shop in another deserted Indian village. All through the coastal forest the Indians had "died on heapes, as they lay in their houses," the English trader Thomas Morton noted. "And the bones and skulls upon the several places of their habitations made such a spectacle" that to Morton the Massachusetts woods seemed to be "a new found Golgotha"—the hill of executions in Roman Jerusalem.

To the Pilgrims' astonishment, one of the corpses they exhumed on Cape Cod had blond hair. A French ship had been wrecked there several years earlier. The Patuxet Indians imprisoned a few survivors. One of them supposedly learned enough of the local language to inform his captors that God would destroy them for their misdeeds. The Patuxet scoffed at the threat. But the Europeans carried a disease, and they bequeathed it to their jailers. The epidemic (probably of viral hepatitis, according to a study by Arthur E. Spiess, an archaeologist at the Maine Historic Preservation Commission, and Bruce D. Spiess, the director of clinical research at the Medical College of Virginia) took years to exhaust itself and may have killed 90 percent of the people in coastal New England. It made huge differences to American history. "The good hand of God favored our beginnings," Bradford mused, by "sweeping away great multitudes of the natives… that he might make room for us."

By the time my ancestor set sail on the *Mayflower*, Europeans had been visiting New England for more than a hundred years. English, French, Italian, Spanish, and Portuguese mariners regularly plied the coastline, trading what they could, occasionally kidnapping the inhabitants for slaves. New England, the Europeans saw, was thickly settled and well defended. In 1605 and 1606 Samuel de Champlain visited Cape Cod, hoping to establish a French base. He abandoned the idea. Too many people already lived there. A year later Sir Ferdinando Gorges—British despite his name—tried to establish an English community in southern Maine. It had more founders than Plymouth and seems to have been better organized. Confronted by numerous well-armed local Indians, the settlers abandoned the project within months. The Indians at Plymouth would surely have been an equal obstacle to my ancestor and his ramshackle expedition had disease not intervened.

Faced with such stories, historians have long wondered how many people lived in the Americas at the time of contact. "Debated since Columbus attempted a partial census on Hispaniola in 1496," William Denevan has written, this "remains one of the great inquiries of history." (In 1976 Denevan assembled and edited an entire book on the subject, *The Native Population of the Americas in 1492*.) The first scholarly estimate of the indigenous population was made in 1910 by James Mooney, a distinguished ethnographer at the Smithsonian Institution. Combing through old documents, he concluded that in 1491 North America had 1.15 million inhabitants. Mooney's glittering reputation ensured that most subsequent researchers accepted his figure uncritically.

That changed in 1966, when Henry F. Dobyns published "Estimating Aboriginal American Population: An Appraisal of Techniques With a New Hemispheric Estimate," in the journal *Current Anthropology*. Despite the carefully neutral title, his argument was thunderous, its impact long-lasting. In the view of James Wilson, the author of *The Earth Shall Weep* (1998), a history of indigenous Americans, Dobyns's colleagues "are still struggling to get out of the crater that paper left in anthropology." Not only anthropologists were affected. Dobyns's estimate proved to be one of the opening rounds in today's culture wars.

Dobyns began his exploration of pre-Columbian Indian demography in the early 1950s, when he was a graduate student. At the invitation of a friend, he spent a few months in northern Mexico, which is full of Spanish-era missions. there he poked through the crumbling leather-bound ledgers in which Jesuits recorded local births and deaths. Right

away he noticed how many more deaths there were. The Spaniards arrived, and then Indians died—in huge numbers at incredible rates. It hit him, Dobyns told me recently, "like a club right between the eyes."

It took Dobyns eleven years to obtain his Ph.D. Along the way he joined a rural-development project in Peru, which until colonial times was the seat of the Incan empire. Remembering what he had seen at the northern fringe of the Spanish conquest, Dobyns decided to compare it with figures for the south. He burrowed into the papers of the Lima cathedral and read apologetic Spanish histories. The Indians in Peru, Dobyns concluded, had faced plagues from the day the conquistadors showed up—in fact, before then: smallpox arrived around 1525, seven years ahead of the Spanish. Brought to Mexico apparently by a single sick Spaniard, it swept south and eliminated more than half the population of the Incan empire. Smallpox claimed the Incan dictator Huayna Capac and much of his family, setting off a calamitous war of succession. So complete was the chaos that Francisco Pizarro was able to seize an empire the size of Spain and Italy combined with a force of 168 men.

Smallpox was only the first epidemic. Typhus (probably) in 1546, influenza and smallpox together in 1558, smallpox again in 1589, diphtheria in 1614, measles in 1618—all ravaged the remains of Incan culture. Dobyns was the first social scientist to piece together this awful picture, and he naturally rushed his findings into print. Hardly anyone paid attention. But Dobyns was already working on a second, related question: If all those people died, how many had been living there to begin with? Before Columbus, Dobyns calculated, the Western Hemisphere held ninety to 112 million people. Another way of saying this is that in 1491 more people lived in the Americas than in Europe.

His argument was simple but horrific. It is well known that Native Americans had no experience with many European diseases and were therefore immunologically unprepared—"virgin soil," in the metaphor of epidemiologists. What Dobyns realized was that such diseases could have swept from the coastlines ini-

tially visited by Europeans to inland areas controlled by Indians who had never seen a white person. The first whites to explore many parts of the Americas may therefore have encountered places that were already depopulated. Indeed, Dobyns argued, they must have done so.

Peru was one example, the Pacific Northwest another. In 1792 the British navigator George Vancouver led the first European expedition to survey Puget Sound. He found a vast charnel house: human remains "promiscuously scattered about the beach, in great numbers." Smallpox, Vancouver's crew discovered, had preceded them. Its few survivors, second lieutenant Peter Puget noted, were "most terribly pitted… indeed many have lost their Eyes." In *Pox Americana* (2001), Elizabeth Fenn, a historian at George Washington University, contends that the disaster on the northwest coast was but a small part of a continental pandemic that erupted near Boston in 1774 and cut down Indians from Mexico to Alaska.

Because smallpox was not endemic in the Americas, colonials, too, had not acquired any immunity. The virus, an equal-opportunity killer, swept through the Continental Army and stopped the drive into Quebec. The American Revolution would be lost, Washington and other rebel leaders feared, if the contagion did to the colonists what it had done to the Indians. "The small Pox! The small Pox!" John Adams wrote to his wife, Abigail. "What shall We do with it?" In retrospect, Fenn says, "One of George Washington's most brilliant moves was to inoculate the army against smallpox during the Valley Forge winter of '78." Without inoculation smallpox could easily have given the United States back to the British.

So many epidemics occurred in the Americas, Dobyns argued, that the old data used by Mooney and his successors represented population nadirs. From the few cases in which before-and-after totals are known with relative certainty, Dobyns estimated that in the first 130 years of contact about 95 percent of the people in the Americas died—the worst demographic calamity in recorded history.

Dobyns's ideas were quickly attacked as politically motivated, a push from the hate-America crowd to inflate the toll of imperialism. The attacks continue to this day. "No question about it, some people want those higher numbers," says Shepard Krech III, a Brown University anthropologist who is the author of *The Ecological Indian* (1999). These people, he says, were thrilled when Dobyns revisited the subject in a book, *Their Numbers Become Thinned* (1983)— and revised his own estimates upward. Perhaps Dobyns's most vehement critic is David Henige, a bibliographer of Africana at the University of Wisconsin, whose *Numbers from Nowhere* (1998) is a landmark in the literature of demographic fulmination. "Suspect in 1966, it is no less suspect nowadays," Henige wrote of Dobyns's work. "If anything, it is worse."

When Henige wrote *Numbers From Nowhere,* the fight about pre-Columbian populations had already consumed forests' worth of trees; his bibliography is ninety pages long. And the dispute shows no sign of abating. More and more people have jumped in. This is partly because the subject is inherently fascinating. But more likely the increased interest in the debate is due to the growing realization of the high political and ecological stakes.

INVENTING BY THE MILLIONS

On May 30, 1539, Hernando de Soto landed his private army near Tampa Bay, in Florida. Soto, as he was called, was a novel figure: half warrior, half venture capitalist. He had grown very rich very young by becoming a market leader in the nascent trade for Indian slaves. The profits had helped to fund Pizarro's seizure of the Incan empire, which had made Soto wealthier still. Looking quite literally for new worlds to conquer, he persuaded the Spanish Crown to let him loose in North America. He spent one fortune to make another. He came to Florida with 200 horses, 600 soldiers, and 300 pigs.

From today's perspective, it is difficult to imagine the ethical system that would justify Soto's actions. For four years his force, looking for gold, wandered through what is now Florida,

Georgia, North and South Carolina, Tennessee, Alabama, Mississippi, Arkansas, and Texas, wrecking almost everything it touched. The inhabitants often fought back vigorously, but they had never before encountered an army with horses and guns. Soto died of fever with his expedition in ruins; along the way his men had managed to rape, torture, enslave, and kill countless Indians. But the worst thing the Spaniards did, some researchers say, was entirely without malice— bring the pigs.

According to Charles Hudson, an anthropologist at the University of Georgia who spent fifteen years reconstructing the path of the expedition, Soto crossed the Mississippi a few miles downstream from the present site of Memphis. It was a nervous passage: the Spaniards were watched by several thousand Indian warriors. Utterly without fear, Soto brushed past the Indian force into what is now eastern Arkansas, through thickly settled land—"very well peopled with large towns," one of his men later recalled, "two or three of which were to be seen from one town." Eventually the Spaniards approached a cluster of small cities, each protected by earthen walls, sizeable moats, and deadeye archers. In his usual fashion, Soto brazenly marched in, stole food, and marched out.

After Soto left, no Europeans visited this part of the Mississippi Valley for more than a century. Early in 1682 whites appeared again, this time Frenchmen in canoes. One of them was Réné-Robert Cavelier, Sieur de la Salle. The French passed through the area where Soto had found cities cheek by jowl. It was deserted—La Salle didn't see an Indian village for 200 miles. About fifty settlements existed in this strip of the Mississippi when Soto showed up, according to Anne Ramenofsky, an anthropologist at the University of New Mexico. By La Salle's time the number had shrunk to perhaps ten, some probably inhabited by recent immigrants. Soto "had a privileged glimpse" of an Indian world, Hudson says. "The window opened and slammed shut. When the French came in and the record opened up again, it was a transformed reality. A civilization crumbled. The question is, how did this happen?"

> *Swine alone can disseminate anthrax, brucellosis, leptospirosis, trichinosis, and tuberculosis. Only a few of Hernando de Soto's pigs would have had to wander off to infect the forest.*

The question is even more complex than it may seem. Disaster of this magnitude suggests epidemic disease. In the view of Ramenofsky and Patricia Galloway, an anthropologist at the University of Texas, the source of the contagion was very likely not Soto's army but its ambulatory meat locker: his 300 pigs. Soto's force itself was too small to be an effective biological weapon. Sicknesses like measles and smallpox would have burned through his 600 soldiers long before they reached the Mississippi. But the same would not have held true for the pigs, which multiplied rapidly and were able to transmit their diseases to wildlife in the surrounding forest. When human beings and domesticated animals live close together, they trade microbes with abandon. Over time mutation spawns new diseases: Avian influenza becomes human influenza, bovine rinderpest becomes measles. Unlike Europeans, Indians did not live in close quarters with animals—they domesticated only the dog, the llama, the alpaca, the guinea pig, and here and there, the turkey and the Muscovy duck. In some ways this is not surprising: the New World had fewer animal candidates for taming than the Old. Moreover, few Indians carry the gene that permits adults to digest lactose, a form of sugar abundant in milk. Non-milk-drinkers, one imagines, would be less likely to work at domesticating milk-giving animals. But this is guesswork. The fact is that what scientists call zoonotic disease was little known in the Americas. Swine alone can disseminate anthrax, brucellosis, leptospirosis, taeniasis, trichinosis, and tuberculosis. Pigs breed exuberantly and can transmit diseases to deer and turkeys. Only a few of

Soto's pigs would have had to wander off to infect the forest.

Indeed, the calamity wrought by Soto apparently extended across the whole Southeast. The Coosa city-states, in western Georgia, and the Caddoan-speaking civilization, centered on the Texas-Arkansas border, disintegrated soon after Soto appeared. The Caddo had had a taste for monumental architecture: public plazas, ceremonial platforms, mausoleums. After Soto's army left, notes Timothy K. Perttula, an archaeological consultant in Austin, Texas, the Caddo stopped building community centers and began digging community cemeteries. Between Soto's and La Salle's visits, Perttula believes, the Caddoan population fell from about 200,000 to about 8,500—a drop of nearly 96 percent. In the eighteenth century the tally shrank further, to 1,400. An equivalent loss today in the population of New York City would reduce it to 56,000—not enough to fill Yankee Stadium. "That's one reason whites think of Indians as nomadic hunters," says Russell Thornton, an anthropologist at the University of California at Los Angeles. "Everything else—all the heavily populated urbanized societies—was wiped out."

Could a few pigs truly wreak this much destruction? Such apocalyptic scenarios invite skepticism. As a rule, viruses, microbes, and parasites are rarely lethal on so wide a scale—a pest that wipes out its host species does not have a bright evolutionary future. In its worst outbreak, from 1347 to 1351, the European Black Death claimed only a third of its victims. (The rest survived, though they were often disfigured or crippled by its effects.) The Indians in Soto's path, if Dobyns, Ramenofsky, and Perttula are correct, endured losses that were incomprehensibly greater.

One reason is that Indians were fresh territory for many plagues, not just one. Smallpox, typhoid, bubonic plague, influenza, mumps, measles, whooping cough—all rained down on the Americas in the century after Columbus. (Cholera, malaria, and scarlet fever came later.) Having little experience with epidemic diseases, Indians had no knowledge of how to combat them. In contrast, Europeans were well versed in the brutal logic of quarantine. They boarded up houses in which plague appeared and fled to the countryside. In Indian New England, Neal Salisbury, a historian at Smith college, wrote in *Manitou and Providence* (1982), family and friends gathered with the shaman at the sufferer's bedside to wait out the illness—a practice that "could only have served to spread the disease more rapidly."

Indigenous biochemistry may also have played a role. The immune system constantly scans the body for molecules that it can recognize as foreign—molecules belonging to an invading virus, for instance. No one's immune system can identify all foreign presences. Roughly speaking, an individual's set of defensive tools is known as his MHC type. Because many bacteria and viruses mutate easily, they usually attack in the form of several slightly different strains. Pathogens win when MHC types miss some of the strains and the immune system is not stimulated to act. Most human groups contain many MHC types; a strain that slips by one person's defenses will be nailed by the defenses of the next. But, according to Francis L. Black, an epidemiologist at Yale University, Indians are characterized by unusually homogeneous MHC types. One out of three South American Indians have similar MHC types; among Africans the corresponding figure is one in 200. The cause is a matter for Darwinian speculation, the effects less so.

In 1966 Dobyns's insistence on the role of disease was a shock to his colleagues. Today the impact of European pathogens on the New World is almost undisputed. Nonetheless, the fight over Indian numbers continues with undiminished fervor. Estimates of the population of North America in 1491 disagree by an order of magnitude—from 18 million, Dobyns's revised figure, to 1.8 million, calculated by Douglas H. Ubelaker, an anthropologist at the Smithsonian. To some "high counters," as David Henige calls them, the low counters' refusal to relinquish the vision of an empty continent is irrational or worse. "Non-Indian 'experts' always want to minimize the size of aboriginal populations," says Lenore Stiffarm, a Native American-education specialist at the University of Saskatchewan. The smaller the numbers of Indians, she believes, the easier it is to regard the continent as having been up for grabs. "It's perfectly acceptable to move into unoccupied land," Stiffarm says. "And land with only a few 'savages' is the next best thing."

"Most of the arguments for the very large numbers have been theoretical," Ubelaker says in defense of low counters. "When you try to marry the theoretical arguments to the data that are available on individual groups in different regions, it's hard to find support for those numbers." Archaeologists, he says, keep searching for the settlements in which those millions of people supposedly lived, with little success. "As more and more excavation is done, one would expect to see more evidence for dense populations than has thus far emerged." Dean Snow, the Pennsylvania State anthropologist, examined Colonial-era Mohawk Iroquois sites and found "no support for the notion that ubiquitous pandemics swept the region." In his view, asserting that the continent was filled with people who left no trace is like looking at an empty bank account and claiming that it must once have held millions of dollars.

The low counters are also troubled by the Dobynsian procedure for recovering original population numbers: applying an assumed death rate, usually 95 percent, to the observed population nadir. Ubelaker believes that the lowest point for Indians in North America was around 1900, when their numbers fell to about half a million. Assuming a 95 percent death rate, the pre-contact population would have been 10 million. Go up one percent, to a 96 percent death rate, and the figure jumps to 12.5 million—arithmetically creating more than two million people from a tiny increase in mortality rates. At 98 percent the number bounds to 25 million. Minute changes in baseline assumptions produce wildly different results.

"It's an absolutely unanswerable question on which tens of thousands of words have been spent to no purpose," Henige says. In 1976 he sat in on a seminar by William Denevan, the Wisconsin geographer. An "epiphanic moment" occurred when he read shortly afterward that scholars had "uncovered" the existence of eight million people in Hispaniola. *Can you just invent millions of people?* he wondered. "We can make of the historical record that there was depopulation and movement of people from internecine warfare and diseases," he says. "But as for how much, who knows? When we start putting numbers to something like that—applying large figures like ninety-five percent—we're saying things we shouldn't say. The number implies a level of knowledge that's impossible."

Nonetheless, one must try—or so Denevan believes. In his estimation the high counters (though not the highest counters) seem to be winning the argument, at least for now. No definitive data exist, he says, but the majority of the extant evidentiary scraps support their side. Even Henige is no low counter. When I asked him what he thought the population of the Americas was before Columbus, he insisted that any answer would be speculation and made me promise not to print what he was going to say next. Then he named a figure that forty years ago would have caused a commotion.

To Elizabeth Fenn, the smallpox historian, the squabble over numbers obscures a central fact. Whether one million or 10 million or 100 million died, she believes, the pall of sorrow that engulfed the hemisphere was immeasurable. Languages, prayers, hopes, habits, and dreams—entire ways of life hissed away like steam. The Spanish and the Portuguese lacked the germ theory of disease and could not explain what was happening (let alone stop it). Nor can we explain it; the ruin was too long ago and too all-encompassing. In the long run, Fenn says, the consequential finding is not that many people died but that many people once lived. The Americas were filled with a stunningly diverse assortment of peoples who had knocked about the continents for millennia. "You have to wonder," Fenn says. "What were all those people *up* to in all that time?"

BUFFALO FARM

In 1810 Henry Brackenridge came to Cahokia, in what is now southwest Illinois, just across the Mississippi from St. Louis. Born close to the frontier, Brack-

enridge was a budding adventure writer; his *Views of Louisiana,* published three years later, was a kind of nineteenth-century *Into Thin Air,* with terrific adventure but without tragedy. Brackenridge had an eye for archaeology, and he had heard that Cahokia was worth a visit. When he got there, trudging along the desolate Cahokia River, he was "struck with a degree of astonishment." Rising from the muddy bottomland was a "stupendous pile of earth," vaster than the Great Pyramid at Giza. Around it were more than a hundred smaller mounds, covering an area of five square miles. At the time, the area was almost uninhabited. One can only imagine what passed through Brackenridge's mind as he walked alone to the ruins of the biggest Indian city north of the Rio Grande.

To Brackenridge, it seemed clear that Cahokia and the many other ruins in the Midwest had been constructed by Indians. It was not so clear to everyone else. Nineteenth-century writers attributed them to, among others, the Vikings, the Chinese, the "Hindoos," the ancient Greeks, the ancient Egyptians, lost tribes of Israelites, and even straying bands of Welsh. (This last claim was surprisingly widespread; when Lewis and Clark surveyed the Missouri, Jefferson told them to keep an eye out for errant bands of Welsh-speaking white Indians.) The historian George Bancroft, dean of his profession, was a dissenter: the earthworks, he wrote in 1840, were purely natural formations.

Bancroft changed his mind about Cahokia, but not about Indians. To the end of his days he regarded them as "feeble barbarians, destitute of commerce and of political connection." His characterization lasted, largely unchanged, for more than a century. Samuel Eliot Morison, the winner of two Pulitzer Prizes, closed his monumental *European Discovery of America* (1974) with the observation that Native Americans expected only 'short and brutish lives, void of hope for any future." As late as 1987 *American History: A Survey,* a standard high school textbook by three well-known historians, described the Americas before Columbus as "empty of mankind and its works." The story of Europeans in the New World, the book explained, "is the story

of the creation of a civilization where none existed."

Alfred Crosby, a historian at the University of Texas, came to other conclusions. Crosby's *The Columbian Exchange: Biological Consequences of 1492* caused almost as much of a stir when it was published, in 1972, as Henry Dobyns's calculation of Indian numbers six years earlier, though in different circles. Crosby was a standard names-and-battles historian who became frustrated by the random contingency of political events. "Some trivial thing happens and you have this guy winning the presidency instead of that guy," he says. He decided to go deeper. After he finished his manuscript, it sat on his shelf—he couldn't find a publisher willing to be associated with his new ideas. It took him three years to persuade a small editorial house to put it out. *The Columbian Exchange* has been in print ever since; a companion, *Ecological Imperialism: The Biological Expansion of Europe, 900–1900,* appeared in 1986.

Human history, in Crosby's interpretation, is marked by two world-altering centers of invention: the Middle East and central Mexico, where Indian groups independently created nearly all of the Neolithic innovations, writing included. The Neolithic Revolution began in the Middle East about 10,000 years ago. In the next few millennia humankind invented the wheel, the metal tool, and agriculture. The Sumerians eventually put these inventions together, added writing, and became the world's first civilization. Afterward Sumeria's heirs in Europe and Asia frantically copied one another's happiest discoveries; innovations ricocheted from one corner of Eurasia to another, stimulating technological progress. Native Americans, who had crossed to Alaska before Sumeria, missed out on the bounty. "They had to do everything on their own," Crosby says. Remarkably, they succeeded.

When Columbus appeared in the Caribbean, the descendants of the world's two Neolithic civilizations collided, with overwhelming consequences for both. American Neolithic development occurred later than that of the Middle East, possibly because the Indians needed more time to build up the requisite population density. Without beasts of burden they could not capitalize on the wheel (for individual workers on uneven terrain skids are nearly as effective as carts for hauling), and they never developed steel. But in agriculture they handily outstripped the children of Sumeria. Every tomato in Italy, every potato in Ireland, and every hot pepper in Thailand came from this hemisphere. Worldwide, more than half the crops grown today were initially developed in the Americas.

Maize, as corn is called in the rest of the world, was a triumph with global implications. Indians developed an extraordinary number of maize varieties for different growing conditions, which meant that the crop could and did spread throughout the planet. Central and Southern Europeans became particularly dependent on it; maize was the staple of Serbia, Romania, and Moldavai by the nineteenth century. Indian crops dramatically reduced hunger, Crosby says, which led to an Old World population boom.

In the Aztec capital Tenochtitlán the Spaniards gawped like hayseeds at the side streets, ornately carved buildings, and markets bright with goods from hundreds of miles away.

Along with peanuts and manioc, maize came to Africa and transformed agriculture there, too. "The probability is that the population of Africa was greatly increased because of maize and other American Indian crops," Crosby says. "Those extra people helped make the slave trade possible." Maize conquered Africa at the time when introduced diseases were leveling Indian societies. The Spanish, the Portuguese, and the British were alarmed by the death rate among Indians, because they wanted to exploit them as workers. Faced with a labor shortage, the Europeans turned their eyes to Africa. The continent's quarrelsome

societies helped slave traders to siphon off millions of people. The maize-fed population boom, Crosby believes, let the awful trade continue without pumping the well dry.

Back home in the Americas, Indian agriculture long sustained some of the world's largest cities. The Aztec capital of Tenochtitlán dazzled Hernán Cortés in 1519; it was bigger than Paris, Europe's greatest metropolis. The Spaniards gawped like hayseeds at the wide streets, ornately carved buildings, and markets bright with goods from hundreds of miles away. They had never before seen a city with botanical gardens, for the excellent reason that none existed in Europe. The same novelty attended the force of a thousand men that kept the crowded streets immaculate. (Streets that weren't ankle-deep in sewage! The conquistadors had never heard of such a thing.) Central America was not the only locus of prosperity. Thousands of miles north, John Smith, of Pocahontas fame, visited Massachusetts in 1614, before it was emptied by disease, and declared that the land was "so planted with Gardens and Corne fields, and so well inhabited with a goodly, strong and well proportioned people... [that] I would rather live here than any where."

Smith was promoting colonization, and so had reason to exaggerate. But he also knew the hunger, sickness, and oppression of European life. France—"by any standards a privileged country," according to its great historian, Fernand Braudel—experienced seven nationwide famines in the fifteenth century and thirteen in the sixteenth. Disease was hunger's constant companion. During epidemics in London the dead were heaped onto carts "like common dung" (the simile is Daniel Defoe's) and trundled through the streets. The infant death rate in London orphanages, according to one contemporary source, was 88 percent. Governments were harsh, the rule of law arbitrary. The gibbets poking up in the background of so many old paintings were, Braudel observed, "merely a realistic detail."

The Earth Shall Weep, James Wilson's history of Indian America, puts the comparison bluntly: "the western hemisphere was larger, richer, and more populous than Europe." Much of it was freer, too. Europeans, accustomed to the serfdom that thrived from Naples to the Baltic Sea, were puzzled and alarmed by the democratic spirit and respect for human rights in many Indian societies, especially those in North America. In theory, the sachems of New England Indian groups were absolute monarchs. In practice, the colonial leader Roger Williams wrote, "they will not conclude of ought... unto which the people are averse."

Pre-1492 America wasn't a disease-free paradise, Dobyns says, although in his "exuberance as a writer," he told me recently, he once made that claim. Indians had ailments of their own, notably parasites, tuberculosis, and anemia. The daily grind was wearing; life-spans in America were only as long as or a little longer than those in Europe, if the evidence of indigenous graveyards is to be believed. Nor was it a political utopia—the Inca, for instance, invented refinements to totalitarian rule that would have intrigued Stalin. Inveterate practitioners of what the historian Francis Jennings described as "state terrorism practiced horrifically on a huge scale," the Inca ruled so cruelly that one can speculate that their surviving subjects might actually have been better off under Spanish rule.

I asked seven anthropologists, archaeologists, and historians if they would rather have been a typical Indian or a typical European in 1491. Every one chose to be an Indian.

I asked seven anthropologists, archaeologists, and historians if they would rather have been a typical Indian or a typical European in 1491. None was delighted by the question, because it required judging the past by the standards of today—a fallacy disparaged as "presentism" by social scientists. But every one chose to be an Indian. Some early colonists gave the same answer. Horrifying the leaders of Jamestown and Plymouth, scores of English ran off to live with the Indians. My ancestor shared their desire, which is what led to the trumped-up murder charges against him—or that's what my grandfather told me, anyway.

As for the Indians, evidence suggests that they often viewed Europeans with disdain. The Hurons, a chagrined missionary reported, thought the French possessed "little intelligence in comparison to themselves." Europeans, Indians said, were physically weak, sexually untrustworthy, atrociously ugly, and just plain dirty. (Spaniards, who seldom if ever bathed, were amazed by the Aztec desire for personal cleanliness.) A Jesuit reported that the "Savages" were disgusted by handkerchiefs: "They say, we place what is unclean in a fine white piece of linen, and put it away in our pockets as something very precious, while they throw it upon the ground." The Micmac scoffed at the notion of French superiority. If Christian civilization was so wonderful, why were its inhabitants leaving?

Like people everywhere, Indians survived by cleverly exploiting their environment. Europeans tended to manage land by breaking it into fragments for farmers and herders. Indians often worked on such a grand scale that the scope of their ambition can be hard to grasp. They created small plots, as Europeans did (about 1.5 million acres of terraces still exist in the Peruvian Andes), but they also reshaped entire landscapes to suit their purposes. A principal tool was fire, used to keep down underbrush and create the open, grassy conditions favorable for game. Rather than domesticating animals for meat, Indians retooled whole ecosystems to grow bumper crops of elk, deer, and bison. The first white settlers in Ohio found forests as open as English parks—they could drive carriages through the woods. Along the Hudson River the annual fall burning lit up the banks for miles on end; so flashy was the show that the Dutch in New Amsterdam boated upriver to goggle at the blaze like children at fireworks. In North America, Indian torches had their biggest impact on the Midwestern prairie,

much or most of which was created and maintained by fire. Millennia of exuberant burning shaped the plains into vast buffalo farms. When Indian societies disintegrated, forest invaded savannah in Wisconsin, Illinois, Kansas, Nebraska, and the Texas Hill Country. Is it possible that the Indians changed the Americas more than the invading Europeans did? "The answer is probably yes for most regions for the next 250 years or so" after Columbus. William Denevan wrote, "and for some regions right up to the present time."

Amazonia has become the emblem of vanishing wilderness—an admonitory image of untouched Nature. But the rain forest itself may be a cultural artifact—that is, an artificial object.

When scholars first began increasing their estimates of the ecological impact of Indian civilization, they met with considerable resistance from anthropologists and archaeologists. Over time the consensus in the human sciences changed. Under Denevan's direction, Oxford University Press has just issued the third volume of a huge catalogue of the "cultivated landscapes" of the Americas. This sort of phrase still provokes vehement objection—but the main dissenters are now ecologists and environmentalists. The disagreement is encapsulated by Amazonia, which has become *the* emblem of vanishing wilderness—an admonitory image of untouched Nature. Yet recently a growing number of researchers have come to believe that Indian societies had an enormous environmental impact on the jungle. Indeed, some anthropologists have called the Amazon forest itself a cultural artifact—that is, an artificial object.

GREEN PRISONS

Northern visitors' first reaction to the storied Amazon rain forest is often

disappointment. Ecotourist brochures evoke the immensity of Amazonia but rarely dwell on its extreme flatness. In the river's first 2,900 miles the vertical drop is only 500 feet. The river oozes like a huge runnel of dirty metal through a landscape utterly devoid of the romantic crags, arroyos, and heights that signify wilderness and natural spectacle to most North Americans. Even the animals are invisible, although sometimes one can hear the bellow of monkey choruses. To the untutored eye—mine, for instance—the forest seems to stretch out in a monstrous green tangle as flat and incomprehensible as a printed circuit board.

The area east of the lower-Amazon town of Santarém is an exception. A series of sandstone ridges several hundred feet high reach down from the north, halting almost at the water's edge. Their tops stand drunkenly above the jungle like old tombstones. Many of the caves in the buttes are splattered with ancient petroglyphs—renditions of hands, stars, frogs, and human figures, all reminiscent of Miró, in overlapping red and yellow and brown. In recent years one of these caves, La Caverna da Pedra Pintada (Painted Rock Cave), has drawn attention in archaeological circles.

Wide and shallow and well lit, Painted Rock Cave is less thronged with bats than some of the other caves. The arched entrance is twenty feet high and lined with rock paintings. Out front is a sunny natural patio suitable for picnicking, edged by a few big rocks. People lived in this cave more than 11,000 years ago. They had no agriculture yet, and instead ate fish and fruit and built fires. During a recent visit I ate a sandwich atop a particularly inviting rock and looked over the forest below. The first Amazonians, thought, must have done more or less the same thing.

In college I took an introductory anthropology class in which I read *Amazonia: Man and Culture in a Counterfeit Paradise* (1971), perhaps the most influential book ever written about the Amazon, and one that deeply impressed me at the time. Written by Betty J. Meggers, the Smithsonian archaeologist, *Amazonia* says that the apparent lushness of the rain forest is a sham. The soils are poor and can't hold nutrients—the jungle flora exists only because it snatches up everything worthwhile before it leaches away in the rain. Agriculture, which depends on extracting the wealth of the soil, therefore faces inherent ecological limitations in the wet desert of Amazonia.

As a result, Meggers argued, Indian villages were forced to remain small—any report of "more than a few hundred" people in permanent settlements, she told me recently, "makes my alarm bells go off." Bigger, more complex societies would inevitably overtax the forest soils, laying waste to their own foundations. Beginning in 1948 Meggers and her late husband, Clifford Evans, excavated a chiefdom on Marajó, an island twice the size of New Jersey that sits like a gigantic stopper in the mouth of the Amazon. The Marajóara, they concluded, were failed offshoots of a sophisticated culture in the Andes. Transplanted to the lush trap of the Amazon, the culture choked and died.

Green activists saw the implication: development in tropical forests destroys both the forests and their developers. Meggers's account had enormous public impact—*Amazonia* is one of the wellsprings of the campaign to save rain forests.

Then Anna C. Roosevelt, the curator of archaeology at Chicago's Field Museum of Natural History, re-excavated Marajó. Her complete report, *Moundbuilders of the Amazon* (1991), was like the anti-matter version of *Amazonia.* Marajó, she argued, was "one of the outstanding indigenous cultural achievements of the New World," a powerhouse that lasted for more than a thousand years, had "possibly well over 100,000" inhabitants, and covered thousands of square miles. Rather than damaging the forest, Marajó's "earth construction" and "large, dense populations" had *improved* it: the most luxuriant and diverse growth was on the mounds formerly occupied by the Marajóara. "If you listened to Meggers's theory, these places should have been ruined," Roosevelt says.

Meggers scoffed at Roosevelt's "extravagant claims," "polemical tone," and "defamatory remarks." Roosevelt, Meggers argued, had committed the beginner's error of mistaking a site that had

been occupied many times by small, unstable groups for a single, long-lasting society. "[Archaeological remains] build up on areas of half a kilometer or so," she told me, "because [shifting Indian groups] don't land exactly on the same spot. The decorated types of pottery don't change much over time, so you can pick up a bunch of chips and say, 'Oh, look, it was all one big site!' Unless you know what you're doing, of course." Centuries after the conquistadors, "the myth of El Dorado is being revived by archaeologists," Meggers wrote last fall in the journal *Latin American Antiquity,* referring to the persistent Spanish delusion that cities of gold existed in the jungle.

The dispute grew bitter and personal; inevitable in a contemporary academic context, it has featured vituperative references to colonialism, elitism, and employment by the CIA. Meanwhile, Roosevelt's team investigated Painted Rock Cave. On the floor of the cave what looked to me like nothing in particular turned out to be an ancient midden: a refuse heap. The archaeologists slowly scraped away sediment, traveling backward in time with every inch. When the traces of human occupation vanished, they kept digging. ("You always go a meter past sterile," Roosevelt says.) A few inches below they struck the charcoal-rich dirt that signifies human habitation—a culture, Roosevelt said later, that wasn't supposed to be there.

For many millennia the cave's inhabitants hunted and gathered for food. But by about 4000 years ago they were growing crops—perhaps as many as 140 of them, according to Charles R. Clement, an anthropological botanist at the Brazilian National Institute for Amazonian Research. Unlike Europeans, who planted mainly annual crops, the Indians, he says, centered their agriculture on the Amazon's unbelievably diverse assortment of trees: fruits, nuts, and palms. "It's tremendously difficult to clear fields with stone tools," Clement says. "If you can plant trees, you get twenty years of productivity out of your work instead of two or three."

Planting their orchards, the first Amazonians transformed large swaths of the river basin into something more pleasing to human beings. In a widely cited article

from 1989, William Balée, the Tulane anthropologist, cautiously estimated that about 12 percent of the nonflooded Amazon forest was of anthropogenic origin—directly or indirectly created by human beings. In some circles this is now seen as a conservative position. "I basically think it's all human-created," Clement told me in Brazil. He argues that Indians changed the assortment and density of species throughout the region. So does Clark Erickson, the University of Pennsylvania archaeologist, who told me in Bolivia that the lowland tropical forests of South America are among the finest works of art on the planet. "Some of my colleagues would say that's pretty radical," he said, smiling mischievously. According to Peter Stahl, an anthropologist at the State University of New York at Binghamton, "lots" of botanists believe that "what the eco-imagery would like to picture as a pristine, untouched Urwelt [primeval world] in fact has been managed by people for millennia." The phrase "built environment," Erickson says, "applies to most, if not all, Neotropical landscapes."

"Landscape" in this case is meant exactly—Amazonian Indians literally created the ground beneath their feet. According to William I. Woods, a soil geographer at Southern Illinois University, ecologists' claims about terrible Amazonian land were based on very little data. In the late 1990s Woods and others began careful measurements in the lower Amazon. They indeed found lots of inhospitable terrain. But they also discovered swaths of *terra preta*—rich, fertile "black earth" that anthropologists increasingly believe was created by human beings.

Terra preta, Woods guesses, covers at least 10 percent of Amazonia, an area the size of France. It has amazing properties, he says. Tropical rain doesn't leach nutrients from *terra preta* fields; instead the soil, so to speak, fights back. Not far from Painted Rock Cave is a 300-acre area with a two-foot layer of *terra preta* quarried by locals for potting soil. The bottom third of the layer is never removed, workers there explain, because over time it will re-create the original soil layer in its initial thickness. The reason, scientists suspect, is that *terra preta* is generated by a special suite of micro-organisms that resists depletion. "Apparently," Woods and the Wisconsin geographer Joseph M. McCann argued in a presentation last summer, "at some threshold level… dark earth attains the capacity to perpetuate—even *regenerate* itself—thus behaving more like a living 'super'-organism than an inert material."

In as yet unpublished research the archaeologists Eduardo Neves, of the University of São Paulo; Michael Heckenberger, of the University of Florida; and other colleagues examined *terra preta* in the upper Xingu, a huge southern tributary of the Amazon. Not all Xingu cultures left behind this living earth, they discovered. But the ones that did generated it rapidly—suggesting to Woods that *terra preta* was created deliberately. In a process reminiscent of dropping microorganism-rich starter into plain dough to create sourdough bread, Amazonian peoples, he believes, inoculated bad soil with a transforming bacterial charge. Not every group of Indians there did this, but quite a few did, and over an extended period of time.

When Woods told me this, I was so amazed that I almost dropped the phone. I ceased to be articulate for a moment and said things like "wow" and "gosh." Woods chuckled at my reaction, probably because he understood what was passing through my mind. Faced with an ecological problem, I was thinking, the Indians *fixed* it. They were in the process of terraforming the Amazon when Columbus showed up and ruined everything.

Scientists should study the microorganisms in *terra preta,* Woods told me, to find out how they work. If that could be learned, maybe some version of Amazonian dark earth could be used to improve the vast expanses of bad soil that cripple agriculture in Africa—a final gift from the people who brought us tomatoes, corn, and the immense grasslands of the Great Plains.

"Betty Meggers would just die if she heard me saying this," Woods told me. "Deep down her fear is that this data will be misused." Indeed, Meggers's recent *Latin American Antiquity* article charged that archaeologists who say the Amazon can support agriculture are effectively

telling "developers [that they] are entitled to operate without restraint." Resuscitating the myth of El Dorado, in her view, "makes us accomplices in the accelerating pace of environmental degradation." Doubtless there is something to this—although, as some of her critics responded in the same issue of the journal, it is difficult to imagine greedy plutocrats "perusing the pages of *Latin American Antiquity* before deciding to rev up the chain saws." But the new picture doesn't automatically legitimize paving the forest. Instead it suggests that for a long time big chunks of Amazonia were used nondestructively by clever people who knew tricks we have yet to learn.

Environmentalists want to preserve as much of the world's land as possible in a putatively intact state. But "intact" may turn out to mean "run by human beings for human purposes."

I visited Painted Rock Cave during the river's annual flood, when it wells up over its banks and creeps inland for miles. Farmers in the floodplain build houses and barns on stilts and watch pink dolphins sport from their doorsteps. Ecotourists take shortcuts by driving motorboats through the drowned forests. Guys in dories chase after them, trying to sell sacks of incredibly good fruit.

All of this is described as "wilderness" in the tourist brochures. It's not, if researchers like Roosevelt are correct. Indeed, they believe that fewer people may be living there now than in 1491. Yet when my boat glided into the trees, the forest shut out the sky like the closing of an umbrella. Within a few hundred years the human presence seemed to vanish. I felt alone and small, but in a way that was curiously like feeling exalted. If that place was not wilderness, how should I think of it? Since the fate of the forest is in our hands, what should be our goal for its future?

NOVEL SHORES

Hernando de Soto's expedition stomped through the Southeast for four years and apparently never saw bison. More than a century later, when French explorers came down the Mississippi, they saw "a solitude unrelieved by the faintest trace of man," the nineteenth-century historian Francis Parkman wrote. Instead the French encountered bison, "grazing in herds on the great prairies which then bordered the river."

To Charles Kay, the reason for the buffalo's sudden emergence is obvious. Kay is a wildlife ecologist in the political-science department at Utah State University. In ecological terms, he says, the Indians were the "keystone species" of American ecosystems. A keystone species, according to the Harvard biologist Edward O. Wilson, is a species "that affects the survival and abundance of many other species." Keystone species have a disproportionate impact on their ecosystems. Removing them, Wilson adds, "results in a relatively significant shift in the composition of the [ecological] community."

When disease swept Indians from the land, Kay says, what happened was exactly that. The ecological ancien régime collapsed, and strange new phenomena emerged. In a way this is unsurprising; for better or worse, humankind is a keystone species everywhere. Among these phenomena was a population explosion in the species that the Indians had kept down by hunting. After disease killed off the Indians, Kay believes, buffalo vastly extended their range. Their numbers more than sextupled. The same occurred with elk and mule deer. "If the elk were here in great numbers all this time, the archaeological sites should be chock-full of elk bones," Kay says. "But the archaeologists will tell you the elk weren't there." On the evidence of middens the number of elk jumped about 500 years ago.

Passenger pigeons may be another example. The epitome of natural American abundance, they flew in such great masses that the first colonists were stupefied by the sight. As a boy, the explorer Henry Brackenridge saw flocks "ten miles in width, by one hundred and twenty in length." For hours the birds darkened the sky from horizon to horizon. According to Thomas Neumann, a consulting archaeologist to Lilburn, Georgia, passenger pigeons "were incredibly dumb and always roosted in vast hordes, so they were very easy to harvest." Because they were readily caught and good to eat, Neumann says, archaeological digs should find many pigeon bones in the pre-Columbian strata of Indian middens. But they aren't there. The mobs of birds in the history books, he says, were "outbreak populations—always a symptom of an extraordinarily disrupted ecological system."

Throughout eastern North America the open landscape seen by the first Europeans quickly filled in with forest. According to William Cronon, of the University of Wisconsin, later colonists began complaining about how hard it was to get around. (Eventually, of course, they stripped New England almost bare of trees.) When Europeans moved west, they were preceded by two waves: one of disease, the other of ecological disturbance. The former crested with fearsome rapidity; the later sometimes took more than a century to quiet down. Far from destroying pristine wilderness, European settlers bloodily *cre-*

ated it. By 1800 the hemisphere was chockablock with new wilderness. If "forest primeval" means a woodland unsullied by the human presence, William Denevan has written, there was much more of it in the late eighteenth century than in the early sixteenth.

Cronon's *Changes in the Land: Indians, Colonists, and the Ecology of New England* (1983) belongs on the same shelf as works by Crosby and Dobyns. But it was not until one of his articles was excerpted in *The New York Times* in 1995 that people outside the social sciences began to understand the implications of this view of Indian history. Environmentalists and ecologists vigorously attacked the anti-wilderness scenario, which they described as infected by postmodern philosophy. A small academic brouhaha ensued, complete with hundreds of footnotes. It precipitated *Reinventing Nature?* (1995), one of the few academic critiques of postmodernist philosophy written largely by biologists. *The Great New Wilderness Debate* (1998), another lengthy book on the subject, was edited by two philosophers who earnestly identified themselves as "Euro-American men [whose] cultural legacy is patriarchal Western civiliza-

tion in its current postcolonial, globally hegemonic form."

It is easy to tweak academics for opaque, self-protective language like this. Nonetheless, their concerns were quite justified. Crediting Indians with the role of keystone species has implications for the way the current Euro-American members of that keystone species manage the forests, watersheds, and endangered species of America. Because a third of the United States is owned by the federal government, the issue inevitably has political ramifications. In Amazonia, fabled storehouse of biodiversity, the stakes are global.

Guided by the pristine myth, mainstream environmentalists want to preserve as much of the world's land as possible in a putatively intact state. But "intact," if the new research is correct, means "run by human beings for human purposes." Environmentalists dislike this, because it seems to mean that anything goes. In a sense they are correct. Native Americans managed the continent as they saw fit. Modern nations must do the same. If they want to return as much of the landscape as possible to its 1491 state, they will have to find it within themselves to create the world's largest garden.

From *The Atlantic Monthly,* March 2002, pp. 41-53. © 2002 by Charles Cameron Mann. Reprinted by permission of the Balkan Agency, Inc.

Mystery Tribe

What happened to the Fremont Indians?
New discoveries may tell their tale at last

Betsy Carpenter

For rent: secure, high-rise dwelling; light, airy rooms; spectacular views; in Utah's striking canyon country.

If archaeologists doubled as real-estate agents, that might be how they would describe the vertiginous, cliff-top settlements in a remote canyon known as Range Creek. (The term "fixer-upper" could be used, too.) But before they could attract tenants, they would have to explain why the previous occupants packed up in a hurry about 700 years ago, leaving arrows scattered on the ground and a granary still holding corn and rye.

The demise of the Fremont Indians is one of North American archaeology's most enduring mysteries. The group, which flourished for 600 years in the rugged terrain between the Rockies and the Sierra Nevada, were adaptable and surprisingly diverse: Some lived in semisubterranean "pit houses," others in rock shelters. They farmed but also hunted and foraged for food. Yet despite their adaptability, things went south for the Fremont around A.D. 1250. Within a century, their culture had virtually vanished.

So, what became of them? The Range Creek site, unveiled this year, holds important clues. The ruins are not visually spectacular like those of the Anasazi, the Fremont's master-builder neighbors to the south. Still, Range Creek is astonishingly pristine and so should provide a rare window into the daily lives—and fears—of these early Americans.

Remote. Range Creek escaped both the predations of looters and the excavations of archaeologists thanks in large part to local rancher Waldo Wilcox, who guarded the site for over half a century until 2001 when he sold it for $2.5 million. (The ranch is now state land.) But its inaccessibility also helped preserve the hundreds of ruins, sprawling across thousands of acres, 34 axle-crunching miles from the closest stretch of unbroken pavement, over a serpentine thriller of a mountain pass.

Researchers have just begun surveying the canyon, but already the ruins are raising tantalizing questions, says archaeologist Jerry Spangler, author of a recent book on the Fremont called *Horned Snakes and Axle Grease.* The stubby circular remains of some pit houses, for instance, are 30 feet in diameter—three times as large as the typical Fremont pit house. Archaeologists have long thought of the Fremont as simple farmers who lived in small family groups, says Spangler. But the Range Creek mini-mansions suggest that some lived with extended families or had strong enough bonds with other families to build communal structures for ceremonial or other purposes.

Range Creek may also reveal more about the relationship between the Anasazi and the Fremont, who have long suffered by comparison with them. Until now, it has been thought that the two groups didn't interact much. But at Range Creek, almost all the settlements are littered with Anasazi as well as Fremont pottery. (The two are easy to tell apart: While the Fremont mostly made utilitarian gray pots, the Anasazi crafted ornate black-and-white ceramics, among other types.) Archaeologists aren't sure what to make of this mingling. One intriguing possibility, however, is that the two groups did, in fact, trade with each other and that evidence of these dealings was expunged from other Fremont ruins by early relic hunters who selectively stole the fancier Anasazi ceramics.

WHAT REMAINS. The Fremont (c. 700-1300) left behind rock art and potsherds in what is now Utah, but little is really known about them—or why they disappeared.

Like the Anasazi, the Fremont raised corn, beans, and squash, but they relied more heavily on wild foods, probably trekking every year between fields near creeks and rivers and foraging grounds. The Fremont left behind distinctive baskets, trapezoidal-shaped clay figurines, and rock art of unparalleled beauty and complexity. "The Anasazi have some interesting rock art," says Spangler, "but the Fremont were absolutely brilliant artists."

War? Although archaeologists are generally reluctant to read too much into rock art, some venture to say that panels in nearby Nine Mile Canyon may give clues as to the demise of the Fremont. "Some appear to depict warfare quite graphically," says Utah state archaeologist Kevin Jones. There are, for example, panels with images of people apparently wielding weapons and shields. Jones also sees evidence of strife in the little granaries tucked way up high into rock faces at Range Creek and the ruins of dwellings perched on pinnacles 900 feet above the canyon floor. "We've had to use technical climbing gear to get to some of these spots," he says.

What had the Fremont climbing the walls? Researchers are still piecing together the story, but the archaeological record shows that the Anasazi ran into trouble about the same time as the Fremont, suggesting, says Jones, "that something was occurring on a large scale across North America." One stress was undoubtedly a drought that began in A.D. 1270 and lasted 25 years. Another may have been the new groups—including ancestors of the Paiute and Ute peoples—moving into their arid territory, competing for plant and animal resources. "When people are starving and looking for ways to survive," says archaeologist David Madsen, author of *Exploring the Fremont*, "there's almost always violence."

Researchers already know how it all turned out: By the time Europeans arrived, the new crowd was in residence, and nearly all traces of the Fremont had disappeared. But what about the last act? Warfare and famine undoubtedly claimed many Fremont. But there's a debate about the fate of the rest of them. Shawn Carlyle, an adjunct professor of anthropology at the University of Utah, believes that, like the Anasazi, many Fremont picked up and moved south, where they became the historic Pueblo people. He has analyzed ancient DNA from Anasazi and Fremont skeletons and found that it is more closely related to DNA from modern-day Pueblos than that from Northern Paiutes.

Madsen also believes that the remnant Fremont moved on. "The sudden replacement of classic Fremont artifacts by different kinds of basketry, pottery, and art styles historically associated with Utah's contemporary native inhabitants suggests that Fremont peoples were for the most part pushed out of the region," he writes. Kevin Jones envisions a somewhat happier ending. He thinks some Fremont families survived on their lands by reverting to full-time hunting and gathering. "Imagine if one day you or I had to leave our homes and strike out on our own," he says. "A thousand years from now, it would look like we'd disappeared when, in fact, we were just doing something different."

---

*With **Paul Foy** in Range Creek, Utah*

Before New England

Richard L. Pflederer visits the site of the first short-lived English colony in Maine set up in competition with Jamestown in Virginia, and considers a remarkable map of it drawn by one of the colonists.

Richard L. Pflederer

IN LATE SEPTEMBER, 1608, a courier arrived at the gates of the Spanish royal residence at Madrid after a journey of several days by road from the coast. He was carrying a dispatch to Philip III from Don Pedro de Zuñiga, Spanish ambassador in London. It contained diplomatic intelligence that he believed would be crucial to Spanish efforts to protect their holdings in North America from encroachment by troublesome British competitors. Twenty years had passed since the unsuccessful attempt by Philip III's father, Philip II, to topple the Protestant Queen of England in the abortive naval invasion known in Spain as the 'Great Enterprise'. Now Elizabeth I was dead, and the crowns of Scotland and England had been united under James VI and I. Spanish unease with the British was now of a more commercial than religious nature, but relations were strained nonetheless, and the ambassador was assiduous in keeping his monarch up to date with worrying developments on both sides of the Atlantic; the previous year he had protested to James about the nascent English colonies of Virginia, and also urged Philip to take action against them—though the King chose not to act on his advice.

The contents of Don Pedro's dispatch were eventually transferred to the royal archives in Simancas, where they were to remain undisturbed for nearly three centuries. When those documents were to come to light in 1888, they would initiate a chain of events leading to what is today one of the most significant archaeological projects of colonial America. For contained in the Zuniga dispatch from London were two maps documenting British efforts aimed at planting colonies uncomfortably close to the Spanish domains in the New World. The first was a general sketch of the Chesapeake Bay and its tributaries, where the British colony of Jamestown was in its infancy; the other a highly detailed plan of Fort St George at what has become known as the Popham Colony on the Kennebec river of Maine. Just how these maps came into the possession of the Spanish ambassador is not known, but espionage was a primary tool of diplomats in those days and it is likely the exchange of a few gold pieces was involved in the transaction.

In the decades following the explorations of Columbus in the 1490s, the Spaniards had been largely free to develop their North American holdings without interference from the other European powers. Thanks to the intervention of Pope Alexander VI who had laid a dividing line between the two in 1494, the Portuguese and Spanish spheres of influence had been relatively well defined, and the consolidation of the Spanish and Portuguese crowns under Philip II in 1580 largely removed competition from that quarter. While Spanish power was firmly established in Mexico, Florida and Cuba, the king of Spain also laid claim to most of the coast of North America, despite maintaining no permanent presence along most of that coast. Other potential European competitors had not become very active in North America, some early exploratory moves notwithstanding. Both the English and French had been early visitors: the Bristol based John Cabot had reached Maine in 1498, while Giovanni da Verrazzano, sailing under a French flag, had explored the same region in 1524. Then, in 1562, French Huguenots under Jean Ribault established a colony, Port Royal, on Parris Island at the mouth of the St John River in what is now South Carolina. The Spaniards felt this colony, along with its fort, Charlesfort, represented a foothold perilously close to their interests in Florida, and in 1566

Don Pedro Menendez, governor at St Augustine, moved to eliminate the colony by force. Further north, Sir Walter Ralegh dreamed of an English colony at Roanoke on North Carolina's Outer Banks in 1585, but this disappeared after a few years. As the sixteenth century drew to a close, Spain could still claim most of North America as its own.

By the early seventeenth century, however, both the French and the English were again active. To the north, Samuel de Champlain undertook extensive explorations of the St Lawrence River area between 1603 and 1607, and explored the coast of New England as far south as Cape Cod, before withdrawing to his base in Acadie (now Nova Scotia). In April 1606, James I signed the charter of the Virginia Company authorizing it to establish colonies in 'Virginia', indicating a vague area between Spanish Florida and French interests in Canada and including what is today considered New England. The Virginia Company was itself divided into two subordinate companies, one based in London, the other in Plymouth. The Plymouth Company was to exploit the northern part of the region while the southern part was assigned to the London Company.

The royal charter envisaged a healthy competition between Plymouth and London, as it created an overlap in their assigned territories, with the more successful company to gain the lands contained in the overlap, i.e., the lands between 38 and 41 degrees north latitude. The two companies responded swiftly, each finding sufficient investors to send out expeditions before the end of the year. The *Richard,* sent by the Plymouth Company in August under the command of Captain Henry Challons, never reached its intended destination in what is now the state of Maine, being intercepted and captured by Spanish forces near Florida in November. The London expedition departed in December 1606 and arrived in the Chesapeake region, settling on what was to be named the

James River on May 14th, 1607. After coming perilously close to failure during the early years, its colony at Jamestown survived and eventually grew to become a successful and lucrative asset of the British empire.

Despite the initial setback, the Plymouth Company wasted no time in organizing its second expedition. It was financed in large part by two influential figures, Sir John Popham, Lord Chief Justice of England, and Sir Ferdinando Gorges, the military governor of Plymouth who had been involved in the promotion of previous explorations of North America. They agreed to appoint George Popham, the nephew of Sir John, as the first president of the colony.

On May 31st, 1607, the ships *Gift of God* and *Mary and John* departed carrying some 120 colonists—a slightly larger group than had travelled from London to Jamestown. Unlike that rival expedition, the Plymouth group took just nine council members and half-a-dozen other notable gentlemen, with the majority being mainly soldiers, craftsmen, farmers and traders, their objective to reach the coast of 'North Virginia' at a latitude of about 43 degrees north. The *Gift of God* arrived at the mouth of the Sagadahoc River (now the Kennebec in Maine) on August 13th, and *Mary and John* followed three days later. Popham immediately began establishing their colony within a fortification sited on the tip of a headland named Sabino, and which they named Fort St George, a site selected by an earlier reconnaissance expedition as a good base for further colonization to the north.

With George Popham, the other leader was the admiral, Raleigh Gilbert, the son of Sir Humphrey Gilbert and a nephew of Sir Walter Ralegh. Gilbert was twenty-five years old and, according to contemporary reports, was rather proud and arrogant, 'desirous of supremacy and rule'. This contrasted markedly with the personality of George Popham, who according to Sir Ferdinando Gorges was:

> ... an honest man, but ould, and of an unwildy body, and timorously fearful to offende, or conteste with others that will oppose him, but otherwayes a discreete, careful man.

As might be expected, there was friction between the two, especially as the hardships increased when the cold winter set in.

The activities of the newly arrived colonists followed the now familiar pattern of Europeans in North America. A settlement was established, and the two ships departed for England fairly quickly—the *Mary and John* in October, as soon as a storehouse had been built to take the provisions (and probably carrying the map that a few months later was to find its way into the hands of Zuniga and thence to Spain), the *Gift of God*, in December carrying home about half the colonists—while the remaining colonists prepared for the rigors of the winter. Popham and Gilbert conducted explorations of the interior to limited distances up river where contact was made with members of the local tribe, the Abenaki. Not surprisingly, their queries to the Abenaki about commercial prospects yielded the answers they hoped to hear. George Popham reported the results of his investigations to King James in a letter, curiously written in Latin, and dated December 13th, 1607, though not taken back to England until the following autumn.

> So far as relates to commerce, all the natives constantly affirm that in these parts there are nutmegs, mace and cinnamon, besides pitch, Brazil wood, cochineal, and ambergris, with many other produces of great importance and value; and these, too, in great abundance. Besides they positively assure me, that there is a certain Sea in the opposite or western part of the province, distant not more than seven day's journey from our fort of St George in Sagadahoc: a sea large, wide and deep of the boundaries of which they are wholly ignorant of; which cannot be other than the Southern Ocean, reaching to the

regions of China, which unquestionably cannot be far from these parts.

One of the first things the colonists did was to build a ship. According to William Strachey, in his *The Historie of Travaile into Virginia Britannia*, (1612):

> The Carpenters framed a pretty Pynnace of about some 30 tonne, which they called the *Virginia*, the chief shipwright being Digby of London.

Little else is known of the details of the construction of the *Virginia*, though a caulking iron was found during excavations of the colony storehouse in 1999. Yet the pinnace, which is shown on the map of the colony drawn in October 1607, must have represented a major drain on the limited manpower of the colony. Just when was the ship completed? It is unlikely it could have been finished by the time the map was drawn, within two months of the expedition's arrival. In any case, the *Virginia* was to prove capable of crossing the Atlantic, carrying the remnants of the colony back to England in the autumn of 1608, and she made at least one subsequent transatlantic voyage, to Jamestown in 1609.

The deaths of three men close to the leadership of the colony were decisive in its failure. First was Sir John Popham, who died in June 1607, just ten days after *Gift of God* and *Mary and John* had cleared Lizard Point on their departure from English waters. Despite this tragedy, of which the colonists themselves remained ignorant, the colony never suffered a shortage of funds during its brief existence; a more immediate threat occurred when George Popham himself—along with a number of other colonists—succumbed to the first cold winter, and died in February 1608.

After the death of George Popham, Raleigh Gilbert was elected president in his place, and the colony survived the harsh winter. Then, when a re-supply ship sent from Plymouth by Gorges arrived in late summer 1608, it brought news that

Gilbert's elder brother, John, had also died. This left Raleigh as heir to the family estate, Compton Castle in Devon. The prospect of another bleak winter in the wilds of Maine seemed less attractive than the idea of returning home and becoming lord of the manor, and Gilbert decided to depart. Faced with the prospect of continuing without his strong leadership, the rest of the surviving colonists decided to leave with him. Fortunately the *Virginia*, along with the re-supply ship, provided sufficient capacity for all to return.

The map is one of the most useful and interesting of the remaining records of the Popham Colony. Its design is typical of British military plans of the period, and it is clear that John Hunt was a professional surveyor/cartographer: his name appears on the list of colonists under the category of 'Notables' and carries the title 'draughtsman'. Little else is known about him, although recently uncovered genealogical records suggest that Hunt was related to Richard Bartlett, a well-known military cartographer who in turn was related by marriage to George Popham.

The plan, an ink-on-paper manuscript measuring 29 x 43cm, depicts the finished fort, complete with battlements, cannon and twenty-five structures within the walls, many of them named. The *Virginia* is shown moored just off the north point of the fort. Although the chart contains no compass rose, the compass directions are indicated alongside the walls of the fort. A scale bar with two scales, 'feet' and 'paces', is included, giving the plan a scale of about 500:1. In the corner is a legend listing the various structures and an inscription crediting the construction of the fort to Captain George Popham, Esquire. It is signed 'John Hunt the viii day of October in the year of our Lord 1607'; the very next day Hunt departed for England in the ship that had delivered the party to the site.

Although the map is effectively a plan view of the site, Hunt depicted the buildings in elevation view, so

that the map-reader could visualize the appearance of the buildings' facades as they would appear from the ground.

As straightforward as it apparently is, the map—and its route into the hands of Philip III in Spain—presents several questions: was the map a documentation of the fort as it existed on that date—just a fifty-two days after the colonists arrived—or was it the plan from which the fort was to be constructed? Is it the original from the hand of John Hunt, or a copy produced by Zuniga's intelligence source in England? How did it reach Spanish hands so quickly?

The other map that Zuniga sent to Philip in September 1608 was a rather rough sketch of the territory around and between the James and Potomac Rivers, including the Chesapeake Bay. It is neither signed nor dated, but is presumed to be the map of Captain John Smith, the *de facto* governor of Virginia, which he had intended as an illustration of his report on Jamestown, A *True Relation* (1608). Smith had sent the map to England with Captain Francis Nelson, who left Virginia on June 6th, 1608, and arrived home in late July. The inclusion of this second map, or a copy of it, in the Zuniga transmittal a mere six weeks after its arrival in London points to the efficiency of the Spaniard ambassador's espionage network in London; but the identity of those who helped him has never been identified.

So what became of the Popham site after Raleigh Gilbert and his party left for England in the autumn of 1608? Three years later, in 1611, a French party under Jean de Biencourt visited the abandoned colony, but periodic visits by local indigenous people in the intervening years must have cleaned out most remaining objects of interest. In 1624 there was another visit, this time by twenty-two-year-old Samuel Maverick, who had recently settled in Massachusetts Bay. Upon his return to Massachusetts, Maverick wrote, 'I found Rootes and Garden hearbs and some old Walles there, ... which shewed it to be the place where they had been...'.

In the years following the Maverick visit, the site lay undisturbed and all but forgotten.

Interest in the Popham colony was rekindled in the twentieth century by Alexander Brown, a historian of early colonial America. In 1888 a researcher at Simancas working for the US Ambassador to Spain came upon the Zuñiga package, while Brown was working on his book, *The Genesis of the United States: a Narrative of the movement in England, 1605-1616*. Brown obtained copies of these papers, including the letter to Philip III, the Hunt map and the map of the James River and the Chesapeake. Brown reproduced the Hunt map in his book, but questions persisted. How accurate was the map, exactly where on the Kennebec River was the colony, and did the map represent the actual constructions or just the plan for projected work?

In the 1990s archaeologist Jeffrey Brain of the Peabody Essex Museum in Salem, Massachusetts, began to bring the colony back to life, using the Hunt map as a primary tool. While walking the site in 1993, he tried to visualize the fit of Hunt's plan onto the topography, and realized that Hunt had aligned his map not to magnetic North but to true North. By rotating the map 20 degrees to the East, superimposing it on a modern topographical map and

adjusting to differing scales, he had the key that was to unlock the secrets of Popham colony. He quickly found the postholes of the largest building, the storehouse. He has subsequently discovered other colonial buildings and artefacts, including the house of Raleigh Gilbert, complete with the stones of its hearth, lying just where the map predicted it to be. According to Brain:

> The map is so reliable that using the scale of feet and paces we can go to a specific location within the fort and expect to find evidence of the feature drawn on the map at that spot. Hunt drew the storehouse in such meticulous detail that we could even predict within centimetres where we would find the individual wall posts.

For the archaeologist, the combination of a relatively undisturbed site which had been constructed, occupied and abandoned within such a short period, plus such an accurate map offers a remarkable opportunity to understand the life of the early colonists. This contrasts with Jamestown, which was occupied continuously for centuries with no map or plan of its early years, other than the simple Smith map of 1608. In many ways, Popham colony's failure to sustain itself makes it a success as an archaeological treasure. Excavations have yielded a large number of artefacts of the lost colony, including musketry and armour, glass beads and buttons,

liquor bottles and drinking glasses, ceramics and a tobacco pipe.

In the end, it turns out that Philip and the Spanish had absolutely nothing to fear from the Popham Colony and little to fear from the longer-lived Jamestown. The early collapse of the northern colony and the long life-and-death struggle for survival at Jamestown meant that the British in North America were to be fully occupied preserving their tenuous foothold for another generation. Nonetheless, these tentative first efforts eventually matured into a strong position. The experience of the Popham colonists contributed directly to the success of the Pilgrims in Massachusetts in 1620. Although he had been intensely disappointed by the collapse of the colony, Ferdinando Gorges remained involved with North America, though he never actually crossed the Atlantic himself. In 1620 he founded the Council for New England and in 1622 with John Mason he was granted the territory that is now Maine, where he established the first system of government in 1636. Although the beleaguered colonists of Popham failed to plant a long-lived establishment at the month of the Kennebec River, their energetic efforts made a significant mark on the history of North America.

Richard Pflederer is an independent scholar of the history of cartography.

"Instruments of Seduction": A Tale of Two Women

Sandra F. VanBurkleo

Ann Hibbens and Anne Hutchinson had much in common. Both hailed from the Puritan hotbed of Lincolnshire, England, where they had married successful merchants before emigrating to New Boston, in 1630 and 1634 respectively. Within a few years, both women stood in the dock, charged with committing crimes against the community and entertaining diabolical religious ideas. And both women lost their contests with government. At issue were Puritan teachings about "godly relations" between husband and wife, minister and church member, and magistrate and subject. In trials of Hibbens, Hutchinson (1), and other "headstrong" women, judicial decisions about whether or not to allow important procedural and substantive freedoms partly depended upon which aspect of Calvinism's two-sided vision of woman held sway at particular moments in the proceeding. On one side, women were potential Saints equal to men in God's eyes; on the other side, they were Eve-like temptresses, peculiarly susceptible to Satanic temptation. In addition, Puritan responses to fallen or treacherous women in courtrooms lay bare the essential masculin-

ity of many freedoms—among them, the right to command one's own body, the right of locomotion, liberty of speech (especially in public), the right to bring witnesses and otherwise engage in self-defense, and the privilege against self-incrimination.

The facts in the two cases differ. The charismatic teacher and spiritist Anne Hutchinson had been admitted in 1635 to the Reverend John Wilson's First Church of Boston, over the objections of several ministers who suspected her of Antinomianism—a belief in the primacy of divine revelation and related skepticism about the authority of clergy and Biblical law. With the encouragement of Governor Harry Vane, the radical theologian John Cotton (her spiritual mentor), and the Reverend John Wheelwright (her intemperate and impolitic brother-in-law), Hutchinson began to hold women's meetings at home. Such meetings were common enough among English gentlewomen, and (contrary to myth) did *not* involve promiscuous mingling of the sexes; instead—and more damagingly—Hutchinson summarized and explicated Biblical texts and criticized sermons, notably Wil-

son's, encouraging women to subject ministers, husbands, and other lawgivers to criticism.

The heyday of Hutchinson's meetings coincided with a colony-wide revival and expansion of church rolls. When spiritual malaise replaced euphoria in 1636, Cotton (2) began castigating other ministers for their abandonment, solely to attract new members, of the "covenant of grace" in favor of a "covenant of works." Hutchinson, who agreed with Cotton and had Vane's ear, emerged as the mainspring of a faction pitted against Wilson's ministry and the political ambitions of John Winthrop. Hutchinson and her followers began walking out of church during sermons; throughout the colony, women rose in mid-service to heckle pastors or to dispute theological points.

In Anglo-America, these were shocking developments: public oratory by women violated both law and custom. Anglican lecturers regularly enjoined women to "obey husbands," to "cease from commanding," and to avoid what Amy Schrager Lang calls "female authorship." The influential English scholar Thomas Hooker permitted public speeches by women only when they supported "*subjection*." And, while Puritans expanded women's sphere to include family governance and church membership, they had qualms about female voices in public spaces. Scholars and preachers hoped to preserve "an inequality in the degree of ... Authority" so that, when push came to shove, husbands might retain "a *Superiority*." Puritan historian Edward Johnson averred that only "silly women laden with diverse lusts and phantastical madness" pursued rhetoric and theology. After the Antinomian crisis, John Cotton similarly proscribed female oratory unless women had in mind "singing forth the praises of the Lord" or confessing crime. Speech "by way of teaching" or "propounding questions ... under pretence of a desire to learn," he said, usurped male prerogatives and unsettled the polity.

On one side, women were potential Saints equal to men in God's eyes; on the other side, they were Eve-like temptresses, peculiarly susceptible to Satanic temptation.

Hutchinson's moment in the sun was fleeting: in mid-1636, the political tides began to turn against the Vane faction. Pretending friendship, Wilson and other clerics visited Hutchinson's home in December, 1636, ostensibly to discuss religion (by Puritan lights, a "private" conversation ordinarily off limits to public scrutiny). Hutchinson spoke freely; Wilson surreptitiously took notes from which record the group compiled a list of doctrinal "errors."

Some weeks later, at John Cotton's invitation, John Wheelwright (3) preached an incendiary fast-day sermon in which, to Cotton's horror, he condemned every minister except his host for practicing a covenant of works, and

called for open warfare against Satan's allies in Bay Colony meetinghouses. His jeremiad revealed, among other things, the ongoing vitality of associations between Woman and the Anti-Christ. Wheelwright said Christians welcomed battles between "Gods people and those that are not"; everyone knew "that the whore [or false church] must be burnt.... [I]t is not shaving of her head and paring her nayles and changing her rayment, that will serve ... but this whore must be burnt."

Fearing rebellion, the General Court confiscated firearms from suspected Wheelwright supporters, who in turn circulated a remonstrance (signed by Wheelwright's friends) threatening an appeal to royal courts. Four months later, Winthrop won the governorship and Vane fled to London. In March, 1637, magistrates commenced proceedings against Wheelwright, Hutchinson, and other minor players in the drama. Convicted of sedition, Wheelwright was exiled, though he returned after a decent interval to preach at Harvard. Significantly, the evidence used against him was a matter of public record (i.e., the contents of a sermon and written, signed remonstrance); magistrates extended a long list of procedural rights at trial—among them, the right to offer witnesses and testimony in self-defense, and the right to be silent.

His sister-in-law fared less well. In September, at an open meeting in Newport, a church-state synod examined Hutchinson, in keeping with English procedure, for evidence of sedition, heresy, blasphemy, and other crimes against authority. Unlike her kinsman, she had never occupied a pulpit, and had neither inspired nor signed petitions. Her crimes—the sowing of rebellious seeds among women, for example—occurred entirely behind the walls of a frame house.

Pregnant and faint, Hutchinson faced three rows of hostile questioners—civil magistrates, elected deputies, and clergy. In Winthrop's words, she had "troubled the peace of the

commonwealth" and "spoken divers things ... prejudicial to the honour of the churches and ministers thereof." She had "maintained a meeting and an assembly" in her home—"a thing not tolerable nor comely in the sight of God" nor "fitting" for her sex. Despite criticism, she had persisted; the court hoped to "understand how things are" and "reduce" her (i.e., force her to acknowledge error). Failing that, she would be condemned for "obstinance."

For a time, Hutchinson prevailed, ably challenging the court's questionable use of evidence taken privately, the curious absence of a criminal charge, the judges' related refusal to let her examine Wilson's notebooks in advance of trial, and their refusal to administer oaths to witnesses (which they technically did not *have* to do, so long as the proceeding still could be termed a magisterial examination and not a trial). Familiar with Biblical law and common law procedure, she saw clearly how weak the governor's case really was. Winthrop, after all, had no hard evidence of sedition—by definition a crime involving public acts—and flimsy evidence of heresy, some of which tended to implicate John Cotton. She had not signed the Wheelwright petition, had criticized ministers at *home*, and had spoken with Wilson as one speaks with "friends." As she put it, Puritans respected private exchanges and "matter(s) of conscience." Nobody came forward to secure liberties for Hutchinson; but, because she managed to assert rights claims accurately and persuasively, the magistrates acceded to her procedural demands.

Gradually, however, Hutchinson lost ground. The focus began to shift from specific theological points to "natural" relations between the sexes, and especially to Hutchinson's alleged violations of the Fifth Commandment and usurpations of male prerogatives. More than once, magistrates reminded her that men need not "discourse" with women—that men need not *hear* what women said as to "facts" or "truth" in self-defense. Winthrop also gained important leverage in the control of Hutchinson's body (e.g., ordering her to stop speaking, to sit while standing, to stand while sitting). A woman could never "call a company together" to preach, he said, nor offer testimony without judicial dispensation. Why had Hutchinson failed to teach young women to "love their husbands and not to make them clash?" Why had she not learned the lesson herself? Surely her meetings, so "prejudicial to the state," led to "families — neglected" by wives who had come to believe, with their teacher, that "the fear of man, is a snare." Domestic sabotage weakened all of political society: as one minister later explained, God chose *not* to create church and state "at one stroke," but to lay "foundations both of State and Church, in a family," the "Mother Hive" from which church and state "issued forth." To attack this "little commonwealth" was to assail political government. For this reason, the court declared Wilson's notebooks a lawful source of evidence: when women attacked the polity at its foundation, confidences "counted for nothing," and private utterances could support charges of sedition (or other "public" crimes). In addition, magistrates imposed banishment instead of censure, against the letter of Bay Colony law.

Because she had been demonized, Hutchinson's decision to tell the truth and be done with it returned to haunt her. She freely described her gift of prophecy, her doctrinal positions, and the content of divine messages; she claimed a God-given ability to distinguish between true and false voices. Sensing an opportunity to gather *public* evidence of heresy, magistrates asked her to say exactly how God communicated with her. "By an immediate voice," she replied truthfully. For good measure, she reminded her accusers that, because Jesus alone controlled her "body and soul," the court could do her no harm, and instead would bring a "curse upon … posterity, and the mouth of the Lord hath spoken it."

Magistrates no doubt breathed a sigh of relief: the "American Jezebel" (as she came to be called) had admitted antinomianism before dozens of witnesses. So long as she refused to recant errors in a separate church trial, they would be rid of her.

Jailed in a private home for the winter, Hutchinson's health steadily declined. John Wilson officiated at the proceeding in March, 1638. There, the congregation would judge whether or not she had violated the First Church covenant by which Saints agreed to "walke in all sincere Conformity" with God's law as interpreted by the clergy. If guilty and unrepentant, she would be excommunicated as well as exiled. Hutchinson was too weak to attend opening sessions, where elders presented yet more evidence "taken from her owne Mouth" over the winter by seeming friends and at least one ex-disciple. As earlier, she had no knowledge of the evidence to be used against her. Because she claimed to be ruled exclusively by God and not by her husband or the clergy, several elders accused her of several obscure heresies and—more damning—of sympathy with Familism (the notorious "family of love" sect in which members collectively married Jesus and dispensed with ordinary matrimony) (4). Hutchinson stoutly denied these charges and recanted several "errors," on the ground that human language garbled God's "true" messages (which came to her *without* language) when she tried to put them into words.

On another day, in another court, recantation might have saved her from severe punishment; but this was not such a day. At one particularly delicate moment, a critic determined to portray Hutchinson as a viper in society's bosom abruptly interjected more talk about "that foule, groce, filthye, and abominable opinion held by Familists, of the Communitie of Weomen." Would she dispense altogether with patriarchal marriages? Cotton reminded parishioners that, while Hutchinson had done "much good," she was

"but a Woman and many unsound and dayngerous principles are held by her." Did she not threaten the "very foundation of Religion" with the "filthie Sinne of the Communitie of Woemen and all promisc[uou]s and filthie cominge togeather of men and Woemen without Distinction or Relation of marriage?" He even accused her of marital infidelity on the ground that Familism always led there.

At closing sessions some days later, Wilson presented a longer list of "errors," some compiled by embittered ex-disciples over the winter. Weakened by pregnancy and long detention, Hutchinson said little; in any case, theology had ceased to be the issue. She had been reconstituted as the "whore of Babylon," charged with violations of Puritan relational ideology, and tarred with Familism, the heresy for which Quakers could be hanged in Massachusetts Bay. One of the elders summarized charges: "[Y]ou have stept out of your place," he said, "you have rather bine a Husband than a Wife and a preacher than a Hearer, and a Magistrate than a Subject." Wilson called her a "dayngerous Instrument of the Divell." Said others, the "Misgovernment of this Woman's tongue" by her husband and other natural rulers portended grave "Disorder." When members objected again to punishment for conscience, Cotton found biblical authority to exile her for perjury, blasphemy, and spiritual "seduction." The writ of excommunication ordered her to leave the parish "as a Leper"; because she "dispised and contemned the Holy Ordinances," she should not "benefit by them."

Hutchinson walked out of church, followed by family members and her friend Mary Dyer (executed in 1660 for Quakerism). In March, 1638, she joined William Hutchinson in Rhode Island, where she experienced what Winthrop soberly termed a "monstrous birth"—in his view, providential evidence of grotesque theology, a "confession" that cast additional doubt upon the woman's own words. The governor noted, too, that Dyer's "familiarity with the devill" earlier had produced a stillborn "monstrous" child, which Hutchinson and Dyer had labored to conceal; both women were unnatural, poisonous, perhaps demonic. Indeed, Winthrop wondered whether or not his old nemesis had been a witch all along. In 1639, church elders (including Ann Hibbens' husband, William) visited Rhode Island to check on the progress of censured members. Hutchinson slammed the door in their faces. She wanted no part of their church, for she was an ecstatic "spouse of Christ." Disconcerted visitors pronounced her a "Harlot," begging the church to "cut her off" once and for all. Wilson gladly obliged.

The tale's end fit neatly into the narrative Winthrop later constructed to justify Hutchinson's exile. In the early 1640's, she moved to New York to find "peace." There, Indians killed the entire Hutchinson family except one child. Surely her assailants had been godly messengers: "I never heard that the Indians ... did ever before this, commit the like outrage," wrote Winthrop. God had made of "this wofull woman" a "heavie example of their cruelty," and confirmed the diabolical nature of her theology.

Meanwhile, Puritans on both sides of the Atlantic had closed ranks, ruling out female ministries and antinomian experimentation. John Brinsley's 1645 sermon in Yarmouth, England, contained a typical announcement of the Puritan decision against woman preachers: "Sure we are," he said, "that ... Women may not teach in publick. And were there no other Reason for it, this alone might be sufficient to silent them. The woman by her taking upon her to teach ... became the Instrument of Seduction, and Author of Transgression to her husband, and consequently of ruine to him....Henceforth then no more Women-Preachers." For women to assume "the office of Teaching," he added, was "no less than a mingling of Heaven and earth together, an inversion of the course and order of nature" (5).

Ann Hibbens, by contrast, did not claim to be a prophet. No sooner had she sailed into Boston harbor than she developed a reputation for "natural crabbedness of ... temper" and squabbling with neighbors (6). But serious trouble awaited 1640, when she locked horns with a joiner (or carpenter) who raised his price after building a fancy bedstead. Hibbens not only disputed the worker's claim and investigated prices charged by other joiners, but also interrogated laborers in neighboring towns and rejected the mediating efforts of another craftsman. Says historian Jane Kamensky, Hibbens "spoke as a woman trying to participate in a rational society with a developing economy; prices, value, and collusion, not inspiration and revelation, were her province." But, after the Hutchinson debacle, wives did business and exhibited a "restless tongue" at some peril. While Puritans despised hustling and gouging, they also hated scolds; in Hibbens' case, they punished the "medium, not the message" (7).

In the autumn of 1640, the First Church commenced a magisterial examination of Hibbens, initially to ferret out evidence of "lying" about her fellows (a felony in Massachusetts); they probably sought evidence as well of scolding (a sex-specific crime punished with a dunking). The trigger had been her seemingly arrogant rejection of a male mediator and related decision to singlehandedly undertake a market survey on horseback. Judges charged Hibbens with laying "infamy, disgrace, and reproach" on the carpenter ("our Brother"). As with Hutchinson, charges multiplied to include neglect of "natural" relations between women and their male "heads."

As in Hutchinson's case, Hibbens refused to submit to false authority; Unlike her forebear, she preferred to *withhold* speech whenever the court demanded testimony, to stand when the court bade her sit, and to smile maddeningly at her accusers. Finally driven to distraction, the magistrates condemned her arrogance and especially her "carriage ... so proud and contemptuous and irreverent ... when

the church is dealing with her." Through a "Brother," Hibbens sardonically told her accusers that she dared not respond to queries in church because God required silence of women.

Also as with Hutchinson, Hibbens's accusers fastened upon ungodly relations—her unwomanly violations of "the rule of the Apostle in usurping authority over him whom God hath made her head and husband," and her anti-Christian decision to take "the power and authority which God hath given to him out of his hands." William had accepted the joiner's price; Ann's insistence that she could "manage it better than her husband" constituted a "plan breach of the rule of Christ," and by implication an indictment of Hibbens' husband for failing to govern his wife. Judges toyed with the possibility that her ability to rile up the neighborhood evidenced witchcraft; but, in 1640, they settled for admonition and (when she refuse to disavow "lusts and covetous distempers") excommunication. The pastor stated that Hibbens merited damnation for "slandering and raising up an evil report of ... Brethren," for the "sowing of discord," and for refusing to remain at home. She had, after all, dashed "with a restless and discontented spirit ... from person to person from house to house, and from place to place." She had rejected governance by the "wise ... head" of her husband, usurped his prerogatives, and "grieved his spirit." Has she not behaved "as if he was a nobody," rejected "the way of obedience," and encouraged "unquietness of the family"? With Hutchinson, Hibbens had little time for "due submission." Unlike her predecessor, she celebrated the commercial spirit and ignored theology—impulse which profoundly troubled her interrogators.

Hibbens vanished from public view until 1654 when her well-respected husband died. One historian thinks that, without his protection, she no longer could fend off the "full weight of her neighbors' hatred" (8). In 1655, the General Court convicted her of witchcraft, but magistrates refused the verdict and ordered a new trial, where jurors again condemned her. In mid-1656, Massachusetts executed

Hibbens as a witch, for being "turbulent in her passion, and discontented," and possessed of a "strange carriage." Years later, a witness to the spectacle told Puritan minister Increase Mather that she had been hanged "for having more wit than her neighbors." She had "guessed that two of her persecutors, whom she saw talking in the street, were talking of her; which, proving true, cost her life."

The trials of Hutchinson and Hibbens—and analogous ordeals to which colonial magistrates subjected other female spiritist and malcontents—lay bare the extent to which gender shaped access to important freedoms, particularly when women threatened to destabilize the "Yoke-fellowship" that governed Puritan families. A reputation for self-sovereignty clearly diminished a woman's liberty prospects. The die was cast when Hutchinson rose to defend herself as God's instrument, immune to the slings and arrows of mere men. Hibbens similarly tossed freedom to the wind when she refused to let magistrates control her body, mind, and tongue. Submissiveness guaranteed nothing, but unruly or aggressive women triggered fears of the Anti-Christ. Puritan divine William Perkins suggested that, in certain cases, and never in cases of witchcraft, women's "weakness" might "lessen both the crime and the punishment"; unruliness or aggression ensured the opposite result. Mercy Brown of Wallingford Massachusetts, escaped the gallows in 1691 after killing her son; however, judges delayed passing sentence because she was "distracted," and finally jailed her. By contrast, Dorothy Talbye of Salem (hanged for child murder) resisted authority, refused to confess until threatened with torture, sat when ordered to stand, and rejected a face-cloth at the gallows. Defiance increased the odds of unmitigated punishment, and often lent credence to suspicions of witchcraft (9).

Comparisons with state trials of men are telling. Magistrates, to give one example, did not interpret Wheelwright's silence as guilt, because regular male ministers (unlike lay female ministers) could be counted on to tell the truth in public and elsewhere, and also because his crime, while heinous, did not weaken political society at its foundation. Anne Hutchinson's brother-in-law brought witnesses on his own behalf, offered testimony for jurors' consideration, and retained sovereign command of his own body. Both Hutchinson and Hibbens confronted judges determined to police their movements and utterances better than husbands had done, and to extract confessions or damning testimony, because they acted from and upon the domestic "Hive." Ann Hibbens's mocking silence bought her a one-way ticket to the gallows; Hutchinson's eleventh-hour recantations at the church trial (which might have saved her, had critics not identified her with Satan) ultimately were used against her, as evidence of bizarre theology and *lying* at the civil trial. For women accused of treachery, public displays of courage, honesty, erudition, and physical autonomy were altogether foolhardy.

Sandra F. VanBurkleo, Associate Professor of History at Wayne State University in Detroit, is completing a book, "Belonging to the World": Women's Rights and American Constitutional Culture. *She teaches and writes in the field of American legal and constitutional history.*

Endnotes

1. For a fuller version of the Hutchinson tale, additional bibliography, and citations to material quoted here, see Sandra F. VanBurkleo, "'To Bee Rooted Out of Her Station': The Ordeal of Anne Hutchinson," in *American Political Trials*, ed. Michal Belknap, rev. ed. (Westport, Conn: Greenwood Press, 1993), 1–24, which in turn relies upon David Hall, ed., *The Antinomian Controversy, 1636–1638: A Documentary History*, 2d ed. (Durham, N.C.: Duke University Press, 1990).
2. Reverend Richard Allestree, quoted in Alice E. Natahews, "Religious Experience of Southern Women," and John Cotton, "Singing of Psalms a Gospel-Ordinance, 1650," in *Women and Religion in America*, ed. Rosemary Radford Ruether and Rosemary Skinner Keller, vol. 2 (New York, 1983), 191–192, 206; Amy Schrager Lang, *Prophetic Woman: Anne Hutchinson and the Problem of Dissent in the Literature of New England* (Berkeley: University of California Press, 1987), 3; Hooker and Cotton quoted in David Leverenz, *Language of Puritan Feeling: An Exploration in Literature, Psychology, and Social History* (New Brunswick, N.J.: Rutgers University Press, 1980), 82; and Edward Johnson quoted in Edgar McManus, *Law and Liberty in Early New England* (Amherst: University of Massachusetts Press, 1993), 199–220.
3. John Wheelwright, "Fast-Day Sermon," in Hall, 158–170.
4. See Christopher W. Marsh, *The Family of Love in English Society, 1550–1630* (New York: Cambridge University Press, 1994).
5. Sermon of Reverend John Brinsely, quoted in Rosemary Skinner Keller, "New England Women: Ideology and Experience in First-Generation Puritanism (1630–1650)," in Ruether and Keller, 189.
6. "[Governor] Thomas Hutchinson on Ann Hibbins [sic]", *Witchhunting in Seventeenth-Century New England*, ed. David Hall (Boston: Northeastern University Press, 1991), 91.
7. [Robert Keayne], "Proceedings of Excommunication against Mistress Ann Hibbens of Boston (1640)," in *Remarkable Providences*, ed. John Demos, rev. ed. (Boston 1991), 262; Jane Kamensky, "Governing the Tongue: Speech and Society in Early New England," (Ph.D. diss., Yale University, 1993), 220. The account of Hibbens's ordeal derives from Demos's transcription supplemented by Hall, *Witchhunting*, 91.
8. Hall, *Witchhunting*, 91.
9. William Perkins, "Discourse on the Damned Art of Witchcraft," (1592) in Ruether and Keller, 154; McManus, 105; Peter Hoffer and N. E. H. Hull, *Murdering Mothers: Infanticide in England and New England, 1558–1803* (New York, 1984), 40–1.

Bibliography

Battis, Emery. *Saints and Sectaries: Anne Hutchinson and the Antinomian Controversy in the Massachusetts Bay Colony.* Chapel Hill: University of North Carolina Press, 1962.

Demos, John. *Remarkable Providences: Readings on Early American History.* Rev. ed. Boston, Mass: 1991.

Hall, David D., ed. *The Antinomian Controversy, 1636–1638: A Documentary History*. 2d ed. Durham, N.C.: Duke University Press, 1990.

———*Witchhunting in Seventeenth-Century New England*. Boston, Mass.: Northeastern University Press, 1991.

Karlsen, Carol F. *The Devil in the Shape of a Woman: Witchcraft in Colonial New England*. New York: W.W. Norton, 1989.

Schrager Lang, Amy. *Prophetic Woman: Anne Hutchinson and the Problem of Dissent in the Literature of New England*. Berkeley: University of California Press, 1987.

Morris, Richard B. "Jezebel Before the Judges." In *Fair Trial*. New York: Macdonald, 1967.

Stoever, William. *"A Faire and Easie Way to Heaven": Covenant Theology and Antinomianism in Early Massachusetts*. Middletown, Conn: Wesleyan University Press, 1978.

VanBurkleo, Sandra F. "'To Bee Rooted Out of Her Station': The Ordeal of Anne Hutchinson." In *American Political Trials*, edited by Michal Belknap. Rev. ed. Westport, Conn: Greenwood Press, 1994.

From *OAH Magazine of History,* Winter 1995, pages 8-13. Copyright © 1995 by Organization of American Historians. Reprinted with permission.

Penning a Legacy

Imprisoned and vilified for his religious views, William Penn, a member of the Society of Friends, sought to establish a colony in the New World where people of all faiths could live in mutual harmony.

By Patricia Hudson

O N A CHILL WINTER DAY in 1668, 24-year-old William Penn paced back and forth in a cramped chamber in the Tower of London. Arrested for blasphemy after publishing a pamphlet that questioned the doctrine of the Trinity, Penn was being held in close confinement. The Bishop of London had decreed that if Penn didn't recant publicly he would remain imprisoned for the rest of his life. Penn's reply was unequivocal: "My prison shall be my grave before I will budge a jot, for I owe my conscience to no mortal man."

W ILLIAM PENN WAS born on October 14, 1644, just a stone's throw from the Tower where he would one day be a prisoner. His father, William, Sr., was an ambitious naval officer who rose to the rank of admiral. Knighted by King Charles II, the elder Penn formed a friendship with the royal family that would play a major role in his son's future.

The Penn family's next-door neighbor on Tower Hill was the diarist Samuel Pepys, who noted in his journal that Admiral Penn was "a merry fellow and pretty good-natured and sings very bawdy songs." Pepys also recorded instances of William, Jr., playing cards with his father, going to the theater, and carelessly leaving his sword in a hired coach and then racing across London to retrieve it.

One incident from Penn's youth foreshadowed his later preoccupation with religious matters—at 17 William was expelled from Oxford University for daring to criticize certain Church of England rituals. Appalled, Admiral Penn packed his overly serious son off to France, hoping that he would grow more worldly amid the glitter of Paris.

When William returned to England after two years abroad, Pepys described him as "a most modish person, grown a fine gentlemen, but [having] a great deal, if not too much, of the vanity of the French garb and affected manner of speech and gait." The admiral, well-pleased with his fashionable son, sent William to Ireland to attend to family business, but it was there, in 1667, that the younger Penn embraced the Quaker faith.

The Society of Friends—dubbed Quakers by their enemies because they admonished listeners to "tremble at the word of the Lord"—had been founded in 1647 by George Fox, a weaver's son-turned-preacher who spoke of the Inner Light and believed that there was "that of God in every man." According to Fox, all people, regardless of their status here on earth, are equal in God's eyes. It was a challenge directed at the very heart of England's class-conscious society, and though all religious dissenters were subject to fines and imprisonments, the establishment singled out Quakers with particular ferocity.

When Penn again returned to London, his family was aghast at the change in him. Not only did young William insist on attending the outlawed Quaker meetings, he also ignored common courtesy by refusing to take off his hat in the presence of his "betters," just one of several methods Friends used to illustrate their belief in equality. In the eyes of acquaintances and family, William had betrayed not only the religious principles of the Church of England but also his social class. Noted Pepys in his diary: "Mr. Will Penn, who is lately come over from Ireland, is a Quaker... or some very melancholy thing."

Better educated than most of the early Friends, Penn quickly became one of their most outspoken advocates, taking part in public debates and writing pamphlets that he published at his own expense. One respected London minister, enraged by the conversion of two female members of his congregation to Quakerism, stated that he would "rather lose them to a bawdy house than a Quaker meeting" and then went on to denounce the group's theology.

When Penn responded to the attack in print, the pamphlet became the talk of the city and led to his imprisonment in the Tower. "Hath got me W. Pen's book against the Trinity," Pepys wrote. "I find it so well writ, as I think it too good for him ever to have writ it—and it is a serious sort of book, and not fit for everybody to read."

Despite the threat of life imprisonment, the cold confines of the Tower failed to dampen Penn's crusading spirit. He spent his time there writing a rough draft of *No Cross, No Crown*, one of his most enduring works. After nine months in custody, William was released, perhaps in part as a favor to Admiral Penn, who had loaned the cash-hungry King Charles II a great deal of money over the years.

In 1672, William married Gulielma Maria Springett. During their more than 21 years of marriage, the couple became the parents of seven children. Family responsibilities, however, did not keep Penn from again risking imprisonment by speaking at Friends' meetings, writing political and religious pamphlets, and refusing to take an oath of allegiance.

By the late 1670s, after more than a decade of clashes with the nation's authorities, Penn had grown pessimistic about the likelihood of religious and civil reforms in

England and so turned his thoughts to the New World. Although the colonies were heavily populated with dissenters from England, many colonial authorities exercised no more tolerance for Quakers than their English counterparts. In Puritan-controlled Boston, for example, two Quaker women were hanged when they refused to stop preaching in public.

Having experienced firsthand the horrors of forced religious conformity, Penn dreamed of showing the world that peaceful coexistence among diverse religious groups was possible and that a single, state-supported religion was not only unnecessary but undesirable. "There can be no reason to persecute any man in this world about anything that belongs to the next," he wrote.

When Admiral Penn died without collecting the money owed to him by the king, William saw a way to make his dream a reality. In 1680, he petitioned King Charles for a grant of land in America to retire the debt. Acceding to his request, the king conferred upon Penn an enormous tract of land, the largest that had ever been granted to an individual. William proposed calling the colony New Wales, it being "a pretty hilly country," but King Charles insisted on calling it "Pennsylvania"—Penn's Woods—in honor of his old friend, the admiral.

At the age of 36, Penn suddenly faced the enormous task of designing a government from scratch. The constitution he created, with its provisions for religious freedom, extensive voting rights, and penal reform, was remarkably enlightened by seventeenth-century standards. Despite the vast power it conferred on him as proprietor, Penn had been careful to leave "to myself and successors no power of doing mischief, that the will of one man may not hinder the good of an whole country...."

Before he set sail for Pennsylvania himself, Penn appointed three commissioners and charged them with establishing the new colony. While William saw nothing wrong with Europeans settling in the New World, he was among the few colonizers of his time who recognized the prior claims of the indigenous people. Thus, he gave the commissioners a letter, dated October 18, 1681, addressed to the people of the Lenni Lenape tribe who inhabited his proprietorship. The letter stated that King Charles had granted him "a great province; but I desire to enjoy it with your love and consent, that we may always live together as neighbours and friends, else what would the great God say to us, who hath made us not to devour and destroy one another but to live soberly and kindly together in the world?"

When he finally arrived in the colony in October 1682, Penn made a treaty with the Indians, in effect purchasing the land he had already been given by the king. Truly wishing to live in peace, he tried to be fair in his dealings with the Lenni Lenape, unmindful that they—like their Delaware kinsmen who "sold" Manhattan Island to Peter Minuit—did not understand the concept of exclusive ownership of the land and believed that the white men simply sought to share its use.

Penn had intended to settle permanently in Pennsylvania, but within two years a boundary dispute with neighboring Maryland required him to return to London, where a web of troubles awaited him. As a result, nearly 16 years passed before he again set foot in his colony. During his long absence, the colonists had grown resentful of his authority, and in 1701, less than two years after his second voyage to Pennsylvania, a disillusioned Penn sailed back to England, never to return. All told, he spent less than five years in America.

From his return to England until his death 16 years later, Penn continually struggled to stave off financial disaster. Never an astute businessman, he discovered, to his horror, that his trusted business manager had defrauded him, leaving him deeply in debt. At the age of 63, Penn was sent to a debtor's prison. Marveled one friend, "The more he is pressed, the more he rises. He seems of a spirit to bear and rub through difficulties." Before long, concerned friends raised enough money to satisfy his creditors.

Prior to his death in 1718 at the age of 73, Penn attempted to sell Pennsylvania back to the Crown, hoping to forge at least a modicum of financial security for his six surviving children. In making the offer, Penn sought to extract a promise from the English Crown that the colony's laws and civil rights would be preserved. But while the negotiations were still in progress, Penn suffered a debilitating stroke, and the transaction was never completed. Penn's descendants thus retained control of the colony until the American Revolution.

Despite imprisonment, vilification, and financial ruin, Penn had labored unceasingly to establish the principle of religious freedom in both his homeland and in America. He espoused such "modern" concepts as civil rights, participatory government, interracial brotherhood, and international peace.

Yet, despite the rich legacy that the founder of the colony of Pennsylvania left to Americans, William Penn remains a shadowy figure in our popular consciousness. For most people, his name conjures up little more than a vague picture that is remarkably similar to the bland, beaming face that adorns boxes of Quaker Oats cereal. The reality, however, was quite different; Penn was an extremely complex individual, whose life was filled with triumph and tragedy and was marked by startling contrasts.

In 1984, more than 300 years after the founding of Pennsylvania, the United States Congress posthumously granted Penn U.S. citizenship. "In the history of this Nation," the proclamation read, "there has been a small number of men and women whose contributions to its traditions of freedom, justice, and individual rights have accorded them a special place of honor... and to whom all Americans owe a lasting debt." The man who pursued his "Holy Experiment" on the shores of the New World was, indeed, one of those men.

Patricia Hudson is a freelance writer from Tennessee and a former contributing editor of Americana *magazine.*

BLESSED AND BEDEVILED

Tales of Remarkable Providences in Puritan New England

Helen Mondloch

On October 31, 2001, Massachusetts Gov. Jane Swift signed a bill exonerating the last five souls convicted of witchcraft during the infamous Salem witch trials of 1692. Rectifying a few of history's wrongs on this Halloween day, the governor's conciliatory gesture was arguably ill-timed, given the frivolous revelry associated with this annual celebration of superstition and frights. In the real-life horror of the witch scare, at least 150 people were imprisoned, including a four-year-old girl who was confined for months to a stone dungeon. Twenty-three men and women, all of whom have now been cleared of their crimes, were hanged or died in prison, and one man was pressed (crushed) to death for his refusal to stand trial.

In probing the underpinnings of this tragic and incredible chapter of American history, New England observers past and present have agreed that the nascent Massachusetts Bay Colony provided a fertile ground for the devil's plagues. Among others, folklore scholar Richard Dorson, author of *America in Legend and American Folklore*, has argued that the frenzy culminating in the witch-hunt was fueled by legends that flourished among the Puritans, a populace that imagined itself both blessed and bedeviled. Of key importance was belief in phenomena called "providences" (more commonly called "remarkable providences"). These were visible, often terrifying, signs of God's will that forged themselves onto the fabric of daily life.

As Dorson explains, "Since, in the Puritan and Reformation concept, God willed every event from the black plague to the sparrow's fall, all events held meaning for errant man." The providences brought rewards or protection for the Lord's followers (generally the Puritans themselves) or vengeance upon His enemies. Sprung from European roots and embraced by intellectuals and common folk alike, they became the subject of a passionate story tradition that enlarged and dramatized events in the manner of all oral legends.

The pursuit of providences was greatly reinforced by those who felt compelled to record their occurrence, including John Winthrop, longtime theocratic governor of Massachusetts Bay Colony. Two prominent New England ministers, Increase Mather and his son Cotton, became the most zealous popularizers of such tales. In 1684 the elder Mather set forth guidelines for their documentation in *An Essay for the Recording of Illustrious Providences*, a study that Cotton Mather would later extend in his own works. The Essay defined "illustrious" providences as the most extraordinary of divinely ordained episodes: "tempests, floods, earthquakes, thunders as are unusual, strange apparitions, or whatever else shall happen that is prodigious." The directives for recording the providences—a duty over which the elder Mather would preside in order to preserve the stories for all posterity—are likened by Dorson to methods observed by modern folklore collectors.

The flip side of the providences were the witchcrafts of the devil, who poised himself with a special vengeance against this citadel of God's elect. Where faith and fear converged, the tales of remarkable providences heightened both.

A 'City Upon a Hill'

In his *Book of New England Legends and Folklore in Prose and Poetry* (1901), Samuel Adams Drake called New England "the child of a superstitious mother." Dorson acknowledges that folk legends in the colonies were "for the most part carbon copies of the folklore in Tudor and Stuart England." But in grafting themselves onto a New World setting, says Dorson, the old beliefs took on a special intensity in the realm of the Puritans.

Many have credited the Mathers with projecting and magnifying this Puritan zeal. Writing at the turn of the last century, historian Samuel McChord Crothers, quoted in B.A. Botkin's *Treasury of New England Folklore*, captured the fervency of the younger Mather, who became a principal driver of the witch-hunt:

> Even Cotton Mather could not avoid a tone of pious boastfulness when he narrated the doings of New England …
>
> … New England had the most remarkable providences, the most remarkable painful preachers, the most remarkable heresies, the most remarkable witches. Even the local devils were in his judgment more enterprising than those of the old country. They had to be in order to be a match for the New England saints.

Perhaps we can gain the proper perspective on the Puritans' passion when we consider the enormous pains they undertook to escape persecution in England and establish their new covenant across the sea. Upholding that covenant was now critical, as evidenced in the lofty proclamations of a sermon delivered in 1630 by John Winthrop. Excerpted in Frances Hill's *Salem Witch Trials Reader*, the governor's words resound with poignant irony given the events that rocked Salem sixty-two years later: "We shall be as a City upon a Hill, the eyes of all people…upon us; so if we shall deal falsely with our God in this work we have undertaken and to cause Him to withdraw His present help from us, we shall be made a story…through the world…and…we shall shame the faces of…God's worthy servants, and cause their prayers to be turned into curses upon us."

Clearly, the task of maintaining this sinless "City Upon a Hill" wrought insecurity among the Puritans, and so, says Dorson, they "searched the providences for continued evidence of God's favor or wrath." As he reveals, popular legends spurred their confidence: "Marvelous escapes from shipwreck, Indian captivity, or starvation reassured the elect that the Lord was guarding their fortunes under His watchful eye."

Cotton Mather recorded many such episodes in his 1702 chronicle titled Magnalia Christi Americana: *The Ecclesiastical History of New England*. In one renowned tale, a spectral ship appeared to an ecstatic crowd of believers in New Haven harbor in 1647. Six months earlier the heavily freighted vessel was presumed lost, after it had sailed from that harbor and never returned. According to Mather's account, quoted by Botkin, the community lost "the best part of their tradable estates…and sundry of their eminent persons." Mather quotes an eyewitness who believed that God had now "condescended" to present the ship's ghostly image as a means of comforting the afflicted souls of the mourners, for whom this remarkable providence affirmed not only their fallen friends' state of grace but also their own.

The Puritans also gleaned affirmation from providences in which the Lord exacted harsh punishments on the enemies of His elect. According to Dorson, the Puritans apparently relished most these tales of divine judg-ment. Those scourged in the tales included Indians, Quakers, and anyone else deemed blasphemous or profane. In the *Magnalia*, Cotton Mather correlates providential offenses to the Ten Commandments. He cites the destruction of the Narragansett Indian nation by a group of white settlers as retribution for the Indians' foul contempt for the Gospel. Oral legends also relayed the fate of Mary Dyer, a Quaker who was sent to the gallows around 1659; Dyer was said to have given birth to a monster, a common curse meted out to nefarious women. Even members of the elect might be struck down by plague or fatal lightning bolts for lapses ranging from the omission of prayer to adultery and murder. The *Magnalia* narrates the doom suffered by various "heretics" who quarreled with village ministers or voted to cut their salaries.

In addition to these ancient themes of reward and punishment, the providence tales incorporated a host of familiar spectacles from an Old World tradition, including apparitions, wild tempests, and corpses that communicated with blood—all magnanimous instruments of an angry but just Lord. Like the spectral ship, apparitions offered hope and solved mysteries; the apparition of a murder victim often disclosed the identity of his killer, a belief that came into play during the witch trials. The age-old notion that a corpse bleeds at the murderer's touch also surfaced abundantly in the tales.

Increase Mather devoted a whole chapter of his *Essay* to thunder and lightning, perceiving in them signs of God's consternation over the advent of secularism in Massachusetts Bay Colony. Mather declared that thunder and lightning had been observed ever since "the English did first settle these American deserts," but warned that only in recent years had they wrought "fatal and fearful slaughters … among us." In the *Magnalia*, Cotton Mather, too, expounded on thunder, a phenomenon that the Harvard scholar and scientist, quoted in Dorson, astutely attributed to the "laws of matter and motion [and] … divers weighty clouds" in collision; lightning, he postulated, derived from "subtil and sulphureos vapours." Like his erudite father, however, Cotton maintained that God was the omnipotent "first mover" of these and other natural forces.

Tales of witchcraft

Dorson explains that "providences issued from God and witchcrafts from the devil, and they marked the tide of battle between the forces of Christ and the minions of Satan." Tales of witchery had their own illustrious elements, including menacing poltergeists, enchantments, and innocent creatures who became possessed and tormented by wicked sorcerers.

He and others have argued that the widely circulated tales of remarkable providences, wherein the Puritans sealed their identity of chosenness, created a fertile climate for witch tales and the witch-hunt. According to

Dorson, "Other Protestants in New York and Virginia, and the Roman Catholics in Maryland, spoke of witchery, but the neurotic intensity of the New England witch scare…grew from the providential aura the Puritans gave their colonial enterprise."

Cotton Mather himself, quoted in Dorson, described the devil's vengeful plot to "destroy the kingdom of our Lord Jesus Christ" in this region that had once been "the Devil's territories" (that is, inhabited by Indians). Both Mathers were implicated as early as the mid-eighteenth-century for promoting bloodlust over witchcraft with their recordings of providence tales. Thomas Hutchinson, governor of Massachusetts Bay in 1771–74, lamented the witch debacle in his *History of the Colony of Massachusetts Bay* (1765). According to Hill, who refers to the governor as a "man of the Enlightenment," Hutchinson's chronicle suggests "that there was widespread disapproval of hanging witches until the *Illustrious Providences and Memorable Providences* [Cotton's later work]…changed the climate of opinion."

Providence lore undoubtedly played a part in the actions of those who spearheaded the witch scare with their clamorous cries of demonic possession. The trouble began in January 1692 when two girls, Betty Parris, the nine-year-old daughter of Salem Village minister Samuel Parris, and her cousin Abigail Williams, age eleven, began experiencing spells of bizarre behavior. In these alarming episodes, the girls convulsed and ranted incoherently. Within a month other neighborhood girls began having similar spells; soon they all began accusing various members of the community of bewitching them.

The cause of these disturbing bouts—which would continue for ten months, until the last of the condemned was pulled down from the gallows—has been the topic of much scholarly speculation and simplistic analysis. Some have theorized, at least as an initiating factor, that the girls suffered from temporary mental illness engendered by eating ergot-infected rye (a theory to which the growing conditions and agricultural practices of the time lend credence, according to Hill). Others have postulated a conspiracy theory incorporating the fierce factionalism that emerged in large part over arguments related to the Reverend Parris' salary and living arrangements.

The most prevalent theory suggests that the girls' hysteria grew from feelings of paranoia and guilt at having dabbled in fortune-telling and other occult practices with Tituba, a native of Barbados who served as the Parris family's slave (and who later confessed, albeit under dubious circumstances, to having engaged in such activities with her young charges). Perhaps one falsehood led to another as the girls struggled to cover up their forbidden deeds; perhaps one or another girl actually believed, for a period, that she had been bewitched; perchance the girls also were pressured by their elders, who were eager to avoid scandal, to reveal the cause of their afflictions. Quite possibly, too, some combination of these factors set into motion the outbursts and subsequent accusations. In

any case, as Hill argues, the girls very likely started out as victims of "human suggestibility" and at some point later became perpetrators of fraud.

This view is supported by the fact that the girls had been reared abundantly on tales of providences and demonic possession. In his popular *Memorable Providences*, quoted by Hill, Mather provided a detailed description of four children who suffered "strange fits, beyond those that attend an epilepsy," as a result of a wicked washer-woman's sorcery. In addition, Hill reveals that Puritans young and old "devoured" sensational pamphlets describing similar demonic episodes, a fact that is hardly surprising, she says, since secular reading was prohibited. In his account of the witch trials, Governor Hutchinson charges that the similarities between these well-known accounts of demonic possession and those of the "supposed bewitched at Salem…is so exact, as to leave no room to doubt the stories had been read by the New England persons themselves, or had been told to them by others who had read them."

One case in particular demonstrates the far-reaching influence of the providence legends: that of Giles Corey, who suffered an excruciating death by pressing for his refusal to stand trial for witchcraft. According to Dorson, as the executions mounted with dreadful fury, the fatal torture of this "sturdy, uncowed farmer" aroused the people's sympathy. Some wondered whether his only crime had been his stubborn silence. Public opinion shifted, however, thanks to the actions of Thomas Putnam, a prominent citizen and the father of twelve-year-old Anne Putnam, one of the principal accusers.

The elder Putnam wrote a letter to Samuel Sewall, one of the trial judges who would later become a famous diarist. The letter reported that on the previous night, Anne had witnessed the apparition of a man who had lived with Giles Corey seventeen years earlier. This "Natural Fool"—perhaps a mentally disabled man—had died suddenly in Corey's house; his ghost now claimed that Corey had murdered him by pressing him to death, causing "clodders of blood about his heart." The apparition reported, moreover, that Corey had escaped punishment for his crime by signing a pact with the devil, whose protective powers were now being usurped by a God who meted out His just desserts—that is, a ghastly punishment precisely matching the crime. Hence, Putnam's letter, now filed by Cotton Mather as an official court document, helped sanctify Corey's execution in the eyes of the citizenry.

By the fall of 1692 the witch crisis had begun to die down. Hill explains that the girls had apparently "overreached themselves by naming as witches several prominent people, including Lady Phipps, the wife of the governor." As the executions began drawing public criticism, Phipps dissolved the witch court and later granted reprieves to the remaining accused. Twelve years later, a sullen Anne Putnam, now twenty-four years old, stood before the congregation in Salem Village Church while the minister read aloud her apology, quoted in Hill, for the "great delusion of Satan" that had caused her to "bring upon…this land the guilt of innocent blood."

A dark legacy

With his strangely circular reasoning, Mather, reflecting on the witch crisis in a 1697 chronicle excerpted by Hill, shaped the tragedies into one great remarkable providence. Oblivious to any possibility of delusion or fraud, he attributed the calamities to God's wrath on New England, ignited by the "little sorceries" practiced by its youth as well as the "grosser" witchcrafts of those condemned: "Although these diabolical divinations are more ordinarily committed perhaps all over the world than they are in the country of New England, yet, that being a country devoted unto the worship and the service of the Lord Jesus Christ above the rest of the world, He signaled His vengeance against such extraordinary dispensations, as have not often been seen in other places."

While post-Enlightenment scholars have generally dismissed Mather's arguments as the rantings of a self-righteous fanatic, his thoughts and actions have left their mark on us. In 1953, the "Red Scare" of the McCarthy era inspired playwright Arthur Miller to re-create the Salem witch-hunt in *The Crucible*. Miller remarked in a 1996 *New Yorker* article, quoted by Hill, that the play's enduring relevance lies in its core subject: "human sacrifice to the furies of fanaticism and paranoia that goes on repeating itself forever."

In our own time, such furies seem painfully present. The era of remarkable providences leaves as its dark legacy a number of lessons not easily reckoned. Now, as the world grapples with the bane of terrorism, Hill's analysis of the Salem trials strikes a contemporary nerve: "The more a group idealizes itself, its own values, and its god, the more it persecutes both other groups and the dissenters in its midst."

Today the American government is repeatedly challenged to implement policies that will prevent the current conflict from turning into a witch-hunt. Moreover, our democratic principles still face the perennial threat of an arrogant religious impulse that has never totally died out. Even now, those among us who boldly stake their claim to the mind of God—like the self-appointed prophets who construed the events of last September 11 as a kind of remarkable providence—risk the resurrection of demons similar to the forces that once ravaged a New England community. The calamities of 1692 entreat us to conquer those demons by loving our neighbor and consigning the will of Providence to the realm of mystery. ■

Additional Reading

B.A. Botkin, ed., *A Treasury of New England Folklore*, Crown Publishers, Inc., New York, 1967.

Richard Dorson, *American Folklore*, University of Chicago Press, Chicage, 1967.

——, *America in Legend: Folklore from the Colonial Period to the Present*, Pantheon Books, New York, 1973.

Samual Adams Drake, *A Book of New England Legends and Folklore in Prose and Poetry*, Little, Brown, 1901.

Frances Hill, *The Salem Witch Trials Reader*, DeCapo Press, Boston, 2000.

Increase Mather, *An Essay for the Recording of Remarkable Providences*, Scholars' Facsimiles and Reprints, Inc., Delmar, N.Y., 1977. Reprint of the 1684 edition printed by J. Green for J. Browning, Boston.

Helen Mondloch is a freelance writer and frequent contributor to the Culture section.

Were American Indians the Victims of Genocide?

Guenter Lewy

On SEPTEMBER 21, the National Museum of the American Indian will open its doors. In an interview early this year, the museum's founding director, W. Richard West, declared that the new institution would not shy away from such difficult subjects as the effort to eradicate American-Indian culture in the 19th and 20th centuries. It is a safe bet that someone will also, inevitably, raise the issue of genocide.

The story of the encounter between European settlers and America's native population does not make for pleasant reading. Among early accounts, perhaps the most famous is Helen Hunt Jackson's *A Century of Dishonor* (1888), a doleful recitation of forced removals, killings, and callous disregard. Jackson's book, which clearly captured some essential elements of what happened, also set a pattern of exaggeration and one-sided indictment that has persisted to this day.

Thus, according to Ward Churchill, a professor of ethnic studies at the University of Colorado, the reduction of the North American Indian population from an estimated 12 million in 1500 to barely 237,000 in 1900 represents a "vast genocide ... , the most sustained on record." By the end of the 19th century, writes David E. Stannard, a historian at the University of Hawaii, native Americans had undergone the "worst human holocaust the world had ever witnessed, roaring across two continents non-stop for four centuries and consuming the lives of countless tens of millions of people." In the judgment of Lenore A. Stiffarm and Phil Lane, Jr., "there can be no more monumental example of sustained genocide—certainly none involving a 'race' of people as broad and complex as this—anywhere in the annals of human history."

The sweeping charge of genocide against the Indians became especially popular during the Vietnam war, when historians opposed to that conflict began drawing parallels between our actions in Southeast Asia and earlier examples of a supposedly ingrained American viciousness toward non-white peoples. The historian

Richard Drinnon, referring to the troops under the command of the Indian scout Kit Carson, called them "forerunners of the Burning Fifth Marines" who set fire to Vietnamese villages, while in *The American Indian: The First Victim* (1972), Jay David urged contemporary readers to recall how America's civilization had originated in "theft and murder" and "efforts toward ... genocide."

Further accusations of genocide marked the run-up to the 1992 quincentenary of the landing of Columbus. The National Council of Churches adopted a resolution branding this event "an invasion" that resulted in the "slavery and genocide of native people." In a widely read book, *The Conquest of Paradise* (1990), Kirkpatrick Sale charged the English and their American successors with pursuing a policy of extermination that had continued unabated for four centuries. Later works have followed suit. In the 1999 *Encyclopedia of Genocide,* edited by the scholar Israel Charny, an article by Ward Churchill argues that extermination was the "express objective" of the U.S. government. To the Cambodia expert Ben Kiernan, similarly, genocide is the "only appropriate way" to describe how white settlers treated the Indians. And so forth.

That American Indians suffered horribly is indisputable. But whether their suffering amounted to a "holocaust," or to genocide, is another matter.

II

It IS A firmly established fact that a mere 250,000 native Americans were still alive in the territory of the United States at the end of the 19th century. Still in scholarly contention, however, is the number of Indians alive at the time of first contact with Europeans. Some students of the subject speak of an inflated "numbers game"; others charge that the size of the aboriginal population has been deliberately minimized in order to make the decline seem less severe than it was.

The disparity in estimates is enormous. In 1928, the ethnologist James Mooney proposed a total count of 1,152,950 Indians in all tribal areas north of Mexico at the time of the European arrival. By 1987, in *American Indian Holocaust and Survival*, Russell Thornton was giving a figure of well over 5 million, nearly five times as high as Mooney's, while Lenore Stiffarm and Phil Lane, Jr. suggested a total of 12 million. That figure rested in turn on the work of the anthropologist Henry Dobyns, who in 1983 had estimated the aboriginal population of North America as a whole at 18 million and of the present territory of the United States at about 10 million.

From one perspective, these differences, however startling, may seem beside the point: there is ample evidence, after all, that the arrival of the white man triggered a drastic reduction in the number of native Americans. Nevertheless, even if the higher figures are credited, they alone do not prove the occurrence of genocide.

To address this issue properly we must begin with the most important *reason* for the Indians' catastrophic decline—namely, the spread of highly contagious diseases to which they had no immunity. This phenomenon is known by scholars as a "virgin-soil epidemic"; in North America, it was the norm.

The most lethal of the pathogens introduced by the Europeans was smallpox, which sometimes incapacitated so many adults at once that deaths from hunger and starvation ran as high as deaths from disease; in several cases, entire tribes were rendered extinct. Other killers included measles, influenza, whooping cough, diphtheria, typhus, bubonic plague, cholera, and scarlet fever. Although syphilis was apparently native to parts of the Western hemisphere, it, too, was probably introduced into North America by Europeans.

About all this there is no essential disagreement. The most hideous enemy of native Americans was not the white man and his weaponry, concludes Alfred Crosby, "but the invisible killers which those men brought in their blood and breath." It is thought that between 75 to 90 percent of all Indian deaths resulted from these killers.

To some, however, this is enough in itself to warrant the term genocide. David Stannard, for instance, states that just as Jews who died of disease and starvation in the ghettos are counted among the victims of the Holocaust, Indians who died of introduced diseases "were as much the victims of the Euro-American genocidal war as were those burned or stabbed or hacked or shot to death, or devoured by hungry dogs." As an example of actual genocidal conditions, Stannard points to Franciscan missions in California as "furnaces of death."

But tight away we are in highly debatable territory. It is true that the cramped quarters of the missions, with their poor ventilation and bad sanitation, encouraged the spread of disease. But it is demonstrably untrue that, like the Nazis, the missionaries were unconcerned with the welfare of their native converts. No matter how difficult the conditions under which the Indians labored—obligatory work, often inadequate food and medical care, corporal punishment—their experience bore no comparison with the fate of the Jews in the ghettos. The missionaries had a poor understanding of the causes of the diseases that afflicted their charges, and medically there was little they could do for them. By contrast, the Nazis knew exactly what was happening in the ghettos, and quite deliberately deprived the inmates of both food and medicine; unlike in Stannard's "furnaces of death," the deaths that occurred there were *meant* to occur.

The larger picture also does not conform to Stannard's idea of disease as an expression of "genocidal war." True, the forced relocations of Indian tribes were often accompanied by great hardship and harsh treatment; the removal of the Cherokee from their homelands to territories west of the Mississippi in 1838 took the lives of thousands and has entered history as the Trail of Tears. But the largest loss of life occurred well before this time, and sometimes after only minimal contact with European traders. True, too, some colonists later welcomed the high mortality among Indians, seeing it as a sign of divine providence; that, however, does not alter the basic fact that Europeans did not come to the New World in order to infect the natives with deadly diseases.

O R DID THEY? Ward Churchill, taking the argument a step further than Stannard, asserts that there was nothing unwitting or unintentional about the way the great bulk of North America's native population disappeared: "it was precisely malice, not nature, that did the deed." In brief, the Europeans were engaged in biological warfare.

Unfortunately for this thesis, we know of but a single instance of such warfare, and the documentary evidence is inconclusive. In 1763, a particularly serious uprising threatened the British garrisons west of the Allegheny mountains. Worried about his limited resources, and disgusted by what he saw as the Indians' treacherous and savage modes of warfare, Sir Jeffrey Amherst, commander-in-chief of British forces in North America, wrote as follows to Colonel Henry Bouquet at Fort Pitt: "You will do well to try to inoculate the Indians [with smallpox] by means of blankets, as well as to try every other method, that can serve to extirpate this execrable race."

Bouquet clearly approved of Amherst's suggestion, but whether he himself carried it out is uncertain. On or around June 24, two traders at Fort Pitt did give blankets and a handkerchief from the forts quarantined hospital to two visiting Delaware Indians, and one of the traders noted in his journal: "I hope it will have the desired effect." Smallpox was already present among the tribes of Ohio; at some point after this episode, there was another outbreak in which hundreds died.

A second, even less substantiated instance of alleged biological warfare concerns an incident that occurred on June 20, 1837. On that day, Churchill writes, the U.S. Army began to dispense "'trade blankets' to Mandans and other Indians gathered at Fort Clark on the Missouri River in present-day North Dakota." He continues:

> Far from being trade goods, the blankets had been taken from a military infirmary in St. Louis quarantined for smallpox, and brought upriver aboard the steamboat St. Peter's. When the first Indians showed symptoms of the disease on July 14, the post surgeon advised those camped near the post to scatter and seek "sanctuary" in the villages of healthy relatives.

In this way the disease was spread, the Mandans were "virtually exterminated," and other tribes suffered similarly devastating losses. Citing a figure of "100,000 or more fatalities" caused by the U.S. Army in the 1836-40 smallpox pandemic (elsewhere he speaks of a toll "several times that number"), Churchill refers the reader to Thornton's *American Indian Holocaust and Survival*.

Supporting Churchill here are Stiffarm and Lane, who write that "the distribution of smallpox-infected blankets by the U.S. Army to Mandans at Fort Clark … was the causative factor in the pandemic of 1836-40." In evidence, they cite the journal of a contemporary at Fort Clark, Francis A. Chardon.

But Chardon's journal manifestly does not suggest that the U.S. Army distributed infected blankets, instead blaming the epidemic on the inadvertent spread of disease by a ship's passenger. And as for the "100,000 fatalities," not only does Thornton fail to allege such obviously absurd numbers, but he too points to infected passengers on the steamboat *St. Peter's* as the cause. Another scholar, drawing on newly discovered source material, has also refuted the idea of a conspiracy to harm the Indians.

Similarly at odds with any such idea is the effort of the United States government at this time to vaccinate the native population. Smallpox vaccination, a procedure developed by the English country doctor Edward Jenner in 1796, was first ordered in 1801 by President Jefferson; the program continued in force for three decades, though its implementation was slowed both by the resistance of the Indians, who suspected a trick, and by lack of interest on the part of some officials. Still, as Thornton writes: "Vaccination of American Indians did eventually succeed in reducing mortality from smallpox."

To sum up, European settlers came to the New World for a variety of reasons, but the thought of infecting the Indians with deadly pathogens was not one of them. As for the charge that the U.S. government should itself be held responsible for the demographic disaster that overtook the American-Indian population, it is unsupported by evidence or legitimate argument. The United States did not wage biological warfare against the Indians; neither can the large number of deaths as a result of disease be considered the result of a genocidal design.

III

STILL, EVEN if up to 90 percent of the reduction in Indian population was the result of disease, that leaves a sizable death toll caused by mistreatment and violence. Should some or all of these deaths be considered instances of genocide?

We may examine representative incidents by following the geographic route of European settlement, beginning in the New England colonies. There, at first, the Puritans did not regard the Indians they encountered as natural enemies, but rather as potential friends and converts. But their Christianizing efforts showed little success, and their experience with the natives gradually yielded a more hostile view. The Pequot tribe in particular, with its reputation for cruelty and ruthlessness, was feared not only by the colonists but by most other Indians in New England. In the warfare that eventually ensued, caused in part by intertribal rivalries, the Narragansett Indians became actively engaged on the Puritan side.

Hostilities opened in late 1636 after the murder of several colonists. When the Pequots refused to comply with the demands of the Massachusetts Bay Colony for the surrender of the guilty and other forms of indemnification, a punitive expedition was led against them by John Endecott, the first resident governor of the colony; although it ended inconclusively, the Pequots retaliated by attacking any settler they could find. Fort Saybrook on the Connecticut River was besieged, and members of the garrison who ventured outside were ambushed and killed. One captured trader, tied to a stake in sight of the fort, was tortured for three days, expiring after his captors flayed his skin with the help of hot timbers and cut off his fingers and toes. Another prisoner was roasted alive.

The torture of prisoners was indeed routine practice for most Indian tribes, and was deeply ingrained in Indian culture. Valuing bravery above all things, the Indians had little sympathy for those who surrendered or were captured. Prisoners, unable to withstand the rigor of wilderness travel were usually killed on the spot. Among those—Indian or European—taken back to the village, some would be adopted to replace slain warriors, the rest subjected to a ritual of torture designed to humiliate them and exact atonement for the tribe's losses. Afterward the Indians often consumed the body or parts of it in a ceremonial meal, and proudly displayed scalps and fingers as trophies of victory.

Despite the colonists' own resort to torture in order to extract confessions, the cruelty of these practices strengthened the belief that the natives were savages who deserved no quarter. This revulsion accounts at least in part for the ferocity of the battle of Fort Mystic in May 1637, when a force commanded by John Mason and assisted by militiamen from Saybrook surprised about half of the Pequot tribe encamped near the Mystic River.

The intention of the colonists had been to kill the warriors "with their Swords," as Mason put it, to plunder the village, and to capture the women and children. But the plan did not work out. About 150 Pequot warriors had arrived in the fort the night before, and when the surprise attack began they emerged from their tents to fight. Fearing the Indians' numerical strength, the English attackers set fire to the fortified village and retreated outside the palisades. There they formed a circle and shot down anyone seeking to escape; a second cordon of Narragansett Indians cut down the few who managed to get through the English line. When the battle was over, the Pequots had suffered several hundred dead, perhaps as many as 300 of these being women and children. Twenty Narragansett warriors also fell.

A number of recent historians have charged the Puritans with genocide: that is, with having carried out a premeditated plan to exterminate the Pequots. The evidence belies this. The use of fire as a weapon of war was not unusual for either Europeans or Indians, and every contemporary account stresses that the burning of the fort was an act of self-protection, not part of a pre-planned massacre. In later stages of the Pequot war, moreover, the colonists spared women, children, and the elderly, further contradicting the idea of genocidal intention.

A SECOND FAMOUS example from the colonial period is King Philip's War (1675-76). This conflict, proportionately the costliest of all American wars, took the life of one in every sixteen men of military age in the colonies; large numbers of women and children also perished or were carried into captivity. Fifty-two of New England's 90 towns were attacked, seventeen were razed to the ground, and 25 were pillaged. Casualties among the Indians were even higher, with many of those captured being executed or sold into slavery abroad.

The war was also merciless, on both sides. At its outset, a colonial council in Boston had declared "that none be Killed or Wounded that are Willing to surrender themselves into Custody." But these rules were soon abandoned on the grounds that the Indians themselves, failing to adhere either to the laws of war or to the law of nature, would "skulk" behind trees, rocks, and bushes rather than appear openly to do "civilized" battle. Similarly creating a desire for retribution were the cruelties perpetrated by Indians when ambushing English troops or overrunning strongholds housing women and children. Before long, both colonists and Indians were dismembering corpses and displaying body parts and heads on poles. (Nevertheless, Indians could not be killed with impunity. In the summer of 1676, four men were tried in Boston for the brutal murder of three squaws and three Indian children; all were found guilty and two were executed.)

The hatred kindled by King Philip's War became even more pronounced in 1689 when strong Indian tribes allied themselves with the French against the British. In 1694, the General Court of Massachusetts ordered all friendly Indians confined to a small area. A bounty was then offered for the killing or capture of hostile Indians, and scalps were accepted as proof of a kill. In 1704, this was amended in the direction of "Christian practice" by means of a scale of rewards graduated by age and sex; bounty was proscribed in the case of children under the age of ten, subsequently raised to twelve (sixteen in Connecticut, fifteen in New Jersey). Here, too, genocidal intent was far from evident; the practices were justified on grounds of self-preservation and revenge, and in reprisal for the extensive scalping carried out by Indians.

IV

WE TURN now to the American frontier. In Pennsylvania, where the white population had doubled between 1740 and 1760, the pressure on Indian lands increased formidably; in 1754, encouraged by French agents, Indian warriors struck, starting a long and bloody conflict known as the French and Indian War or the Seven Years' War.

By 1763, according to one estimate, about 2,000 whites had been killed or vanished into captivity. Stories of real, exaggerated, and imaginary atrocities spread by word of mouth, in narratives of imprisonment, and by means of provincial newspapers. Some British officers gave orders that captured Indians be given no quarter, and even after the end of formal hostilities, feelings continued to run so high that murderers of Indians, like the infamous Paxton Boys, were applauded rather than arrested.

As the United States expanded westward, such conflicts multiplied. So far had things progressed by 1784 that, according to one British traveler, "white Americans have the most rancorous antipathy to the whole race of Indians; and nothing is more common than to hear them talk of extirpating them totally from the face of the earth, men, women, and children."

Settlers on the expanding frontier treated the Indians with contempt, often robbing and killing them at will. In 1782, a militia pursuing an Indian war party that had slain a woman and a child massacred more than 90 peaceful Moravian Delawares. Although federal and state officials tried to bring such killers to justice, their efforts, writes the historian Francis Prucha, "were no match for the singular Indian-hating mentality of the frontiersmen, upon whom depended conviction in the local courts."

But that, too, is only part of the story. The view that the Indian problem could be solved by force alone came under vigorous challenge from a number of federal commissioners who from 1832 on headed the Bureau of Indian Affairs and supervised the network of agents and subagents in the field. Many Americans on the eastern seaboard, too, openly criticized the rough ways of the frontier. Pity for the vanishing Indian, together with a sense of remorse, led to a revival of the 18th-century concept of the noble savage. America's native inhabitants were romanticized in historiography, art, and literature, notably by James Fenimore Cooper in his *Leatherstocking Tales* and Henry Wadsworth Longfellow in his long poem, *The Song of Hiawatha.*

On the western frontier itself, such views were of course dismissed as rank sentimentality; the perceived nobility of the savages, observed cynics, was directly proportional to one's geographic distance from them. Instead, settlers vigorously complained that the regular army was failing to meet the Indian threat more aggressively. A large-scale uprising of the Sioux in Minnesota in 1862, in which Indian war parties killed, raped, and pillaged all over the countryside, left in its wake a climate of fear and anger that spread over the entire West.

Colorado was especially tense. Cheyenne and Arapahoe Indians, who had legitimate grievances against the encroaching white settlers, also fought for the sheer joy of combat, the desire for booty, and the prestige that accrued from success. The overland route to the East was particularly vulnerable: at one point in 1864, Denver was cut off from all supplies, and there were several butcheries of entire families at outlying ranches. In one gruesome case, all of the victims were scalped, the throats of the two children were cut, and the mother's body was ripped open and her entrails pulled over her face.

Writing in September 1864, the Reverend William Crawford reported on the attitude of the white population of Colorado: "There is but one sentiment in regard to the final disposition which shall be made of the Indians: 'Let them be exterminated—men, women, and children together.'" Of course, he added, "I do not myself share in such views." The *Rocky Mountain News,* which at first had distinguished between friendly and hostile Indians, likewise began to advocate extermination of this "dissolute, vagabondish, brutal, and ungrateful race."

With the regular army off fighting the Civil War in the South, the western settlers depended for their protection on volunteer regiments, many lamentably deficient in discipline. It was a local force of such volunteers that committed the massacre of Sand Creek, Colorado on November 29, 1864. Formed in August, the regiment was made up of miners down on their luck, cowpokes tired of ranching, and others itching for battle. Its commander, the Reverend John Milton Chivington, a politician and ardent Indian-hater, had urged war without mercy, even against children. "Nits make lice," he was fond of saying. The ensuing orgy of violence in the course of a surprise attack on a large Indian encampment left between 70 and 250 Indians dead, the majority women and children. The regiment suffered eight killed and 40 wounded.

News of the Sand Creek massacre sparked an outcry in the East and led to several congressional inquiries. Although some of the investigators appear to have been biased against Chivington, there was no disputing that he had issued orders not to give quarter, or that his soldiers had engaged in massive scalping and other mutilations.

THE SORRY tale continues in California. The area that in 1850 became admitted to the Union as the 31st state had once held an Indian population estimated at anywhere between 150,000 and 250,000. By the end of the 19th century, the number had dropped to 15,000. As elsewhere, disease was the single most important factor, although the state also witnessed an unusually large number of deliberate killings.

The discovery of gold in 1848 brought about a fundamental change in Indian-white relations. Whereas formerly Mexican ranchers had both exploited the Indians and provided them with a minimum of protection, the new immigrants, mostly young single males, exhibited animosity from the start, trespassing on Indian lands and often freely killing any who were in their way. An American officer wrote to his sister in 1860: "There never was a viler sort of men in the world than is congregated about these mines."

What was true of miners was often true as well of newly arrived farmers. By the early 1850's, whites in California outnumbered Indians by about two to one, and the lot of the natives, gradually forced into the least fertile parts of the territory, began to deteriorate rapidly. Many succumbed to starvation; others, desperate for food, went on the attack, stealing and killing livestock. Indian women who prostituted themselves to feed their families contributed to the demographic decline by removing themselves from the reproductive cycle. As a solution to the growing problem, the federal government sought to confine the Indians to reservations, but this was opposed both by the Indians themselves and by white ranchers fearing the loss of labor. Meanwhile, clashes multiplied.

One of the most violent, between white settlers and Yuki Indians in the Round Valley of Mendocino County, lasted for several years and was waged with great ferocity. Although Governor John B. Weller cautioned against an indiscriminate campaign— "[Y]our operations against the Indians," he wrote to the commander of a volunteer force in 1859, "must be confined strictly to those who are known to have been engaged in killing the stock and destroying the property of our citizens ... and the women and children under all circumstances must be spared"— his words had little effect. By 1864 the number of Yukis had declined from about 5,000 to 300.

The Humboldt Bay region, just northwest of the Round Valley, was the scene of still more collisions. Here too Indians stole and killed cattle, and militia companies retaliated. A secret league, formed in the town of Eureka, perpetrated a particularly hideous massacre in February 1860, surprising Indians sleeping in their houses and killing about sixty, mostly by hatchet. During the same morning hours, whites attacked two other Indian rancherias, with the same deadly results. In all, nearly 300 Indians were killed on one day, at least half of them women and children.

Once again there was outrage and remorse. "The white settlers," wrote a historian only 20 years later, "had received great provocation.... But nothing they had suffered, no depredations the savages had committed, could justify the cruel slaughter of innocent women and children." This had also been the opinion of a majority of the people of Eureka, where a grand jury condemned the massacre, while in cities like San Francisco all such killings repeatedly drew strong criticism. But atrocities continued: by the 1870's, as one historian has summarized the situation in California, "only remnants of the aboriginal populations were still alive, and those who had survived the maelstrom of the preceding quarter-century were dislocated, demoralized, and impoverished."

LASTLY WE come to the wars on the Great Plains. Following the end of the Civil War, large waves of white migrants, arriving simultaneously from East and West, squeezed the Plains Indians between them. In response, the Indians attacked vulnerable white outposts; their "acts of devilish cruelty," reported one officer on the scene, had "no parallel in savage warfare." The trails west were in similar peril: in December 1866, an army detachment of 80 men was lured into an ambush on the Bozeman Trail, and all of the soldiers were killed.

To force the natives into submission, Generals Sherman and Sheridan, who for two decades after the Civil War commanded the Indian-fighting army units on the Plains, applied the same strategy they had used so successfully in their marches across Georgia and in the Shenandoah Valley. Unable to defeat the Indians on the open prairie, they pursued them to their winter camps, where numbing cold and heavy snows limited their mobility. There they destroyed the lodges and stores of food, a tactic that inevitably resulted in the deaths of women and children.

Genocide? These actions were almost certainly in conformity with the laws of war accepted at "the time. The principles of limited war and of noncombatant immunity had been codified in Francis Lieber's *General Order No. 100,* issued for the Union Army on April 24, 1863. But the villages of warring Indians who refused to surrender were considered legitimate military objectives. In any event, there was never any order to exterminate the Plains Indians, despite heated pronouncements on the subject by the outraged Sherman and despite Sheridan's famous quip that "the only good Indians I ever saw were dead." Although Sheridan did not mean that all Indians should be shot on sight, but rather that none of the warring Indians on the Plains could be trusted, his words, as the historian James Axtell rightly suggests, did "more to harm straight thinking about Indian-white relations than any number of Sand Creeks or Wounded Knees."

As for that last-named encounter, it took place on December 29, 1890 on the Pine Ridge Reservation in South Dakota. By this time, the 7th Regiment of U.S. Cavalry had compiled a reputation for aggressiveness, particularly in the wake of its surprise assault in 1868 on a Cheyenne village on the Washita river in Kansas, where about 100 Indians were killed by General George Custer's men.

Still, the battle of Washita, although one-sided, had not been a massacre: wounded warriors were given first aid, and 53 women and children who had hidden in their lodges survived the assault and were taken prisoner. Nor were the Cheyennes unarmed innocents; as their chief Black Kettle acknowledged, they had been conducting regular raids into Kansas that he was powerless to stop.

The encounter at Wounded Knee, 22 years later, must be seen in the context of the Ghost' Dance religion, a messianic movement that since 1889 had caused great excitement among Indians in the area and that was interpreted by whites as a general call to war. While an encampment of Sioux was being searched for arms, a few young men created an incident; the soldiers, furious at what they considered an act of Indian treachery, fought back furiously as guns surrounding the encampment opened fire with deadly effect. The Army's casualties were 25 killed and 39 wounded, mostly as a result of friendly fire. More than 300 Indians died.

Wounded Knee has been called "perhaps the best-known genocide of North American Indians." But, as Robert Utley has concluded in a careful analysis, it is better described as a regrettable, tragic accident of war," a bloodbath that neither side intended. In a situation where women and children were mixed with men, it was inevitable that some of the former would be killed. But several groups of women and children were in fact allowed out of the encampment, and wounded Indian warriors, too, were spared and taken to a hospital. There may have been a few deliberate killings of noncombatants, but on the whole, as a court of inquiry ordered by President Harrison established, the officers and soldiers of the unit made supreme efforts to avoid killing women and children.

On January 15, 1891, the last Sioux warriors surrendered. Apart from isolated clashes, America's Indian wars had ended.

V

THE GENOCIDE Convention was approved by the General Assembly of the United Nations on December 9, 1948 and came into force on January 12, 1951; after a long delay, it was ratified by the United States in 1986. Since genocide is now a technical term in international criminal law, the definition established by the convention has assumed prima-facie authority, and it is with this definition that we should begin in assessing the applicability of the concept of genocide to the events we have been considering.

According to Article II of the convention, the crime of genocide consists of a series of acts "committed *with intent* to destroy, in whole or in part, a national, ethnical, racial, or religious group as a such" (emphases added). Practically all legal scholars accept the centrality of this clause. During the deliberations over the convention, some argued for a clear specification of the reasons, or motives, for the destruction of a group. In the end, instead of a list of such motives, the issue was resolved by adding the words "as such"—i.e., the motive or reason for the destruction must he the ending of the group as a national, ethnic, racial, or religious entity. Evidence of such a motive, as one legal scholar put it, "will constitute an integral part of the proof of a genocidal plan, and therefore of genocidal intent."

The crucial role played by intentionality in the Genocide Convention means that under its terms the huge number of Indian deaths from epidemics cannot be considered genocide. The lethal diseases were introduced inadvertently, and the Europeans cannot be blamed for their ignorance of what medical science would discover only centuries later. Similarly, military engagements that led to the death of noncombatants, like the battle of the Washita, cannot be seen as genocidal acts, for the loss of innocent life was not intended and the soldiers did not aim at the destruction of the Indians as a defined group. By contrast, some of the massacres in California, where both the perpetrators and their supporters openly acknowledged a desire to destroy the Indians as an ethnic entity, might indeed be regarded under the terms of the convention as exhibiting genocidal intent.

Even as it outlaws the destruction of a group "in whole or in part," the convention does not address the question of what percentage of a group must be affected in order to qualify as genocide. As a benchmark, the prosecutor of the International Criminal Tribunal for the Former Yugoslavia has suggested "a reasonably significant number, relative to the total of the group as a whole," adding that the actual or attempted destruction should also relate to "the factual opportunity of the accused to destroy a group in a specific geographic area within the sphere of his control, and not in relation to the entire population of the group in a wider geographic sense." If this principle were adopted, an atrocity like the Sand Creek massacre, limited to one group in a specific single locality, might also be considered an act of genocide.

OF COURSE, it is far from easy to apply a legal concept developed in the middle of the 20th century to events taking place many decades if not hundreds of years earlier. Our knowledge of many of these occurrences is incomplete. Moreover, the malefactors, long since dead, cannot be tried in a court of law, where it would be possible to establish crucial factual details and to clarify relevant legal principles.

Applying today's standards to events of the past raises still other questions, legal and moral alike. While history has no statute of limitations, our legal system rejects the idea of retroactivity (*ex post facto* laws). Morally, even if we accept the idea of universal principles transcending particular cultures and periods, we must exercise caution in condemning, say, the conduct of war during America's colonial period, which for the most part conformed to then-prevailing notions of right and wrong. To understand all is hardly to forgive all, but historical judgment, as the scholar Gordon Leff has correctly stressed, "must always be contextual: it is no more reprehensible for an age to have lacked our values than to have lacked forks."

The real task, then, is to ascertain the context of a specific situation and the options it presented. Given circumstances, and the moral standards of the day, did the people on whose conduct we are sitting in judgment have a choice to act differently? Such an approach would lead us to greater indulgence toward the Puritans of New England, who fought for their survival, than toward the miners and volunteer militias of California who often slaughtered Indian men, women, and children for no other reason than to satisfy their appetite for gold and land. The former, in addition, battled their Indian adversaries in an age that had little concern for humane standards of warfare, while the latter committed their atrocities in the face of vehement denunciation not only by self-styled humanitarians in the faraway East but by many of their fellow citizens in California.

Finally, even if some episodes can be considered genocidal—that is, tending toward genocide—they certainly do not justify condemning an entire society. Guilt is personal, and for good reason the Genocide Convention provides that only "persons" can be charged with the crime, probably even ruling out legal proceedings against governments. No less significant is that a massacre like Sand Creek was undertaken by a local volunteer militia and was not the expression of official U.S. policy. No regular U.S. Army unit was ever implicated in a similar atrocity. In the majority of actions, concludes Robert Utley, "the Army shot noncombatants incidentally and accidentally, not purposefully." As for the larger society, even if some elements in the white population, mainly in the West, at times advocated extermination, no official of the U.S. government ever seriously proposed it. Genocide was never American policy, nor was it the result of policy.

THE VIOLENT collision between whites and America's native population was probably unavoidable. Between 1600 and 1850, a dramatic surge in population led to massive waves of emigration from Europe, and many of the millions who arrived in the New World gradually pushed westward into America's seemingly unlimited space. No doubt, the 19th-century idea of America's "manifest destiny" was in part a rationalization for acquisitiveness, but the resulting dispossession of the Indians was as unstoppable as other great population movements of the past. The U.S. government could not have prevented the westward movement even if it had wanted to.

In the end, the sad fate of America's Indians represents not a crime but a tragedy, involving an irreconcilable collision of cultures and values. Despite the efforts of well-meaning people in both camps, there existed no good solution to this clash. The Indians were not prepared to give up the nomadic life of the hunter for the sedentary life of the farmer. The new Americans, convinced of their cultural and racial superiority, were unwilling to grant the original inhabitants of the continent the vast preserve of land required by the Indians' way of life. The consequence was a conflict in which there were few heroes, but which was far from a simple tale of hapless victims and merciless aggressors. To fling the charge of genocide at an entire society serves neither the interests of the Indians nor those of history.

GUENTER LEWY, *who for many years taught political science at the University of Massachusetts, has been a contributor to* COMMENTARY *since 1964. His books include* The Catholic Church & Nazi Germany, Religion & Revolution, America in Vietnam, *and* The Cause that Failed: Communism in American Political Life.

From *Commentary*, September 2004, pp. 55-63. Copyright © 2004 by American Jewish Committee. Reprinted by permission of the publisher and author.

UNIT 2

Revolutionary America

Unit Selections

Key Points to Consider

- Discuss the differences between those colonists who wished to pry concessions from the British but who still wanted to remain in the empire, and those who sought nothing less than independence. How did the latter group prevail?

- What purposes was the Declaration of Independence meant to serve? How have perceptions of this document changed over the years?

- It has been said that George Washington lost more battles than any other victorious general. What were his strengths and weaknesses as a general? What was his symbolic importance?

- Why is the debate over the Second Amendment so emotional? Examine both sides of the issue. Does the amendment guarantee the unlimited possession of firearms or does it refer only to the establishment of militias?

Student Website

www.mhcls.com/online

Internet References

Further information regarding these websites may be found in this book's preface or online.

The Early America Review
http://www.earlyamerica.com/review/

House of Representatives
http://www.house.gov

National Center for Policy Analysis
http://www.public-policy.org/web.public-policy.org/index.php

Supreme Court/Legal Information Institute
http://supct.law.cornell.edu/supct/index.html

U.S. Senate
http://www.senate.gov

The White House
http://www.whitehouse.gov/

The World of Benjamin Franklin
http://www.fi.edu/franklin/

We live in an age of instant communication. Our call to complain about a credit card may be answered by someone in India. Television satellites permit the simultaneous viewing of events all over the world. Imagine what it was like in the 18th Century when it took weeks for a message to be delivered from London to one of the colonies, and weeks more to receive a reply. Under such circumstances the British understandably gave wide latitude to royal governors who were on the scene and who knew more about local conditions than could the bureaucrats at home. The fact that the American colonies were but part of the British world empire also discouraged attempts to micromanage their affairs.

According to economic theory at the time, an empire could be likened to an organism with each part functioning in such a way as to benefit the whole. The ideal role of a colony, aside from helping to defend the empire when the need arose, was to serve as a protected market for the mother country's manufactured goods and as a provider of raw materials for its mills and factories. Because imperial rivalries often led to war, particular emphasis was placed on achieving self-sufficiency. An imperial power did not wish to be dependent on another empire for materials—especially those of strategic value such as the shipbuilding materials mentioned in the previous unit—that might be cut off if the two came into conflict.

With regard to the American colonies, those in the South most nearly fit the imperial model. Southern colonies produced goods such as cotton and tobacco that could not be grown in Great Britain, and Southerners were disinclined to become involved in activities that would compete with British manufactures. The New England and the middle colonies were another matter. Individuals in both areas often chafed at imperial restrictions that prevented them from purchasing products more cheaply from other countries or from engaging in manufacturing their own. What served to temper discontent among the colonists was the knowledge that they depended on the protection of the British army and navy against threats by other powers, most notably the French.

During the middle decades of the 1700s, London permitted the colonists to exercise a great deal of control over their own internal affairs so long as they played their designated economic role within the empire. This attitude, which came to be known as "benign neglect," meant that the colonies for all practical purposes became nearly autonomous. The passage of time and the great distances involved combined to make British rule more of a abstraction rather than a day-to-day relationship. Most colonists never visited the mother country, and they might go months or years without seeing any overt signs of British authority. They came to regard this as the normal order of things.

This casual relationship was altered in 1763 when what the colonists called the French and Indian war came to an end after seven years of fighting. The peace brought two results that had enormous consequences. First, British acquisition of French possessions in North America meant that the military threat to the colonists had ended. Second, the war had been enormously costly to the British people who were suffering under staggering tax burdens. The government in London, taking the understandable view that the colonists ought to pay their fair share of the costs, began levying a variety of new taxes and enforcing shipping regulations that previously had been ignored.

The new British crackdown represented to the colonists an unwarranted assault on the rights and privileges they had long enjoyed. Disputes over economic matters escalated into larger concerns about rights and freedoms in other areas. Many colonists who regarded themselves as loyal subjects of the Crown at first looked upon the situation as a sort of family quarrel that could be smoothed out provided there was good will on both sides. When clashes escalated instead, more and more people who now regarded themselves as "Americans" began calling for independence from the motherland. The British, of course, had no intention of handing over portions of their hardwon empire to the upstart colonists. War became inevitable.

"Info Highwayman" treats Benjamin Franklin's early years as author, printer, and publisher. Franklin retired from this business at an early age, but retained his interest in the postal system and in 1753 was appointed Britain's deputy postmaster general for North America. By 1774, the postal system he helped create was earning 4,500 pounds per year of which he kept 1500 pounds for himself.

Much has been made of Paul Revere's ride in April 1775 to warn the Sons of Liberty in Concord that the British were coming. The man who actually completed that mission, Dr. Samuel Prescott, has been unknown except to professional historians. "Midnight Riders" not only pays Prescott the attention he deserves, but also describes the events leading up to the British advance on Concord and Lexington. Even after these battles, and the one at Bunker Hill, many colonists sought a negotiated settlement with Great Britain rather than to embark on the uncertain quest for independence. "The Rocky Road to Revolution" analyzes the debate, and shows how those who wanted to break with the mother country triumphed. Their victory, embodied in the Declaration of Independence, is analyzed in Pauline Maier's "Making Sense of the Fourth of July." She also explains how the meaning and function of the Declaration has changed over the course of time.

Two essays deal with the conduct of the Revolutionary War. "Hamilton Takes Command" shows how the 20-year old Alexander Hamilton's intelligence and courage propelled him into rapid advancement and, most important for his future, brought him to the attention of George Washington. Washington, a towering figure in this nation's history, was almost single-handidly responsible for keeping the colonial armies intact during extremely difficult times. His first command was to preside over the siege of Boston, where he hoped to deal the British a decisive blow. He failed to do so then, but accomplished his goal six years later at the Battle of Yorktown.

The last essay in this unit treats the American Constitution. "Your Constitution is Killing You" discusses changing interpretations of the Second Amendment. The issue continues to be hotly debated between those who believe the amendment guarantees the unconditional right to own guns, and those who believe it was originally intended primarily to provide for the arming of militias.

Flora MacDonald

By a twist of fate, the Scottish heroine who helped Bonnie Prince Charlie escape the British in 1746 immigrated to North Carolina in 1774, only to find herself allied with the Crown during the American Revolution.

By Jean Creznic

"… FLORA MACDONALD, a name that will be mentioned in history, and if courage and fidelity be virtues, mentioned with honour," wrote Doctor Samuel Johnson in *Journey to the Western Isles* after he and his friend James Boswell visited her in Scotland in September 1773. As Johnson predicted, her name is honored among her fellow Scots, and her life has become legend, a story that took this eighteenth-century heroine from the islands of Scotland to the colony of North Carolina, on the eve of America's Revolutionary War.

Flora MacDonald gained renown and the affection of her Scottish Highland countrymen when she helped Prince Charles Edward, the Stuart pretender to the British throne, escape capture in 1746. Her later association with America, though brief, placed her in the thick of the Revolutionary War.

Flora was born in 1722 in Milton, South Uist, one of the Hebrides Islands that lie off the western coast of Scotland.

Her father died when she was a child, and her mother remarried in 1728 and moved to the Hebridean Isle of Skye. Ever the independent thinker, six-year-old Flora declared that she would stay in Milton with her older brother, Angus, rather than go to her mother's new home. She said that she would be happier with him there than in a house that was strange to her. Later, an aunt and uncle took charge and sent her to school in Edinburgh, after which, she lived as a member of a privileged family, spending her time in ladylike pursuits, frequently traveling to visit relatives and friends.

The adventure that brought Flora fame began as she was staying with relatives at Ormaclade, on South Uist. The talk in Scotland was all about Prince Charles Edward Stuart, known by the Scots as Bonnie Prince Charlie, and how he might reestablish the Catholic Stuarts as Great Britain's rightful rulers. The prince was the grandson of the Stuart King James II, who had reigned in Britain during 1685–88. English sentiment against Catholicism ran high during his reign, and James, whose sympathies leaned more and more toward Rome, fled to France in 1688 when the overthrow of the throne appeared imminent. His son, also named James, spent his life in France and Italy, plotting to regain his father's throne.

During the first half of the eighteenth century, the pressure on James's son, Charles Edward, to succeed to the throne

was enormous, but England under Protestant King George II had no intention of allowing the Catholic Stuarts to wear the crown. Despite the fact there was no encouragement for Prince Charles Edward from that quarter, agents of the exiled Stuarts traveled the Scottish Highlands, striving to enlist the support of the Highland clans. They succeeded in rallying a small band of Jacobites (supporters of the House of Stuart), most of them MacDonalds, to the cause.

Arriving in Scotland in August 1745, the prince and his followers launched their long awaited campaign. Although well begun, the effort was nevertheless doomed to failure and ended the next year on April 16, 1746, at the Battle of Culloden, where the prince and his five thousand Highland supporters were crushed by some nine thousand infantrymen led by George II's son, William, the Duke of Cumberland.

The English showed the weakened Scots no mercy, and this defeat sealed the fate of the prince and of the resurgence of the House of Stuart. Charles Edward fled for his life after the battle, hiding from the Duke of Cumberland's soldiers wherever he could, finally making his way to the western isles, and Flora MacDonald.

Some say that Flora's stepfather, Hugh MacDonald—a sympathizer of Prince Charles Edward despite his position as the commander of the government militia in South Uist—suggested her participation in the escape. Others credit the scheme to the prince's comrade and fellow soldier, Captain Felix O'Neill, who was acquainted with Flora and knew her to be a young woman of admirable common sense. Still other accounts say that her actions were entirely spontaneous. Whichever version of the events is accurate, the facts surrounding the plan that Flora devised and carried out have never been disputed.

With a bounty of £30,000 offered for his capture, the Bonnie Prince was hunted by British troops as well as local militia. Every traveler was suspect, and a passport was required of anyone wishing to leave the island or to come ashore. Careful planning would be required to effect the escape of such a notorious fugitive.

Flora, who already had her passport, built a scheme around her intended trip to see her sick mother at Armadale on the Isle of Skye. Once she succeeded in getting the prince to Skye, he would make his way to mainland Scotland and be picked up by a French naval vessel, which would transport him to safety in Europe.

Hugh MacDonald supplied the passports that Flora needed for the several boatmen, a manservant, and an Irish spinning maid who would help care for his ailing wife. According to the plan, Betty Burke, the Irish maid, would make the crossing bundled up against the wind and sea in a bonnet, cloak, and shawl, making it difficult for anyone to have a close look at her face—all for the best since "Betty," an ignorant and ungainly looking servant girl, would indeed be the Bonnie Prince.

Daylight lingers in June in the Hebrides, which increased the risk of the travelers being discovered by government scouts. The prince's party decided to hide themselves on shore until dark, when there would be less chance of being intercepted by British patrol vessels. In spite of high winds and stormy seas, they set out for the Isle of Skye on the night of June 28. En route, they narrowly avoided at least one British boat that passed so close they could hear the sailors' voices.

Landing on Skye the following morning, they made their way to Portree, where friends hid the prince until he could exchange his female attire for kilt and plaid, then sail to the mainland, and on to France. At Portree, Prince Charles Edward and Flora parted, never to meet again.[1]

Flora spent a few days with her mother, then went to visit her brother at Milton. But word of the adventure got out. The authorities quickly apprehended Flora, and after questioning her, imprisoned her aboard a British sloop-of-war. In July, the ship made for Leith, just beside Edinburgh on the Firth of Forth, where it lay for several weeks.

By this time, all of Scotland seemed to have learned of Flora's part in the prince's escape, and many people, proclaiming her a heroine, came to visit her on the prison ship. November found her in the Tower of London, but she was soon paroled to the house of a Mr. Dick, an official Messenger at Arms in whose home prisoners of war who could pay for their keep were permitted to stay. Virtually free, Flora was allowed to visit friends, albeit always accompanied by Mr. Dick's daughters. She became something of a celebrity in London, and wealthy benefactors soon appeared with funds for her support at Mr. Dick's home.

Freed once and for all in July 1747, Flora headed straight for Scotland and home. She went to stay with her mother at Armadale, but her adventures had brought her such renown that she was a coveted visitor about Skye.

On November 6, 1750, Flora—reportedly dressed in a gown of Stuart tartan—married Allen MacDonald. But living happily ever after was not to be the lot of Flora and Allen. Hard times for the Highlanders increased after the short-lived campaign that had ended at Culloden, and those who had sided with Prince Charles Edward, especially the few who had given him shelter as he fled, seemed to face the most difficulties.

Over the years, the financial situation of Flora and Allen and their seven children steadily worsened. Feeling they had nothing to look forward to in Scotland but more oppression, the couple decided to leave for America. In 1774, they followed a growing number of their neighbors on Skye, including their married daughter, Anne, to North Carolina.[2] Leaving their youngest son and daughter with friends in Scotland who would see to the youngsters' education, they took two of their older boys with them.

Flora and Allen were met in North Carolina with great fanfare and ceremony; friends held a ball in her honor at Wilmington. When the festivities subsided after several days, the new immigrants moved on to Cross Creek (now Fayetteville), where Flora stayed while Allen searched for a site on which to establish their new home. Near Rockingham, he found a place that would suit them and named it "Killiegrey." The property already had a dwelling and several outbuildings, so Flora, in her fifties by now, settled in, perhaps thinking she had found peace and security at last.

Their neighbors treated the famous Flora and her husband with great respect, and they came to occupy a prominent position in the community. Aside from one claim that Allen built and operated a grist mill on their land, almost nothing is known of their everyday life. J. P. MacLean's *Flora MacDonald in America*, published in 1909, does say, however, that "their influence was everywhere felt and acknowledged."

The peace that Flora was enjoying proved to be momentary; the American War for Independence erupted, and even remote Killiegrey soon became entangled in the troubles. At first it seemed that the North Carolina Scots would take up the American cause, urged on by a committee of patriots who conferred "with the gentlemen who have lately arrived from the Highlands in Scotland to settle in this province... to explain to them the nature of our unhappy controversy with Great Britain, and to advise and urge them to unite with the other inhabitants of America in defense of their rights...."

But Josiah Martin, royal governor of North Carolina, did everything in his power to persuade the Highlanders to remain loyal to the Crown. In view of the treatment they had suffered at home at the hands of the British, it seemed unlikely they would ally themselves with the British cause in America. But threats, propaganda, and coercion from Governor Martin and his agents prevailed, and the

Scots, many of them MacDonalds, were won over. They organized a sizable army of volunteers, with Allen as a colonel.

In February 1776, events rushed toward a climax for the Highlanders. Word came that they were to meet a British fleet scheduled to land at Cape Fear and then nip the revolution in North Carolina in the bud. Although they were as secretive as possible, the difficulty inherent in concealing the movements of groups of armed men soon led to the patriots learning what was taking place.

An estimated 1,500 to 3,000 Highlanders assembled for the march, and Flora came out to cheer them on their way. Mounted on a white horse, she reviewed the troops, and then rode along for a short distance with Allen and their son-in-law, Alexander MacLeod, a captain in the regiment. With all attempts at maintaining secrecy apparently forgotten, the marching column made a dramatic departure, "drums beating, pipes playing, flags flying."

The Highlanders headed east to the coast, marching at night and criss-crossing creeks along the way in an attempt to evade opposing forces. They eluded Colonel James Moore, who, with about 650 troops from the First North Carolina Continentals, had been sent to head them off at Corbett's Ferry on the Black River.

When he realized that he had been outmaneuvered, Moore ordered Colonel Richard Caswell, commanding some eight hundred Parisan Rangers from New Bern, to cut the Scots off at Moore's Creek Bridge. Caswell and his men, along with 150 other troops commanded by Colonel Alexander Lillington, reached the bridge and quickly constructed earthworks on the west side of the creek. Deciding to abandon these works and meet the loyalist troops on the other side of the creek, they crossed the bridge, removing a section of flooring behind them as they went. After digging new entrenchments, they waited for the Scots to arrive.

Seeing the abandoned earthworks, the Highlanders assumed that their crossing of the bridge would be unopposed. Nonetheless, Colonel Donald McLeod, the Scots' senior officer, led a charge, shouting "King George and Broadswords" as he ran toward the bridge. Shielded by breastworks, the Americans, who had two cannon to assist them, opened fire, almost immediately shattering the attack.

The first battle of the Revolution fought in North Carolina, "the Insurrection of the MacDonalds" left many Highlanders dead or wounded; a number of the loyalist troops drowned after losing their footing while trying to cross the section of the bridge where the flooring had been removed.[3] Many of the Highlanders were taken prisoner, among them Allen MacDonald and his son Alexander, a lieutenant in the loyalist regiment, who were jailed in the town of Halifax.

Things went badly for Flora after the Battle of Moore's Creek Bridge. Recognizing the part she had played in recruiting Highlanders and her influential role in the Scottish settlements, the revolutionaries were not about to allow her to escape punishment. She was viewed with suspicion by those who took the patriot side and deeply resented by the families who had lost men in the battle at Moore's Creek. Summoned to appear before the local Committee of Safety, Flora answered the charges against her with dignity and courage, defending her activities among her Scottish countrymen. Although the committee permitted her to return to Killiegrey, her property was confiscated a year later.

In August 1777, after having been moved several times by his captors, Allen was permitted to go to New York City to negotiate an exchange for himself and his son, Alexander. He was on his honor "not to convey to the enemy or bring back any intelligence whatever of a political nature, and to return [to Reading, Pennsylvania] in a certain time to be fixed by his parole or when called for, on behalf of the United States."

By November, he had succeeded in his mission and soon joined his battalion in Nova Scotia, where he was stationed at Fort Edward, in Windsor. Flora, having first made her way to British-held New York City with her daughter and grandsons, arrived there the next year. Her health had suffered from her ordeal, and in late 1779, Flora, her daughter, and the children sailed for Scotland.

Home at last, Flora went to stay in a cottage on her brother's property in Milton. In 1784, the war over and his regiment disbanded, Allen returned home to Flora. The couple went back to Kingsburgh House on Skye, where they had started their marriage. Less than six years later, on March 5, 1790, Flora died. One of the bed sheets on which Prince Charles Edward had slept so many years before served as her shroud. She had kept the sheet with her during her North American sojourn and carried it back again to Skye, requesting that she be buried in it when the time came.

By all accounts, Flora's funeral was the grandest ever seen on the Isle of Skye. The procession to the cemetery stretched for more than a mile. People had traveled from all the islands and from the mainland to pay their last respects to the patriotic lady in whose heart Scotland was always first.

NOTES

1. Charles Edward Stuart spent the next twenty years in Europe, devising futile plots to establish his claim to the British throne. He returned to Rome, the city of his birth, at the time of his father's death in 1766. He remained there until he died in 1788. His remains are entombed in the vaults of St. Peter's Basilica in Rome.
2. More than 23,000 Highland Scots left their homeland for the American colonies between 1764 and '76.
3. The surviving loyalist troops claimed that the Americans had greased the wooden girders of the bridge with soft soap and tallow after removing the flooring, causing the attackers to slip while trying to cross.

Jean Creznic is senior editor of Early American Homes *magazine and a student of Scottish lore.*

Info Highwayman

As a media baron, Ben Franklin did well by doing good

WALTER ISAACSON

IN HIS SPEECHES ABOUT THE NATION'S EMERGING "information superhighway," Vice President Al Gore sometimes cites the patron saint of American networking. Ever since Benjamin Franklin consolidated the U.S. postal system, Gore says, "open access" has been a basic principle of the way we distribute information. His point is that cable and phone companies should open their new networks to anyone—including competitors—who wants to use them to distribute movies, news and other products. Opponents say that builders of new networks have a right to decide what goes on them and that they must be allowed some economic advantage or there will be no incentive to build them.

The vice president may be right about information technologies. But he is mistaken, I think, about where Ben Franklin might stand in the open-access debate. Although he was, as our schoolbooks tell us, a public-spirited man who put his genius at the service of the common good, the wily Philadelphia printer lived by the maxim that one could "do well by doing good." He was, in fact, the nation's first "info highwayman," a creative and competitive entrepreneur with an instinct for profits. He would have fit right in with John Malone, Ted Turner and Barry Diller at a cable-industry trade show.

When Franklin became postmaster of Philadelphia in 1737, the key issue was the right of a distributor to play gatekeeper, just as it is with media barons and cable operators today. In other words, to what extent should the manager of a network be allowed to determine what goes on it? The previous postmaster, Andrew Bradford, had been sending his newspaper through the mail for free while preventing Franklin's from getting carriage. When Franklin took over as postmaster, "my old competitor's newspaper declined," he wrote, "and I was satisfied without retaliating his refusal, while postmaster, to permit my papers being carried?"

Franklin's open-access policy lasted less than two years. His battle with Bradford for control of the posts was part of a publishing rivalry that had begun in the 1720s and would culminate in 1740 with a fevered competition to launch America's first magazine. The story of

their rivalry sheds light on the relationship between public networks and private commerce—and the mix of public and private control of the info highway—that has existed, as Vice President Gore would say, ever since Benjamin Franklin.

IN 1723, THE DAY AFTER HE ARRIVED IN PHILADELPHIA AS A 17-year-old runaway from Boston, Benjamin Franklin walked into Andrew Bradford's printing shop and applied for a job. Bradford, a prosperous gentleman, instead offered breakfast and a referral: He told Franklin he should visit the town's other printer, a newcomer to the trade named Samuel Keimer, who might be looking for a journeyman. If not, Bradford generously offered, Franklin could come back and lodge at his house until "fuller business should offer?"

The incident offered Franklin an early glimpse of the odd mix of cooperation and competition among Philadelphia businessmen. Bradford's father accompanied young Franklin to Keimer's shop, and Keimer assumed that the old man was merely a kindly stranger rather than the father of his competitor. So Keimer, garrulous and naive, began boasting how he would soon become the town's dominant printer. The elder Bradford, Franklin recalled, "drew him on by artful questions and starting little doubts to explain all his views, what interest he relied on, and in what manner he intended to proceed?" Only later did Keimer discover who the old man was.

Franklin treated Keimer less like a boss than like a dotty but beloved uncle. He was a dabbler in odd religions and had once belonged to a sect called the French Prophets, whose adherents spoke in tongues and preached the coming of doomsday. "He retained a great deal of his enthusiasms and loved argumentation," Franklin wrote. Franklin used to practice confounding him through Socratic questioning, asking Keimer innocent-sounding queries until he was so tangled in his logic that he would give up arguing. In fact, he almost gave up answering any of Franklin's questions. "He grew ridiculously cautious and would hardly answer me the most common question without asking first, What do you intend to infer from that?"

So impressed was Keimer with Franklin's rhetorical skills that he proposed they start a religion together. "He was to preach the doctrines, I was to confound the opponents," Franklin wrote. Franklin agreed on one condition: A tenet of the religion must be to forbid eating meat. "He was usually a great glutton," Franklin said of Keimer, "and I promised myself some diversion in half-starving him." Surprisingly, the pact lasted three months. Finally, Keimer decided to abandon the enterprise and order a roasted pig to be shared by himself, Franklin and two "women friends." Keimer, however, ended up not sharing his feast, as Franklin recalled: "It being brought too soon upon [the] table, he could not resist the temptation, and ate it all before we came."

Such a partnership was not destined to last. Franklin traveled to England in hopes of buying his own printing presses and supplies, and when his credit fell through he returned to Philadelphia to find another partner. By 1728, he was able to open a printing shop of his own. His first project, he decided, would be to launch a lively newspaper to compete with the only one that existed in Philadelphia, Andrew Bradford's *American Weekly Mercury*. Bradford's paper, Franklin ungenerously (and rather unfairly) said, "was a paltry thing, wretchedly managed, and no way entertaining; and yet was profitable to him."

"If thou proceed any further, we intend to have thy right ear for it"

But Franklin made the mistake of confiding his plan to a friend, who passed it along to Keimer. Keimer than decided to preempt his former employee by starting a newspaper himself. "I resented this," Franklin wrote, "and to counteract them, as I could not yet begin our paper, I wrote several pieces of entertainment for Bradford's paper." The goal was to run Keimer's paper out of business by enlivening Bradford's pages with a series of anonymous pieces along the lines of the "Silence Dogood" essays that Franklin had written as a teenage apprentice for his brother's paper in Boston.

Thus were born the delightful "Busy-Body" essays, which began appearing in Bradford's *Mercury* in February 1729, just weeks after Keimer's rival weekly was launched. "I have often observed with concern that your *Mercury* is not always equally entertaining," Franklin declared in his first article, cleverly establishing the inadequacies of Bradford's paper and his own intent to make it—at least temporarily—better. And the way to do that, Franklin noted, was to report on "the growing vices and follies" of his neighbors. He readily admitted that such matters are "nobody's business," but upon "mature deliberation" and "out of zeal for the public good," he announced himself willing "to take nobody's business wholly into my own hands."

Franklin waited until the third Busy-Body essay to skewer Keimer. He did so by creating a fictional character named Cretico who was clearly (especially to Philadelphia readers at the time) based on Keimer in his temperament and style. "Thou art crafty, but far from being wise," the Busy-Body wrote about Cretico. The cringing demeanor of Cretico's apprentices, the essay continued, was "like the worship paid by Indians to the devil," motivated more by fear than gratitude.

Keimer responded with a blustery admonition against "gaining popular applause" by defaming others, and he warned the Busy-Body to avoid "gross descriptions." Although the Busy-Body never mentioned Keimer by name, Franklin and his writing partner continued to nettle him, provoking responses in Keimer's paper that served only to shore up the circulation of Bradford's.

Even more pointedly, Franklin used two other pen names to catch Keimer in what today would be called a gaffe. Keimer had been filling up the pages of his papers each week by reprinting, in alphabetical order, entries from an English encyclopedia. By the fifth week, he had gotten to the entry on abortion, which he methodically reprinted. The following week there appeared in Bradford's *Mercury*—on the front page—two letters of feigned outrage signed with names that, as subsequent scholarship has established, sprang from Franklin's own pen: "Martha Careful" and "Caelia Shortface."

"If he proceed further to expose the secrets of our sex," Martha Careful wrote about Keimer, "my sister Molly and myself, with some others, are resolved to take him by the beard at the next place we meet him and make an example of him for his immodesty" Caelia Shortface, on the other hand, threatened, "If thou proceed any further in that scandalous manner, we intend very soon to have thy right ear for it."

Franklin's plan worked: "Keimer's credit and business declining daily," Franklin noted, "he was at last forced to sell his printing-house to satisfy his creditors." Franklin bought the paper and renamed it *The Pennsylvania Gazette*. He promptly quit writing for Bradford and became, instead, a tough competitor.

The Franklin-Bradford newspaper war included disputes over scoops and stolen stories. In 1730, Franklin, then only 24, wrote in an editor's note: "When Mr. Bradford publishes after us, and has occasion to take an article or two out of the *Gazette*, which he is always welcome to do, he is desired not to date his paper a day before ours lest distant readers should imagine we take from him, which we always carefully avoid?"

The rivalry was heightened later that year when Franklin set out to win from Bradford the job of being official printer for the Pennsylvania Assembly. After Bradford printed a message of the assembly in a sloppy fashion, Franklin saw his opening. He printed the same message "elegantly and correctly," as he put it, and sent it to each of the members. "It strengthened the hands of our friends in the house," Franklin later recalled, "and they voted us their printers."

The rivalry turned more personal when Franklin, then a young bachelor, began courting the daughter of one of the town's merchants. To Franklin, marriage (like much else) was a business matter, and he began to negotiate the size of his dowry. He let it be known that he "expected as much money with their daughter as would payoff my remaining debt for the printing-house," which was about 100 pounds. The family sent back word that they had no such sum to spare, so Franklin suggested they "might mortgage their house in the loan office." As brash as this might sound, it was not unusual for eligible men to demand a dowry to set themselves up in business.

At this point the family decided to ask Andrew Bradford for his opinion. The older printer replied, not without some conflicting self-interest, that the business was not a profitable one, that Philadelphia could not support two printers and that Franklin would probably soon go bankrupt. So the family broke off negotiations and barred their daughter from seeing Franklin. (Franklin soon after had an illegitimate son and entered into a common-law marriage with the daughter of his first landlord.)

There was also a political basis to the rivalry: Bradford was aligned with Pennsylvania's "proprietary faction," which supported the Penn family and their appointed governors, while Franklin was more populist and tended to support the rights of the elected assembly. Politics and personality combined during the 1733 reelection campaign of the assembly's speaker, Andrew Hamilton, an anti-proprietary leader who had helped Franklin wrest the government printing job away from Bradford.

Hamilton had opposed the reappointment of the current governor, who in turn fought Hamilton's reelection. Bradford's *Mercury* jumped in with fervent attacks against Hamilton. Among them was an essay, "On Infidelity," that was pointed at both Hamilton and Franklin. There followed a piece accusing Hamilton of insulting the Penn family, attempting to depose the governor and abusing his power as head of the loan office. Franklin came to Hamilton's defense with a dignified yet damning rebuttal in the *Gazette*. Cast as an account of a "Half-Hour's Conversation" with Hamilton, the piece skewered the *Mercury* article for sins ranging from malapropism (using "contemptibly" when the author meant "contemptuously") to hiding behind the cloak of anonymity ("seeing it was commonly agreed to be wrote by nobody, he thought nobody should regard it").

Bradford's most vicious assault on Franklin arose out of a prank that turned into a tragedy. The apprentice of one of the town's druggists wanted to become a Freemason, and his employer decided to have some fun with him. A group of businessmen devised a fake Masonic ritual and oath, which they showed to Franklin, who was active in Philadelphia's Masonic order. Franklin was amused, and he even read the fake oath to some of his friends. But he did not participate in the prank and was not present when the businessmen continued their trickery with an initiation ceremony involving burning brandy. The lad was accidentally caught in the flames and suffered a lingering and agonizing death. Franklin was initially able to avoid the ensuing public outcry and criminal charges, but Bradford subsequently printed a venomous letter attacking him. It claimed, with some justification, that Franklin had known about the prank when it began and had even laughed when shown the oath. In his own paper, Franklin had to concede that he knew of the joke, but he claimed he tried to dissuade the perpetrators from going further with it. He felt compelled to include in his paper testimonials about his character by two of his prominent supporters.

Bradford made it necessary for Franklin to bribe postal riders

During the press war, Franklin's business flourished. In 1732 he began publishing *Poor Richard's Almanac*, which became a bestseller (10,000 copies a year), and he started creating franchises and partnerships (some of them secret) with printers in South Carolina, Rhode Island, Connecticut, New York, Antigua, Dominica and Jamaica. Through these partnerships, Franklin was able to build up a regular income while extending his influence over newspapers and post offices around the Colonies, and beyond.

There was, however, one problem: Bradford was the postmaster of Philadelphia, and he used that position to deny Franklin the right, at least officially, to send his *Gazette* through the mail. Because Bradford controlled the post office, Franklin noted, "it was imagined he had better opportunities of obtaining news, his paper was thought a better distributor of advertisements than mine, and therefore had many more." Nowadays, even with a myriad of regulations to govern the relationship between "content providers" and "transport providers" on the info highway, the two groups continue to come into conflict. Back then, the conflict took place with almost no rules of the road.

At one point Franklin persuaded Col. Alexander Spotswood, the Crown-appointed deputy postmaster general for the Colonies, to order Bradford to run an open system and carry rival newspapers. In the *Gazette* in 1735, Franklin ran an announcement of Spotswood's order. But Bradford continued to make it difficult for Franklin's papers to get carriage, forcing him to bribe the postal riders. Not only was this expensive; as was often the case, Franklin was worried about public perception. "Tho' I did indeed receive and send papers by the post, yet the public opinion was otherwise; for what I did send was by bribing the riders who took them privately."

Franklin, who admitted that this "occasioned some resentment on my part," was determined to wrest the Philadelphia postmastership away. That became possible because Bradford did a poor job of keeping his records. Colonel Spotswood, with Franklin's encouragement, withdrew Bradford's commission in 1737 and offered the job to Franklin. "I accepted it readily," Franklin noted, "and found it to great advantage." The *Gazette* began to gain in both circulation and advertising.

Instead of reciprocating with a closed-network policy of his own, Franklin allowed Bradford's *Mercury* to be carried through the mails along with the *Gazette* and others at least initially. In his *Autobiography*, Franklin congratulated himself for being so open. "I thought so meanly of him for it," Franklin wrote, referring to Bradford's closed-network policy, "that when I afterwards came into his situation, I took care never to imitate it."

Because Bradford never settled the accounts from his tenure as Philadelphia postmaster, Spotswood sent Franklin an order to "commence suit against him" and "no longer suffer to be carried by the post any of his newspapers." Bradford had to resort to Franklin's old practice of bribing the riders to deliver his papers unofficially. Franklin knew this and tolerated it, just as Bradford had earlier tolerated the same from Franklin. But even this indulgence by Franklin was not to last.

In 1740, he and Bradford became involved in a race to start the first magazine in America. Franklin came up with the idea first, but once again he was betrayed by a confidant. This time the culprit was a lawyer, John Webbe, who had contributed essays to the *Gazette* and who had been chosen by Franklin to file the suit against Bradford that Spotswood had ordered. Franklin described the magazine and offered him the job of editor.

Stunning Franklin, Webbe took the idea to Bradford because he wanted a better partnership deal that would give him more of the profits. On November 6, 1740, Bradford announced the prospectus for *The American Magazine*. One week later, Franklin published his own plan for *The General Magazine*. (Copies of *The General Magazine*, *The Pennsylvania Gazette* and *Poor Richard's Almanac*, along with many books and personal papers, are in the Benjamin Franklin Collection at the Library of Congress.) In his announcement, Franklin denounced Webbe's betrayal. "This magazine … was long since projected," he wrote in the *Gazette*. "It would not, indeed, have been published quite so soon, were it not that a person, to whom the scheme was communicated in confidence, has thought fit to advertise it in the last *Mercury* … and reap the advantage of it wholly to himself." The ensuing spat led Franklin to bar completely Bradford's paper from the mails. It also turned the question of postal access into a public issue.

Webbe responded in the *Mercury* the next week with a sharp counterattack of his own titled "The Detection." He particularly objected to what was indeed one of Franklin's less endearing traits: his clever way of implying allegations rather than making them outright. Franklin's indirection, "like the slyness of a pickpocket," was more "dastardly" than the audacity of a direct liar, Webbe

wrote. As far as defending himself, Webbe was more muted. His best excuse was that Franklin had indeed confided his "desire" to print a magazine, "but surely his making the proposal neither obliged me to the writing of one for him to print, nor restrained me from the printing of it at any other press."

Franklin did not respond. With an exquisite sense of how to goad Webbe and Bradford, he merely reprinted his original notice in the next issue of the *Gazette*, including the same allegation of Webbe's duplicity. This led Webbe to publish another screed in the next edition of Bradford's *Mercury*. Once again Franklin showed infuriating restraint: He again reprinted his original notice.

Webbe responded in the December 4 *Mercury* by escalating the dispute in a way guaranteed to draw a response from Franklin. "Since my first letter," Webbe wrote, referring to his missive two weeks earlier, Franklin had "taken upon him to deprive the *Mercury* of the benefit of the post."

In the next *Gazette*, Franklin gave a somewhat disingenuous reply. It had been a year, he said, since Bradford's *Mercury* had been barred use of the mails. This had nothing to do with the dispute over the magazines. Instead, it was at the order of Spotswood. To prove his point, Franklin printed the Spotswood letter that told him to file suit against Bradford and not carry his paper. He said that both Bradford and Webbe knew this to be the case, Webbe in particular, since he had been the lawyer Franklin retained to file the suit.

Webbe replied by laying out the history of the postal practices. Yes, he conceded, Spotswood had ordered Franklin to stop carrying Bradford's paper a year earlier. But as Franklin well knew, the riders had continued to carry the papers unofficially. Moreover, Webbe charged, Franklin had confided to people that he permitted this arrangement because it helped assure that Bradford would take care not to print anything too harmful to Franklin. "He had declared," wrote Webbe, "that as he favored Mr. Bradford by permitting the postman to distribute his papers, he had him therefore under his thumb."

The debate over postal practices quieted down as both sides raced to put out America's first magazine. Bradford and Webbe's *American Magazine* came off the press February 13, 1741, and Franklin's *General Magazine* appeared on the 16th. Neither was a success; Bradford's folded in three months, Franklin's in six. The most distinguished of Franklin's literary contributions to come out of the venture was a poem in Irish dialect parodying one of Bradford's *American Magazine* advertisements.

Franklin's interest in printing and publishing was in fact winding down. But his interest in the postal system and in networks for the distribution of information continued to grow. He held the Philadelphia postmaster job until 1753, when the Crown appointed him Britain's deputy postmaster general for North America.

It was in this capacity that Franklin created the operating protocols that led to the growth of an open and standardized national network, one that permitted universal access. After he retired from the printing business at 42, he dedicated himself more to public service. He even refused to take patents on his most famous inventions—including the lightning rod and the Franklin stove—because he felt the public would be better served by opening up the ideas to anyone who wanted to manufacture and market them.

Still, Franklin continued to view the postal system as a family business. Throughout his life, he installed his relatives and newspaper partners in key postmaster jobs, including passing along the Philadelphia position to his illegitimate son, William, whom he later made comptroller of the whole system. During one Christmas visit to Boston, he gave his older brother John the post office there. When his sister's son complained about being slighted, he was given the job in New Haven.

Franklin viewed the Colonies' new information highway much the way a modern media baron would: a system operated not merely for the common good but also for private profit. When he took the job, it paid only 150 pounds per year, yet he had authorized a friend in London to spend 300 pounds to help him secure it. Then Franklin and the other deputy postmaster invested 900 pounds to overhaul the system so that it could become profitable. By 1774, the system was clearing 4,500 pounds per year, 1,500 pounds of which Franklin kept as his cut. For him, the link between communication and commerce was always clear, just as was the potential link between the public good and private gain.

MIDNIGHT RIDERS

Following a convoluted series of events, Paul Revere and William Dawes were sent to alert Lexington and Concord that the British were coming. But it was a virtually forgotten third rider who would complete their mission.

Charles J. Caes

In the days leading up to April 15, 1775, Dr. Joseph Warren had been receiving reports of unsual movements within the Bristish army as well as increased activity aboard the king's ships in Boston Harbor. On that Sunday, Warren, now nearly in complete charge of the radical groups increasingly protesting British rule, including the action-oriented Sons of Liberty, decided that the reported movements were suspicious enough to be brought to the attention of John Hancock and John Adams in Lexington. The man Warren called on to give that warning was none other than Paul Revere, one of the leaders of the Sons.

Revere was a popular and often recruited messenger: He was swift, intelligent and dependable. An engraver and silversmith by profession, Revere longed for a military commission but found he could best serve the colonies as a courier, printer and gunpowder manufacturer. He would eventually get his chance to command troops, but that opportunity would not present itself until the war was 3 years old.

For now, Revere was satisfied to work with the Sons of Liberty, the group of freedom fighters who had banded together a decade earlier in response to British taxation. Since 1765, the Sons had been threatening and harassing British officials, ostracizing or punishing supporters of the king, and coercing merchants to stop buying goods from the mother country. Samuel Adams, who was looking for every opportunity to break with England, and other leaders of the revolutionary element were gaining impressive ground, though the true extent of their popular support remained unsure. Colonials were an independent lot.

Revere made haste to Lexington, trying to attract as little attention as possible. He knew that the British commander, General Thomas Gage, had at least one spy among the Sons and that this spy and other Gage men always kept an eye on his movements. Nevertheless, Revere made the 15-mile journey without incident. He duly reported at his destination, "Boats belonging to the trans-ports were all launched and carried under the Sterns of Men of War." He may also have reported that, the day before, British troops in Boston had been taken off regular duties and might be preparing to march the 18 miles to Concord, where they could seize or destroy the arms and ammunition in the town's well-known arsenal.

"I returned at night through Charlestown," Revere recalled in a 1798 account given to Dr. Jeremy Belknap, founder of the Massachusetts Historical Society. "There I agreed with a Colonel [William] Conant, and some other gentleman, that if the British went out by water, we would shew two lanthorns in the Old North Church steeple; and if by land, one, as a signal; for we were apprehensive it would be difficult to cross the Charles River, or get over Boston neck."

Dr. Warren probably realized that he would soon have to ask Revere to carry another message from him, and it might be one that would forever change the course of Colonial history. Warren was well aware the conflict between England and its colonies might soon come to blows. He knew that the majority of colonists still saw themselves as citizens of England, and although they might support the protests against the crown, simply sought the same political and economic rights as full British subjects rather than a complete break with the motherland. Warren also realized that some of the more outspoken Colonial leaders sought full independence. What he didn't know was whether or not the independent citizens-at-large would give their support to the Sons of Liberty and other Patriots who might decide to take up arms against the British.

Relations between England and the colonies had been deteriorating rapidly following an event that had occurred some 16 months before. On the evening of December 16, 1773, about 60 men disguised as Mohawk braves had raided three ships in Boston Harbor. Two thousand others from Boston and neighboring towns watched as the raiders went into the ships' holds, carried out more than 300 chests of tea, and for the next three or four hours tossed the tea overboard and destroyed the chests. Their well-rehearsed mission was carried out with the discipline of highly trained operatives, and, except for the splashing water, there was hardly a whisper or even much noise resulting from their numbers and hard work. When most of the cargo of tea had been destroyed, the "Mohawks" lined up on the wharf, dusted themselves off, and filed away. They left silently, leaving behind no one hurt and no property damage but the tea.

Of this event John Adams, who would one day become president, wrote in his diary, using the chaotic capitalization of the time: "The people should never rise without doing something to be remembered—something notable and striking. The Destruction of the Tea is so bold, so daring, so firm, intrepid and inflexible, and it must have so important Consequences, and so lasting, that I can't but consider it as an Epocha in History."

Not everyone, however, shared Adams' view, and Revere and most of the Boston Patriots were surprised to learn that their Tea Party, as it came to be called, was condemned not only by the Tories—those loyal to the British crown—but also by some of the more radical members of the Patriots' cause. In fact, even Ben Franklin chided them publicly, calling what they had done "an act of violent injustice." He insisted Boston should be required to make the necessary restitution.

The reasons for the decision to target tea for a defiant display of resentment had been many. In May 1773, the British Parliament had passed the Tea Act, intended to bolster the privately owned and financially troubled East India Company. The act provided that tea could be shipped to the colonies only in East India vessels, was to be stored in company warehouses to be built in the colonies, and could be sold directly to retailers only by East India agents. It also adjusted import duties to allow East India to undercut the prices of Colonial merchants and smugglers who had offered strong competition. In essence, the East India Company was granted a monopoly on the tea trade to the colonies.

Colonists were angered because Parliament had again passed legislation that meddled in Colonial affairs without giving voice, vote or legal recourse to those most affected. In addition, the legislated monopoly immediately threatened to put legitimate Colonial tea merchants out of business and to undersell the smugglers. (By the time of the Boston Tea Party, some estimates suggest that 90 percent of the tea consumed in the colonies was smuggled in, and many noted patriots, including John Hancock, found that trade both adventurous and highly profitable.)

In late 1773, with three British tea-laden vessels, *Dartmouth, Eleanor* and *Beaver,* waiting to be offloaded in Boston Harbor, Patriot spokesmen attempted to negotiate with Royal Governor of Massachusetts Thomas Hutchinson and the East India Company's agents—two of whom were Hutchinson's sons—to have the tea sent back to England. When those negotiations failed, a general boycott of English tea was called for and it was decided that the raid on the three ships was the best way to express how serious the matter was to the colonists.

When news of the Tea Party reached England, King George III declared that the Colonials had finally gone too far and petitioned Parliament to design measures for a suitable response. The result was a series of acts specifically designed to punish Massachusetts. Among other provisions, the English closed the port of Boston until the tea was paid for, made illegal any town meeting except those authorized by the governor or necessary for the regular election of officers, and allowed public buildings so designated to be used to house the military. Called the "Intolerable Acts" by the colonists, they were intrinsically punitive measures, and the other colonies feared that if the British were to get away with punishing Massachusetts in this way, a precedent would be set for dealing with all the colonies.

The result was demonstrations in all major cities. The protests and demands of the colonists increased, and before long mere protests became outcries for the colonies to unite. These events led to a proposal in the Massachusetts House of Representatives that a Congress be convened in Philadelphia that year to respond to British demands. The First Continental Congress went into session on September 3 and continued to October 26. Representatives from all the colonies except Georgia attended.

Each colony was given one vote, and it became quite clear that when the votes were counted, they would reflect a Congress well resolved to fight the British Acts. As it turned out, the Congress declared the Intolerable Acts had no constitutional foundation and recommended that Massachusetts should form an independent government and withhold payment of any taxes until the Acts were repealed. It also established the Continental Association to promote boycotts of British goods and recommended that each colony establish an armed militia.

The Tea Act, the Tea Party, the Intolerable Acts and the First Continental Congress had created a political tide that could not be avoided. Dr. Warren probably realized that there was no way of sailing against it, and all he could do was command as best he could while being driven by its force. That General Gage had increased his Boston garrison to about 10,000 men was a sign to the Patriot leadership that the British were ready to move against the colony.

If Gage had his way, he would have had 20,000 men in the garrison, but Parliament winced at this request, thinking there was hardly any real threat of a rebellion. After all, they believed, Gage's true threat was simply a small number of disorganized radicals egged on by Colonial money, with profit as motive. It was preposterous to think that the entire Massachusetts colony would ever consider taking up arms against the motherland.

Parliament made one thing very clear to Gage: He had to crush the Sons of Liberty and other radical groups once and for all, and soon. By the time of Revere's April 15 dispatch to Adams and Hancock, Gage already had in his possession direct orders from British Secretary of State Lord Dartmouth to act with force.

Gage was not enthusiastic about his orders. Like most soldiers of rank and experience, he knew no one could ever be sure just how a battle might turn out. Besides, in this case, it would be friend against friend in many instances: Mutual respect had developed between British officials and soldiers and the colonists with whom they had entered congenial social and business relationships. Gage had hoped that a show of force on his part would make the Colonials realize that armed resistance was of no avail and was therefore disappointed when Parliament would not allow him more troops. Nevertheless, if he were to fight, he would do so with all skill and determination, and with all the force he could command.

Organizing his best troops for what he advertised as a training exercise, Gage prepared them for a search-and-destroy mission to Concord. At the same time he would also attempt to find, and capture or kill, Hancock and Adams. To command the forces against Concord, he selected Colonel Francis Smith. Second-in-command was Major John Pitcairn, whose surname is best recognized outside of England for its attachment to the Pacific island named for his son Robert.

Expecting only token opposition, Gage gave no specific orders on how to handle armed resistance. He only advised his commanders to move swiftly on the evening of April 18, 1775, for he knew the citizens of Concord were relocating their munitions. To stop them, he planned to move light infantry and grenadiers by longboat across Boston's Back Bay, and then march them to Concord. Meanwhile, he put patrols on the roads from both Boston and Charlestown with orders to lay hold of anyone attempting to warn Concord. The plan would have been seamless except that there were not enough boats to keep the schedule. Ferrying could not be completed until after midnight.

Early in the evening of the 18th, as soon as Dr. Warren was aware that Gage's men were marching to Boston Common, he called for two messengers to carry word to Lexington and Concord. The warning had to get out, and two messengers on different pathways increased the odds of success.

Warren called for the first, William Dawes Jr., a tanner and neighbor who lived on Ann Street no more than 300 yards from Warren, and Dawes responded instantly. He either arrived with his uncle Josiah Waters or met him at Warren's house. Once there, Dawes received instructions to take a very specific route to deliver messages at Roxbury, Cambridge, Menotomy (now Arlington), Lexington and Concord. But his journey would not end there. From Concord, he was to proceed to Waltham, where he would instruct the militia to prepare an ambush. Once this mission was complete, Dawes was to return to Menotomy for additional instructions from Warren.

Dawes wasted no time in riding off, but proceeded slowly at first since his uncle was following on foot at a distance to see that Dawes got past the British checkpoints at Boston Neck. Uncle Josiah reported the successful passage to Dr. Warren as his nephew rode on to Roxbury. There, Dawes reported to Patriot General William Heath and instructed him to meet Warren and the Committee of Safety in Menotomy, explaining that from there Heath and Warren would proceed on to Lexington, where Heath would assume command of the militia.

The second rider called was Revere, who would be given a shorter route. Why Warren waited until 10 p.m. to summon him is hard to discern. In any event, by the time Revere appeared, Dawes had already been to Roxbury and was on his way to Cambridge. Warren was in an anxious mood when Revere arrived and implored him to leave immediately for Lexington to report on the latest news about British troop movements.

Revere was quickly on his way. He assumed he had been given the same instructions as Dawes, but later realized their missions were not exactly the same. He no doubt also realized that his own high profile often worked against him, and that Warren, well aware of this, was using him as backup.

Popular literature leaves the impression of a quick dash to his horse and a gallop to Lexington. The start of Revere's journey was actually far less theatrical. "I left Dr. Warren, called upon a friend, and desired him to make the signals," Revere recalled. The friend was Robert Newman, and the signal was to be that of the two lanterns. "I then went home took my boots and surtout [a tight-fitting coat], and went to the north part of town, where I kept a boat; two friends rowed me across the river..." and past a man-of-war. When they arrived on the Charlestown side, he hurried into town, where he met Colonel William Conant and some others. Revere learned they were already advised of the British strategy thanks to the double-lantern signal from Newman. Reporting all he knew about Gage's movements and possible intentions, Revere borrowed a horse, possibly named Brown Beauty, and raced off toward Lexington. At one point around Charlestown Neck, he was chased by two British officers, but some talented riding and a soft-bottomed pond that trapped one of the Britons allowed Revere to escape capture.

By this time, Dawes had already been to Cambridge to warn that British troops were on their way over water to Concord from Charlestown, but that the majority of the force was traveling by land with heavier battle equipment. In order to further thwart the British, the townspeople tore up most of the planks from the Great Bridge and left them stacked at the Cambridge end.

Revere went on to Medford and then Menotomy. "In Medford," he recorded, "I awaked the Captain of the minutemen; and after that, I alarmed almost every house, till I got to Lexington. I found Messrs. Hancock and Adams at the Rev. Mr. Clark's. I told them of my errand, and inquired of Mr. Dawes."

Revere was afraid that Dawes might have been captured by the British, perhaps by the same two officers who had chased him. In fact, Dawes was in Menotomy warning the Committee of Safety that they might be taken prisoner if found. Dawes, however, did indeed come close to capture but avoided it by entering into conversation and riding along with some British soldiers. He finally arrived in Lexington to warn Hancock and Adams about a half-hour after Revere.

After allowing themselves time to refresh, Revere and Dawes set off to warn Concord and tell its militia to move its arsenals to safer places. Along the way, they heard a rider approaching, and at first both were apprehensive, for little that night could be predictable. But the rider was alone and friendly enough.

He was 24-year-old Dr. Samuel Prescott, who had just spent the evening with a young lady with whom he was evidently quite smitten. Prescott's personality, mannerisms, voice and knowledge of the Sons of Liberty—in which he claimed membership—won the trust of Dawes and Revere. While Prescott was not another of Warren's official messengers, when he learned of the mission Revere and Dawes were on, he was eager to play his role in warning the people of Concord.

"I likewise mentioned, that we had better alarm all the inhabitants till we got to Concord," Revere noted in his account for the Massachusetts Historical Society. "The young doctor much approved of it, and said, he would stop with either of us, for the people between [there] and Concord knew him. And would give the more credit to what we said."

The three horsemen continued on their journey, Revere riding perhaps a 100 yards ahead of Dawes and Prescott, probably to scout or draw out trouble in time for the others to get away. As it turned out, the strategy paid off. They were riding right into a British patrol commanded by Major Edward Mitchell.

Revere called out a warning to Dawes and Prescott. Dawes immediately turned his horse and started for Lexington. Prescott galloped toward Revere, instinctively intent on facing whatever challenge was at hand, but by the time he reached Revere, the British were too well positioned, their guns or swords drawn for the kill. Prescott knew the terrain, however; he wheeled his horse about suddenly and, riding pell-mell, jumped a stone wall and raced off toward Concord. Two British horsemen sped after him.

An expert horseman, the young doctor fearlessly guided his horse through the forest, leading his pursuers toward a swamp too threatening for the British to enter. They feared being led into a trap or finding themselves and their mounts sinking deep into mud and water. Prescott, on the other hand, knowing the terrain, guided his horse swiftly through the mud and water or around it.

Prescott pushed through a thicket, on the other side of which he knew was the home of a fellow minuteman. After quietly riding around to the rear of the house, he began banging on the kitchen door until he had awakened every one. When Sergeant Samuel Hartwell, of the Lincoln Minute Men, recognized Prescott, he came to the window and asked why he was there. The young physician explained that the British were on the march and told Hartwell to alert his fellow militiamen. He then turned his mount toward his hometown, and, as he raced away, the sergeant prepared himself to spread the word on the road back toward Lexington.

Mitchell's men captured Revere, but Mitchell, worried that he and his men were in harm's way or insufficiently prepared to take advantage of an opportunity, was extremely angry that the other two riders had escaped. He had Revere brought to him and quickly put a gun to Revere's head. "I'm about to ask you some questions," he warned. "If I do not get the true answers, I will blow your brains out."

Revere made up a story that Mitchell was in greater danger than he, claiming he had already warned the entire colony about what Gage was planning, and that hundreds of men were between Mitchell and Boston. Most important, Revere pointed out, Mitchell could expect no reinforcements; the troops he was expecting from across the river had run aground.

Mitchell could not decide if Revere was lying, but thought it best to retreat to Lexington. On their way, Mitchell heard a shot, then a volley of shots. He feared that it might be the result of a skirmish and that, perhaps, Revere was telling the truth after all. In fact, the shots had been fired by members of the local militia testing their firearms.

Unsure of the reason for the gunfire, Mitchell decided his best course of action was to cut across Lexington Common with maximum speed. Movement, he decided, would be safer and swifter without prisoners, so he reluctantly released Revere and others he was holding.

Although Revere's horse had been given to one of Mitchell's men, Revere knew the area well and took little time running through a cemetery and across pastures to reach the Hancock-Clarke House. There he found both Hancock and Adams eagerly awaiting the latest news while debating whether to stay and fight or head for safety. Since they were the brains behind the revolt, their capture would be costly to the cause as well as devastating to morale.

Hancock wanted to join the militia and stand against the British; Adams argued that they were better off retreating to Philadelphia. Hancock eventually agreed that Adams' judgment was, perhaps, the better, and the leaders asked Revere to see to their safe escort for part of their journey to Philadelphia. They were pleased when he agreed.

While Revere and another man were moving a chest of papers from a tavern room for Hancock, Captain John Parker, a veteran of the French and Indian War, was mustering about 80 minutemen onto Lexington Green. As they assembled, Colonel Pitcairn marched a column of light infantry up the road toward Parker. It was shortly after 5 a.m., and there was enough light for Revere and his friend to see what poor Parker was up against. Revere, a veteran soldier, must have wondered if the minutemen had any chance at all.

When the minutemen realized the British were fearless, determined and well-armed, they considered that this might be their very last day on earth, so they began to back away. Parker ordered them to stand fast. The minutemen on Lexington Green watched the determined and well-armed British troops march toward them, counted their far superior number, and heard Pitcairn call out for Parker and his men to lay down their arms and disperse. Parker's instinct told him the odds were against him, and he responded by ordering his men to put down their weapons and leave the scene.

As they began to do so, a shot rang out, followed by more. The British answered with a volley and charged with bayonets drawn. When it was over, eight minutemen lay dead, another 10 wounded. The war for independence had begun.

Because Revere had been captured by Mitchell, he was never able to complete in its entirety the mission for which he was recruited. Dawes was instrumental in bringing the necessary warnings to Roxbury, Cambridge, Menotomy and Lexington (though here, after Revere), but after his escape from Mitchell and his men, Dawes was unable to race on to Concord. In fact, records are unclear on just where he finally wound up on the morning of the 19th. However, thanks to the swashbuckling young Dr. Prescott, Warren's message did reach Concord in time for its arsenal to be moved to safer ground. By the time the British marched on Concord, they found only a small number of arms and supplies.

Boston born and bred, Paul Revere remains the most historically popular of the three riders. He fought in the French and Indian War and was, to name a few of his talents and skills, a silversmith, an engraver, a printer and even a dentist before the revolution. After the revolution, he served as a lieutenant colonel of artillery, designed the first seal for the united colonies, and managed to stay employed in lucrative ventures.

After the famous ride, Dawes fought in the war and possibly at Bunker Hill. Afterward, he and his brother-in-law, John Coolidge, opened a general store in Worcester, Mass. From 1786 to 1787, he saw duty as a clerk in the Ancient and Honorable Artillery Company of Massachusetts. Life after the war was not particularly easy for William, for he had aged parents to take care of as well as his own family, and his meager finances provided only a minimum amount of security. About 1790, he began raising cash by selling properties he owned in Boston (his birthplace) and Worcester. Widowed and remarried, he died in Marlboro.

Samuel Prescott, who remains mostly a mystery to historians, received little recognition for his famous ride. Up until the time of the revolution, he was a practicing physician, having served his apprenticeship under the tutelage of his father, Abel Prescott, a successful doctor. Even less is known about his life after the war began, except that he was a surgeon in the Ticonderoga campaign, and later served aboard a privateer. Two stories have emerged about his death. One says that he was captured at Ticonderoga, there to die in prison. Another tells that he was captured at sea and died in British custody at Halifax. There is no record of his having married.

Prescott's courage, daredevil riding and strong voice did more than bring timely warning to his friends and neighbors in Concord. His rousing of other Sons of Liberty along the way increased the network of "expresses" who rapidly and thoroughly spread the message in outlying areas that the British were on their way. As the records show, only Prescott finished the midnight ride to Concord; not Dawes, not Revere.

The Rocky Road to Revolution

While most members of Congress sought a negotiated settlement with England, independence advocates bided their time.

John Ferling

We hold these truths to be self-evident, that all men are created equal, that they are endowed by their Creator with certain unalienable Rights, that among these are Life, Liberty and the pursuit of Happiness— That to secure these rights, Governments are instituted among Men, deriving their just powers from the consent of the governed ...

LABORING AT HIS DESK in the midst of a Philadelphia heat wave in June 1776, Thomas Jefferson hastened to complete a pressing assignment. A Congressional committee, recognizing his "happy talent for composition," had given the 33-year-old Jefferson responsibility for drafting a declaration of independence, a document that Congress needed almost immediately. Jefferson, one of Virginia's seven delegates to the Second Continental Congress, worked in his two-room apartment on the second floor of a tradesman's house at Market and Seventh streets, a heavily trafficked corner. He rose before sunrise to write and, after the day's long Congressional session, he returned to his lodging to take up his pen again at night. Toward the end of his life, Jefferson would say that his purpose had been to "place before mankind the common sense of the subject." Congress, he recalled, required an "expression of the American mind."

Jefferson well knew that America was at a defining moment in its history. Independence would sever ties with a long colonial past and propel the 13 states—and the new American nation to which they would belong—into an extremely uncertain future. Jefferson also knew that Congress wanted the declaration completed by July 1, less than three weeks after he was given the assignment.

No one appreciated better than he the irony in the sudden desire for haste. Jefferson had been prepared to declare independence perhaps as much as a year earlier, from the moment that war against the mother country erupted on April 19, 1775. Yet Congress had refused. In the 14 months since American blood had been shed at Lexington and Concord, American soldiers had also died at Bunker Hill, in the siege of Bos-

ton, and during an ill-fated invasion of Canada. In addition, the Royal Navy had bombarded and burned American towns, and the colonists' commerce had been nearly shut down by a British blockade. Still, Congress had not declared independence.

But not even Jefferson, passionate advocate of independence that he was, fully grasped the importance of the document he was preparing. Nor did his colleague, John Adams of Massachusetts, who had masterminded the arduous struggle within Congress to declare independence. Focused single-mindedly on that contentious undertaking, Adams regarded the actual statement itself as a mere formality—he would call it "a theatrical show"—a necessary instrument of propaganda. Jefferson, for his part, said little about his accomplishment. Not long after his work was completed, he would depart Philadelphia to return to his responsibilities in the Virginia legislature. Still, he was more than mildly vexed that Congress had made revisions—or "mutilations," as he put it—to the language of his original draft. Historians now agree that Congress' alterations and excisions enhanced the Declaration's power. Jefferson's magisterial opening passage, and indeed, much of his original language, actually survived intact.

Today, the passage of time has dulled our memory of the extent to which many Americans, including a majority in the Continental Congress, were, for a very long period, reluctant to break ties completely and irrevocably with Britain. The creation of the document we have come to regard as the seminal expression of revolutionary ardor was by no means inevitable. More than two-and-a-quarter centuries after the Declaration was signed, this eloquent assertion of individual rights, reinstalled last September in a state-of-the-art glass encasement at the National Archives in Washington, D.C., can be assessed in all of its complexity—as the product of the protracted political debate that preceded its formulation.

BY THE SUMMER of 1776, the patience of many congressmen had been sorely tried by bitter wrangling over the question of whether or not to declare independence. Many of the legislators thought it nonsensical to fight a war for any purpose other than independence, yet others disagreed. For month after bloody month Congress had sat on its hands, prompting John Adams to exclaim early in 1776 that America was caught "between Hawk and Buzzard," fighting a war it could not win unless it declared independence from Britain, thereby prompting England's enemies, most prominently France, to aid in the struggle.

America's war with the mother country had commenced when a British army of nearly 900 men, acting on orders from London, had marched from Boston to Concord, intending to destroy a colonial arsenal and, if possible, capture ringleaders John Hancock and Samuel Adams. The Second Continental Congress, which assembled in Philadelphia just three weeks later, had barely been gaveled to order when John Rutledge of South Carolina, a 35-year-old lawyer from Charleston, raised the critical question: "Do We aim at independancy? or do We only ask for a Restoration of Rights & putting of Us on Our old footing [as subjects of the crown]?" It would take Congress 14 months to answer that question.

Congress quickly divided into two factions. One felt that the British actions at Lexington and Concord in April required nothing less than a clean break from the motherland; they believed colonists would always be second-class citizens in the British Empire. This faction would have declared independence in May or June 1775. But a second faction, which comprised a substantial majority in Congress, yearned to be reconciled with Britain. These delegates believed in waging war only to compel London to accept America's terms—Rutledge's "old footing"—to return to the way things were before Parliament tried to tax Americans and claim unlimited jurisdiction over them.

Opposition to Parliament had been growing since it enacted the first American tax, the Stamp Act of 1765. At the First Continental Congress, which met in Philadelphia in September 1774, some delegates wanted to force repeal of it and other repressive measures through a trade embargo. A more conservative faction had pushed for a compromise to provide American representation in Parliament. In the end, Congress adopted the trade boycott, and war had come. "Nothing," wrote John Adams, "but Fortitude, Vigour, and Perseverance can save Us."

Most who had attended the First Continental Congress now sat in the Second, where they were joined by several fresh faces. For instance, Hancock, who had escaped capture at Lexington thanks to Paul Revere's timely warning, was now a member of the Massachusetts delegation. Sixty-nine-year-old Benjamin Franklin, who had just returned to Philadelphia after a decade in London, had been named a delegate from Pennsylvania. Gone were those from the First Continental Congress who refused to countenance a war against Britain, prompting Richard Henry Lee of Virginia to observe that a "perfect unanim-

ity" existed in the Second Continental Congress, at least on the war issue.

John Adams concurred that a "military Spirit" that was "truly amazing" had seized the land. Militiamen were "as thick as Bees," he said, marching and drilling everywhere, including in the steamy streets outside the Pennsylvania State House where Congress met. His cousin, Samuel Adams, believed an equally militant spirit gripped Congress and that every member was committed to "the Defence and Support of American Liberty." The Adams cousins soon discovered, however, that while all in Congress supported the war, sentiment for severing ties with Britain was strong only in New England and Virginia. Reconciliationists prevailed everywhere else.

John Adams counseled patience. "We must Suffer People to take their own Way," he asserted in June 1775, even though that path might not be the "Speedyest and Surest." He understood that to push too hard for independence was to risk driving conservative Americans back into Britain's arms. Thus, for most of 1775, the pro-independence faction never spoke openly of a break with Britain. Adams likened America to that of "a large Fleet sailing under Convoy. The fleetest Sailors must wait for the dullest and slowest." For the foreseeable future, he lamented, "Progress must be slow."

But Adams was confident that those who favored reconciliation would be driven inexorably toward independence. In time, he believed, they would discover that London would never give in to America's demands. Furthermore, he expected that war would transform the colonists' deep-seated love for Britain into enmity, necessitating a final break.

Reconciliationists were strongest in the Middle Atlantic colonies (New York, New Jersey, Pennsylvania, Maryland and Delaware) and in South Carolina, all of which had long since been drawn into the economic web of the Atlantic world. Before the war, the products of the backcountry—furs, hides and lumber—as well as grain, had moved through New York and Philadelphia to markets in the Caribbean and England. Charleston exported indigo and rice. In return, English-manufactured goods entered the colonies through these ports. Business had flourished during most of the 18th century; in recent years Philadelphia's merchants had routinely enjoyed annual profits of more than 10 percent.

The great merchants in Philadelphia and New York, who constituted a powerful political force, had other compelling reasons for remaining within the empire. Many relied upon credit supplied by English bankers. The protection afforded to transatlantic trade by the Royal Navy minimized insurance and other overhead costs. Independence, Philadelphia merchant Thomas Clifford asserted in 1775, would "assuredly prove unprofitable." The "advantages of security and stability," said another, "lie with ... remaining in the empire."

And there was fear of the unknown. Some in Congress spoke of a break with Britain as a "leap in the dark," while others likened it to being cast adrift on "an Unknown Ocean." To be sure, many things *could* miscarry should America try to go it alone. After all, its army was composed of untried soldiers led, for the most part, by inexperienced officers. It possessed neither a navy nor allies and lacked the funds to wage a lengthy conflict. The most immediate danger was that the fledgling nation might lose a war for independence. Such a defeat could unleash a series of dire consequences that, the reconciliationists believed, might be avoided only if the colonies, even in the midst of war, were to negotiate a settlement *before* breaking absolutely with Britain. The reconciliationists held that it was still possible to reach a middle ground; this view seemed, to men such as John Adams, a naive delusion. Finally, the anti-independence faction argued, losing the war might well result in retaliation, including the loss of liberties the colonists had long enjoyed.

Even victory could have drawbacks. Many felt independence could be won only with foreign assistance, which raised the specter of American dependence on a European superpower, most likely autocratic and Roman Catholic France. But Adams believed that fear of anarchy accounted for most conservative opposition to independence. More than anything, said Adams, it rendered "Independency ... an Hobgoblin, of so frightfull Mein" to the reconciliationists.

PENNSYLVANIA'S JOHN DICKINSON soon emerged as the leader of those who sought rapprochement with Britain. Dickinson, who was 43 in 1775, had been raised on plantations in Maryland and Delaware. One of the few supporters of the war to have actually lived in England, where he had gone to study law, in London, he had not been impressed by what he found there. The English, he concluded, were intemperate and immoral; their political system was hopelessly corrupt and run by diabolical mediocrities. Returning to Philadelphia to practice law in 1757, he was soon drawn to politics.

Tall and thin, Dickinson was urbane, articulate and somewhat prickly. A patrician accustomed to having his way, he could be quick-tempered with those who opposed him. He had once brawled with a political adversary and challenged him to a duel. Early in the Second Continental Congress, following an incendiary speech by Adams, Dickinson pursued him into the State House yard and, in a venomous outburst, as recounted by Adams, demanded: "What is the reason, Mr. Adams, that you New Englandmen oppose our Measures of Reconciliation. ... Look Ye," he threatened, "If you don't concur with Us, in our pacific System, I, and a Number of Us, will break off from you ... and We will carry on the Opposition by ourselves in our own Way." Adams was infuriated by Dickinson's invective: the two never spoke again.

Dickinson had a distinguished record. In 1765 he had served in the Stamp Act Congress convened to protest that measure. Two years later, he published his cogent and illuminating *Letters from a Farmer in Pennsylvania,*

America's most popular political tract before 1776, which assumed that Parliament, though possessed of the right to regulate trade, lacked authority to tax the colonists. That was the very stand taken by 1774's First Continental Congress, and a constitutional settlement along those lines—not independence—was what the reconciliationists hoped to achieve through war. Dickinson charged that London had launched an "inexpressibly cruel War." Its "Sword is opening our Veins," he said, compelling Americans to fight for their freedom.

But he also warned that a war for independence would be interminable. British prime minister Lord Frederick North had pledged an implacable fight to maintain "every Advantage" that Britain derived from its control of the colonies. Before any war for independence ended, Dickinson prophesied, Americans would have "tasted deeply of that bitter Cup called the Fortunes of War." Not only would they have to "wade thro Seas of Blood," but in due course, hostilities would bring on massive unemployment within the maritime trades, heinous cruelties along the frontier, slave insurrections in the South and the relentless spread of disease from armies to civilians. And even in the unlikely event independence was achieved, Dickinson argued, yet another catastrophe might well lie in store: France and Spain would destroy the infant United States. In contrast, a war for reconciliation would be short-lived. Confronted with "a bloody & tedious Contest attended with Injury to their Trade," Lord North's government would collapse. Its successor would be compelled to accept Congress' terms: American "Dependence & Subordination" on the Crown, but with it a recognition from London that Parliament's only power over the colonies was the regulation of American trade.

Given Dickinson's position as a longtime foe of Parliamentary taxation, it was only to be expected that he would emerge as a leader in Congress. Adams' rise, however, was a different story. When he became leader of the independence forces—what one contemporary observer, Dr. Benjamin Rush, described as the "first man in the House"—many were caught by surprise. Before his election to Congress in 1774, Adams was largely inexperienced in public life. He had served only one term in the Massachusetts assembly and had not even headed the Massachusetts delegation at the First Congress—cousin Sam had assumed that responsibility.

Forty years old in 1775, John Adams had grown up on a small farm just south of Boston, where his father moonlighted as a shoemaker to earn the money to send his oldest son to Harvard. Like Dickinson, Adams had practiced law, and also like him, had advanced rapidly. Within a dozen years of opening his law office, Adams maintained the heaviest caseload of any attorney in Boston. Unlike Dickinson, Adams was initially wary of the American protest against British policies, believing that the ministry had simply erred in its actions and might be expected to mend its ways. He had been converted to open support of the popular cause only in 1773.

Adams came to keenly desire a leadership role, but feared that his physical limitations—he was portly and balding—and irascible manner would frustrate his ambitions. Furthermore, he was no jovial backslapper. Gruff and argumentative, he was maladroit when it came to talking about what he regarded as the favorite topics of men: dogs, horses and women. Nevertheless, those who penetrated his churlish exterior discovered a good-natured, self-effacing and exceptionally bright individual. And he possessed the skills needed to be an effective legislator. He was tireless, a skilled debater, an incisive, if not flamboyant, orator and a trenchant thinker. He quickly won a reputation as the Congressional authority on diplomacy and political theory. His colleagues found him to be unfailingly well prepared, prudent, honest and trustworthy—in short, just the man to follow in this high-stakes endeavor.

THE FIRST ISSUE TO TRULY DIVIDE the Second Continental Congress arose early on. In May 1775, as it considered the creation of the Continental Army, Dickinson insisted on petitioning the king with what he characterized as a "Measure of Peace." Adams privately branded it a "Measure of Imbecility" and raged that some delegates, at least those from the mercantile colonies of New York and Pennsylvania, were "selfish and avaricious." For those congressman, he charged, "a ship [was] dearer than" the lives of Continental soldiers. In October 1774, the First Continental Congress had petitioned the monarch; Adams feared that to do so again was to risk appearing weak. Franklin concurred. "It is a true old saying," he remarked, "that *make yourselves sheep and the wolves will eat you.*"

Nevertheless, the independence faction wanted no confrontation with Dickinson's at this crucial juncture of the war, and the Olive Branch Petition, as the peace measure was known, was approved, though only after a contentious debate over its wording. Richard Penn, a former governor of Pennsylvania, carried it to England. Franklin advised a London friend, a director of the Bank of England, that this was Britain's last hope for preventing "a total Separation" by the colonies. To another friend in England he wrote: "If you flatter yourselves with beating us into submission, you know neither the [American] people nor the country."

At about the same time, Congress created a committee to draft a "Declaration of the Causes and Necessity of Taking Up Arms." Among others, it appointed Jefferson, who had only recently joined the Virginia delegation, and Dickinson to the committee. Jefferson, who enjoyed a reputation as a facile writer, was asked to draft the document. With views similar to Adams', he produced a paper that reiterated the charges of British tyranny and harshly cataloged the ministry's "avowed course of murder and devastation." Dickinson was appalled. He feared that such a provocative statement would make a measured response to the Olive Branch Petition impossible. He demanded, and obtained, an opportunity to tone down

Jefferson's draft. Dickinson's softer proclamation stipulated that "we mean not to dissolve that Union" with Britain. It was adopted in July 1775.

The reconciliationists held sway through the summer of 1775, but as hostilities unfolded and Congress was required to prosecute the war, their hold gradually weakened. By the end of 1775, Congress had issued a Continental currency, drawn up regulations applying to all militia, created a Continental post office and taken control of Indian relations. Feeling "a little of the Seafaring Inclination," as Adams put it, Congress also established an American navy and two battalions of marines. It regulated American trade, assumed responsibility for the enforcement of the embargo of British commerce, attempted to resolve intercolonial territorial disputes and even acted as the national judiciary, hearing appeals from state courts in cases that involved the seizure of British ships.

Congress additionally began to conduct foreign policy. It created a Secret Committee to contract for arms imports and a Committee of Secret Correspondence to establish contact with "our friends" throughout the world. In March 1776, Congress dispatched one of its own, Silas Deane of Connecticut, to Versailles to pursue talks with the French government. In fact, if not in name, the Second Continental Congress had become the government of an autonomous union of American provinces.

Back in November 1775, word had arrived that George III had branded the colonists rebels and traitors and had contemptuously refused to accept the Olive Branch Petition. Two months later, the full text of the king's speech to Parliament reached Philadelphia. In it the monarch unsparingly assailed those colonists who supported hostilities, charging that they were part of a "wicked" and "desperate conspiracy." In addition, he revealed his intention to obtain foreign mercenaries to help suppress the rebellion. Hancock, by now president of Congress, wryly remarked that the Crown's actions "don't look like a Reconciliation." John Adams gleefully noted that Dickinson "sinks ... in the public opinion."

Indeed, evidence was mounting that the mood of the country was changing. Already, by the summer of 1775, when Congress began authorizing the colonies to create their own governments, supplanting those chartered by the Crown, it had taken its most radical step since the creation of the army. Dickinson and his principal ally, James Wilson of Pennsylvania, fought back. In January 1776 they proposed that Congress adopt yet another "humble & dutiful Petition" disclaiming independence to the king. This time Congress refused. Some members, such as Samuel Adams, had begun to see the reconciliationists as "Tools of a Tyrant."

Yet Congress still remained unwilling to declare independence. Had a vote been taken in early January 1776, the measure would likely have failed. On the 17th of that month, however, word reached Philadelphia of a devastating military setback, the young army's first. The news was instrumental in propelling Congress on its final journey toward independence.

AS WASHINGTON'S ARMY besieged British regulars in Boston during the summer of 1775, Congress had authorized an invasion of lightly defended Canada in order to defeat British forces there. It was a troubled campaign from the start, and on December 31 disaster struck. An attack on Quebec was repulsed; 500 men, half of America's invading army, were lost: 100 were killed or wounded and another 400 taken prisoner. So much for any expectation of a short-lived war. Overnight, many in Congress came to believe that no victory would ever be possible without foreign assistance; all understood that no aid from any outside power would be forthcoming so long as America fought for the "purpose of repairing the breach [with Britain]," as Thomas Paine had observed in his incendiary pamphlet *Common Sense*, published in January 1776.

Soon after the debacle at Quebec, John Adams observed that there now existed "no Prospect, no Probability, no Possibility" of reconciliation. Late in February came still more stunning news. Congress learned that Parliament had enacted the American Prohibitory Act, shutting down all trade with the colonies and permitting seizure of colonial vessels. John Adams called the law "a Gift" to the pro-independence party. Virginia's Richard Henry Lee concurred, saying that it severed the last ties with the mother country. It was "curious," he stated, that Congress yet hesitated to declare independence when London had already "put the two Countries asunder."

As spring foliage burst forth in Philadelphia in 1776, ever larger numbers of Americans were coming round to independence. The "Sighing after Independence" in Massachusetts, said James Warren, speaker of the colony's House of Representatives, had become nearly "Universal." By mid-May every Southern colony had authorized its delegates to vote for breaking off ties with Britain.

Within Congress, emotions ran high. "I cannot conceive what good Reason can be assignd against [independence]," Samuel Adams railed in mid-April. He exclaimed that the "Salvation of the Country depends on its being done speedily. I am anxious to have it done." John Adams maintained that had independence been declared months earlier, America's armies would already possess French arms. Elbridge Gerry, a Massachusetts delegate, complained that "timid Minds are terrified at the Word Independency," while Franklin deplored those who clutched at the "vain Hope of Reconciliation." As for General Washington, he said he believed that Congress had "long, & ardently sought for reconciliation upon honourable terms," only to be rebuffed at every turn. He had long been of the opinion that "all Connexions with a State So unjust" should be broken.

Still, the reconciliationists held out, encouraged by a passage in the Prohibitory Act that authorized the monarch to appoint commissioners to grant pardons and to receive the grievances of colonists. Dickinson and his followers viewed the appointees as peace commissioners and held out hope that they were being sent to resolve differences. Many in Congress refused to budge until they learned just what the envoys had to offer. John Adams disdainfully predicted that this was "a Bubble" and a misbegotten "Messiah that will never come." Samuel Adams said that he was "disgusted" both with the "King & his Junto," who spoke of peace while making "the most destructive Plans," and with the reconciliationists who were willing to be "Slaves" to "a Nation so lost to all Sense of Liberty and Virtue."

In May, as American newspapers published the text of Britain's treaties with several German principalities, authorizing the hiring of mercenaries, outrage toward the Crown skyrocketed. Many were now convinced, as Richard Henry Lee said, that the action proved Britain was bent "upon the absolute conquest and subduction of N. America." Nearly simultaneously, word arrived of yet more calamities in Canada. Congress had dispatched reinforcements following the failed attack in December, but smallpox and desertions soon thinned their ranks. With the arrival of British reinforcements in May, the American army commenced a long, slow retreat that lasted until mid-June. Now, said Lee, it "is not choice then but necessity that calls for Independence, as the only means by which a foreign Alliance can be obtained."

One final matter helped the slowest sailors in Congress catch up with the swiftest. Month after month had passed with no sign of the so-called peace commissioners. Then, in the spring, it was learned that, although some commissioners had been named, they had been ordered not to treat with Congress. That proved a final blow; all but the most ardent reconciliationists were persuaded that the king's envoys were coming for the sole purpose of dividing American opinion and derailing the war effort.

With the tide so turned, in mid-May, Congress declared that "every kind of authority under the ... Crown should be totally suppressed" and instructed each colony to adopt a new government suitable for providing for the "happiness and safety of their constituents and ... America in general." John Adams, who called this the "last Step," believed this was tantamount to a declaration of independence. Even Maryland's Thomas Stone, a foe of separation, disconsolately allowed that the "Dye is cast. The fatal Stab is given to any future Connection between this Country & Britain." Only a formal declaration of independence remained, and that could not now be long in coming.

On June 7, three weeks after Congress urged changes in the provincial governments, Lee introduced a motion for independence: "*Resolved*, That these United Colonies are, and of right ought to be, free and independent States, that they are absolved from all allegiance to the British Crown, and that all political connection between them and the State of Great Britain is, and ought to be, totally dissolved."

© Getty Images/Hisham F. Ibrahim

Congress rancorously debated Lee's motion for two days. Several reconciliationists from the Middle-Atlantic colonies made their final stand, even threatening to "secede from the Union" if Congress declared independence. But their threats and recriminations no longer frightened the majority, including Oliver Wolcott of Connecticut, who recognized that America was in the "Midst of a great Revolution ... leading to the lasting Independancy of these Colonies." On June 11, Congress created a five-member committee to prepare a statement on independence. Adams, Franklin, Jefferson, Roger Sherman of Connecticut and Robert Livingston of New York were given until July 1 to complete their work. Once again it was to Jefferson that a panel turned, this time for the fateful task of drafting the declaration.

Jefferson and his colleagues beat the deadline by two days, submitting on June 28 a document that explained and defended independence. By July 1, the final consideration of Lee's motion to declare independence was taken up. That day's session, John Adams told a friend in a letter written early that morning, would see "the greatest Debate of all." With the outcome no longer in doubt, he said that he prayed for "the new born Republic" about to be created.

When debate began midmorning on that hot, steamy Monday, Dickinson was first on his feet to make one last speech against independence. Speaking emotionally for perhaps as much as two hours in the stifling heat of the closed room (windows were kept shut to keep spies from listening in), Dickinson reviewed the familiar arguments: America could not win the war; at best, it could fight Britain to a stalemate, and deadlocked wars often ended in partition treaties in which territory is divided among the belligerents; therefore, after all the killing, some colonies would remain part of the British Empire, while others would pass under the control of France or Spain.

It was John Adams—soon to be christened "the Atlas of Independence" by New Jersey's Richard Stockton—who rose to answer Dickinson. Striving to conceal his contempt for his adversary, Adams spoke extemporaneously in subdued tones. Once again, he reviewed the benefits of independence. Although his speech was not transcribed, he surely invoked the ideas he had expressed and the phrases he had used on many another occasion. Breaking ties with Britain, he argued, would ensure freedom from England's imperial domination; escape from the menace of British corruption; and the opportunity to create a republic based on equality of representation.

Others then took the floor. The speeches stretched past the customary 4 o'clock adjournment and into the evening. The business was "an idle Mispence of Time," Adams remarked sourly, as "nothing was Said, but what had been repeated and hackneyed in that Room an hundred Times for Six Months past." After the Congress reconvened the next morning, July 2, the delegates cast their momentous votes. Twelve states—the colonies would become states with the vote—voted for independence. Not one voted against the break with Britain. New York's delegation, which had not yet been authorized by the New York legislature to separate from the mother country, did not vote. (Dickinson and Robert Morris did not attend, and Pennsylvania cast its vote for independence by a three-to-two margin.)

Adams predicted that July 2 would ever after "be solemnized with Pomp and Parade, with Shews, Games, Sports, Guns, Bells, Bonfires and Illuminations from one End of this Continent to the other." He was wrong, of course, for July 4, the date that Congress approved the formal Declaration of Independence, would become the commemorative day. But Adams had made one prediction that would prove tellingly correct. With the Union intact after a 15-month battle for independence, and with the step finally taken that could secure foreign assistance in America's desperate war, Adams declared he could "see the Rays of ravishing Light and Glory" that would accompany military victory.

Historian **John Ferling** is the author of A Leap in the Dark: The Struggle to Create the American Republic.

Making Sense of the Fourth of July

The DECLARATION OF INDEPENDENCE is not what Thomas Jefferson thought it was when he wrote it—and that is why we celebrate it

By Pauline Maier

JOHN ADAMS THOUGHT AMERICANS would commemorate their Independence Day on the second of July. Future generations, he confidently predicted, would remember July 2, 1776, as "the most memorable Epocha, in the History of America" and celebrate it as their "Day of Deliverance by solemn Acts of Devotion to God Almighty. It ought to be solemnized with Pomp and Parade, with Shews, Games, Sports, Guns, Bells, Bonfires and Illuminations from one End of this Continent to the other from this Time forward forever more."

His proposal, however odd it seems today, was perfectly reasonable when he made it in a letter to his wife, Abigail. On the previous day, July 2, 1776, the Second Continental Congress had finally resolved "That these United Colonies are, and of right ought to be, free and independent States, that they are absolved from all allegiance to the British Crown, and that all political connection between them and the State of Great Britain is, and ought to be, totally dissolved." The thought that Americans might instead commemorate July 4, the day Congress adopted a "Declaration on Independency" that he had helped prepare, did not apparently occur to Adams in 1776. The Declaration of Independence was

one of those congressional statements that he later described as "dress and ornament rather than Body, Soul, or Substance," a way of announcing to the world the fact of American independence, which was for Adams the thing worth celebrating.

In fact, holding our great national festival on the Fourth makes no sense at all—unless we are actually celebrating not just independence but the Declaration of Independence. And the declaration we celebrate, what Abraham Lincoln called "the charter of our liberties," is a document whose meaning and function today are different from what they were in 1776. In short, during the nineteenth century the Declaration of Independence became not just a way of announcing and justifying the end of Britain's power over the Thirteen Colonies and the emergence of the United States as an independent nation but a statement of principles to guide stable, established governments. Indeed, it came to usurp in fact if not in law a role that Americans normally delegated to bills of rights. How did that happen? And why?

According to notes kept by Thomas Jefferson, the Second Continental Congress did not discuss the resolution on in-

dependence when it was first proposed by Virginia's Richard Henry Lee, on Friday, June 7, 1776, because it was "obliged to attend at that time to some other business." However, on the eighth, Congress resolved itself into a Committee of the Whole and "passed that day & Monday the 10th in debating on the subject." By then all contenders admitted that it had become impossible for the colonies ever again to be united with Britain. The issue was one of timing.

John and Samuel Adams, along with others such as Virginia's George Wythe, wanted Congress to declare independence right away and start negotiating foreign alliances and forming a more lasting confederation (which Lee also proposed). Others, including Pennsylvania's James Wilson, Edward Rutledge of South Carolina, and Robert R. Livingston of New York, argued for delay. They noted that the delegates of several colonies, including Maryland, Pennsylvania, Delaware, New Jersey, and New York, had not been "impowered" by their home governments to vote for independence. If a vote was taken immediately, those delegates would have to "retire" from Congress, and their states might secede from the union, which would seriously weaken the Americans' chance of realizing their independence. In the past, they said, members of Congress had followed the "wise & proper" policy of putting off major decisions "till the voice of the people drove us into it," since "they were our power, & without them our declarations could not be carried into effect." Moreover, opinion on independence in the critical middle colonies was "fast ripening & in a short time," they predicted, the people there would "join in the general voice of America."

CONGRESS DECIDED TO GIVE THE laggard colonies time and so delayed its decision for three weeks. But it also appointed a Committee of Five to draft a declaration of independence so that such a document could be issued quickly once Lee's motion passed. The committee's members included Jefferson, Livingston, John Adams, Roger Sherman of Connecticut, and Pennsylvania's Benjamin Franklin. The drafting committee met, decided what the declaration should say and how it would be organized, then asked Jefferson to prepare a draft.

Meanwhile, Adams—who did more to win Congress's consent to independence than any other delegate—worked feverishly to bring popular pressure on the governments of recalcitrant colonies so they would change the instructions issued to their congressional delegates. By June 28, when the Committee of Five submitted to Congress a draft declaration, only Maryland and New York had failed to allow their delegates to vote for independence. That night Maryland fell into line.

Even so, when the Committee of the Whole again took up Lee's resolution, on July 1, only nine colonies voted in favor (the four New England states, New Jersey, Maryland, Virginia, North Carolina, and Georgia). South Carolina and Pennsylvania opposed the proposition, Delaware's two delegates split, and New York's abstained because their twelve-month-old instructions precluded them from approving anything that impeded reconciliation with the mother country. Edward Rutledge now asked that Congress put off its decision until the next day, since he thought that the South

Carolina delegation would then vote in favor "for the sake of unanimity." When Congress took its final tally on July 2, the nine affirmative votes of the day before had grown to twelve: Not only South Carolina voted in favor, but so did Delaware—the arrival of Caesar Rodney broke the tie in that delegation's vote— and Pennsylvania. Only New York held out. Then on July 9 it, too, allowed its delegates to add their approval to that of delegates from the other twelve colonies, lamenting still the "cruel necessity" that made independence "unavoidable."

Once independence had been adopted, Congress again formed itself into a Committee of the Whole. It then spent the better part of two days editing the draft declaration submitted by its Committee of Five, rewriting or chopping off large sections of text. Finally, on July 4, Congress approved the revised Declaration and ordered it to be printed and sent to the several states and to the commanding officers of the Continental Army. By formally announcing and justifying the end of British rule, that document, as letters from Congress's president, John Hancock, explained, laid "the Ground & Foundation" of American self-government. As a result, it had to be proclaimed not only before American troops in the hope that it would inspire them to fight more ardently for what was now the cause of both liberty and national independence but throughout the country, and "in such a Manner, that the People may be universally informed of it."

Not until four days later did a committee of Congress—not Congress itself—get around to sending a copy of the Declaration to its emissary in Paris, Silas Deane, with orders to present it to the court of France and send copies to "the other Courts of Europe." Unfortunately the original letter was lost, and the next failed to reach Deane until November, when news of American independence had circulated for months. To make matters worse, it arrived with only a brief note from the committee and in an envelope that lacked a seal, an unfortunately slipshod way, complained Deane, to announce the arrival of the United States among the powers of the earth to "old and powerfull states." Despite the Decla-

ration's reference to the "opinions of mankind," it was obviously meant first and foremost for a home audience.

As copies of the Declaration spread through the states and were publicly read at town meetings, religious services, court days, or wherever else people assembled, Americans marked the occasion with appropriate rituals. They lit great bonfires, "illuminated" their windows with candles, fired guns, rang bells, tore down and destroyed the symbols of monarchy on public buildings, churches, or tavern signs, and "fixed up" on the walls of their homes broadside or newspaper copies of the Declaration of Independence.

BUT WHAT EXACTLY WERE THEY celebrating? The news, not the vehicle that brought it; independence and the assumption of self-government, not the document that announced Congress's decision to break with Britain. Considering how revered a position the Declaration of Independence later won in the minds and hearts of the people, Americans' disregard for it in the first years of the new nation verges on the unbelievable. One colonial newspaper dismissed the Declaration's extensive charges against the king as just another "recapitulation of injuries," one, it seems, in a series, and not particularly remarkable compared with earlier "catalogues of grievances." Citations of the Declaration were usually drawn from its final paragraph, which said that the united colonies "are and of Right ought to be Free and Independent states" and were "Absolved of all Allegiance to the British Crown"—words from the Lee resolution that Congress had inserted into the committee draft. Independence was new; the rest of the Declaration seemed all too familiar to Americans, a restatement of what they and their representatives had already said time and again.

The adoption of independence was, however, from the beginning confused with its declaration. Differences in the meaning of the word *declare* contributed to the confusion. Before the Declaration of Independence was issued—while, in fact, Congress was still editing Jefferson's draft—Pennsylvania newspapers announced that on July 2 the Continental Congress had "declared the United Colonies Free and Independent States," by which it meant simply that it had officially accepted that status. Newspapers in other colonies repeated the story. In later years the "Anniversary of the United States of America" came to be celebrated on the date Congress had approved the Declaration of Independence. That began, it seems, by accident. In 1777 no member of Congress thought of marking the anniversary of independence at all until July 3, when it was too late to honor July 2. As a result, the celebration took place on the Fourth, and that became the tradition. At least one delegate spoke of "celebrating the Anniversary of the Declaration of Independence," but over the next few years references to the anniversary of independence and of the Declaration seem to have been virtually interchangeable.

> *The Fourth of July was rarely celebrated during the Revolution and seems actually to have declined in popularity once the war was over.*

Accounts of the events at Philadelphia on July 4, 1777, say quite a bit about the music played by a band of Hessian soldiers who had been captured at the Battle of Trenton the previous December, and the "splendid illumination" of houses, but little about the Declaration. Thereafter, in the late 1770s and 1780s, the Fourth of July was not regularly celebrated; indeed, the holiday seems to have declined in popularity once the Revolutionary War ended. When it was remembered, however, festivities seldom, if ever—to judge by newspaper accounts—involved a public reading of the Declaration of Independence. It was as if that document had done its work in carrying news of independence to the people, and it neither needed nor deserved further commemoration. No mention was made of Thomas Jefferson's role in composing the document, since that was not yet public knowledge, and no sug-

gestion appeared that the Declaration itself was, as posterity would have it, unusually eloquent or powerful.

IN FACT, ONE OF THE VERY FEW PUBLIC comments on the document's literary qualities came in a Virginia newspaper's account of a 1777 speech by John Wilkes, an English radical and a long-time supporter of the Americans, in the House of Commons. Wilkes set out to answer a fellow member of Parliament who had attacked the Declaration of Independence as "a wretched composition, very ill written, drawn up with a view to captivate the people." Curiously, Wilkes seemed to agree with that description. The purpose of the document, he said, was indeed to captivate the American people, who were not much impressed by "the polished periods, the harmonious, happy expressions, with all the grace, ease, and elegance of a beautiful diction" that Englishmen valued. What they liked was "manly, nervous sense… even in the most awkward and uncouth dress of language."

ALL THAT BEGAN TO CHANGE IN THE 1790s, when, in the midst of bitter partisan conflict, the modern understanding and reputation of the Declaration of Independence first emerged. Until that time celebrations of the Fourth were controlled by nationalists who found a home in the Federalist party, and their earlier inattention to the Declaration hardened into a rigid hostility after 1790. The document's anti-British character was an embarrassment to Federalists who sought economic and diplomatic rapprochement with Britain. The language of equality and rights in the Declaration was different from that of the Declaration of the Rights of Man issued by the French National Assembly in 1789, but it still seemed too "French" for the comfort of Federalists, who, after the execution of Louis XVI and the onset of the Terror, lost whatever sympathy for the French Revolution they had once felt. Moreover, they understandably found it best to say as little as possible about a fundamental American text that had been

drafted by a leader of the opposing Republican party.

It was, then, the Republicans who began to celebrate the Declaration of Independence as a "deathless instrument" written by "the immortal Jefferson." The Republicans saw themselves as the defenders of the American Republic of 1776 against subversion by pro-British "monarchists," and they hoped that by recalling the causes of independence, they would make their countrymen wary of further dealings with Great Britain. They were also delighted to identify the founding principles of the American Revolution with those of America's sister republic in France. At their Fourth of July celebrations, Republicans read the Declaration of Independence, and their newspapers reprinted it. Moreover, in their hands the attention that had at first focused on the last part of the Declaration shifted toward its opening paragraphs and the "self-evident truths" they stated. The Declaration, as a Republican newspaper said on July 7, 1792, was not to be celebrated merely "as affecting the separation of one country from the jurisdiction of another"; it had an enduring significance for established governments because it provided a "definition of the rights of man, and the end of civil government."

The Federalists responded that Jefferson had not written the Declaration alone. The drafting committee—including John Adams, a Federalist—had also contributed to its creation. And Jefferson's role as "the scribe who penned the declaration" had not been so distinguished as his followers suggested. Federalists rediscovered similarities between the Declaration and Locke's *Second Treatise of Government* that Richard Henry Lee had noticed long before and used them to argue that even the "small part of that memorable instrument" that could be attributed to Jefferson "he stole from *Locke's Essays.*" But after the War of 1812, the Federalist party slipped from sight, and with it, efforts to disparage the Declaration of Independence.

When a new party system formed in the late 1820s and 1830s, both Whigs and Jacksonians claimed descent from Jefferson and his party and so accepted the old Republican position on the Declaration and Jefferson's glorious role in its creation. By then, too, a new generation of Americans had come of age and made preservation of the nation's revolutionary history its particular mission. Its efforts, and its reverential attitude toward the revolutionaries and their works, also helped establish the Declaration of Independence as an important icon of American identity.

THE CHANGE CAME SUDDENLY. AS late as January 1817 John Adams said that his country had no interest in its past. "I see no disposition to celebrate or remember, or even Curiosity to enquire into the Characters, Actions, or Events of the Revolution," he wrote the artist John Trumbull. But a little more than a month later Congress commissioned Trumbull to produce four large paintings commemorating the Revolution, which were to hang in the rotunda of the new American Capitol. For Trumbull, the most important of the series, and the one to which he first turned, was the Declaration of Independence. He based that work on a smaller painting he had done between 1786 and 1793 that showed the drafting committee presenting its work to Congress. When the new twelve-by-eighteen-foot canvas was completed in 1818, Trumbull exhibited it to large crowds in Boston, Philadelphia, and Baltimore before delivering it to Washington; indeed, *The Declaration of Independence* was the most popular of all the paintings Trumbull did for the Capitol.

Soon copies of the document were being published and sold briskly, which perhaps was what inspired Secretary of State John Quincy Adams to have an exact facsimile of the Declaration, the only one ever produced, made in 1823. Congress had it distributed throughout the country. Books also started to appear: the collected biographies of those who signed the Declaration in nine volumes by Joseph M. Sanderson (1823–27) or one volume by Charles A. Goodrich (1831), full biographies of individual revolutionaries that were often written by descendants who used family papers, and collections of revolutionary docu-

ments edited by such notable figures as Hezekiah Niles, Jared Sparks, and Peter Force.

Postwar efforts to preserve the memories and records of the Revolution were undertaken in a mood of near panic. Many documents remained in private hands, where they were gradually separated from one another and lost. Even worse, many revolutionaries had died, taking with them precious memories that were gone forever. The presence of living remnants of the revolutionary generation seemed so important in preserving its tradition that Americans watched anxiously as their numbers declined. These attitudes first appeared in the decade before 1826, the fiftieth anniversary of independence, but they persisted on into the Civil War. In 1864 the Reverend Elias Brewster Hillard noted that only seven of those who had fought in the Revolutionary War still survived, and he hurried to interview and photograph those "venerable and now sacred men" for the benefit of posterity. "The present is the last generation that will be connected by living link with the great period in which our national independence was achieved," he wrote in the introduction to his book *The Last Men of the Revolution.* "Our own are the last eyes that will look on men who looked on Washington; our ears the last that will hear the living voices of those who heard his words. Henceforth the American Revolution will be known among men by the silent record of history alone."

Most of the men Hillard interviewed had played modest roles in the Revolution. In the early 1820s, however, John Adams and Thomas Jefferson were still alive, and as the only surviving members of the committee that had drafted the Declaration of Independence, they attracted an extraordinary outpouring of attention. Pilgrims, invited and uninvited, flocked particularly to Monticello, hoping to catch a glimpse of the author of the Declaration and making nuisances of themselves. One woman, it is said, even smashed a window to get a better view of the old man. As a eulogist noted after the deaths of both Adams and Jefferson on, miraculously, July 4, 1826, the world had not waited for death to "sanctify" their names. Even while they

remained alive, their homes became "shrines" to which lovers of liberty and admirers of genius flocked "from every land."

ADAMS, IN TRUTH, WAS MIFFED BY Jefferson's celebrity as the penman of Independence. The drafting of the Declaration of Independence, he thought, had assumed an exaggerated importance. Jefferson perhaps agreed; he, too, cautioned a correspondent against giving too much emphasis to "mere composition." The Declaration, he said, had not and had not been meant to be an original or novel creation; his assignment had been to produce "an expression of the American mind, and to give that expression the proper tone and spirit called for by the occasion."

Jefferson, however, played an important role in rescuing the Declaration from obscurity and making it a defining event of the revolutionary "heroic age." It was he who first suggested that the young John Trumbull paint *The Declaration of Independence.* And Trumbull's first sketch of his famous painting shares a piece of drawing paper with a sketch by Jefferson, executed in Paris sometime in 1786, of the assembly room in the Old Pennsylvania State House, now known as Independence Hall. Trumbull's painting of the scene carefully followed Jefferson's sketch, which unfortunately included architectural inaccuracies, as Trumbull later learned to his dismay.

Jefferson forgot, as the years went by, how substantial a role other members of the committee had played in framing the Declaration's text.

Jefferson also spent hour after hour answering, in longhand, letters that he said numbered 1,267 in 1820, many of which asked questions about the Declaration and its creation. Unfortunately, his responses, like the sketch he made for Trumbull, were inaccurate in many details. Even his account of the drafting process, retold in an important letter to James Madison of 1823 that has been accepted by one authority after another, conflicts with a note he sent Benjamin Franklin in June 1776. Jefferson forgot, in short, how substantial a role other members of the drafting committee had played in framing the Declaration and adjusting its text before it was submitted to Congress.

INDEED, IN OLD AGE JEFFERSON FOUND enormous consolation in the fact that he was, as he ordered inscribed on his tomb, "Author of the Declaration of American Independence." More than anything else he had done, that role came to justify his life. It saved him from a despair that he suffered at the time of the Missouri crisis, when everything the Revolution had accomplished seemed to him in jeopardy, and that was later fed by problems at the University of Virginia, his own deteriorating health, and personal financial troubles so severe that he feared the loss of his beloved home, Monticello (those troubles, incidentally, virtually precluded him from freeing more than a handful of slaves at his death). The Declaration, as he told Madison, was "the fundamental act of union of these States," a document that should be recalled "to cherish the principles of the instrument in the bosoms of our own citizens." Again in 1824 he interpreted the government's re-publication of the Declaration as "a pledge of adhesion to its principles and of a sacred determination to maintain and perpetuate them," which he described as a "holy purpose."

But just which principles did he mean? Those in the Declaration's second paragraph, which he understood exactly as they had been understood in 1776—as an assertion primarily of the right of revolution. Jefferson composed the long sentence beginning "We hold these truths to be self-evident" in a well-known eighteenth-century rhetorical style by which one phrase was piled on another and the meaning of the whole became clear only at the end. The sequence ended with an assertion of the "Right of the People to alter or to abolish" any government that failed to secure their inalienable rights and to institute a new

form of government more likely "to effect their Safety and Happiness." That was the right Americans were exercising in July 1776, and it seemed no less relevant in the 1820s, when revolutionary movements were sweeping through Europe and Latin America. The American example would be, as Jefferson said in the last letter of his life, a "signal arousing men to burst the chains under which monkish ignorance and superstition had persuaded them to bind themselves, and to assume the blessings and security of self-government."

Others, however, emphasized the opening phrases of the sentence that began the Declaration's second paragraph, particularly "the memorable assertion, that 'all men are created equal, that they are endowed by their Creator with certain unalienable rights, and that to secure these rights, governments are instituted among men, deriving their just powers from the consent of the governed.'" That passage, the eulogist John Sergeant said at Philadelphia in July 1826, was the "text of the revolution," the "ruling vital principle" that had inspired the men of the 1770s, who "looked forward through succeeding generations, and saw stamped upon all their institutions, the great principles set forth in the Declaration of Independence." In Hallowell, Maine, another eulogist, Peleg Sprague, similarly described the Declaration of Independence as an assertion *"by a whole people,* of… *the native equality of the human race,* as the true foundation of all political, of all human institutions."

AND SO AN INTERPRETATION OF THE declaration that had emerged in the 1790s became ever more widely repeated. The equality that Sergeant and Sprague emphasized was not, however, asserted for the first time in the Declaration of Independence. Even before Congress published its Declaration, one revolutionary document after another had associated equality with a new American republic and suggested enough different meanings of that term—equal rights, equal access to office, equal voting power—to keep Americans busy sorting them out and fighting over inegalitarian practices far

into the future. Jefferson, in fact, adapted those most remembered opening lines of the Declaration's second paragraph from a draft Declaration of Rights for Virginia, written by George Mason and revised by a committee of the Virginia convention, which appeared in the *Pennsylvania Gazette* on June 12, 1776, the day after the Committee of Five was appointed and perhaps the day it first met. Whether on his own inspiration or under instructions from the committee, Jefferson began with the Mason draft, which he gradually tightened into a more compressed and eloquent statement. He took, for example, Mason's statement that "all men are born equally free and independent," rewrote it to say they were "created equal & independent," and then cut out the "& independent."

Jefferson was not alone in adapting the Mason text for his purposes. The Virginia convention revised the Mason draft before enacting Virginia's Declaration of Rights, which said that all men were "by nature" equally free and independent. Several other states—including Pennsylvania (1776), Vermont (1777), Massachusetts (1780), and New Hampshire (1784)—remained closer to Mason's wording, including in their state bill of rights the assertions that men were "born free and equal" or "born equally free and independent." Unlike the Declaration of Independence, moreover, the state bills or "declarations" of rights became (after an initial period of confusion) legally binding. Americans' first efforts to work out the meaning of the equality written into their founding documents therefore occurred on the state level.

IN MASSACHUSETTS, FOR EXAMPLE, several slaves won their freedom in the 1780s by arguing before the state's Supreme Judicial Court that the provision in the state's bill of rights that all men were born free and equal made slavery unlawful. Later, in the famous case of *Commonwealth* v. *Aves* (1836), Justice Lemuel Shaw ruled that those words were sufficient to end slavery in Massachusetts, indeed that it would be difficult to find others "more precisely adapted to the abolition of negro slavery." White Americans also found the equality provisions in their state bills of rights useful. In the Virginia constitutional convention of 1829–30, for example, a delegate from the trans-Appalachian West, John R. Cooke, cited that "sacred instrument" the Virginia Declaration of Rights against the state's system of representing all counties equally in the legislature regardless of their populations and its imposition of a property qualification for the vote, both of which gave disproportional power to men in the eastern part of the state. The framers of Virginia's 1776 constitution allowed those practices to persist despite their violation of the equality affirmed in the Declaration of Rights, Cooke said, because there were limits on how much they dared change "in the midst of war." They therefore left it for posterity to resolve the inconsistency "as soon as leisure should be afforded them." In the hands of men like Cooke, the Virginia Declaration of Rights became a practical program of reform to be realized over time, as the Declaration of Independence would later be for Abraham Lincoln.

But why, if the states had legally binding statements of men's equality, should anyone turn to the Declaration of Independence? Because not all states had bills of rights, and not all the bills of rights that did exist included statements on equality. Moreover, neither the federal Constitution nor the federal Bill of Rights asserted men's natural equality or their possession of inalienable rights or the right of the people to reject or change their government. As a result, contenders in national politics who found those old revolutionary principles useful had to cite the Declaration of Independence. It was all they had.

THE SACRED STATURE GIVEN THE Declaration after 1815 made it extremely useful for causes attempting to seize the moral high ground in public debate. Beginning about 1820, workers, farmers, women's rights advocates, and other groups persistently used the Declaration of Independence to justify their quest for equality and their opposition to the "tyranny" of factory owners or railroads or

great corporations or the male power structure. It remained, however, especially easy for the opponents of slavery to cite the Declaration on behalf of their cause. Eighteenth-century statements of equality referred to men in a state of nature, before governments were created, and asserted that no persons acquired legitimate authority over others without their consent. If so, a system of slavery in which men were born the subjects and indeed the property of others was profoundly wrong. In short, the same principle that denied kings a right to rule by inheritance alone undercut the right of masters to own slaves whose status was determined by birth, not consent. The kinship of the Declaration of Independence with the cause of antislavery was understood from the beginning—which explains why gradual emancipation acts, such as those in New York and New Jersey, took effect on July 4 in 1799 and 1804 and why Nat Turner's rebellion was originally planned for July 4, 1831.

Even in the eighteenth century, however, assertions of men's equal birth provoked dissent. As slavery became an increasingly divisive issue, denials that men were naturally equal multiplied. Men were not created equal in Virginia, John Tyler insisted during the Missouri debates of 1820: "No, sir, the principle, although lovely and beautiful, cannot obliterate those distinctions in society which society itself engenders and gives birth to." Six years later the acerbic, self-styled Virginia aristocrat John Randolph called the notion of man's equal creation "a falsehood, and a most pernicious falsehood, even though I find it in the Declaration of Independence." Man was born in a state of "perfect helplessness and ignorance" and so was from the start dependent on others. There was "not a word of truth" in the notion that men were created equal, repeated South Carolina's John C. Calhoun in 1848. Men could not survive, much less develop their talents, alone; the political state, in which some exercised authority and others obeyed, was in fact man's "natural state," that in which he "is born, lives and dies." For a long time the "false and dangerous" doctrine that men were created equal had lain "dormant," but by the late 1840s Americans had begun "to ex-

perience the danger of admitting so great an error... in the Declaration of Independence," where it had been inserted needlessly, Calhoun said, since separation from Britain could have been justified without it.

FIVE YEARS LATER, IN SENATE DEBATES over the Kansas-Nebraska Act, Indiana's John Pettit pronounced his widely quoted statement that the supposed "self-evident truth" of man's equal creation was in fact "a self-evident lie." Ohio's senator Benjamin Franklin Wade, an outspoken opponent of slavery known for his vituperative style and intense patriotism, rose to reply. Perhaps Wade's first and middle names gave him a special bond with the Declaration and its creators. The "great declaration cost our forefathers too dear," he said, to be so "lightly thrown away by their children." Without its inspiring principles the Americans could not have won their independence; for the revolutionary generation the "great truths" in that "immortal instrument," the Declaration of Independence, were "worth the sacrifice of all else on earth, even life itself." How, then, were men equal? Not, surely, in physical power or intellect. The "good old Declaration" said "that all men are equal, and have inalienable rights; that is, [they are] equal in point of right; that no man has a right to trample on another." Where those rights were wrested from men through force or fraud, justice demanded that they be "restored without delay."

Abraham Lincoln, a little-known forty-four-year-old lawyer in Springfield, Illinois, who had served one term in Congress before being turned out of office, read these debates, was aroused as by nothing before, and began to pick up the dropped threads of his political career. Like Wade, Lincoln idealized the men of the American Revolution, who were for him "a forest of giant oaks," "a fortress of strength," "iron men." He also shared the deep concern of his contemporaries as the "silent artillery of time" removed them and the *living history* they embodied from this world. Before the 1850s, however, Lincoln seems to have had relatively little interest in the Declaration of Independence. Then, suddenly, that document and its assertion that all men were created equal became his "ancient faith," the "father of all moral principles," an "axiom" of free society. He was provoked by the attacks of men such as Pettit and Calhoun. And he made the arguments of those who defended the Declaration his own, much as Jefferson had done with Mason's text, reworking the ideas from speech to speech, pushing their logic, and eventually, at Gettysburg in 1863, arriving at a simple statement of profound eloquence. In time his understanding of the Declaration of Independence would become that of the nation.

Lincoln's position emerged fully and powerfully during his debates with Illinois's senator Stephen Douglas, a Democrat who had proposed the Kansas-Nebraska Act and whose seat Lincoln sought in 1858. They were an odd couple, Douglas and Lincoln, as different physically—at full height Douglas came only to Lincoln's shoulders—as they were in style. Douglas wore well-tailored clothes; Lincoln's barely covered his limbs. Douglas was in general the more polished speaker; Lincoln sometimes rambled on, losing his point and his audience, although he could also, especially with a prepared text, be a powerful orator. The greatest difference between them was, however, in the positions they took on the future of slavery and the meaning of the Declaration of Independence.

Douglas defended the Kansas-Nebraska Act, which allowed the people of those states to permit slavery within their borders, as consistent with the revolutionary heritage. After all, in instructing their delegates to vote for independence, one state after another had explicitly retained the exclusive right of defining its domestic institutions. Moreover, the Declaration of Independence carried no implications for slavery, since its statement on equality referred to white men only. In fact, Douglas said, it simply meant that American colonists of European descent had equal rights with the King's subjects in Great Britain. The signers were not thinking of "the negro or… savage Indians, or the Feejee, or the Malay, or any other inferior or degraded race." Otherwise they would

have been honor bound to free their own slaves, which not even Thomas Jefferson did. The Declaration had only one purpose: to explain and justify American independence.

Lincoln believed the Declaration "contemplated the progressive improvement in the condition of all men everywhere." Otherwise, it was "mere rubbish."

To LINCOLN, DOUGLAS'S ARGUMENT left only a "mangled ruin" of the Declaration of Independence, whose "plain, unmistakable language" said *"all* men" were created equal. In affirming that government derived its "just powers from the consent of the governed," the Declaration also said that no man could rightly govern others without their consent. If, then, "the negro is a man," was it not a "total destruction of self-government, to say that he too shall not govern *himself?"* To govern a man without his consent was "despotism." Moreover, to confine the Declaration's significance to the British peoples of 1776 denied its meaning, Lincoln charged, not only for Douglas's "inferior races" but for the French, Irish, German, Scandinavian, and other immigrants who had come to America after the Revolution. For them the promise of equality linked new Americans with the founding generation; it was an "electric cord" that bound them into the nation "as though they were blood of the blood, and flesh of the flesh of the men who wrote that Declaration," and so made one people out of many. Lincoln believed that the Declaration "contemplated the progressive improvement in the condition of all men everywhere." If instead it was only a justification of independence "without the *germ,* or even the *suggestion* of the individual rights of man in it," the document was "of no practical use now— mere rubbish—old wadding left to rot on the battlefield after the victory is won,"

an "interesting memorial of the dead past… shorn of its vitality, and practical value."

LIKE WADE, LINCOLN DENIED THAT the signers meant that men were equal in *"all respects,"* including "color, size, intellect, moral developments, or social capacity." He, too, made sense of the Declaration's assertion of man's equal creation by eliding it with the next, separate statement on rights. The signers, he insisted, said men were equal in having "'certain inalienable rights.…' This they said, and this they meant." Like John Cooke in Virginia three decades before, Lincoln thought the Founders allowed the persistence of practices at odds with their principles for reasons of necessity: to establish the Constitution demanded that slavery continue in those original states that chose to keep it. "We could not secure the good we did if we grasped for more," but that did not "destroy the principle that is the charter of our liberties." Nor did it mean that slavery had to be allowed in states not yet organized in 1776, such as Kansas and Nebraska.

Again like Cooke, Lincoln claimed that the authors of the Declaration understood its second paragraph as setting a standard for free men whose principles should be realized "as fast as circumstances… permit." They wanted that standard to be "familiar to all, and revered by all; constantly looked to, and constantly labored for, and even though never perfectly attained, constantly approximated and thereby constantly spreading and deepening its influence, and augmenting the happiness and value of life to all people of all colors everywhere." And if, as Calhoun said, American independence could have been declared without any assertion of human equality and inalienable rights, that made its inclusion all the more wonderful. "All honor to Jefferson," Lincoln said in a letter of 1859, "to the man who… had the coolness, forecast, and capacity to introduce into a merely revolutionary document, an abstract truth, applicable to all men and all times, and to embalm it there," where it would remain "a rebuke and a stumbling-block to the very harbingers of re-appearing tyranny and oppression."

JEFFERSON AND THE MEMBERS OF THE second contInental Congress did not understand what they were doing in quite that way on July 4, 1776. For them, it was enough for the Declaration to be "merely revolutionary." But if Douglas's history was more accurate, Lincoln's reading of the Declaration was better suited to the needs of the Republic in the mid-nineteenth century, when the standard of revolution had passed to Southern secessionists and to radical abolitionists who also called for disunion. In his hands the Declaration became first and foremost a living document for an established society, a set of goals to be realized over time, the dream of "something better, than a mere change of masters" that explained why "our fathers" fought and endured until they won the Revolutionary War. In the Civil War, too, Lincoln told Congress on July 4, 1861, the North fought not only to save the Union but to preserve a form of government "whose leading object is to elevate the condition of men—to lift artificial weights from all shoulders—to clear the paths of laudable pursuit for all." The rebellion it opposed was at base an effort "to overthrow the principle that all men were created equal." And so the Union victory at Gettysburg in 1863 became for him a vindication of that proposition, to which the nation's fathers had committed it in 1776, and a challenge to complete the "unfinished work" of the Union dead and bring to "this nation, under God, a new birth of freedom."

The Declaration Lincoln left was not Jefferson's Declaration, although Jefferson and other revolutionaries shared the values Lincoln stressed.

Lincoln's Gettysburg Address stated briefly and eloquently convictions he had developed over the previous decade, convictions that on point after point echoed earlier Americans: Republicans of the 1790s, the eulogists Peleg Sprague and John Sergeant in 1826, John Cooke in the Virginia convention a few years later, Benjamin Wade in 1853. Some of those men he knew; others were unfamiliar to him, but they had also struggled to understand the practical implications of their revolutionary heritage and followed the same logic to the same conclusions. The Declaration of Independence Lincoln left was not Jefferson's Declaration, although Jefferson and other revolutionaries shared the values Lincoln and others stressed: equality, human rights, government by consent. Nor was Lincoln's Declaration of Independence solely his creation. It remained an "expression of the American mind," not, of course, what all Americans thought but what many had come to accept. And its implications continued to evolve after Lincoln's death. In 1858 he had written a correspondent that the language of the Declaration of Independence was at odds with slavery but did not require political and social equality for free black Americans. Few disagreed then. How many would agree today?

The Declaration of Independence is in fact a curious document. After the Civil War members of Lincoln's party tried to write its principles into the Constitution by enacting the Thirteenth, Fourteenth, and Fifteenth Amendments, which is why issues of racial or age or gender equality are now so often fought out in the courts. But the Declaration of Independence itself is not and has never been legally binding. Its power comes from its capacity to inspire and move the hearts of living Americans, and its meaning lies in what they choose to make of it. It has been at once a cause of controversy, pushing as it does against established habits and conventions, and a unifying national icon, a legacy and a new creation that binds the revolutionaries to descendants who confronted and continue to confront issues the Founders did not know or failed to resolve. On Independence Day, then, Americans celebrate not simply the birth of their nation or the legacy of a few great men. They also commemorate a Declaration of Independence that is their own collective work now and through time. And that, finally, makes sense of the Fourth of July.

Pauline Maier is William Rand Kenan, Jr., Professor of American History at the Massachusetts Institute of Technology.

This article originally appeared in *American Heritage,* July/August 1997, pp. 54–65. Adapted from AMERICAN SCRIPTURE: MAKING THE DECLARATION OF INDEPENDENCE, by Pauline Maier. © 1997 by Pauline Maier. Used by permission of Alfred A. Knopf, a division of Random House, Inc.

Hamilton Takes Command

In 1775, the 20-year-old Alexander Hamilton took up arms to fight the British. Soon the brash young soldier would display the courage and savvy that would take him to the apex of power in the new U.S. government.

"ALEXANDER HAMILTON is the least appreciated of the founding fathers because he never became president," says Willard Sterne Randall, a professor of humanities at Champlain College in Burlington, Vermont, and the author of Alexander Hamilton: A Life, *released this month from HarperCollins Publishers. "Washington set the mold for the presidency, but the institution wouldn't have survived without Hamilton."*

Hamilton was born January 11, 1755, on the island of Nevis in the West Indies, the illegitimate son of James Hamilton, a merchant from Scotland, and Rachel Fawcett Levine, a doctor's daughter who was divorced from a plantation owner. His unmarried parents separated when Hamilton was 9, and he went to live with his mother, who taught him French and Hebrew and how to keep the accounts in a small dry goods shop by which she supported herself and Hamilton's older brother, James. She died of yellow fever when Alexander was 13.

After her death, Hamilton worked as a clerk in the Christiansted (St. Croix) office of a New York-based import-export house. His employer was Nicholas Cruger, the 25-year-old scion of one of colonial America's leading mercantile families, whose confidence he quickly gained. And in the Rev. Hugh Knox, the minister of Christiansted's first Presbyterian church, Hamilton found another patron. Knox, along with the Cruger family, arranged a scholarship to send Hamilton to the United States for his education. At age 17, he arrived in Boston in October 1772 and was soon boarding at the Elizabethtown Academy in New Jersey, where he excelled in English composition, Greek and Latin, completing three years' study in one. Rejected by Princeton because the college refused to go along with his demand for accelerated study, Hamilton went instead in 1773 to King's College (now Columbia University), then located in Lower Manhattan. In events leading up to the excerpt that follows, Hamilton was swept up by revolutionary fervor and, at age 20, dropped out of King's College and formed his own militia unit of about 25 young men.

In JUNE 1775, the Continental Congress in Philadelphia chose Virginia delegate Col. George Washington as commander in chief of the Continental Army then surrounding British-occupied Boston. Hurrying north, Washington spent a day in New York City where, on Sunday June 25, 1775, Alexander Hamilton braced at attention for Washington to inspect his militiamen at the foot of Wall Street.

Two months later, the last hundred British troops withdrew from Manhattan, going aboard the 64-gun man-of-war *Asia.* At 11 o'clock on the night of August 23, Continental Army Artillery captain John Lamb gave orders for his company supported by Hamilton's volunteers and a light infantry unit, to seize two dozen cannons from the battery at the island's southern tip. The *Asia's* captain, having been warned by Loyalists that the Patriots would raid the fort that night, posted a patrol barge with redcoats just offshore. Shortly after midnight, the British spotted Hamilton, his friend Hercules Mulligan, and about 100 comrades tugging on ropes they had attached to the heavy guns. The redcoats opened a brisk musket fire from the barge. Hamilton and the militiamen returned fire, killing a redcoat. At this, the *Asia* hoisted sail and began working in close to shore, firing a 32-gun broadside of solid shot. One cannonball pierced the roof of Fraunces Tavern at Broad and Pearl Streets. Many years later Mulligan would recall: "I was engaged in hauling off one of the cannons, when Mister Hamilton came up and gave me his musket to hold and he took hold of the rope.... Hamilton [got] away with the cannon. I left his musket in the Battery and retreated. As he was returning, I met him and he asked for his piece. I told him where I had left it and he went for it, notwithstanding the firing continued, with as much concern as if the [*Asia*] had not been there."

Hamilton's cool under fire inspired the men around him: they got away with 21 of the battery's 24 guns, dragged them uptown to City Hall Park and drew them up around the Liberty Pole under guard for safekeeping.

On January 6, 1776, the New York Provincial Congress ordered that an artillery company be raised to defend the colony; Hamilton, unfazed that virtually all commissions were going to native colonists of wealth and social position, leaped at the opportunity. Working behind the scenes to advance his candidacy, he won the support of Continental Congressmen John Jay and William Livingston. His mathematics teacher at King's College vouched for his mastery of the necessary trigonometry, and Capt. Stephen Bedlam, a skilled artillerist, certified that he had "examined Alexander Hamilton and judges him qualified."

While Hamilton waited to hear about his commission, Elias Boudinot, a leader of the New Jersey Provincial Congress, wrote from Elizabethtown to offer him a post as brigade major and aide-de-camp to Lord Stirling (William Alexander), commander of the newly formed New Jersey Militia. It was tempting. Hamilton had met the wealthy Scotsman as a student at Elizabethtown Academy and thought highly of him. And if he accepted, Hamilton would likely be the youngest major in the Revolutionary armies. Then Nathanael Greene, a major general in the Continental Army, invited Hamilton to become *his* aide-de-camp as well. After thinking the offers over, Hamilton declined both of them, gambling instead on commanding his own troops in combat.

Sure enough, on March 14, 1776, the New York Provincial Congress ordered Alexander Hamilton "appointed Captain of the Provincial Company of Artillery of this colony." With the last of his St. Croix scholarship money, he had his friend Mulligan, who owned a tailor shop, make him a blue coat with buff cuffs and white buckskin breeches.

He then set about recruiting the 30 men required for his company "We engaged 25 men [the first afternoon]," Mulligan remembered, even though, as Hamilton complained in a letter to the provincial congress, he could not match the pay offered by Continental Army recruiters. On April 2, 1776, two weeks after Hamilton received his commission, the provincial congress ordered him and his fledgling company to relieve Brig. Gen. Alexander McDougall's First New York Regiment, guarding the colony's official records, which were being shipped by wagon from New York's City Hall to the abandoned Greenwich Village estate of Loyalist William Bayard.

In late May 1776, ten weeks after becoming an officer, Hamilton wrote to New York's provincial congress to contrast his own meager payroll with the pay rates spelled out by the Continental Congress: "You will discover a considerable difference," he said. "My own pay will remain the same as it is now, but I make this application on behalf of the company, as I am fully convinced such a disadvantageous distinction will have a very pernicious effect on the minds and behavior of the men. They do the same duty with the other companies and think themselves entitled to the same pay."

The day the provincial congress received Captain Hamilton's missive, it capitulated to all his requests. Within three weeks, the young officer's company was up to 69 men, more than double the required number.

Meanwhile, in the city, two huge bivouacs crammed with tents, shacks, wagons and mounds of supplies were taking shape. At one of them, at the juncture of present-day Canal and Mulberry Streets, Hamilton and his company dug in. They had been assigned to construct a major portion of the earthworks that reached halfway across Manhattan Island. Atop Bayard's Hill, on the highest ground overlooking the city, Hamilton built a heptagonal fort, Bunker Hill. His friend Nicholas Fish described it as "a fortification superior in strength to any my imagination could ever have conceived." When Washington inspected the works, with its eight 9-pounders, four 3-pounders and six cohorn mortars, in mid-April, he commended Hamilton and his troops "for their masterly manner of executing the work."

Hamilton also ordered his men to rip apart fences and cut down some of the city's famous stately elm trees to build barricades and provide firewood for cooking. In houses abandoned by Loyalists, his soldiers propped muddy boots on damask furniture, ripped up parquet floors to fuel fireplaces, tossed garbage out windows and grazed their horses in gardens and orchards. One Loyalist watched in horror as army woodcutters, ignoring his protests, chopped down his peach and apple orchards on 23rd Street. Despite a curfew, drunken soldiers caroused with prostitutes in the streets around Trinity Church. By midsummer, 10,000 American troops had transformed New York City into an armed camp.

T HE VERY DAY—July 4, 1776—that the founding fathers of the young nation-to-be were signing the Declaration of Independence in Philadelphia, Captain Hamilton watched through his telescope atop Bayard's Hill as a forest of ship masts grew ominously to the east; in all, some 480 British warships would sail into New York Harbor. One of Washington's soldiers wrote in his diary that it seemed "all London was afloat." Soon they had begun to disgorge the first of what would swell to 39,000 troops—the largest expeditionary force in English history—onto Staten Island. On July 9, at 6 o'clock in the evening, Hamilton and his men stood to attention on the commons to hear the declaration read aloud from the balcony of City Hall. Then the soldiers roared down Broadway to pull down and smash the only equestrian statue of King George III in America.

Three days later, British Vice Admiral Lord Richard Howe detached two vessels from his flotilla, the 44-gun *Phoenix* and the 28-gun *Rose*, to sail up the Hudson and probe shore defenses. The captain of the *Rose* coolly sipped claret on his quarterdeck as his vessel glided past the battery on Lower Manhattan—where an ill-trained American gun crew immediately blew itself up. The ships sailed unmolested up the river to Tarrytown as colonial troops abandoned their posts to watch. An appalled Washington fumed: "Such unsoldierly conduct gives the enemy a mean opinion of the army." On their return, the two British ships passed within cannon range of Hamilton's company at Fort Bunker Hill. He ordered his 9-pounders to fire, which the British warships returned. In the brief skirmish, one of Hamilton's cannons burst, killing one man and severely wounding another.

On August 8, Hamilton tore open orders from Washington: his company was to be on round-the-clock alert against an imminent invasion of Manhattan. "The movements of the enemy and intelligence by deserters give the utmost reason to believe that the great struggle in which we are contending for everything dear to us and our posterity, is near at hand," Washington wrote.

But early on the morning of August 27, 1776, Hamilton watched, helpless, as the British ferried 22,000 troops from Staten Island, not to Manhattan at all, but to the village of Brooklyn, on Long Island. Marching quickly inland from a British beachhead that stretched from Flatbush to Gravesend, they met little resistance. Of the 10,000 American troops on Long Island, only 2,750 were in Brooklyn, in four makeshift forts spread over four miles. At Flatbush, on the American east flank, Lord Charles Cornwallis quickly captured a mounted patrol of five young militia officers, including Hamilton's college roommate, Robert Troup, enabling 10,000 redcoats to march stealthily behind the Americans. Cut off by an 80-yard-wide swamp, 312 Americans died in the ensuing rout; another 1,100 were wounded or captured. By rowboat, barge, sloop, skiff and canoe in a howling northeaster, a regiment of New England fishermen transported the survivors across the East River to Manhattan.

At a September 12, 1776, council of war, a grim-faced Washington asked his generals if he should abandon New York City to the enemy. Rhode Islander Nathanael Greene, Washington's second-in-command, argued that "a general and speedy retreat is absolutely necessary" and insisted, as well, that "I would burn the city and suburbs," which, he maintained, belonged largely to Loyalists.

But Washington decided to leave the city unharmed when he decamped. Before he could do so, however, the British attacked again, at Kip's Bay on the East River between present-day 30th and 34th Streets, two miles north of Hamilton's hill fort, leaving his company cut off and in danger of capture. Washington sent Gen. Israel Putnam and his aide-de-camp, Maj. Aaron Burr, to evacuate them. The pair reached Fort Bunker Hill just as American militia from Lower Manhattan began to stream past Hamilton heading north on the Post Road (now Lexington Avenue). Although Hamilton had orders from Gen. Henry Knox to rally his men for a stand, Burr, in the name of Washing-

ton, countermanded Knox and led Hamilton, with little but the clothes on his back, two cannons and his men, by a concealed path up the west side of the island to freshly dug entrenchments at Harlem Heights. Burr most likely saved Hamilton's life.

THE BRITISH BUILT defenses across northern Manhattan, which they now occupied. On September 20, fanned by high winds, a fire broke out at midnight in a frame house along the waterfront near Whitehall Slip. Four hundred and ninety-three houses—one-fourth of the city's buildings—were destroyed before British soldiers and sailors and townspeople put out the flames. Though the British accused Washington of setting the fire, no evidence has ever been found to link him to it. In a letter to his cousin Lund at Mount Vernon, Washington wrote: "Providence, or some good honest fellow, has done more for us than we were disposed to do for ourselves."

By mid-October, the American army had withdrawn across the Harlem River north to White Plains in Westchester County. There, on October 28, the British caught up with them. Behind hastily built earthworks, Hamilton's artillerymen crouched tensely as Hessians unleashed a bayonet charge up a wooded slope. Hamilton's gunners, flanked by Maryland and New York troops, repulsed the assault, causing heavy casualties, before being driven farther north.

Cold weather pinched the toes and numbed the fingers of Hamilton's soldiers as they dug embankments. His pay book indicates he was desperately trying to round up enough shoes for his barefoot, frostbitten men. Meanwhile, an expected British attack did not materialize. Instead, the redcoats and Hessians stormed the last American stronghold on Manhattan Island, Fort Washington, at present-day 181st Street, where 2,818 besieged Americans surrendered on November 16. Three days later, the British force crossed the Hudson and attacked Fort Lee on the New Jersey shore near the present-day George Washington Bridge. The Americans escaped, evacuating the fort so quickly they left behind 146 precious cannons, 2,800 muskets and 400,000 cartridges.

In early November, Captain Hamilton and his men had been ordered up the Hudson River to Peekskill to join a column led by Lord Stirling. The combined forces crossed the Hudson to meet Washington and, as the commander in chief observed, his 3,400 "much broken and dispirited" men, in Hackensack, New Jersey.

Hamilton hitched horses to his two remaining 6-pound guns and marched his gun crews 20 miles in one day to the Raritan River. Rattling through Elizabethtown, he passed the Elizabethtown Academy where, only three years earlier, his greatest concern had been Latin and Greek declensions.

Dug in near Washington's Hackensack headquarters on November 20, Hamilton was startled by the sudden appearance of his friend Hercules Mulligan, who, to

Hamilton's great dismay, had been captured some three months early at the Battle of Long Island. Mulligan had been determined a "gentleman" after his arrest and released on his honor not to leave New York City. After a joyous reunion, Hamilton evidently persuaded Mulligan to return to New York City and to act, as Mulligan later put it, as a "confidential correspondent of the commander-in-chief"—a spy.

After pausing to await Gen. Sir William Howe, the British resumed their onslaught. On November 29, a force of about 4,000, double that of the Americans, arrived at a spot across the Raritan River from Washington's encampment. While American troops tore up the planks of the New Bridge, Hamilton and his guns kept up a hail of grapeshot.

For several hours, the slight, boyish-looking captain could be seen yelling, "Fire! Fire!" to his gun crews, racing home bags of grapeshot, then quickly repositioning the recoiling guns. Hamilton kept at it until Washington and his men were safely away toward Princeton. Halfway there, the general dispatched a brief message by express rider to Congress in Philadelphia: "The enemy appeared in several parties on the heights opposite Brunswick and were advancing in a large body toward the [Raritan] crossing place. We had a smart cannonade whilst we were parading our men."

Washington asked one of his aides to tell him which commander had halted his pursuers. The man replied that he had "noticed a youth, a mere stripling, small, slender, almost delicate in frame, marching, with a cocked hat pulled down over his eyes, apparently lost in thought, with his hand resting on a cannon, and every now and then patting it, as if it were a favorite horse or a pet plaything." Washington's stepgrandson Daniel Parke Custis later wrote that Washington was "charmed by the brilliant courage and admirable skill" of the then 21-year-old Hamilton, who led his company into Princeton the morning of December 2. Another of Washington's officers noted that "it was a model of discipline; at their head was a boy, and I wondered at his youth, but what was my surprise when he was pointed out to me as that Hamilton of whom we had already heard so much."

AFTER LOSING New Jersey to the British, Washington ordered his army into every boat and barge for 60 miles to cross the Delaware River into Pennsylvania's Bucks County. A shivering Hamilton and his gunners made passage in a Durham ore boat, joining artillery already ranged along the western bank. Whenever British patrols ventured too near the water, Hamilton's and the other artillerymen repulsed them with brisk fire. The weather grew steadily colder. General Howe said he found it "too severe to keep the field." Remming to New York City with his redcoats, he left a brigade of Hessians to winter at Trenton.

In command of the brigade, Howe placed Col. Johann Gottlieb Rall, whose troops had slaughtered retreating Americans on Long Island and at Fort Washington on Manhattan. His regiments had a reputation for plunder and worse. Reports that the Hessians had raped several women, including a 15-year-old girl, galvanized New Jersey farmers, who had been reluctant to help the American army. Now they formed militia bands to ambush Hessian patrols and British scouting parties around Trenton. "We have not slept one night in peace since we came to this place," one Hessian officer moaned.

Washington now faced a vexing problem: the enlistments of his 3,400 Continental troops expired at midnight New Year's Eve; he decided to attack the Trenton Hessians while they slept off the effects of their Christmas celebration. After so many setbacks, it was a risky gambit; defeat could mean the end of the American cause. But a victory, even over a small outpost, might inspire lagging Patriots, cow Loyalists, encourage reenlistments and drive back the British—in short, keep the Revolution alive. The main assault force was made up of tested veterans. Henry Knox, Nathanael Greene, James Monroe, John Sullivan and Alexander Hamilton, future leaders of America's republic, huddled around a campfire at McKonkey's Ferry the frigid afternoon of December 25, 1776, to get their orders. Hamilton and his men had blankets wrapped around them as they hefted two 6-pounders and their cases of shot and shells onto the 9-foot-wide, 60-foot-long Durham iron-ore barges they had commandeered, then pushed and pulled their horses aboard. Nineteen-year-old James Wilkinson noted in his journal that footprints down to the river were "tinged here and there with blood from the feet of the men who wore broken shoes." Ship captain John Glover ordered the first boatloads to push off at 2 a.m. Snow and sleet stung Hamilton's eyes.

Tramping past darkened farmhouses for 12 miles, Hamilton's company led Nathanael Greene's division as it swung off to the east to skirt the town. One mile north of Trenton, Greene halted the column. At precisely 8 in the morning, Hamilton unleashed his artillery on the Hessian outpost. Three minutes later, American infantry poured into town. Driving back Hessian pickets with their bayonets, they charged into the old British barracks to confront groggy Hessians at gunpoint. Some attempted to regroup and counterattack, but Hamilton and his guns were waiting for them. Firing in tandem, Hamilton's cannons cut down the Hessians with murderous sheets of grapeshot. The mercenaries sought cover behind houses but were driven back by Virginia riflemen, who stormed into the houses and fired down from upstairs windows. Hessian artillerymen managed to get off only 13 rounds from two brass fieldpieces before Hamilton's gunners cut them in two. Riding back and forth behind the guns, Washington saw for himself the brutal courage and skillful discipline of this youthful artillery captain.

The Hessians' two best regiments surrendered, but a third escaped. As the Americans recrossed the Delaware, both they and their prisoners, nearly 1,000 in all, had to stomp their feet to break up the ice that was forming on the river. Five men froze to death.

Stung by the defeat, British field commander Lord Cornwallis raced across New Jersey with battle-seasoned grenadiers to retaliate. Americans with $10 gold reenlistment bonuses in their pockets recrossed the river to intercept them. When the British halted along a three-mile stretch of Assunpink Creek outside Trenton and across from the Americans, Washington duped British pickets by ordering a rear guard to tend roaring campfires and to dig noisily through the night while his main force slipped away.

At 1 a.m., January 2, 1777, their numbers reduced from 69 to 25 by death, desertion and expired enlistments, Hamilton and his men wrapped rags around the wheels of their cannons to muffle noise, and headed north. They reached the south end of Princeton at sunrise, to face a brigade—some 700 men—of British light infantry. As the two forces raced for high ground, American general Hugh Mercer fell with seven bayonet wounds. The Americans retreated from a British bayonet charge. Then Washington himself galloped onto the battlefield with a division of Pennsylvania militia, surrounding the now outnumbered British. Some 200 redcoats ran to Nassau Hall, the main building at Princeton College. By the time Hamilton set up his two cannons, the British had begun firing from the windows of the red sandstone edifice. College tradition holds that one of Hamilton's 6-pound balls shattered a window, flew through the chapel and beheaded a portrait of King George II. Under Hamilton's fierce cannonade, the British soon surrendered.

IN THE WAKE of twin victories within ten days, at Trenton and Princeton, militia volunteers swarmed to the American standard, far more than could be fed, clothed or armed. Washington's shorthanded staff was ill-equipped to coordinate logistics. In the four months since the British onslaught had begun, 300 American officers had been killed or captured. "At present," Washington complained, "my time is so taken up at my desk that I am obliged to neglect many other essential parts of my duty. It is absolutely necessary for me to have persons [who] can think for me as well as execute orders.... As to military knowledge, I do not expect to find gentlemen much skilled in it. If they can write a good letter, write quick, are methodical and diligent, it is all I expect to find in my aides."

He would get all that and more. In January, shortly after the army was led into winter quarters at Morristown, New Jersey, Nathanael Greene invited Hamilton, who had just turned 22, to dinner at Washington's headquarters. There, Washington invited the young artillery officer to join his staff. The appointment carried a promotion from captain to lieutenant colonel, and this time Hamilton did not hesitate. On March 1, 1777, he turned over the command of his artillery company to Lt. Thomas Thompson—a sergeant whom, against all precedent, he had promoted to officer rank—and joined Washington's headquarters staff.

It would prove a profound relationship.

"During a long series of years, in war and in peace, Washington enjoyed the advantages of Hamilton's eminent talents, integrity and felicity, and these qualities fixed [Hamilton] in [Washington's] confidence to the last hour of his life," wrote Massachusetts Senator Timothy Pickering in 1804. Hamilton, the impecunious abandoned son, and Washington, the patriarch without a son, had begun a mutually dependent relationship that would endure for nearly 25 years—years corresponding to the birth, adolescence and coming to maturity of the United States of America.

HAMILTON WOULD BECOME inspector general of the U.S. Army and in that capacity founded the U.S. Navy. Along with James Madison and John Jay, he wrote the Federalist Papers, *essays that helped gain popular support for the then-proposed Constitution. In 1789, he became the first Secretary of the Treasury, under President Washington and almost single-handedly created the U.S. Mint, the stock and bond markets and the concept of the modern corporation.*

After the death of Washington on December 14, 1799, Hamilton worked secretly, though assiduously, to prevent the reelection of John Adams as well as the election of Thomas Jefferson and Aaron Burr. Burr obtained a copy of a Hamilton letter that branded Adams an "eccentric" lacking in "sound judgment" and got it published in newspapers all over America. In the 1801 election, Jefferson and Burr tied in the Electoral College, and Congress made Jefferson president, with Burr his vice president. Hamilton, his political career in tatters, founded the New York Evening Post *newspaper, which he used to attack the new administration. In the 1804 New York gubernatorial election, Hamilton opposed Aaron Burr's bid to replace Governor George Clinton. With Hamilton's help, Clinton won.*

When he heard that Hamilton had called him "a dangerous man, and one who ought not to be trusted with the reins of government," Burr demanded a written apology or satisfaction in a duel. On the morning of Thursday, July 11, 1804, on a cliff in Weehawken, New Jersey, Hamilton faced the man who had rescued him 28 years earlier in Manhattan. Hamilton told his second, Nathaniel Pendleton, that he intended to fire into the air so as to end the affair with honor but without bloodshed. Burr made no such promise. A shot rang out. Burr's bullet struck Hamilton in the right side, tearing through his liver. Hamilton's pistol went off a split second later, snapping a twig overhead. Thirty-six hours later, Alexander Hamilton was dead. He was 49 years old.

Willard Sterne Randall is the Historical Scholar in Residence at Champlain College, Burlington, VT. Article from *Smithsonian,* January 2003, pages 64–71. This article is adapted from ALEXANDER HAMILTON: A LIFE, by Willard Sterne Randall. Copyright © 2003 by Willard Sterne Randall. Reprinted with permission of the author.

Winter of Discontent

Even as he endured the hardships of Valley Forge, George Washington
faced another challenge: critics who questioned his fitness to lead

BY NORMAN GELB

GEORGE WASHINGTON'S TROOPS could easily be followed as they trudged through the wintry expanse of southeastern Pennsylvania in late December 1777. The soldiers, many of them ragged and shoeless, left bloody footprints in the snow, marking the grueling progress of this army of the American Revolution toward winter quarters at Valley Forge.

There was no shelter for the men when they reached the exposed, hilly landscape of that misnamed redoubt, actually a plateau Washington chose largely for its defensibility. (A nearby hollow had once been the site of a smithy hence the designation.) Tents provided their only barrier against frost and wind. Their commander in chief insisted that he, too, would shelter in a tent until his troops were able to cut down trees and construct log huts for themselves.

Washington despaired for the fate of his army. "The whole of them," said his comrade in arms, Gen. John Sullivan, were "without watch coats, one half without blankets, and more than one third without shoes ... many of them without jackets ... and not a few without shirts." None had enough to eat: some had gone hungry for days. Exhausted and ill, men were deserting in great numbers, heading home to their families and farms. It was a dark moment for the Revolution and for Washington. From his makeshift headquarters, he wrote to warn Congress: "unless some great and capital change suddenly takes place ... this army must inevitably... starve, dissolve or disperse."

At that instant, stays Revolutionary era historian Edmund Morgan, Washington was indeed "giving Congress the facts of life: you can't fight a war without an army. He was operating at a big disadvantage; the state militias offered larger bounties than Congress did for serving in the Continental army."

Yet even as Washington attempted to keep his army from disintegrating, he found himself challenged on another front. Prominent figures in the independence movement—most notably, some members of Congress—had begun to question his very fitness to command. Over the course of the next several months—until mid-March—Washington would be plagued by a small but vocal contingent calling for his ouster. They engineered a very real distraction at a moment of grave crisis.

More than two years before, on June 15, 1775, Congress had unanimously chosen the tall, 43-year-old Virginia plantation owner and gentleman farmer "to command all the continental forces, raised or to be raised, for the defense of American liberty." During the French and Indian War two decades earlier, he had proved himself a courageous and levelheaded officer, serving under British command and as a colonel in the Virginia militia.

Washington had immediately justified the confidence placed in him by bringing order to the hodgepodge of militia contingents he led in what was becoming America's war of national liberation. From disarray and muddle, he created an American army and, in March 1776, orchestrated its first significant achievement, besieging the British and causing them to withdraw from Boston, the principal redcoat base in America at the time. "This was the moment," says historian John Ferling, author of the definitive Washington biography *The First of Men*, "that George Washington first captured the imagination of the American people."

But after Boston, his army suffered a series of serious reverses, including defeat at Brooklyn Heights on August 27, 1776, and the loss of New York. "At this point," says Ferling, "Washington was on the run. He nearly got trapped two or three times. During this period the British, under the command of General Howe, could have defeated him."

Washington's daring strikes against the enemy at Trenton on December 26 and Princeton on January 3, 1777, in New Jersey, boosted morale, but otherwise had little lasting military importance. Then came Brandywine Creek, in Pennsylvania. on September 11, 1777, where Washington failed to stop the British from advancing on Philadelphia, the capital of the Revolution. Members of Congress, who faced execution if taken prisoner, fled the city. This fiasco was followed by the Battle of Germantown, Pennsylvania, on October 4, where the Continental army snatched defeat from the jaws of victory through blunders in the field. Washington's four-pronged attack for taking the city proved too complex for inexperienced troops to carry out. As his soldiers maneuvered in a dense fog, they accidentally fired on one another. Given this turn of events, few in Congress observed the progress of the war without growing anxiety.

In the small Pennsylvania market town of York, about 100 miles west of Philadelphia, where Congress reconvened, there was talk that the commander in chief was indecisive and overly dependent on the advice of his senior subordinates. Congressman Thomas Burke of North Carolina decried what he called the "want of abilities in our superior officers and want of order and discipline in our army." Pennsylvania's new attorney general, Jonathan Dickinson Sergeant, a former congressman, charged that Washington was responsible for "such blunders as might have disgraced a soldier of three months' standing." In a moment of despair, John Adams, although ever fearful that a tyrant might emerge to fill the gap left by the discarded British king, pleaded in his diary while en route from Philadelphia to York, "Oh, Heaven! grant Us one great Soul! … One leading Mind would extricate the best Cause, from that Ruin which seems to await it."

Suddenly, it seemed, that desperate prayer had been answered: a patriot paladin appeared on the scene. Less than nine weeks before Washington's troops retreated to Valley Forge—the main column arrived there on December 19—the Continental army had scored a decisive victory. On October 17, at Saratoga in eastern New York, American forces, under the command of Gen. Horatio Gates, inflicted the first major defeat of the war on the redcoats, their German mercenary auxiliaries and Indian allies. For Gates, the 49-year-old English-born son of a duke's housekeeper, it was a moment of both tactical and symbolic triumph. The dashing John Burgoyne, campaigning down from Canada to split the states and crush the Revolution, was ignominiously forced to surrender himself and his army to the gruff, battle-hardened American, himself a former British officer. "One cannot underestimate the importance of Saratoga," says Ferling. "It is this victory that induces France to come into the war."

Gates' success greatly lifted American spirits. But his victory also drew attention to the fact that Washington, his superior officer, could claim no equivalent battle honors. Within Congress, criticism of Washington's performance escalated. Perhaps, some legislators suggested, the victor at Saratoga would make a better commander in chief than the general who had not prevented the British from taking Philadelphia.

Massachusetts Congressman James Lovell was scarcely alone in his view, as he wrote Gates, "The army will be totally lost unless you…, collect the virtuous band who wish to fight under your banner." Dr. Benjamin Rush, a signer of the Declaration of Independence, contrasted Gates, "exulting in the success of schemes planned with wisdom and executed with vigor and bravery," with Washington, "outgeneralled and twice beaten."

Most of the delegates at York, however, along with the majority of the Continental army's officers and its ordinary soldiers, continued to esteem their commander in chief. They were well aware that it was Washington who had kept the army from dissolving, despite the paucity of resources provided by either the strapped and deeply shaken Congress or the newly independent states. When it was suggested to hulking Gen. Daniel Morgan, whose corps of riflemen had played a decisive role at Saratoga, that a handful of senior officers intended to resign unless Washington was removed, he unhesitatingly responded, "Under no other man than Washington as Commander-in-Chief would I ever serve."

Dr. Benjamin Rush, a signer of the Declaration of Independence, referred to Washington as "outgeneralled and twice beaten."

Washington knew well that he was blamed, in certain quarters, for the poor performance of his army. But he was fitted with far more pressing matters. He had troops to feed, clothe, prepare for battle—and, most important, inspire: he understood that he must rally his remaining troops—about 11,000 all told at Valley Forge—and dissuade them from deserting. The commander of the Continental army was, according to Philander D. Chase, editor of *The Papers of George Washington* at the University, of Virginia, "astute enough to take a longer view of things. He understood that criticism, fair or unfair, real or apprehended, was part of the price that he had to pay to remain an effective leader and to achieve the aims of the Revolution."

In addition, Washington was engaged in planning offensive campaigns against a powerful, well-supplied foe. "The British were indeed formidable," says Ferling. "They had defeated the French in the French and Indian War; they also had the best navy in the world."

To add to Washington's concerns, for months he had contended with an assortment of European military officers, most of them French, who had converged on America to volunteer their services. They were recruited in Paris by Silas Deane, America's first official diplomat.

Some of the officers Deane commissioned may have shared the principles that had sparked the American Revolution. But most had signed on to further their own military careers, hoping to leapfrog into higher ranks back in Europe. Washington welcomed some of those volunteers, who would prove of great value to the American cause. Notable among them were the Marquis de Lafayette, the 19-year-old French nobleman who became one of Washington's most trusted aides; Friedrich von Steuben, the German soldier who would transform Washington's ragged army into a disciplined fighting force at Valley Forge; and Tadeusz Kosciuszko, the Polish military engineer who contributed greatly to the American victory at Saratoga.

But some foreign officers who laid claim to senior command in the Continental army were a nuisance or worse—none more so than Col. Thomas Conway. He would figure prominently among Washington's detractors, whom history would come to designate the Conway Cabal. A French officer of Irish origin, the 42-year-old Conway, high browed, thin lipped and supercilious, made it plain that he had come to America "to increase my fortune and that of my family." He was a seasoned soldier who joined the French Army at the age of 14. Gen. John Sullivan, under whom he served in the ill-fated Battle of Germantown, believed "his knowledge of military matters in general far exceeds any officer we have."

Congress quickly awarded Conway the rank of brigadier general; his military background and charisma earned him many an admirer in York. When he threatened to return to France unless promoted to major general, more than a few congressmen, convinced that Washington needed experienced commanders, took up Conway's cause.

At first, Washington, too, had been impressed by Conway's credentials. Over time, however, he had come to believe that the French officer's "importance in this Army, exists more in his imagination than in reality." What troubled him most was Congress's readiness to promote Conway over the heads of Washington's own loyal brigadiers. Many of his officers, he warned, would refuse to serve under Conway and would simply go home. "I have been a slave to the service," Washington informed Virginia Congressman Richard Henry Lee on October 17, 1777. "But it will be impossible for me to be of any further service if such insuperable obstacles are thrown in my way."

While some in Congress would have welcomed Washington's resignation in favor of Gates, the prospect of sowing confusion in the ranks, or even of causing an already demoralized army to disband, was alarming. The Continental army embodied the Revolution.

At this juncture, during the fall of 1777, Washington prevailed and Congress failed to act on Conway's promotion. But Congress also, at this moment, reorganized its Board of War. That Congressional committee, charged with overseeing the struggle for independence, was in fact composed of members who possessed little understanding of military matters. Until then, the board had intervened only minimally when it came to the army. Now the committee would include senior officers; Washington, the commander in chief, was not consulted about whom they would be.

It was rumored that Conway might be among them. From the moment of his arrival in America in the spring of 1777, Conway had found that the organization of the Continental army clashed with his European understanding of how military units should be commanded, trained and deployed. He did not hesitate in express his deprecating views. After Congress, acting on the basis of Washington's firm intercession, had failed to support his promotion to major general, Conway stepped up his campaign to defame the commander in chief. He informed General Gates that he wished to serve under him because "the more I see of [Washington's] army the less I think it fit for general action."

Recognizing the delicacy of the situation, Congress did not name Conway to the board. But it did appoint Thomas Mifflin, the army's former quartermaster general. Once Washington's friend, Mifflin had differed sharply on strategy and was now among the general's most acerbic critics. He jealously asserted that the commander's "favourites … had an undue influence on

him" and told Gates that Conway's criticism of Washington contained "just sentiments."

But the most significant appointment to the board turned out to be none other than the hero of Saratoga himself: it was a decision bound to create problems. Ever since his victory only a matter of weeks earlier, Gates had behaved disdainfully toward Washington, his superior officer. He even failed to formally notify the commander in chief of the triumph at Saratoga. Instead, Gates reported directly to Congress, a gesture that implied he claimed equal status with Washington. He had been slow to respond to Washington's request that some of Gates' troops, no longer essential for much-reduced northern operations, be released to the south, where they were desperately needed. Now Gates emerged as the leader of the board that would superintend the operations of Washington and his ragtag army.

Conway informed General Gates that "the more I see of Washington's army the less I think it fit for general action."

Although Washington surely must have been offended by this high-handed treatment, he refused to engage in a squabble over the appointments. Whatever his complaints about Congress's shortcomings in providing supplies and pay for his men, he recognized the legislature's authority over the military wing of the Revolution.

Substantial changes, too, in the character of the Congress that had ringingly declared American independence more than a year earlier, on July 4, 1776, intensified the divisiveness. Many of the original founding fathers had already left the legislature or were soon to depart. Thomas Jefferson had returned to Virginia to assist its transition from a royal colony to an independent state. Benjamin Franklin was in Paris seeking French assistance for America in the war. John Adams was preparing to join him there. Twenty-one-year-old Lt. Col. Alexander Hamilton, Washington's aide-de-camp, angrily demanded, "The great men who composed our first council; are they dead, have they deserted the cause, or what has become of them?"

Among the new delegates, few were as gifted, or would prove as memorable, as their predecessors. Much time was wasted in futile bickering. Henry Laurens of South Carolina, president of Congress during much of its York exile, grumbled, "Some sensible things have been said [here], and as much nonsense as ever I heard in so short a space." Charles Carroll of Maryland complained, "We murder time, and chat it away in idle impertinent talk."

Meanwhile, detractors in Congress were becoming increasingly critical of Washington. After visiting York, Lafayette returned to Valley Forge and declared himself outraged by "stupid men who without knowing a single word about war, undertake to judge you."

The move to replace the commander in chief with Gates—or even, it was muttered, with Conway—came to a head early in

1778 after the Continental army had arrived at the glacial hell of Valley Forge. One of every four soldiers who wintered in that place would die there. Even hardened veterans, among them Albigence Waldo of Connecticut, an army surgeon who had served since 1775, were appalled by what they saw: "There comes a soldier," Waldo wrote, "his bare feet are seen thro' his worn-out shoes, his legs nearly naked from the tattered remains of an only pair of stockings, his Breeches not sufficient to cover his nakedness…. He crys … I am Sick, my feet lame, my legs are sore, my body covered with this tormenting Itch."

Reluctantly, Washington sent troops to seize food from nearby farmers. Already weighed down with dire anxieties, he suffered another blow. On December 13, he learned Congress had reversed itself and decided to appoint Conway to the Board of War, as inspector general of the army. What was more, Congress elevated Conway to the rank of major general—the promotion previously denied because of Washington's objections.

Conway wasted no time in presenting himself at army headquarters, where, predictably, he was received with cold formality. Washington informed Conway that the newly conferred rank—a promotion the commander in chief dryly referred to as "extraordinary"—would offend many senior officers; he then asked to see specific instructions Conway had received from the Board of War. When Conway failed to produce such a communique, Washington had him shown out.

Upon his departure from Valley Forge, Conway sent Washington a letter barbed with sarcasm and self-justification, complaining their meeting had been a reception "as I never met with before with any general during the course of thirty years in a very respectable [French] Army."

His patience exhausted, Washington decided to confront the Conway issue. He passed the new inspector general's comments on to Congress, along with a bitter rebuttal of each accusation. Washington denied that he had received Conway with anything less than "proper respect to his official character" as an appointee of Congress. Nevertheless, he concluded, "My feelings will not permit me to make professions of friendship to a man I deem my enemy."

All the while, despite reports from friends that members of Congress were maneuvering to install Gates in his place, Washington had not sought to clash with the victor of Saratoga. He refused to believe that the new president of the Board of War was conspiring against him. "Being honest himself," Joseph Reed, Washington's former military secretary wrote, "he will not readily suspect the virtue of others." However, recognition of the challenge to his position became unavoidable.

Washington's trusted friend Dr. James Craik, a senior army medical officer, wrote to inform him that although "they dare not appear openly as your enemies … the new Board of War is composed of such leading men as will throw such obstacles and difficulties in your way as to force you to resign." Without consulting Washington, Gates' board secured Congressional approval of a campaign to pursue the English into Canada (the plans were later aborted). Patrick Henry, the governor of Virginia, forwarded to Washington a disturbing anonymous letter warning that "unless a Moses or a Joshua are raised up in our behalf, we must perish before we reach the promised land."

Increasingly exasperated by such taunts, Washington told a friend he would be happy to resign his command. "There is not an Officer in the Service of the United States," he declared, "that would return to the sweets of domestic life with more heartfelt joy than I should." But he would do so, he added, only if the will of the people ordained it: he feared destabilizing consequences if he stepped down.

"My Enemies take an ungenerous advantage of me," Washington wrote. "I cannot combat their insinuations."

The unkindest cut, however, came from those who suggested he had concealed the appalling condition of his army in order to deflect criticism of his command. "My Enemies take an ungenerous advantage of me," Washington protested to Henry Laurens. "They know I cannot combat their insinuations, however injurious, without disclosing secrets it is of the utmost moment to conceal." Had they known its state, the redcoats, a mere 18 miles away in Philadelphia, might well have launched an attack.

While Washington hoped that the British commander, Lord William Howe, remained ignorant of the extent of the patriot army's vulnerability as it bivouacked on frozen ground, members of Congress began arriving at Valley Forge to survey conditions for themselves. A shocked John Harvie of Virginia told Washington, "My dear General, if you had given some explanation, all these rumors [denigrating Washington] would have been silenced a long time ago."

Within Congress, a growing recognition of Washington's extraordinary leadership at Valley Forge—not only was he preventing the Continental army from dissolving, he was somehow inspiring his men under the cruelest of conditions— made a profound impression. Joseph Jones, a congressman from Virginia and a long-standing friend to Washington, wrote to offer his support: "The same equal and disinterested conduct, the same labor and attention, which you have manifested in the public service from the first of the contest, will shield and protect you from the shafts of envy and malevolence."

Still, Washington decided the time had come to take up the festering matter of a letter that Conway had written to Gates that autumn, which referred to a "weak general" who might prove the ruin of America.

He had learned of the letter when one of Gates' own aides had disclosed its contents to an officer loyal to Washington. When Gates discovered that the letter had been leaked to Washington, he wrote to him, demanding the identity of the "wretch" who had "stealingly copied" his private correspondence. Bent on dramatizing his challenge to the commander in chief's integrity, Gates sent a copy of this letter to Congress.

It would prove an enormous blunder. Washington was, quite rightly, able to take the high ground when he replied to the slander. Why, he inquired of Congress, would anyone want to add needlessly to the burdens on the beleaguered legislature, pestering it with details of a personal disagreement? He pointed out that he had learned of the malicious Conway letter to Gates through an indiscretion by one of Gates' own aides. Washington added that he had not previously gone public with the matter because he was "desirous ... of concealing every matter that could give the smallest interruption to the tranquility of this army." In the end, the episode caused the hero of Saratoga, and Conway along with him, to appear small-minded and vindictive.

But what conclusively undermined Washington's critics was the recognition that, whatever his shortcomings, Washington remained the individual who most represented the cause of liberty in the minds of the American people and its army. Mercy Otis Warren reported to her husband, Continental Navy Board member James Warren, that "The toast among the soldiers" is "Washington or no Army." Thomas Paine, the conscience mad primary propagandist of the Revolution, expressed the fervent hope that he could "shame [Washington's critics]" or at least "convince them of their error."

Congressman Jones accurately foretold that whatever the conspirators had intended, "it will redound to their own disgrace." Men who had spoken belittlingly of the commander in chief would later deny they had ever held him in anything but the highest regard. Gates soon tried to effect a reconciliation with Washington, but his attempt was rebuffed. Congress later removed him from the Board of War and assigned him to a succession of field commands. His reputation as a military hero would soon come to grief in South Carolina where, at the Battle of Camden on August 16, 1780, his troops were routed by the British. During a hasty retreat, Gates' undisguised anxiety for his own personal safety made him an object of ridicule among his men. "The general's frantic dash from the scene," says historian John Ferling, "proved his ruination."

Mifflin also suffered a measure of disgrace. Charged with having contributed to the troops' hardships at Valley Forge through mismanagement of funds as quartermaster general, he was forced to resign from the Board of War. He denied conspiring against Washington, insisting he had always "dearly loved and greatly admired" him.

As for Conway, who was scarcely the most significant figure in the Conway Cabal—despite the name by which it became known—Congress acted with crushing decisiveness. Still denied a senior command in the army, he offered his resignation April 1778 and was surprised when it was accepted. Before returning to France, he wrote Washington "You are in my eyes the great and the good man. May you long enjoy the love, veneration and esteem of these States, whose liberties you have asserted by your virtues." In that, at least, his wish would be realized.

Historians disagree over the significance of the attacks on Washington. In his monumental biography of Washington, Douglas S. Freeman stated that "the imperative reason for defeating [the cabal] was to keep the Army and the country united in the hard battle for freedom." But Ferling tends to minimize its importance. "I don't really think the cabal existed as an organized conspiracy," he says. "It existed more in Washington's mind than in reality." Certainly, Washington was convinced that a "malignant faction" had conspired to remove him. So, too, was Patrick Henry, who, along with others, feared for the patriot cause if such efforts had succeeded.

Whatever the strength of those who considered Washington a liability, it is impossible to calculate the consequences for the Continental army, the American Revolution and the embryonic United States of America had their sentiments found greater resonance in Congress—and forced or provoked the man who would later be called the Father of the Country to resign his command.

NORMAN GELB, author of numerous histories, is currently working on a study of military leadership in the American Revolution.

Your Constitution Is Killing You

A reconsideration of the right to bear arms

By Daniel Lazare

A well regulated Militia, being necessary to the security of a free State, the right of the people to keep and bear Arms, shall not be infringed.

—Second Amendment to the Constitution of the United States

On June 17, in the aftermath of the massacre at Columbine High School and a similar, if less grisly, incident the following month in Conyers, Georgia, the House of Representatives passed a "juvenile crime bill" steadfast in its refusal to limit the ease with which juveniles can lay their hands on firearms. House Republicans, it was clear, were determined to avoid making any connection between the fact that there are an estimated 240 million guns in the United States, nearly one per person, a number that is increasing by some 5 to 7 million a year, and the increase of violence in our culture. Instead, the problem was that we had forgotten the importance of "family values," that our children had become "spoiled with material things," that we had given in to "liberal relativism." Guns weren't the problem; the problem was

"the abandonment of God" in the public sphere.

Representatives Henry Hyde (R., Ill.) and Tom DeLay (R., Tex.) were particularly enthusiastic in their efforts to look beyond guns for a solution. Hyde put the blame on the entertainment industry and tried to push through an amendment to the crime bill that would have made it a jailable offense to sell overtly violent or sexual material to minors. Even when 127 of his fellow Republicans voted against the measure, Hyde refused to let go. "People were misled," he said, "and disinclined to oppose the powerful entertainment industry." DeLay's approach was even more entertaining. At a "God Not Guns" rally, he read aloud an e-mail he claimed to have received that very morning: "The student writes, 'Dear God, Why didn't you stop the shootings at Columbine?' And God writes, 'Dear student, I would have, but I wasn't allowed in school.'" (So much for divine omnipotence.) An hour later DeLay was on the House floor, telling his colleagues that "our school systems teach the children that they are nothing but glorified apes who are evolutionized out of some primordial soup of mud." Other DeLayisms: "We place our children in daycare centers where they learn their socializa-

tion skills... under the law of the jungle..."; "Our children, who historically have been seen as a blessing from God, are now viewed as either a mistake created when contraception fails or inconveniences that parents try to raise in their spare time." A proposal to allow the display of the Ten Commandments in public schools was subsequently voted into the bill.

Liberals cannot bear to admit the truth about gun control; the right wing is right. The second amendment confers an individual right

---

Among the further futile gestures housed in a second piece of crime legislation that failed the next day was a measure to reduce the Senate's proposed waiting time for purchases at gun shows and to limit the number of gun shows subject to any waiting period whatsoever. All this despite polls showing two-to-one support for stricter gun control even before Columbine. Two centuries ago, the great fear among the men who drew up the United States Constitution was of a popularly elected legislature falling all over itself to do the public's bidding; today we are witness to a popularly elected body falling all over itself not to carry out the democratic will. Why?

The standard liberal response is that the National Rifle Association made them do it. The NRA has used its immense campaign war chest to punish gun-control advocates and stifle dissent. It has twisted and distorted the Constitution. It has cleared a path for troglodytes like Hyde and DeLay. But the real problem is more disconcerting. The reason that Hyde and Co. are able to dominate the gun debate, the reason that the gun lobby is so powerful, is not the NRA but the basis on which the NRA's power rests; i.e., the Second Amendment. The truth about the Second Amendment is something that liberals cannot bear to admit: The right wing is right. The amendment does confer an individual right to bear arms, and its very presence makes effective gun control in this country all but impossible.

F or decades liberal constitutional scholars have maintained that, contrary to the NRA, the Second Amendment does not guarantee an individual's right to own guns, merely a right to participate in an official state militia. The key phrase, they have argued, is "[a] well regulated Militia," which the introductory clause describes as nothing less than essential to "the security of a free State." A well-regulated militia is not just a goal, consequently, but *the* goal, the amendment's raison d'être. Everything else is subordinate. The right "to keep and bear Arms" is valid only to the degree that it serves this all-important end. There is therefore no *individual right* to bear arms in and of itself, only a *collective* right on the part of the citizens of the states to do so as members of the various official state militias. The right to own the assault weapon of one's choice exists only in the fevered imagination of the National Rifle Association. Its constitutional basis is nil. The only right that the Second Amendment confers is the right

to emulate Dan Quayle and join the National Guard.

This is the cheerful, anodyne version of the Second Amendment we're used to from the American Civil Liberties Union and other liberal groups. But as the gun issue has heated up since the Sixties and Seventies, constitutional scholars have taken a second look. The result has been both a renaissance in Second Amendment studies and a remarkable about-face in how it is interpreted. The purely "collectivist" interpretation has been rejected across the board by liberals and conservatives as ahistorical and overly pat. The individualist interpretation, the one that holds that Americans have a right to bear arms whether they're serving in an official state militia or not, has been more or less vindicated. In fact, some academics have gone so far as to compare the NRA's long campaign in behalf of an expansive interpretation of the Second Amendment to the ACLU's long campaign in behalf of an expansive reading of the First. As the well-known constitutional scholar William Van Alstyne put it, "The constructive role of the NRA today, like the role of the ACLU in the 1920s,... ought itself not lightly to be dismissed. Indeed, it is largely by the 'unreasonable' persistence of just such organizations in this country that the Bill of Rights has endured." Language like this is what one might expect at some Texas or Colorado gun show, not in the pages of the Duke Law Journal.

With day traders and students shooting citizens, the implications of an individual right to bear arms are profound

---

No less strikingly, the Second Amendment renaissance has also led to a renewed appreciation for the amendment's ideological importance. Previously, scholars were inclined to view the Second Amendment as little more than a historical curiosity, not unlike the Third Amendment, which, as almost no one remembers, prohibits the peacetime quartering of troops in private homes without

the owners' consent. Harvard's Laurence Tribe gave the Second Amendment no more than a footnote in the 1988 edition of his famous textbook *American Constitutional Law,* but a new edition, published this August, treats the subject much more extensively. It is now apparent that the amendment, despite its brevity, encapsulates an entire worldview concerning the nature of political power, the rights and duties of citizenship, and the relationship between the individual and the state. It *is* virtually a constitution-within-the-Constitution, which is undoubtedly why it fuels such fierce passions.

With crazed day traders and resentful adolescents mowing down large numbers of their fellow citizens every few weeks, the implications of this new, toughened-up version of the Second Amendment would seem to be profound. Politically, there's no doubt that it has already had an effect by encouraging the gun lobby to dig in its heels after Littleton, Conyers, the Mark Barton rampage in Atlanta, and the earlier shootings in Kentucky, Arkansas, and elsewhere. When Joyce Lee Malcolm, professor of history at Bentley College in Waltham, Massachusetts, and the author of a path-breaking 1994 study, *To Keep and Bear Arms: The Origins of an Anglo-American Right* (Harvard University Press), told a congressional committee a year later that "[i]t is very hard, sir, to find a historian who now believes that it is only a collective right... [t]here is no one for me to argue against anymore," it was just the sort of thing that pro-gun forces on Capitol Hill wanted to hear. If it wasn't a sign that God was on their side, then it was a sign that the Constitution was, which in American politics is more or less the same thing.

The judicial impact is a bit harder to assess. Although the Supreme Court has not ruled on the Second Amendment since the 1930s, it has repeatedly upheld gun control measures. But there is evidence that judicial sentiment is beginning to take heed of the academic change of heart. Two years ago, Supreme Court Justice Clarence Thomas indicated that he thought it was time to rethink the Second Amendment; Justice Antonin Scalia apparently thinks so as well. Then, just this past April, two weeks before Eric

Harris and Dylan Klebold shot up Columbine High School, a federal judge in a Texas gun case issued a ruling so enthusiastically "individualist" that it was virtually a brief in favor of what is now known in academic circles as the "Standard Model" of the Second Amendment. "The plain language of the amendment," declared Judge Sam R. Cummings, "shows that the function of the subordinate clause [i.e., the portion referring to a well-regulated militia] was not to qualify the right [to keep and bear arms], but instead to show why it must be protected." Rather than mutually exclusive, the collective right to join a state militia and the individual right to own a gun are, according to Cummings, mutually reinforcing. Although anti-gun groups predicted that the decision would soon be overturned, it is clear that a purely collectivist reading is becoming harder and harder to defend; the individualist interpretation, harder and harder to deny.

W e have long been in the habit of seeing in the Constitution whatever it is we want to see. Because liberals want a society that is neat and orderly, they tell themselves that this is what the Constitution "wants" as well. This is a little like a nineteenth-century country vicar arguing that the Bible stands for moderation, reform, and other such Victorian virtues when in fact, as anyone who actually reads the text can see, it is filled with murder, mayhem, and the arbitrary vengeance of a savage god. By the same token, the increasingly sophisticated scholarship surrounding the Second Amendment has led to renewed respect for the constitutional text as it is rather than as we would like it to be. The Constitution, it turns out, is not neat and orderly but messy and unruly. It is not modern but pre-modern. It is not the product of a time very much like our own but reflects the unresolved contradictions of a time very different from our own.

Could it be that the Constitution is not the greatest plan on earth, that it contains notions that are repugnant to the modern sensibility? "When we are lost, the best thing for us to do is to look to our Constitution as a beacon of light and a guide to

get us through trying times." So declaimed Representative Zoe Lofgren (D., Calif.) during the House impeachment debate last October. Considering how we've all been taught since childhood to revere this document, probably not one American in a thousand would disagree. But what if Zoe Lofgren is wrong—what if the sacred text is seriously, if not fatally, flawed? Could it be that constitutional faith is not enough to get us through trying times? In a faithbound republic like the United States, this is pretty heretical stuff. Yet one of the nice things about the Second Amendment renaissance is the way it forces us to grapple with such heresy. Instead of allowing us to go on blindly trusting in the wisdom of a group of tribal patriarchs known as the Founding Fathers, it compels us to think for ourselves.

Could it be that the constitution is not the greatest plan, that it contains notions repugnant to the modern sensibility?

The framers, as it turns out, were of two minds where the power of the people was concerned. The Preamble to the Constitution implies a theory of unbounded popular sovereignty in which "we the people" are so powerful that we can "ordain and establish" new constitutions and, in the process, abrogate old ones such as the disastrous Articles of Confederation. The rest of the document implies that "we the people" are so powerless that when it comes to an anachronism such as the Second Amendment, the democratic majority is effectively precluded from changing a Constitution made in the people's name. We the people can move mountains, but we cannot excise one troublesome twenty-seven-word clause. Because we have chained ourselves to a premodern Constitution, we are unable to deal with the modern problem of a runaway gun culture in a modern way. Rather than binding society together, the effort to force society to conform to the dictates of an outmoded

plan of government is tearing it apart. Each new crazed gunman is a symptom of our collective—one might say our constitutional—helplessness. Someday soon, we will have to emancipate ourselves from our eighteenth-century Constitution. The only question is how.

A mericans tend to give history short shrift; after all, when your Constitution is a timeless masterpiece, who needs to bother with something as boring as the past? But in order to unlock the meaning of the Second Amendment, it is necessary to know a little about the world in which it was created. The most important thing to understand is the eighteenth century's role as the great transitional period. Capitalism, industrialism, the rise of the great metropolis, the creation of new kinds of politics—these were beginning to make themselves felt, and as they did so they were creating shock waves and counter shock waves from one end of the English-speaking world to the other. Urbanization fueled passionate defenses of the old agrarian way of life. A new system of government centered on a prime minister, a cabinet, and an all-powerful House of Commons provoked endless screeds in favor of the old system of checks and balances among a multitude of coequal governing institutions.

This is the source of the great eighteenth-century polarization between what was known as Court and Country—the powerbrokers, influence-wielders, and political fixers on one side, and all those who felt shut out by the new arrangement on the other. Since the 1960s, historians have made immense strides in reconstructing this Anglo-American ideological world. In essence, we now know that it was dominated by fierce controversy over the nature of political power: whether it was harmful or beneficial, oppressive or liberating, whether it should be concentrated in a single legislative chamber or distributed among many. The Country opposition believed passionately in the latter. As a couple of coffeehouse radicals named John Trenchard and Thomas Gordon put it in their hugely popular *Cato's Letters* in the 1720s, "Power is like fire; it warms, scorches, or destroys according as it is watched, provoked, or increased." The solution was to divide power among so many competitive institutions that politicians' "emulation, envy, fear, or interest, always made them spies and checks upon one another." Since power was growing, oppression was growing also. "Patriots," therefore, were continually fighting a rear-guard action against corruption and tyranny, which were forever on the increase.

Guns were a big part of the eighteenth-century Anglo-American debate, in which the popular militia represented freedom at its most noble

---

We can recognize in eighteenth-century beliefs like these such modern U.S. attitudes as the cult of checks and balances, hostility to "big gummint," and the Zoe Lofgrenesque conviction that everything will turn out well so long as we remain true to the constitutional faith of our forefathers. Guns, as it turns out, were also a big part of the eighteenth-century Anglo-American debate. "Standing armies," the great bugaboo of the day, represented concentrated power at its most brutal; the late-medieval institution of the popular militia represented freedom at its most noble and idealistic. Beginning with the highly influential Niccolò Machiavelli, a long line of political commentators stressed the special importance of the popular militias in the defense of liberty. Since the only ones who could defend popular liberty were the people themselves, a freedom-loving people had to maintain themselves in a high state of republican readiness. They had to be strong and independent, keep themselves well armed, and be well versed in the arts of war. The moment they allowed themselves to surrender to the wiles of luxury, the cause of liberty was lost.

Thus, we have Sir Walter Raleigh warning that the first goal of a would-be tyrant is to "unarm his people of weapons, money, and all means whereby they may resist his power." In the mid-

seventeenth century, we have the political theorist James Harrington stressing the special importance of an armed yeomanry of self-sufficient small farmers, while in the early eighteenth we have Trenchard and Gordon warning that "[t]he Exercise of despotick Power is the unrelenting War of an armed Tyrant upon his unarmed Subjects." In the 1770s, James Burgh, another writer in this long Country tradition, advised that "[n]o kingdom can be secured [against tyranny] otherwise than by arming the people. The possession of arms is the distinction between a freeman and a slave." A pro-American English radical named Richard Price added in 1784 that

> [T]he happiest state of man is the middle state between the *savage* and the *refined,* or between the wild and the luxurious state. Such is the state of society in CONNECTICUT, and in some others of the *American* provinces; where the inhabitants consist, if I am rightly informed, of an independent and hardy YEOMANRY, all nearly on a level—trained to arms,—instructed in their rights—cloathed in home-spun—of simple manners—strangers to luxury—drawing plenty from the ground—and that plenty, gathered easily by the hand of industry.

Not only were guns needed for self-defense but their widespread possession confirmed America's self-image as Homeland of Liberty

---

This was the Country myth in all its glory, the image of the roughhewn, liberty-loving "republican" as someone who called no one master, equated freedom and independence, and was not afraid to fight in defense of either or both. Joyce Lee Malcolm points out that where English patriots were content to pay lip service to the importance of arming the people, their cousins across the sea took the notion quite literally. A law

passed by the Plymouth Colony in 1623 required "that every freeman or other inhabitant of this colony provide for himselfe and each under him able to beare arms a sufficient musket and other serviceable peece for war." A 1639 law in Newport ordered that "noe man shall go two miles from the Towne unarmed, eyther with Gunn or Sword; and that none shall come to any public Meeting without his weapon." Measures like these were both practical and symbolic. Not only were guns necessary for self-defense but their widespread possession confirmed America's self-image as a homeland of liberty.

Ideas like these do not seem to have abated the least bit during the colonial period; indeed, by the 1770s they were at full boil. By the time British Redcoats faced off against heavily armed colonial irregulars at the Battle of Lexington and Concord in April 1775, it was as if both sides were actors in a political passion play that had been centuries in the making. It was the standing army versus the people's militia, the metropolis versus the hinterlands, centralized imperial power versus the old balanced constitution. Although the militias performed less than brilliantly in the Revolutionary War—Washington, professional soldier that he was, thought that the ragtag volunteer outfits were more trouble than they were worth—the myth lingered on. Americans needed to believe that amateur citizen-soldiers had won the war because their ideology told them that it was only via a popular militia that republican virtue could be established.

It is worth noting that even among those who were skeptical about the militias' military worth, the concept of a people in arms does not seem to have been at all problematic. Although Alexander Hamilton argued against separate state militias at the Constitutional Convention in 1787, for example, he seemed to have had nothing against popular militias per se. In 1788, he argued in *The Federalist Papers* that in the unlikely event that the proposed new national government used what was known at the time as a "select" militia—i.e., an elite corps—to oppress the population at large, the rest of the militia would be more than enough to fight them off. Such "a large body of citizens," he wrote, "little if at all inferior to them in discipline and the use of arms,... [would] stand ready to defend their own rights and those of their fellow-citizens." This is one reason why the argument that the Second Amendment confers only a collective right to join the National Guard is specious: today's National Guard is far closer to the eighteenth-century concept of a select militia than to the broad, popular militia the Framers clearly had in mind. And if the Second Amendment was nothing more than a guarantee of a right on the part of the states to organize state militias, it would imply that only the federal government was potentially tyrannical. Yet it is clear from James Madison's writings in *The Federalist Papers* that he saw state governments as potential sources of tyranny as well. Madison wrote that "the advantage of being armed" was one of the things that distinguished Americans from all other nations and helped protect them against abuse of power at all levels of government, federal and state. Antifederalists quite agreed. Their only quibble was that they demanded a Bill of Rights; they wanted the right to bear arms put in writing for all to see.

T he meaning of what is now the Second Amendment becomes clearer still if we take a look at how its wording evolved. Madison's original version, which he drew up in 1789 as a member of the newly created House of Representatives, was on the wordy side but at least had the merit of clarity:

> The right of the people to keep and bear arms shall not be infringed; a well armed and well regulated militia being the best security of a free country; but no person religiously scrupulous of bearing arms shall be compelled to render military service in person.

By reversing the order between the right to bear arms and a well-regulated militia, Madison reversed the priority. Rather than a precondition, his original version suggested that a well-ordered militia was merely one of the good things that flowed from universal gun ownership. A committee to which the amendment was referred, however, changed the order so that the amendment now read,

> A well regulated militia, composed of the body of the people, being the best security of a free State, the right of the people to keep and bear arms shall not be infringed, but no person religiously scrupulous shall be compelled to bear arms.

This was confusing but at least made plain that a militia was essentially synonymous with the people at large. Unfortunately, that notion, too, was lost when the Senate got hold of the amendment and began chopping out words right and left. The reference to "the body of the people" wound up on the cutting-room floor, as did the final clause. The effect was to deprive later generations of an important clue as to what a well-regulated militia actually meant. Although the final version was leaner and more compact, it was also a good deal less clear.

If the Framers were less than explicit about the nature of a well-regulated militia, it was because they didn't feel they had to be

Nonetheless, a few things seem evident. If the Framers were less than explicit about the nature of a well-regulated militia, it was because they didn't feel they had to be. The idea of a popular militia as something synonymous with the people as a whole was so well understood in the eighteenth century that it went without saying, which is undoubtedly why the Senate felt that the reference to "the body of the people" could be safely eliminated. It is also important to note that the flat-out declaration "[t]he right of the people to keep and bear arms shall not be infringed" remained unchanged throughout the drafting process. As Joyce Lee Malcolm has noted, the Second Amendment is a reworking of a provision contained in the English Bill of Rights of 1689. But whereas the English

Bill of Rights specified that subjects "may have arms for their defense suitable to their conditions, and as allowed by law," the American version avoided any such restrictions. Since all Americans (or, rather, members of the white male minority) were of the same rank, they possessed the same rights. They could bear arms for any purpose. And since the amendment was now part of the Constitution, the right was not limited by ordinary law but was over and above it. It was the source of law rather than the object. In this regard, as in virtually all others, Americans saw their role as taking ancient liberties and strengthening them so as to render tyranny all the more unlikely.

In the search for the meaning of the second amendment, we must recognize that "meaning" is problematic across the span of centuries

A lthough members of the legal academy assume that this is where the discussion ends, they're wrong: it's where the real questions begin. In attempting to nail down the meaning of the Second Amendment, we are therefore forced to recognize that "meaning" itself is problematic, especially across the span of more than two centuries. Once we have finished dissecting the Second Amendment, we are still left with a certain tension that necessarily exists between a well-regulated militia on the one hand and a right to bear arms on the other. One suggests order and discipline, if not government control; the other suggests voluntarism and a welling up from below. Eighteenth-century Country ideology tried to resolve this contradiction by envisioning the popular militia as a place where liberty and discipline would converge, where a freedom-loving people would enjoy the right to bear arms while proving their republican mettle by voluntarily rising to the defense of liberty. But although this certainly sounded nice, a harrowing eight-year war for independence had demonstrated the limits of such voluntarism. No-nonsense Federalists such as Washington and Hamilton recognized that there was no substitute for a professional army, not to mention a strong, centralized nation-state. But they also recognized that they had to get along with elements for whom such ideas were anathema. As a result, they felt they had no choice but to put aside their scruples and promise effective discipline from above and spontaneous self-organization from below, strong national government and states' rights, as contradictory as those notions might now seem.

The *meaning* of the Second Amendment, therefore, incorporates the contradictions in the Founders' thinking. But what's true for the Second Amendment is true for the Constitution as a whole. In June, William Safire rather naively suggested in his *New York Times* column that the solution to the problem of "the Murky Second" was to use the constitutional amending process to clarify its meaning. Did Americans have an unqualified right to bear arms or merely a right to enlist in the National Guard? Since the Founders had "botched" the wording, the solution was simply to fix it. This is indeed logical, but the problem is that the amending process is entirely useless in this instance. Because Article V stipulates that two thirds of each house, plus three fourths of the states, are required to change so much as a comma, as few as thirteen states—representing, by the way, as little as 4.5 percent of the total U.S. population—would be sufficient to block any change. Since no one would have any trouble coming up with a list of thirteen states in the South or the West for whom repealing the sacred Second Amendment would be akin to repealing the four Gospels, the issue is moot.

Since "we the people" are powerless to change the Second Amendment, we must somehow learn to live within its confines. But since this means standing by helplessly while ordinary people are gunned down by a succession of heavily armed maniacs, it is becoming more and more difficult to do so. As a result, politicians from President Clinton on down are forever coming up with ways of reconciling the irreconcilable, of reining in the gun trade without challenging the Second Amendment-fueled gun culture. The upshot is an endless series of ridiculous proposals to ban some kinds of firearms but not others, to limit handgun purchases to one a month, or to provide for background checks at otherwise unregulated traveling gun bazaars. Instead of cracking down on guns, the administration has found it easier to crack down on video games and theater owners who allow sixteen-year-olds to sneak into adult movies. The moral seems to be that guns don't kill people—fart jokes in the R-rated *South Park: Bigger, Longer & Uncut* do.

Why must we subordinate ourselves to a 208-year-old law that, if the latest scholarship is correct, is contrary to what we want?

This is the flip side of the unbounded faith of a Zoe Lofgren or a Barbara Jordan, who famously declared during Watergate, "My faith in the Constitution is whole, it is complete, it is total...." If one's faith in the Constitution is total, then one's faith in the Second Amendment is total as well, which means that one places obedience to ancient law above the needs of modern society. Once all the back-and-forth over the meaning of the Second Amendment is finished, the question we're left with is: So what? No one is suggesting that the Founders' thinking on the gun issue is irrelevant, but because they settled on a certain balance between freedom and order, are we obliged to follow suit? Or are we free to strike a different balance? Times change. From a string of coastal settlements, the United States has grown into a republic of 270 million people stretching across the entire North American continent. It is a congested, polluted society filled with traffic jams, shopping malls, and anomic suburbs in which an eighteenth-century right to bear arms is as out of place as silk knee britches and tricornered hats. So why must we subordinate ourselves to a 208-year-old law that, if the latest scholarship is correct, is contrary to what the democratic majority believes is in its best interest? Why can't *we* create the kind of society we want as opposed to living with laws meant to create the kind of society *they* wanted? They are dead and buried and will not be around to suffer the consequences. We the living will.

There is simply no solution to the gun problem within the confines of the U.S. Constitution. As the well-known Yale law professor Akhil Reed Amar put it recently, the Constitution serves to "structure the conversation of ordinary Americans as they ponder the most fundamental and sometimes divisive issues in our republic." In other words, the Constitution's hold on our society is so complete that it controls the way we discuss and debate, even the way we think. Americans are unable to conceive of an alternative framework, to think "outside the box," as the corporate strategists put it. Other countries are free to change their constitutions when it becomes necessary. In fact, with the exception of Luxembourg, Norway, and Great Britain, there is not one advanced industrial nation that has not thoroughly revamped its constitution since 1900. If they can do it, why can't we? Why must Americans remain slaves to the past?

Daniel Lazare is the author of The Frozen Republic: How the Constitution Is Paralyzing Democracy, *published by Harcourt Brace. His book about the prospects for re-urbanization in the twenty-first century,* America's Undeclared War, *was published on April 23, 2001.*

UNIT 3

National Consolidation and Expansion

Unit Selections

Key Points to Consider

- Discuss the opposing visions of Thomas Jefferson and Alexander Hamilton as the new government got underway. Were they reconcilable? Who tended to win out during the Washington administrations?

- There is no provision in the Constitution for political parties. How did this cause such chaos in electing a president in 1800? How was the situation rectified in later years?

- Why can the Louisiana Purchase be considered "The Revolution of 1803?" Discuss the ramifications of this acquisition at the time and for the future course of American history?

- Discuss some of the new findings about blacks during and after the American Revolution. Be sure to include in your discussion the rise of free-black communities and early abolitionism.

- How did President Andrew Jackson remove the Cherokee Indians from Georgia, and why? Why was the Indians' migration referred to as "the trail of tears?"

- What did the phrase "manifest destiny" mean to people at the time? How could Americans insist that their desire to expand was fundamentally different from European imperialism?

Student Website

www.mhcls.com/online

Internet References

Further information regarding these websites may be found in this book's preface or online.

Consortium for Political and Social Research
http://www.icpsr.umich.edu

Department of State
http://www.state.gov

Mystic Seaport
http://amistad.mysticseaport.org/

Social Influence Website
http://www.workingpsychology.com/intro.html

University of Virginia Library
http://www.lib.virginia.edu/exhibits/lewis_clark/

Women in America
http://xroads.virginia.edu/~HYPER/DETOC/FEM/

Women of the West
http://www.wowmuseum.org/

The individuals who wrote the American Constitution could only provide a general structure under which the government would work. Those involved in actually making the system function had to venture into uncharted territory. There were no blueprints as to exactly which body had what powers, or what their relationships with one another would be. And, if disputes arose, which individual or group would act as arbiter? Officials during the first few years after 1789 were conscious that practically everything they did would be regarded as setting precedents for the future. Even such apparently trivial matters as the proper form of addressing the president caused debate. From hindsight of more than 200 years, it is difficult to appreciate how tentative they had to be in establishing this newborn government.

The most fundamental difference over the Constitution arose over whether it should be interpreted strictly or loosely. That is, should governmental powers be limited to those expressly granted in the document, or were there "implied" powers that could be exercised as long as they were not expressly prohibited? Many of the disputes were argued on principles, but the truth is that most individuals were trying to promote programs that would benefit the interests they represented.

George Washington, as first president, was a towering figure who provided a stabilizing presence during the seemingly endless squabbles. He believed that he served the entire nation, and that there was no need for political parties (he disdainfully referred to them as "factions") which he regarded as divisive. Despite his disapproval, nascent political parties did begin to develop fairly early on in his first administration. Washington's first Secretary of the Treasury, Alexander Hamilton, almost invariably favored those measures that would benefit the commercial and manufacturing interests of the Northeast. Secretary of State Thomas Jefferson and his ally James Madison just as often spoke for the rural and agricultural interests of the West and the South. These two groups frequently clashed over what the Constitution did or did not permit, what sources of revenue should be tapped to pay for government, and a host of other issues. The fact that Washington most often sided with Hamilton's views made him a partisan despite his wish to remain above the fray. "The Best of Enemies" analyzes the Hamilton-Jefferson struggle.

Washington's enormous prestige delayed the creation of formal political parties until he was out of office. "Cliffhanger: The Election of 1800" shows how this changed after John Adams became president in 1797. Because the Constitution did not provide for political parties, Aaron Burr and Thomas Jefferson wound up in a tie even though both were Republicans. "Federalists and Republicans appeared to agree on one thing only," author John Ferling writes, "that the victor in 1800 would set America's course for generations to come, perhaps forever."

The United States already was a large country by 1803, stretching from the Atlantic Ocean to the Mississippi River. Some said it was too large. Propertied Easterners complained that the Western migration lowered property values and raised wages, and they feared population shifts would weaken their section's influence in government. Others thought that the great distances involved might cause the system to fly apart, given the primitive means of communication and transportation at the time. When Thomas Jefferson had the unexpected opportunity to double the nation's size by purchasing the huge Lousiana Territory, as discussed in "The Revolution of 1803," he altered the course of American history. "Paddle a Mile in Their Canoes" describes the Lewis-Clark expedition, a Jefferson-sponsored effort to find out just what had been acquired and whether there were water routes to the Pacific coast.

Coverage of African-Americans in high school and college textbooks is far more comprehensive than it was a few decades ago, according to Gary B. Nash, but some areas still merit greater concentration. "African Americans in the Early Republic" describes some of these, such as the rise of free-Black communities and early abolitionism. Another article on African-Americans, "How American Slavery Led to the Birth of Liberia," shows how the American Colonization Society's efforts to create a haven for blacks was doomed to failure. Detractors of this project argued that it actually would benefit slavery by drawing off the most vigorous and independent blacks, who could provide leadership in the struggle against the institution in the United States.

Pirates from rogue states along the northern coast of Africa had for centuries highjacked ships and cargoes, and enslaved crews in the Atlantic and the Mediterranean. Most European nations and the United States attempted to alleviate these depredations by paying bribes or "tribute" to these pirates. Under the administrations of Thomas Jefferson and James Madison, naval expeditions were mounted against the predators. "Pirates!" argues that these expeditions did more than merely address the problem, they helped establish the United States as a world power.

Accounts of settling the West also have changed over the years. Once presented in the relatively simplistic terms of "taming the wilderness," the westward movement was far more complicated than the story of hardy pioneers overcoming obstacles. "Andrew Jackson Versus the Cherokee Nation" tells of the forcible removal of the Cherokees from Georgia to west of the Mississippi. The trek had such awful consequences that it became known as "the trail of tears." The phrase "Manifest Destiny" became popular during the 1840s. Advocates believed that the United States was destined to dominate Mexico and the Caribbean. "Storm Over Mexico" examines this phenomenon, with particular reference to one of its most ardent advocates, a woman named Jane McManus. She was a dynamo who was a political journalist, a land speculator, and a pioneer settler in Texas.

The Best of Enemies

Jefferson was visionary and crafty. In Hamilton, he met his match. How the rivalry lives on.

Ron Chernow

ON MARCH 21, 1790, THOMAS JEFFERSON BELATEDLY arrived in New York City to assume his duties as the first Secretary of State after a five-year ministerial stint in Paris. Tall and lanky, with a freckled complexion and auburn hair, Jefferson, 46, was taken aback by the adulation being heaped upon the new Treasury Secretary, Alexander Hamilton, who had streaked to prominence in his absence. Few people knew that Jefferson had authored the Declaration of Independence, which had yet to become holy writ for Americans. Instead, the Virginian was eclipsed by the 35-year-old wunderkind from the Caribbean, who was a lowly artillery captain in New York when Jefferson composed the famous document. Despite his murky background as an illegitimate orphan, the self-invented Hamilton was trim and elegant, carried himself with an erect military bearing and had a mind that worked with dazzling speed. At first, Hamilton and Jefferson socialized on easy terms, with little inkling that they were destined to become mortal foes. But their clash inside George Washington's first Cabinet proved so fierce that it would spawn the two-party system in America. It also produced two divergent visions of the country's future that divide Americans to the present day.

For Hamilton, the first Treasury Secretary, the supreme threat to liberty arose from insufficient government power. To avert that, he advocated a vigorous central government marked by a strong President, an independent judiciary and a liberal reading of the Constitution. As the first Secretary of State, Jefferson believed that liberty was jeopardized by concentrated federal power, which he tried to restrict through a narrow construction of the Constitution. He favored states' rights, a central role for Congress and a comparatively weak judiciary.

At first glance, Hamilton might seem the more formidable figure in that classic matchup. He took office with an ardent faith in the new national government. He had attended the Constitutional Convention, penned the bulk of the Federalist papers to secure passage of the new charter and spearheaded ratification efforts in New York State. He therefore set to work at Treasury with more unrestrained gusto than Jefferson—who had monitored the Constitutional Convention from his post in Paris—did at State. Jefferson's enthusiasm for the new political order was tepid at best, and when Washington crafted the first government in 1789, Jefferson didn't grasp the levers of power with quite the same glee as Hamilton, who had no ideological inhibitions about shoring up federal power.

Hamilton—brilliant, brash and charming—had the self-reliant reflexes of someone who had always had to live by his wits. His overwhelming intelligence petrified Jefferson and his followers. As an orator, Hamilton could speak extemporaneously for hours on end. As a writer, he could crank out 5,000- or 10,000-word memos overnight. Jefferson never underrated his foe's copious talents. At one point, a worried Jefferson confided to his comrade James Madison that Hamilton was a one-man army, "a host within himself."

Despite Jefferson's policy battles, **there was a playful side to his politics.** On New Year's Day 1802, supporters in Cheshire, Mass., sent him, as a gift, a mammoth cheese that measured more than 4 ft. in diameter and 17 in. in height and weighed 1,235 lbs. President Jefferson took the pungent present in good humor. Reportedly, he stood in the White House doorway, arms outstretched, waiting for the cheese's delivery. The smelly gift was served to guests for at least a year, perhaps more.

Whether in person or on paper, Hamilton served up his opinions promiscuously. He had a true zest for debate and never left anyone guessing where he stood. Jefferson, more than a decade older, had the quiet, courtly manner of a Virginia planter. He was emphatic in his views—Hamilton labeled him "an atheist in religion and a *fanatic in politics*"—but shrank from open conflict. Jefferson, a diffident speaker, mumbled his way through his rare speeches in a soft, almost inaudible voice and reserved his most scathing strictures for private correspondence.

The epic battle between these two Olympian figures began not long after Jefferson came to New York City to assume his State Department duties in March 1790. By then Hamilton was in the thick of a contentious campaign to retire massive debt inherited from the Revolution. America had suspended principal and interest payments on its obligations, which had traded as low as 15¢ on the dollar. In an audacious scheme to restore public credit, Hamilton planned to pay off that debt at face value, causing the securities to soar from depressed levels. Jefferson and Madison thought the original holders of those securities—many of them war veterans—should profit from that appreciation even if they had already sold their paper to traders at depressed prices. Hamilton thought it would be impractical to track them down. With an eye on future U.S. capital markets, he wanted to enshrine the cardinal principle that current owners of securities incurred all profits and losses, even if that meant windfall gains for rapacious speculators who had only recently bought the securities.

That skirmish over Hamilton's public credit plan was part of a broader tussle over the U.S.'s economic future. Jefferson was fond of summoning up idyllic scenes of an agrarian America peopled by sturdy yeoman farmers. That poetic vision neglected the underlying reality of large slave plantations in the South. Jefferson was a fine populist on paper but not in everyday life, and his defense of Virginia interests was inextricably bound up with slavery. Hamilton—derided as a pseudo aristocrat, an elitist, a crypto-monarchist—was a passionate abolitionist with a far more expansive economic vision. He conceded that agriculture would persist for decades as an essential component of the economy. But at the same time he wanted to foster the rudiments of a modern economy—trade, commerce, banks, stock exchanges, factories and corporations—to enlarge economic opportunity. Hamilton dreamed of a meritocracy, not an aristocracy, while Jefferson retained the landed gentry's disdain for the vulgar realities of trade, commerce and finance. And he was determined to undermine Hamilton's juggernaut.

Because we celebrate Jefferson for his sonorous words in the Declaration of Independence—Hamilton never matched Jefferson's gift for writing ringing passages that were at once poetic and inspirational—we sometimes overlook Jefferson's consummate skills as a practicing politician. A master of subtle, artful indirection, he was able to marshal his forces without divulging his general-

ship. After Hamilton persuaded President Washington to create the Bank of the United States, the country's first central bank, Jefferson was aghast at what he construed as a breach of the Constitution and a perilous expansion of federal power. Along with Madison, he recruited the poet Philip Freneau to launch an opposition paper called the *National Gazette*. To subsidize the paper covertly, he hired Freneau as a State Department translator. Hamilton was shocked by such flagrant disloyalty from a member of Washington's Cabinet, especially when Freneau began to mount withering assaults on Hamilton and even Washington. Never one to suffer in silence, Hamilton retaliated in a blizzard of newspaper articles published under Roman pseudonyms. The backbiting between Hamilton and Jefferson grew so acrimonious that Washington had to exhort both men to desist.

Instead, the feud worsened. In early 1793, a Virginia Congressman named William Branch Giles began to harry Hamilton with resolutions ordering him to produce, on short deadlines, stupendous amounts of Treasury data. With prodigious bursts of energy, Hamilton complied with those inhuman demands, foiling his opponents. Jefferson then committed an unthinkable act. He secretly drafted a series of anti-Hamilton resolutions for Giles, including one that read, "Resolved, That the Secretary of the Treasury has been guilty of maladministration in the duties of his office and should, in the opinion of Congress, be removed from his office by the President of the United States." The resolution was voted down, and the effort to oust Hamilton stalled. Jefferson left the Cabinet in defeat later that year.

Throughout the 1790s, the Hamilton-Jefferson feud continued to fester in both domestic and foreign affairs. Jefferson thought Hamilton was "bewitched" by the British model of governance, while Hamilton considered Jefferson a credulous apologist for the gory excesses of the French Revolution. Descended from French Huguenots on his mother's side, Hamilton was fluent in French and had served as Washington's liaison with the Marquis de Lafayette and other French aristocrats who had rallied to the Continental Army. The French Revolution immediately struck him as a bloody affair, governed by rigid, Utopian thinking. On Oct. 6, 1789, he wrote a remarkable letter to Lafayette, explaining his "foreboding of ill" about the future course of events in Paris. He cited the "vehement character" of the French people and the "reveries" of their "philosophic politicians," who wished to transform human nature. Hamilton believed that Jefferson while in Paris "drank deeply of the French philosophy in religion, in science, in politics." Indeed, more than a decade passed before Jefferson fully realized that the French Revolution wasn't a worthy sequel to the American one so much as a grotesque travesty.

If Jefferson and Hamilton define opposite ends of the political spectrum in U.S. history and seem to exist in perpetual conflict, the two men shared certain traits, feeding a mutual cynicism. Each scorned the other as excessively

According to the new book *Jefferson's Second Revolution,* by Susan Dunn, for more than a week in early July 1800, Federalist newspapers gleefully carried the (false) story that Jefferson had died. **"I am much indebted to my enemies,"** Jefferson said, "for proving, by their recitals of my death, that I have friends."

ambitious. In his secret diary, or *Anas*, Jefferson recorded a story of Hamilton praising Julius Caesar as the greatest man in history. (The tale sounds dubious, as Hamilton invariably used Caesar as shorthand for "an evil tyrant.") Hamilton repaid the favor. In one essay he likened Jefferson to "Caesar *coyly refusing* the proffered diadem" and rejecting the trappings, but "tenaciously grasping the substance of imperial domination."

Similarly, both men hid a potent hedonism behind an intellectual facade. For all their outward differences, the two politicians stumbled into the two great sex scandals of the early Republic. In 1797 a journalist named James T. Callender exposed that Hamilton, while Treasury Secretary and a married man with four children, had entered into a yearlong affair with grifter Maria Reynolds, who was 23 when it began. In a 95-page pamphlet, Hamilton confessed to the affair at what many regarded as inordinate length. He wished to show that the money he had paid to Reynolds' husband James had been for the favor of her company and not for illicit speculation in Treasury securities, as the Jeffersonians had alleged. Forever after, the Jeffersonians tagged Hamilton as "the amorous Treasury Secretary" and mocked his pretensions to superior morality.

By an extraordinary coincidence, during Jefferson's first term as President, Callender also exposed Jefferson's relationship with Sally Hemings. Callender claimed that "Dusky Sally," a.k.a. the "African Venus," was the President's slave concubine, who had borne him five children. "There is not an individual in the neighborhood of Charlottesville who does not believe the story," Callender wrote, "and not a few who know it." Jefferson never confirmed or denied Callender's story. But the likely truth of the Hemings affair was dramatically bolstered by DNA tests published in 1998, which indicated that a Jefferson male had sired at least one of Hemings' children.

The crowning irony of the stormy relations between Hamilton and Jefferson is that Hamilton helped install his longtime foe as President in 1801. Under constitutional rules then in force, the candidate with the majority of electoral votes became President; the runner-up became Vice

HAMILTON

Favored a strong Federal Government
Pushed for an economy in which trade, finance and manufacturing supplemented agriculture
Feared closer relations with France and was an Anglophile
Wanted the U.S. to have a professional federal army

JEFFERSON

Argued strongly for states' rights
Admired farming and the simple, rural life and hoped America would remain an agrarian nation
Favored warm, fraternal relations with France and was an Anglophobe
Thought the country should rely on state militias

President. That created an anomalous situation in which Jefferson, his party's presumed presidential nominee, tied with Aaron Burr, its presumed vice presidential nominee. It took 36 rounds of voting in the House to decide the election in Jefferson's favor. Faced with the prospect of Burr as President, a man he considered unscrupulous, Hamilton not only opted for Jefferson as the lesser of two evils but also was forced into his most measured assessment of the man. Hamilton said he had long suspected that as President, Jefferson would develop a keen taste for the federal power he had deplored in opposition. He recalled that a decade earlier, in Washington's Cabinet, Jefferson had seemed like a man who knew he was destined to inherit an estate—in this case, the presidency—and didn't wish to deplete it. In fact, Jefferson, the strict constructionist, freely exercised the most sweeping powers as President. Nothing in the Constitution, for instance, permitted the Louisiana Purchase. Hamilton noted that with rueful mirth.

Chernow is the author of The House of Morgan, Titan *and the recent best-selling biography Alexander Hamilton*

Cliffhanger

Presidential candidates Thomas Jefferson and Aaron Burr were deadlocked in the House of Representatives with no majority for either. For seven days, as they maneuvered and schemed, the fate of the young republic hung in the ballots.

John Ferling

On the afternoon of September 23, 1800, Vice President Thomas Jefferson, from his Monticello home, wrote a letter to Benjamin Rush, the noted Philadelphia physician. One matter dominated Jefferson's thoughts: that year's presidential contest. Indeed, December 3, Election Day—the date on which the Electoral College would meet to vote—was only 71 days away.

Jefferson was one of four presidential candidates. As he composed his letter to Rush, Jefferson paused from time to time to gather his thoughts, all the while gazing absently through an adjacent window at the shimmering heat and the foliage, now a lusterless pale green after a long, dry summer. Though he hated leaving his hilltop plantation and believed, as he told Rush, that gaining the presidency would make him "a constant butt for every shaft of calumny which malice & falsehood could form," he nevertheless sought the office "with sincere zeal."

He had been troubled by much that had occurred in incumbent John Adams' presidency and was convinced that radicals within Adams' Federalist Party were waging war against what he called the "spirit of 1776"—goals the American people had hoped to attain through the Revolution. He had earlier characterized Federalist rule as a "reign of witches," insisting that the party was "adverse to liberty" and "calculated to undermine and demolish the republic." If the Federalists prevailed, he believed, they would destroy the states and create a national government every bit as oppressive as that which Great Britain had tried to impose on the colonists before 1776.

The "revolution ... of 1776," Jefferson would later say, had determined the "form" of America's government; he believed the election of 1800 would decide its "principles." "I have sworn upon the altar of God eternal hostility against every form of tyranny over the mind of Man," he wrote.

Jefferson was not alone in believing that the election of 1800 was crucial. On the other side, Federalist Alexander Hamilton, who had been George Washington's secretary of treasury, believed that it was a contest to save the new nation from "the fangs of Jefferson." Hamilton agreed with a Federalist newspaper essay that argued defeat meant "happiness, constitution and laws [faced] endless and irretrievable ruin." Federalists and Republicans appeared to agree on one thing only: that the victor in 1800 would set America's course for generations to come, perhaps forever.

Only a quarter of a century after the signing of the Declaration of Independence, the first election of the new 19th century was carried out in an era of intensely emotional partisanship among a people deeply divided over the scope of the government's authority. But it was the French Revolution that had imposed a truly hyperbolic quality upon the partisan strife.

That revolution, which had begun in 1789 and did not run its course until 1815, deeply divided Americans. Conservatives, horrified by its violence and social leveling, applauded Great Britain's efforts to stop it. The most conservative Americans, largely Federalists, appeared bent on an alliance with London that would restore the ties between America and Britain that had been severed in 1776. Jeffersonian Republicans, on the other hand, insisted that these radical conservatives wanted to turn back the clock to reinstitute much of the British colonial template. (Today's Republican Party traces its origins not to Jefferson and his allies but to the party formed in 1854-1855, which carried Lincoln to the presidency in 1860.)

A few weeks before Adams' inauguration in 1796, France, engaged in an all-consuming struggle with England for world domination, had decreed that it would not permit America to trade with Great Britain. The French Navy soon swept American ships from the seas, idling port-city workers and plunging the economy toward depression. When Adams sought to negotiate a settlement, Paris spurned his envoys.

Adams, in fact, hoped to avoid war, but found himself riding a whirlwind. The most extreme Federalists, known as Ultras, capitalized on the passions unleashed in this crisis and scored great victories in the off-year elections of 1798, taking charge of both the party and Congress. They created a provisional army and pressured Adams into putting Hamilton in charge. They passed heavy taxes to pay for the army and, with Federalist sympathizers in the press braying that "traitors must be silent," enacted the Alien and Sedition Acts, which provided jail terms and exorbitant fines for anyone who uttered or published "any false, scandalous, and malicious" statement against the United States government or its officials. While Federalists defended the Sedition Act as a necessity in the midst of a grave national crisis, Jefferson and his followers saw it as a means of silencing Republicans—and a violation of the Bill of Rights. The Sedition Act, Jefferson contended, proved there was no step, "however atrocious," the Ultras would not take.

All along, Jefferson had felt that Federalist extremists might overreach. By early 1799, Adams himself had arrived at the same conclusion. He, too, came to suspect that Hamilton and the Ultras wanted to precipitate a crisis with France. Their motivation perhaps had been to get Adams to secure an alliance with Great Britain and accept the Ultras' program in Congress. But avowing that there "is no more prospect of seeing a French Army here, than there is in Heaven," Adams refused to go along with the scheme and sent peace envoys to Paris. (Indeed, a treaty would be signed at the end of September 1800.)

It was in this bitterly partisan atmosphere that the election of 1800 was conducted. In those days, the Constitution stipulated that each of the 138 members of the Electoral College cast two votes for president, which allowed electors to cast one vote for a favorite son and a second for a candidate who actually stood a chance of winning. The Constitution also stipulated that if the candidates tied, or none received a majority of electoral votes, the House of Representatives "shall chuse by Ballot one of them for President." Unlike today, each party nominated two candidates for the presidency.

Federalist congressmen had caucused that spring and, without indicating a preference, designated Adams and South Carolina's Charles Cotesworth Pinckney as the party's choices. Adams desperately wanted to be re-elected. He was eager to see the French crisis through to a satisfactory resolution and, at age 65, believed that a defeat would mean he would be sent home to Quincy, Massachusetts, to die in obscurity. Pinckney, born into Southern aristocracy and raised in England, had been the last of the four nominees to come around in favor of American independence. Once committed, however, he served valiantly, seeing action at Brandywine, Germantown and Charleston. Following the war, he sat in the Constitutional Convention; both Washington and Adams had sent him to France on diplomatic missions.

In addition to Jefferson, Republicans chose Aaron Burr as their candidate, but designated Jefferson as the party's first choice. Jefferson had held public office intermittently since 1767, serving Virginia in its legislature and as a wartime governor, sitting in Congress, crossing to Paris in 1784 for a five-year stint that included a posting as the American minister to France, and acting as secretary of state under Washington. His second place finish in the election of 1796 had made him vice president, as was the custom until 1804. Burr, at age 44 the youngest of the candidates, had abandoned his legal studies in 1775 to enlist in the Continental Army; he had experienced the horrors of America's failed invasion of Canada and the miseries of Valley Forge. After the war he practiced law and represented New York in the U.S. Senate. In 1800, he was serving as a member of the New York legislature.

In those days, the Constitution left the manner of selecting presidential electors to the states. In 11 of the 16 states, state legislatures picked the electors; therefore, the party that controlled the state assembly garnered all that state's electoral votes. In the other five states, electors were chosen by "qualified" voters (white, male property owners in some states, white male taxpayers in others). Some states used a winner-take-all system: voters cast their ballots for the entire slate of Federalist electors or for the Republican slate. Other states split electors among districts.

Presidential candidates did not kiss babies, ride in parades or shake hands. Nor did they even make stump speeches. The candidates tried to remain above the fray, leaving campaigning to surrogates, particularly elected officials from within their parties. Adams and Jefferson each returned home when Congress adjourned in May, and neither left their home states until they returned to the new capital of Washington in November.

But for all its differences, much about the campaign of 1800 was recognizably modern. Politicians carefully weighed which procedures were most likely to advance their party's interests. Virginia, for instance, had permitted electors to be elected from districts in three previous presidential contests, but after Federalists carried 8 of 19 congressional districts in the elections of 1798, Republicans, who controlled the state assembly, switched to the winner-take-all format, virtually guaranteeing they would get every one of Virginia's 21 electoral votes in 1800. The ploy was perfectly legal, and Federalists in Massachusetts, fearing an upsurge in Republican strength, scuttled district elections—which the state had used previously—to select electors by the legislature, which they controlled.

Though the contest was played out largely in the print media, the unsparing personal attacks on the character and temperament of the nominees resembled the studied incivility to which today's candidates are accustomed on television. Adams was portrayed as a monarchist who had turned his back on republicanism; he was called senile, a poor judge of character, vain, jealous and driven by an "ungovernable temper." Pinckney was labeled a mediocrity, a man of "limited talents" who was "illy suited to the exalted station" of the presidency. Jefferson was accused of cowardice. Not only, said his critics, had he lived in luxury at Monticello while others sacrificed during the War of Independence, but he had fled like a jack rabbit when British soldiers raided Charlottesville in 1781. And he had failed egregiously as Virginia's governor, demonstrating that his "nerves are too weak to bear anxiety and difficulties." Federalists further insisted Jefferson had been transformed into a dangerous radical during his residence in France and was a "howling atheist." For his part, Burr was depicted as without principles, a man who would do anything to get his hands on power.

Also like today, the election of 1800 seemed to last forever. "Electioneering is already begun," the first lady, Abigail Adams, noted 13 months before the Electoral College was to meet. What made it such a protracted affair was that state legislatures were elected throughout the year; as these assemblies more often than not chose presidential electors, the state contests to determine them became part of the national campaign. In 1800 the greatest surprise among these contests occurred in New York, a large, crucial state that had given all 12 of its electoral votes to Adams in 1796, allowing him to eke out a three-vote victory over Jefferson.

The battle for supremacy in the New York legislature had hinged on the outcome in New York City. Thanks largely to lopsided wins in two working-class wards where many voters owned no property, the Republicans secured all 24 of New York's electoral votes for Jefferson and Burr. For Abigail Adams, that was enough to seal Adams' fate. John Dawson, a Republican congressman from Virginia, declared: "The Republic is safe…. The [Federalist] party are in rage & despair."

But Adams himself refused to give up hope. After all, New England, which accounted for nearly half the electoral votes needed for a majority, was solidly in his camp, and he felt certain he would win some votes elsewhere. Adams believed that if he could get South Carolina's eight votes, he would be virtually certain to garner the same number of electoral votes that had put him over the top four years earlier. And, at first, both parties were thought to have a shot at carrying the state.

When South Carolina's legislature was elected in mid-October, the final tally revealed that the assembly was about evenly divided between Federalists and Republicans—though unaffiliated representatives, all pro-Jefferson, would determine the outcome. Now Adams' hopes were fading fast. Upon hearing the news that Jefferson was assured of South Carolina's eight votes, Abigail Adams remarked to her son Thomas that the "consequence to us personally is that we retire from public life." All that remained to be determined was whether the assembly would instruct the electors to cast their second vote for Burr or Pinckney.

The various presidential electors met in their respective state capitals to vote on December 3. By law, their ballots were not to be opened and counted until February 11, but the outcome could hardly be kept secret for ten weeks. Sure enough, just nine days after the vote, Washington, D.C.'s *National Intelligencer* newspaper broke the news that neither Adams nor Pinckney had received a single South Carolina vote and, in the voting at large, Jefferson and Burr had each received 73 electoral votes. Adams had gotten 65, Pinckney 64. The House of Representatives would have to make the final decision between the two Republicans.

Adams thus became the first presidential candidate to fall victim to the notorious clause in the Constitution that counted each slave as three-fifths of one individual in calculating population used to allocate both House seats and electoral votes. Had slaves, who had no vote, not been so counted, Adams would have edged Jefferson by a vote of 63 to 61. In addition, the Federalists fell victim to the public's perception that the Republicans stood for democracy and egalitarianism, while the Federalists were seen as imperious and authoritarian.

In the House, each state would cast a single vote. If each of the 16 states voted—that is, if none abstained—9 states would elect the president. Republicans controlled eight delegations—New York, New Jersey, Pennsylvania, Virginia, North Carolina, Georgia, Kentucky and Tennessee. The Federalists held six: New Hampshire, Massachusetts, Rhode Island, Connecticut, Delaware and South Carolina. And two delegations—Maryland and Vermont—were deadlocked.

Though Jefferson and Burr had tied in the Electoral College, public opinion appeared to side with Jefferson. Not only had he been the choice of his party's nominating caucus, but he had served longer at the national level than Burr, and in a more exalted capacity. But if neither man was selected by noon on March 4, when Adams' term ended, the country would be without a chief executive until the newly elected Congress convened in December, nine months later. In the interim, the current, Federalist-dominated Congress would be in control.

Faced with such a prospect, Jefferson wrote to Burr in December. His missive was cryptic, but in it he appeared to suggest that if Burr accepted the vice presidency, he would be given greater responsibilities than previous vice presidents. Burr's response to Jefferson was reassuring. He pledged to "disclaim all competition" and spoke of "your administration."

Meanwhile, the Federalists caucused to discuss their options. Some favored tying up the proceedings in order to hold on to power for several more months. Some wanted to try to invalidate, on technical grounds, enough electoral votes to make Adams the winner. Some urged the party to throw its support to Burr, believing that, as a native of mercantile New York City, he would be more friendly than Jefferson to the Federalist economic program. Not a few insisted that the party should support Jefferson, as he was clearly the popular choice. Others, including Hamilton, who had long opposed Burr in the rough and tumble of New York City politics, thought Jefferson more trustworthy than Burr. Hamilton argued that Burr was "without Scruple," an "unprincipled … voluptuary" who would plunder the country. But Hamilton also urged the party to stall, in the hope of inducing Jefferson to make a deal. Hamilton proposed that in return for the Federalist votes that would make him president, Jefferson should promise to preserve the Federalist fiscal system (a properly funded national debt and the Bank), American neutrality and a strong navy, and to agree to "keeping in office all our Foederal Friends" below the cabinet level. Even Adams joined the fray, telling Jefferson that the presidency would be his "in an instant" should he accept Hamilton's terms. Jefferson declined, insisting that he "should never go into the office of President … with my hands tied by any conditions which should hinder me from pursuing the measures" he thought best.

In the end, the Federalists decided to back Burr. Hearing of their decision, Jefferson told Adams that any attempt "to defeat the Presidential election" would "produce resistance by force, and incalculable consequences."

Burr, who had seemed to disavow a fight for the highest office, now let it be known that he would accept the presidency if elected by the House. In Philadelphia, he met with several

Republican congressmen, allegedly telling them that he intended to fight for it.

Burr had to know that he was playing a dangerous game and risking political suicide by challenging Jefferson, his party's reigning power. The safest course would have been to acquiesce to the vice presidency. He was yet a young man, and given Jefferson's penchant for retiring to Monticello—he had done so in 1776, 1781 and 1793—there was a good chance that Burr would be his party's standard-bearer as early as 1804. But Burr also knew there was no guarantee he would live to see future elections. His mother and father had died at ages 27 and 42, respectively.

Burr's was not the only intrigue. Given the high stakes, every conceivable pressure was applied to change votes. Those in the deadlocked delegations were courted daily, but no one was lobbied more aggressively than James Bayard, Delaware's lone congressman, who held in his hands the sole determination of how his state would vote. Thirty-two years old in 1800, Bayard had practiced law in Wilmington before winning election to the House as a Federalist four years earlier. Bayard despised Virginia's Republican planters, including Jefferson, whom he saw as hypocrites who owned hundreds of slaves and lived "like feudal barons" as they played the role of "high priests of liberty." He announced he was supporting Burr.

THE CITY OF Washington awoke to a crippling snowstorm Wednesday, February 11, the day the House was to begin voting. Nevertheless, only one of the 105 House members did not make it in to Congress, and his absence would not change his delegation's tally. Voting began the moment the House was gaveled into session. When the roll call was complete, Jefferson had carried eight states, Burr six, and two deadlocked states had cast uncommitted ballots; Jefferson still needed one more vote for a majority. A second vote was held, with a similar tally, then a third. When at 3 a.m. the exhausted congressmen finally called it a day, 19 roll calls had been taken, all with the same inconclusive result.

By Saturday evening, three days later, the House had cast 33 ballots. The deadlock seemed unbreakable.

For weeks, warnings had circulated of drastic consequences if Republicans were denied the presidency. Now that danger seemed palpable. A shaken President Adams was certain the two sides had come to the "precipice" of disaster and that "a civil war was expected." There was talk that Virginia would secede if Jefferson were not elected. Some Republicans declared they would convene another constitutional convention to restructure the federal government so that it reflected the "democratical spirit of America." It was rumored that a mob had stormed the arsenal in Philadelphia and was preparing to march on Washington to drive the defeated Federalists from power. Jefferson said he could not restrain those of his supporters who threatened "a dissolution" of the Union. He told Adams that many Republicans were prepared to use force to prevent the Federalists' "legislative usurpation" of the executive branch.

In all likelihood, it was these threats that ultimately broke the deadlock. The shift occurred sometime after Saturday's final ballot; it was Delaware's Bayard who blinked. That night, he sought out a Republican close to Jefferson, almost certainly John Nicholas, a member of Virginia's House delegation. Were Delaware to abstain, Bayard pointed out, only 15 states would ballot. With eight states already in his column, Jefferson would have a majority and the elusive victory at last. But in return, Bayard asked, would Jefferson accept the terms that the Federalists had earlier proffered? Nicholas responded, according to Bayard's later recollections, that these conditions were "very reasonable" and that he could vouch for Jefferson's acceptance.

The Federalists caucused behind doors on Sunday afternoon, February 15. When Bayard's decision to abstain was announced, it touched off a firestorm. Cries of "Traitor! Traitor!" rang down on him. Bayard himself later wrote that the "clamor was prodigious, the reproaches vehement," and that many old colleagues were "furious" with him. Two matters in particular roiled his comrades. Some were angry that Bayard had broken ranks before it was known what kind of deal, if any, Burr might have been willing to cut. Others were upset that nothing had been heard from Jefferson himself. During a second Federalist caucus that afternoon, Bayard agreed to take no action until Burr's answer was known. In addition, the caucus directed Bayard to seek absolute assurances that Jefferson would go along with the deal.

Early the next morning, Monday, February 16, according to Bayard's later testimony, Jefferson made it known through a third party that the terms demanded by the Federalists "corresponded with his views and intentions, and that we might confide in him accordingly." The bargain was struck, at least to Bayard's satisfaction. Unless Burr offered even better terms, Jefferson would be the third president of the United States.

At some point that Monday afternoon, Burr's letters arrived. What exactly he said or did not say in them—they likely were destroyed soon after they reached Washington and their contents remain a mystery—disappointed his Federalist proponents. Bayard, in a letter written that Monday, told a friend that "Burr has acted a miserable paultry part. The election was in his power." But Burr, at least according to Bayard's interpretation, and for reasons that remain unknown to history, had refused to reach an accommodation with the Federalists. That same Monday evening a dejected Theodore Sedgwick, Speaker of the House and a passionate Jefferson hater, notified friends at home: "the gigg is up."

The following day, February 17, the House gathered at noon to cast its 36th, and, as it turned out, final, vote. Bayard was true to his word: Delaware abstained, ending seven days of contention and the long electoral battle.

Bayard ultimately offered many reasons for his change of heart. On one occasion he claimed that he and the five other Federalists who had held the power to determine the election in their hands—four from Maryland and one from Vermont—had agreed to "give our votes to Mr. Jefferson" if it became clear that Burr could not win. Bayard also later insisted that he had acted from what he called "imperious necessity" to prevent a civil war or disunion. Still later he claimed to have been swayed by the public's preference for Jefferson.

Had Jefferson in fact cut a deal to secure the presidency? Ever afterward, he insisted that such allegations were "absolutely false." The historical evidence, however, suggests otherwise. Not only did many political insiders assert that Jefferson had indeed agreed to a bargain, but Bayard, in a letter dated February 17, the very day of the climactic House vote—as well as five years later, while testifying under oath in a libel suit—insisted that Jefferson had most certainly agreed to accept the Federalists' terms. In another letter written at the time, Bayard assured a Federalist officeholder, who feared losing his position in a Republican administration: "I have taken good care of you.... You are safe."

Even Jefferson's actions as president lend credence to the allegations. Despite having fought against the Hamiltonian economic system for nearly a decade, he acquiesced to it once in office, leaving the Bank of the United States in place and tolerating continued borrowing by the federal government. Nor did he remove most Federalist officeholders.

The mystery is not why Jefferson would deny making such an accord, but why he changed his mind after vowing never to bend. He must have concluded that he had no choice if he wished to become president by peaceful means. To permit the balloting to continue was to hazard seeing the presidency slip from his hands. Jefferson not only must have doubted the constancy of some of his supporters, but he knew that a majority of the Federalists favored Burr and were making the New Yorker the same offer they were dangling before him.

Burr's behavior is more enigmatic. He had decided to make a play for the presidency, only apparently to refuse the very terms that would have guaranteed it to him. The reasons for his action have been lost in a confounding tangle of furtive transactions and deliberately destroyed evidence. It may have been that the Federalists demanded more of him than they did of Jefferson. Or Burr may have found it unpalatable to strike a bargain with ancient enemies, including the man he would kill in a duel three years later. Burr may also have been unwilling to embrace Federalist principles that he had opposed throughout his political career.

The final mystery of the election of 1800 is whether Jefferson and his backers would have sanctioned violence had he been denied the presidency. Soon after taking office, Jefferson claimed that "there was no idea of [using] force." His remark proves little, yet during the ongoing battle in the House, he alternately spoke of acceding to the Federalists' misconduct in the hope that their behavior would ruin them, or of calling a second Constitutional Convention. He probably would have chosen one, or both, of these courses before risking bloodshed and the end of the Union.

In the days that followed the House battle, Jefferson wrote letters to several surviving signers of the Declaration of Independence to explain what he believed his election had meant. It guaranteed the triumph of the American Revolution, he said, ensuring the realization of the new "chapter in the history of man" that had been promised by Thomas Paine in 1776. In the years that followed, his thoughts often returned to the election's significance. In 1819, at age 76, he would characterize it as the "revolution of 1800," and he rejoiced to a friend in Virginia, Spencer Roane, that it had been effected peacefully "by the rational and peaceful instruments of reform, the suffrage of the people."

Historian **JOHN FERLING** *is the author of* Adams vs. Jefferson: The Tumultuous Election of 1800 (*Oxford University Press*).

The Revolution of 1803

The Louisiana Purchase of 1803 was "the event which more than any other, after the foundation of the Government and always excepting its preservation, determined the character of our national life." So said President Theodore Roosevelt on the 100th anniversary of this momentous acquisition. As we celebrate the 200th anniversary, it's clear that the extraordinary real estate deal also shaped America's perception of its role in the world.

by Peter S. Onuf

If there was one thing the United States did not seem to need in 1803, it was more land. The federal government had plenty to sell settlers in the new state of Ohio and throughout the Old Northwest (stretching from the Ohio and Mississippi rivers to the Great Lakes), as did New York, Pennsylvania, and other states. New Englanders were already complaining that the westward exodus was driving up wages and depressing real estate prices in the East.

The United States then consisted of 16 states: the original 13, strung along the Atlantic seaboard, and three recent additions on the frontier: Vermont, which had declared its independence from New York during the Revolution, was finally recognized and admitted in 1791, and Kentucky and Tennessee, carved out of the western reaches of Virginia and North Carolina in 1792 and 1796, respectively, extended the union of states as far as the Mississippi River. The entire area east of the Mississippi had been nominally secured to the United States by the Peace of Paris in 1783, though vast regions remained under the control of Indian nations and subject to the influence of various European imperial powers.

Many skeptical commentators believed that the United States was already too big and that the bonds of union would weaken and snap if new settlements spread too far and too fast. "No paper engagements" could secure the connection of East and West, Massachusetts congressman Rufus King wrote in 1786, and separatist movements and disunionist plots kept such concerns alive in subsequent years. Expansionists had a penchant for naturalistic language: At best, the "surge" or "tide" of white settlement might be channeled, but it was ultimately irresistible.

Though President Thomas Jefferson and the American negotiators who secured the Louisiana Purchase in 1803 had not even dreamed of acquiring such a vast territory, stretching from the Mississippi to the Rockies, the expansion of the United States has the retrospective feel of inevitability, however much

some modern Americans may bemoan the patriotic passions and imperialistic excesses of "Manifest Destiny" and its "legacies of conquest." Indeed, it's almost impossible for us to imagine any other outcome now, or to recapture the decidedly mixed feelings of Americans about their country's expansion at the start of the 19th century.

Jefferson and his contemporaries understood that they were at a crossroads, and that the American experiment in republican self-government and the fragile federal union on which it depended could easily fail. They understood that the United States was a second-rate power, without the "energy" or military means to project—or possibly even to defend—its vital interests in a world almost constantly at war. And they understood all too well that the loyalties of their countrymen—and, if they were honest with themselves, their own loyalties—were volatile and unpredictable.

There were good reasons for such doubts about American allegiances. Facing an uncertain future, patriotic (and not so patriotic) Americans had only the dimmest sense of who or what should command their loyalty. The Union had nearly collapsed on more than one occasion, most recently during the presidential succession crisis of 1800-01, which saw a tie in the Electoral College and 36 contentious ballots in the House of Representatives before Jefferson was elevated to the presidency. During the tumultuous 1790s, rampant partisan political strife between Federalists and Jefferson's Republicans roiled the nation, and before that, under the Articles of Confederation (1781-89), the central government ground to a virtual halt and the Union almost withered away before the new constitution saved it. Of course, everyone professed to be a patriot, dedicated to preserving American independence. But what did that mean? Federalists such as Alexander Hamilton preached fealty to a powerful, consolidated central government capable of doing the people's will (as they loosely construed it); Republican oppositionists championed a strictly construed federal constitution that left power in the hands of the people's (or peoples') state governments. Each side accused the other of being subject to the corrupt influence of a foreign power: counterrevolutionary England in the case of Federalist "aristocrats" and "monocrats"; revolutionary France for Republican "Jacobins."

In Jefferson's mind, and in the minds of his many followers, the new Republican dispensation initiated by his ascension to power in "the Revolution of 1800" provided a hopeful answer to all these doubts and anxieties. Jefferson's First Inaugural Address, which the soft-spoken, 57-year-old president delivered to Congress in a nearly inaudible whisper in March 1801, seemed to his followers to herald a new epoch in American affairs. "We are all republicans, we are all federalists," he insisted in the speech. "Let us, then, unite with one heart and one mind." The president's inspiring vision of the nation's future augured, as he told the English radical Joseph Priestley, then a refugee in republican Pennsylvania, something "new under the sun."

While Jefferson's conciliatory language in the inaugural address famously helped mend the partisan breach—and, not coincidentally, helped cast Hamilton and his High Federalist minions far beyond the republican pale—it also anticipated the issues that would come to the fore during the period leading up to the Louisiana Purchase.

First, the new president addressed the issue of the nation's size. Could an expanding union of free republican states survive without jeopardizing the liberties won at such great cost by the revolutionary generation? Jefferson reassured the rising, post-revolutionary generation that it too had sufficient virtue and patriotism to make the republican experiment work and to pass on its beneficent legacy. "Entertaining a due sense of our equal right to the use of our own faculties" and "enlightened by a benign religion, professed, indeed, and practiced in various forms, yet all of them inculcating honesty, truth, temperance, gratitude, and the love of man; acknowledging and adoring an over-ruling Providence, which by all its dispensations proves that it delights in the happiness of man here and his greater happiness hereafter," Americans were bound to be "a happy and a prosperous people."

Jefferson congratulated his fellow Americans on "possessing a chosen country, with room enough for our descendants to the thousandth and thousandth generation," a vast domain that was "separated by nature and a wide ocean from the exterminating havoc of one quarter of the globe." Jefferson's vision of nationhood was inscribed on the American landscape: "An overruling Providence, which by all its dispensations proves that it delights in the happiness of man here and his greater happiness hereafter" provided this fortunate people with land enough to survive and prosper forever. But Jefferson knew that he was not offering an accurate description of the nation's current condition. Given the frenzied pace of westward settlement, it would take only a generation or two—not a thousand—to fill out the new nation's existing limits, which were still marked in the west

by the Mississippi. Nor was the United States as happily insulated from Europe's "exterminating havoc" as the new president suggested. The Spanish remained in control of New Orleans, the key to the great river system that controlled the continent's heartland, and the British remained a powerful presence to the north.

Jefferson's vision of the future was, in fact, the mirror opposite of America's present situation at the onset of the 19th century. The nation was encircled by enemies and deeply divided by partisan and sectional differences. The domain the president envisioned was boundless, continent-wide, a virgin land waiting to be taken up by virtuous, liberty-loving American farmers. In this providential perspective, Indian nations and European empires simply disappeared from view, and the acquisition of new territory and the expansion of the Union seemed preordained. It would take an unimaginable miracle, acquisition of the entire Louisiana territory, to begin to consummate Jefferson's inaugural promise.

Jefferson's expansionist vision also violated the accepted axioms of contemporary political science. In his *Spirit of the Laws* (1748), the great French philosopher Montesquieu taught that the republican form of government could survive only in small states, where a virtuous and vigilant citizenry could effectively monitor the exercise of power. A large state, by contrast, could be sustained only if power were concentrated in a more energetic central government; republicanism in an expanding state would give way to more "despotic," aristocratic, and monarchical regimes. This "law" of political science was commonly understood in mechanical terms: Centrifugal forces, pulling a state apart, gained momentum as territory expanded, and they could be checked only by the "energy" of strong government.

James Madison had grappled with the problem in his famous *Federalist* 10, in which he argued that an "extended republic" would "take in a greater variety of parties and interests," making it "less probable that a majority of the whole will have a common motive to invade the rights of other citizens." Modern pluralists have embraced this argument, but it was not particularly persuasive to Madison's generation—or even to Madison himself a decade later. During the struggle over ratification of the Constitution, Antifederalists effectively invoked Montesquieu's dictum against Federalist "consolidationism," and in the 1790s, Jeffersonian defenders of states' rights offered the same arguments against Hamiltonian High Federalism. And Jefferson's "Revolution of 1800," vindicating the claims of (relatively) small state-republics against an overly energetic central government, seemed to confirm Montesquieu's wisdom. Montesquieu's notion was also the basis for the popular interpretation of what had caused the rise of British tyranny in the colonies before the American Revolution.

At the same time, however, Montesquieu's logic posed a problem for Jefferson. How could he imagine a continental republic in 1801 and negotiate a land cession that doubled the country's size in 1803? To put the problem somewhat differently, how could Jefferson—who had, after all, drafted the controversial Kentucky Resolutions of 1798, which threatened state nullification of federal authority—overcome his own disunionist tendencies?

Jefferson's response in his inaugural was to call on his fellow Americans to "pursue our own federal and republican principles, our attachment to union and representative government," with "courage and confidence." In other words, a sacred regard for states' rights ("federal principles") was essential to the preservation and strength of a "union" that depended on the "attachment" of a people determined to secure its liberties ("republican principles"). This conception of states as republics would have been familiar and appealing to many Americans, but Jefferson's vision of the United States as a *powerful* nation, spreading across the continent, was breathtaking in its boldness. How could he promise Americans that they could have it both ways, that they could be secure in their liberties yet have a federal government with enough "energy" to preserve itself? How could he believe that the American government, which had only recently endured a near-fatal succession crisis and which had a pathetically small army and navy, was "the strongest Government on earth"?

Jefferson responded to these questions resoundingly by invoking—or perhaps more accurately, inventing—an American people or nation, united in devotion to common principles, and coming together over the course of succeeding generations to constitute one great family. Thus, the unity the president imagined was prospective. Divided as they might now be, Americans would soon come to realize that they were destined to be a great nation, freed from "the throes and convulsions of the ancient world" and willing to sacrifice everything in defense of their country. In Jefferson's vision of progressive continental development, the defensive vigilance of virtuous republicans, who were always ready to resist the encroachments of power from any and every source, would be transformed into a patriotic devotion to the transcendent community of an inclusive and expanding nation, "the world's best hope." "At the call of the law," Jefferson predicted, "every man ... would fly to the standard of the law, and would meet invasions of the public order as his own personal concern.

Jefferson thus invoked an idealized vision of the American Revolution, in which patriotic citizen-soldiers rallied against British tyranny, as a model for future mobilizations against internal as well as external threats. (It was an extraordinary—and extraordinarily influential—exercise in revisionist history. More dispassionate observers, including those who, unlike Jefferson, actually had some military experience, were not inclined to give the militias much, if any, credit for winning the war.)

Jefferson's conception of the American nation imaginatively countered the centrifugal forces, the tendency toward anarchy and disunion, that republicanism authorized and unleashed. Devotion to the Union would reverse this tendency and draw Americans together, even as their private pursuits of happiness drew them to the far frontiers of their continental domain. It was a paradoxical, mystifying formulation. What seemed to be weakness—the absence of a strong central government—was, in fact, strength. Expansion did not attenuate social and political ties; rather, it secured a powerful, effective, and affective union. The imagined obliteration of all possible obstacles to the enactment of this great national story—the removal of Indians and

foreigners—was the greatest mystification of all, for it disguised how the power of the federal state was to be deployed to clear the way for "nature's nation."

In retrospect, the peaceful acquisition of the Louisiana Territory, at the bargain-basement price of $15 million, seemed to conform to the expansionist scenario in Jefferson's First Inaugural Address. The United States bought land from France, just as individuals bought land from federal and state land offices, demonstrating good intentions (to be fruitful and multiply, to cultivate the earth) and their respect for property rights and the rule of law. Yet the progress of settlement was inexorable, a "natural" force, as the French wisely recognized in ceding their claims.

The threat of armed conflict was, nonetheless, never far below the surface. When the chilling news reached America in 1802 that Spain had retroceded Louisiana to France, under pressure from Napoleon Bonaparte, some Federalists agitated for a preemptive strike against New Orleans before Napoleon could land troops there and begin to carry out his plan for a reinvigorated French empire in the Western Hemisphere. As if to provide a taste of the future, Spanish authorities in New Orleans revoked the right of American traders to store goods in the city for export, thereby sending ripples of alarm and economic distress through farms and plantations of the Mississippi valley. Americans might like to think, with Jefferson, that the West was a vast land reserve for their future generations, but nature would issue a different decree if the French gained control of the Mississippi River system.

As Senator William Wells of Delaware warned the Senate in February 1803, if Napoleon were ensconced in New Orleans, "the whole of your Southern States" would be at his mercy; the French ruler would not hesitate to foment rebellion among the slaves, that "inveterate enemy in the very bosom of those States." A North Carolina congressman expected the French emperor to do even worse: "The tomahawk of the savage and the knife of the negro would confederate in the league, and there would be no interval of peace." Such a confederation—a powerful, unholy alliance of Europeans, Indians, and slaves—was the nightmarish antithesis of the Americans' own weak union. The French might even use their influence in Congress to revive the vicious party struggles that had crippled the national government during the 1790s.

Jefferson had no idea how to respond to the looming threat, beyond sending his friend and protégé James Monroe to join U.S. Minister to France Robert R. Livingston in a desperate bid to negotiate a way out of the crisis. At most, they hoped that Napoleon would sell New Orleans and the Floridas to the United States, perhaps with a view to preempting an Anglo-American alliance. Jefferson dropped a broad hint to Livingston (undoubtedly for Napoleon's edification) that if France ever took "possession of N. Orleans ... we must marry ourselves to the British fleet and nation." For the Anglophobe Jefferson this must have been a horrible thought, even if it was a bluff. But then, happily for Jefferson—and crucially for his historical reputation—fortune intervened.

Napoleon's intentions for the New World hinged on control of Saint-Domingue (now Haiti), but a slave revolt there, led by the brilliant Toussaint L'Ouverture, complicated the emperor's plans. With a strong assist from yellow fever and other devastating diseases, the rebels fought a French expeditionary force of more than 20,000 to a standstill. Thwarted in his western design and facing the imminent resumption of war in Europe, Napoleon decided to cut his losses. In April 1803, his representative offered the entire Louisiana Territory to a surprised Livingston. By the end of the month, the negotiators had arrived at a price. For $15 million, the United States would acquire 828,000 square miles of North America, stretching from the Mississippi River to the Rocky Mountains and from the Gulf of Mexico to the Canadian border. Over time 13 states would be carved from the new lands.

When the news reached America in July, it proved a great deal more than anyone had been contemplating but was met with general jubilation. There was widespread agreement that national security depended on gaining control of the region around New Orleans; and Spanish Florida, occupying the critical area south of Georgia and the territory that the state had finally ceded to Congress in 1802, was high on southern planters' wish list of territorial acquisitions. But it was hard to imagine any immediate use for the trans-Mississippi region, notwithstanding Jefferson's inspiring rhetoric, and there was some grumbling that the negotiators had spent more than Congress had authorized. A few public figures, mostly New England Federalists, even opposed the transaction on political and constitutional grounds.

The Lewis and Clark expedition, authorized before the Purchase was completed, testifies to Americans' utter ignorance of the West in 1803. The two explorers were sent, in effect, to feel around in the dark. Perhaps, Jefferson mused, the trans-Mississippi region could be used as a kind of toxic waste dump, a place to send emancipated slaves beyond harm's way. Or, a more portentous thought, Indian nations might be relocated west of the river—an idea President Andrew Jackson later put into effect with his infamous removal policy.

What gripped most commentators as they celebrated the news of the Purchase in 1803 was simply that the Union had survived another awful crisis. They tended to see the new lands as a buffer. "The wilderness itself," Representative Joseph Nicholson of Maryland exclaimed, "will now present an almost insurmountable barrier to any nation that inclined to disturb us in that quarter." And another congressman exulted that America was now "insulated from the rest of the world."

David Ramsay, the South Carolina historian and devout Republican, offered the most full-blown paean to the future of the "chosen country" as Jefferson had envisioned it. Echoing Jefferson's First Inaugural, he asked, "What is to hinder our extension on the same liberal principles of equal rights till we have increased to twenty-seven, thirty-seven, or any other number of states that will conveniently embrace, in one happy union, the whole country from the Atlantic to the Pacific ocean, and from the lakes of Canada to the Gulf of Mexico?" In his Second Inaugural, in 1805, Jefferson himself would ask, "Who can limit the extent to which the federative principle may operate effectively?" Gone were his doubts about the uses to which the new

lands could be put. "Is it not better that the opposite bank of the Mississippi should be settled by our own brethren and children, than by strangers of another family?"

Jefferson's vision of the American future has ever since provided the mythic master narrative of American history. In the western domains that Jefferson imagined as a kind of blank slate on which succeeding generations would inscribe the image of American nationhood, it would be all too easy to overlook other peoples and other possibilities. It would be all too easy as well to overlook the critical role of the state in the progress of settlement and development. When Americans looked back on events, they would confuse effects with causes: War and diplomacy eliminated rival empires and dispossessed native peoples; an activist federal state played a critical role in pacifying a "lawless" frontier by privatizing public lands and promoting economic development. In the mythic history of Jefferson's West, an irresistible westward tide of settlement appears to be its own cause, the manifest destiny of nature's nation.

Yet if the reality of power remains submerged in Jefferson's thought, it's not at any great depth. The very idea of the nation implies enormous force, the power of a people enacting the will of "an overruling Providence." In Jefferson's Declaration of Independence, Americans claimed "the separate & equal station to which the laws of nature and of nature's God entitle them." The first law of nature, the great natural law proclaimed by writers of the day, was self-preservation, and the defining moment in American history was the great mobilization of American power to secure independence in the Revolution. President Jefferson's vision of westward expansion projected that glorious struggle into the future and across the continent. It was a kind of permanent revolution, re-enacting the nation's beginnings in the multiplication of new, self-governing republican states.

Born in war, Jefferson's conception of an expanding union of free states constituted a peace plan for the New World. But until it was insulated from Europe's "exterminating havoc," the new nation would remain vulnerable, unable to realize its historic destiny. By eliminating the clear and present danger of a powerful French presence at the mouth of the Mississippi, the Louisiana Purchase guaranteed the survival of the Union—for the time being, at least. By opening the West to white American settlers, it all but guaranteed that subsequent generations would see their own history in Jefferson's vision of their future, a mythic, nation-making vision yoking individual liberty and national power and promising a future of peace and security in a dangerous world. Two hundred years later, that vision remains compelling to many Americans.

PETER S. ONUF *is a professor of history at the University of Virginia. His most recent book is* Jefferson's Empire: The Language of American Nationhood (2001). *Copyright © 2003 by Peter Onuf.*

Paddle a mile in their canoes

Gregory M. Lamb

"We shall delineate with correctness the great arteries of this great country: those who come after us will fill up the canvas we begin."
—Thomas Jefferson, May 1804

Peter Geery isn't satisfied with just reading about the exploits of American explorers Lewis and Clark. He's been living them.

In his role as Sgt. John Ordway, Mr. Geery has reenacted small pieces of the team's epic journey.

"I've been on the river at 106 degrees, and I've been on the river at 36 degrees in wind and rain, standing in the bow of the boat and watching for semi- submerged debris," he says. "You can read the journals, but when you're wearing the clothing, and you're on the site, and you're living the talk, the journals take on a different presence."

Now Geery's reenactment group, The Discovery Expedition of St. Charles (Mo.), has a bigger prize in mind. Starting in 2004, exactly 200 years after the two Army officers set out across the western American wilderness to seek a water passage to the Pacific, the group will trace all the river-based portions of the trip, traveling in a painstakingly accurate replica keelboat and two authentic pirogues (large dugout canoes).

They won't often find the solitude encountered by Meriwether Lewis and William Clark and their party of about 40—including American soldiers, a young Indian woman, and an African-American slave. According to early estimates, 25 million to 30 million Americans will explore some aspect of the 28-month, 8,000-mile trek that Lewis and Clark made by foot, boat, and horseback between St. Louis and the mouth of the Columbia River near Astoria, Ore.

The Lewis and Clark bicentennial officially begins on Jan. 18 at Thomas Jefferson's home at Monticello near Charlottesville, Va. That's the day when President Jefferson sent a confidential letter to Congress urging it to provide $2,500 for an expedition to the Northwest in search of a river passage to the Pacific Ocean. He appointed his personal secretary, Lewis, an Army captain, to lead the expedition. Lewis, in turn, invited friend and fellow officer Clark to be co-leader.

THE CORPS OF DISCOVERY, the group led by Meriwether Lewis and William Clark, helped chart a course for national expansion. When President Jefferson brought the Louisiana Territory from France in 1803, Lewis and Clark were charged with documenting plants and animals, mapping the region, and making overtures to the Indians that would expand trade. Their journey symbolizes bravery and a thirst for knowledge to many, but it also set in motion a series of dire changes for native peoples and the environment. Starting in January, commemorations throughout the country will give people opportunities to make their own explorations of this watershed in American history.

Exploring America's course today

Starting in 2003 and continuing into 2006, organizations and cities will engage in what planners say may be the biggest historical celebration in the United States since the bicentennial of the Declaration of Independence in 1976. The festivities will mark every step of the expedition's progress. Public-service ads will tell how it raised issues still important today, and students from elementary schools to colleges will study it from every angle.

Books are in the works, and hundreds of Lewis and Clark websites already have sprung up. A new large-format film takes visitors soaring over dramatic landscapes and plunks them into the frigid river rapids the explorers had to run. Maya Lin, architect of the Vietnam Veterans Memorial in Washington, has been commissioned to design four memorials to Lewis and Clark at sites in Washington State.

The bicentennial should be a way to "engage in a deeper conversation about what it means to be an American" and ask "what kind of course corrections should we be making in the 21st century," says Robert Archibald, who serves as president of the National Council of the Lewis and Clark Bicentennial and is also president of the Missouri Historical Society in St. Louis.

All the attention to what transpired 200 years ago will push people to ask themselves, "Can we stand in other people's shoes and see this land differently?"

Dr. Archibald says. "That seems to be one of the powerful possible outcomes of this."

For Maurice Isserman, a professor of history at Hamilton College in Clinton, N.Y., standing in Lewis and Clark's shoes went so far as tracing part of their route last summer—in an Isuzu Trooper instead of a canoe. He was scouting the route for a group of students he plans to take along in 2004. As he watched eagles drift overhead and pelicans wade nearby in Montana's Missouri Breaks region, Mr. Isserman felt he was experiencing "the scenes of visionary enchantment" Clark mentions in his journals.

Isserman followed a dirt Forest Service road up a trail that Lewis and three others had climbed in August of 1805. At the Lemhi Pass on the Continental Divide, Lewis had expected to look down on another river valley that would quickly lead to the Pacific. Instead, he saw the soaring Rockies, "row after row after row of snowcapped mountains," Isserman says. Quickly, Lewis realized that an unexpected and incredibly difficult journey still lay ahead. "That was the moment I really felt for Lewis," Isserman says.

Isserman is teaming up with geologist Todd Rayne and, they hope, a biologist, to travel with 24 to 48 students. He says Lewis and Clark, who kept journals about what they saw, provide great examples for his students.

"They were naturalists, geographers, biologists, folklorists, ethnologists," he says. "We want students to learn *about* Lewis and Clark. But, in a way, we want them to become Lewis and Clark. We want them to be able to see the world with eyes open to new experiences."

Tales of the men's "undaunted courage" (as the late historian Stephen Ambrose described it in his popular book) have become a kind of American Odyssey—full of strange encounters, heroic suffering, and ultimate survival.

Some observers note that the expedition of nearly 2½ years took about the same time it would take today to reach Mars by spaceship. Others have called the expedition a greater achievement than landing a man on the moon, because Lewis and Clark were isolated from any communication with their home base.

But those involved in the bicentennial hope it will do more than celebrate the heroism and courage of the expedition members. It's seen as a time to raise important issues about not only America's past, but also its future.

Native American perspectives

One prominent theme will be the role of native Americans. The best-known Indian in the Lewis and Clark saga is Sacagawea, the young woman whose assistance as a guide and interpreter was crucial to the expedition's success.

"Sacagawea is my hero," says Bruce Neibaur, director of "Lewis and Clark: Great Journey West," a giant-screen film produced by Destination Cinema for the National Geographic Society.

The expedition, Mr. Neibaur says, forged a way for the US to become a nation that stretched from sea to sea.

"How do you measure the impact of that?" he asks. "It's enormous. Now was that good or bad? It depends on your point of view. If you're a native American, [your] point of view might well be, 'It's not so good: Look what happened to us.' "

Americans may be surprised to learn that Lewis and Clark encountered some 60 tribes on their journey, and nearly all the contacts were friendly—in some cases life-saving.

"It was far from an empty continent," says Roger Kennedy, past director of the National Park Service and author of the forthcoming book "Mr. Jefferson's Lost Cause: Land, Farmers, Slavery, and the Louisiana Purchase." The expedition headed across land that, from the Indians' point of view, was already occupied. "So it's a pretty imperial activity.... We commenced our 'Big Stick' activity not with Theodore Roosevelt but with Thomas Jefferson."

As Lewis and Clark traveled, they weren't actually naming things, "they were renaming things," says Bobbie Conner, a member of Confederated Tribes of Umatilla near Pendleton, Ore., and a co-chairwoman of the council of tribal advisers appointed by the national bicentennial group. "That's a simple idea to convey, but it has vast consequence when you explore it. All these places [already] had names, identities, and populations. But most people think of this as the unbounded, unoccupied wilderness in the West.... We were civilized. We were complex. We were diverse."

Many hope that Americans' knowledge will expand beyond what little they've heard about Sacagawea. "As native American people, we know everything about Americans," says Wilma Mankiller, a social activist and former chief of the Cherokee Nation in Oklahoma. "We go to their schools, we attend their churches, we read their literature, we see their films, partake in their popular culture. But they know very little about our government, our history. They have no context to use to understand our contemporary lives."

She adds that as the bicentennial approaches, she's looking forward to "having some genuine dialogue ... about the aftermath of Lewis and Clark."

Ms. Conner says she hopes this bicentennial will fare better than 1992's 500-year commemoration of Columbus landing in the New World, which was seen as bringing disease and enslavement to native peoples. "It could be a debacle," she says, adding, "We don't use the Big C—'celebration' —word here." The anniversary should be a more neutral "commemoration" or "observance," she says.

"We want to tell our own stories," Conner says. "We don't want people to tell them for us."

One issue native Americans plan to raise is the protection of burial grounds and other sacred sites: An increase in water and foot traffic along the route could expose old graves.

Conner does expect that tourism could have a positive effect, as well. "We want to share in the economic boom that will occur," she says.

Another piece of the Lewis and Clark story—how Sacagawea and Clark's African-American slave, York, were allowed to vote along with the white men on the crucial question of where to build winter shelter along the Columbia—may strike many as a poignant reminder of the belated enfranchisement of blacks and women into the American political system. After playing an important role in the expedition, York chafed at returning to his life of servitude, and he eventually persuaded Clark to give him his freedom.

Reconnecting with the rivers

Conservation issues will top many people's bicentennial agendas.

Lewis and Clark documented 70 to 75 plant species, numerous bird species (including Clark's nutcracker and Lewis's woodpecker), four kinds of salmon, the grizzly bear, and bighorn sheep, all of which were unknown to Europeans. Today the men are often seen as "proto-environmentalists" who waxed rhapsodic in their journals about the natural beauty and abundance they encountered. While escaping from a party of angry Blackfeet Indians, Lewis famously jumped down from his horse to grab a sample of a plant that was unfamiliar to him.

With much of the journey taking place on the Missouri, Yellowstone, Snake, and Columbia Rivers, attention inevitably will be focused on their condition today.

The bicentennial is a "chance to do something meaningful to restore these great rivers," says Rebecca Wodders, president of American Rivers. The nonprofit conservation organization is urging the breaching of dams on the Missouri and Snake to return them to a condition closer to their natural flow and provide habitat for species like the piping plover and least tern. The Missouri, in particular, Ms. Wodders says, "is just a shadow of what Lewis and Clark saw."

The potential extinction of the Pacific salmon in the Snake River, if it should happen during the bicentennial, would be "a travesty," she says. Restoring these rivers would be the "highest tribute to the [Lewis and Clark] expedition."

Some cities along the Missouri River are taking this opportunity to reconnect with and improve their riverfronts. Among larger cities, Wodders praises Omaha, Neb., and among smaller cities she points to Nebraska City, Neb.

One clear legacy: awe

The Lewis and Clark story has always meant different things at different times in American history, says Archibald, president of the bicentennial council.

The history textbooks of the 1830s made almost no mention of the expedition. "It was a footnote," he says. "If there was something America had too much of [then], it was wilderness."

But then a young historian named Frederick Jackson Turner looked at the 1890 census and got up at a meeting of the American Historical Society and said, "It's all gone," Archibald says. The frontier had vanished. "That's amazing to me. Eighty-six years after the Lewis and Clark expedition set out and Jefferson [thought] he'd endowed America with land forever, it's gone."

While lively debates may develop over just what is the legacy of the expedition today, few observers deny that its participants were heroic.

"The Lewis and Clark Expedition will stand forever as a monument to the American spirit, a spirit of optimism and courage and persistence in the face of adversity," President Bush said last July 4 as he declared 2003 to 2006 to be the Lewis and Clark Bicentennial.

Those involved in making the film about the journey in remote areas of the American West "just came away in awe of what these people went through and endured," director Neibaur says. "You got a sense of how incredibly tough people were back in that age. Just tough, tough, tough people."

As for Geery and his Discovery Corps of St. Charles mates, they plan to recruit some 300 people to reenact the trip. Almost no one will be allowed to participate for more than three weeks at a time without taking a break to rest.

Referring to participants in the original expedition, he says, "The least of them have become very, very big men in our eyes."

African Americans in the Early Republic

by Gary B. Nash

Any teacher using a textbook published before the 1980s would find virtually nothing on African Americans—slave or free, North or South—in the era of the American Revolution and the early republic. Though about 20 percent of the population, African Americans simply did not exist in the pre-1980s story of how the Revolution proceeded and how the search for "life, liberty, and the pursuit of happiness" affected those most deprived of these unalienable rights. Nor did textbooks take any notice of the free black churches, schools, and benevolent societies created by an emerging cadre of black leaders after the Revolution. A cursory examination of pre-1980s texts shows black history beginning when the first Africans arrived in Virginia in 1619 and then jumping magically over about two hundred years until the Missouri Compromise in 1820 produced heated arguments among white legislators over the spread of slavery. While older textbooks treat antebellum slavery and the rise of abolitionism after 1820 in some detail, they leave unnoticed the fast-growing free black communities of the North and upper South.

The outpouring of scholarship on African and African American history in the last third of this century, prompted by the civil rights movement and the opening up of the historical profession, has gradually remedied the astounding erasure of one-fifth of the American population in the nation's formative years. Yet many school textbooks today still lag a decade or more behind current scholarship on African Americans. Today, most students learn something about such figures as Olaudah Equiano, Crispus Attucks, and Richard Allen and have at least some notion that slaves and free blacks fought heartily in the American Revolution, began to throw off the shackles of slavery before the Emancipation Proclamation, and resisted slavery before Nat Turner's rebellion of 1831. Yet there is much still to be learned before the student graduating from high school can claim a basic grasp of both race relations during the nation's formative decades and the role of free and enslaved blacks in the nation's explosive growth. Five African American topics—some historians

might add more—ought to be essential parts of the history curriculum that young Americans learn as they study the years between 1760 and 1830.

The Black American Revolution

African Americans, most born in the colonies but many in Africa, were deeply involved in the American Revolution and were deeply affected by it. The earliest black historians, wanting to stimulate racial pride and counter white hostility, focused on the few thousand blacks who fought with white Americans to gain their independence. Crispus Attucks, Salem Poor, and James Forten were typical of those who made blood sacrifices for "the glorious cause." But now, in a latter era when we can be more realistic about the American Revolution, students will readily understand why ten to twenty times as many slaves (along with some free blacks) fought with the British as with the American patriots. While white Americans discouraged or forbade black enlistment in state militias and the Continental Army, the British promised to grant perpetual freedom to any slave (or indentured servant) who fled his or her master to join the British forces.

The wholesale flight to the British, Benjamin Quarles wrote in his mold-breaking *Negro in the American Revolution*, had "one common origin, one set purpose—the achievement of liberty." This book, first published in 1961 and republished with an introduction by this author in 1996, is still the best one-volume account of the African Americans' American Revolution. In ringing phrases, Quarles wrote of how the "major loyalty" of blacks "was not to a place nor a people, but to a principle" and "insofar as he had freedom of choice, he was likely to join the side that made him the quickest and best offer in terms of those 'unalienable rights' of which Mr. Jefferson had spoken." This little secret about African American history ought to become common knowledge, without embarrassment or anger.

Much scholarship since Quarles's book has deepened our understanding of the massive slave rebellion that occurred during the American Revolution and the effect of white rhetoric about unalienable rights and British oppression on early abolitionists, white and black. Teachers wanting to present heroic figures who stood with the Americans can bring alive figures such as James Armistead Lafayette, the double spy who helped win the climactic battle at Yorktown, and the men of Rhode Island's black regiment. But those who struggled for freedom with the British present equally heroic stories, and their travails after the war, as they sought refuge in Nova Scotia and then returned to Africa to join the Sierra Leone experiment, are remarkable examples of endurance and unextinguishable hopes for the future. Sidney Kaplan's *Black Presence in the Era of the American Revolution*, first published in 1976 and republished in an expanded edition with Emma Nogrady Kaplan in 1989, is a teacher's goldmine. Little-known black figures leap off the pages of this fine book, which is studded with short primary sources suitable for classroom use and includes nearly every image of African Americans in the revolutionary generation that has come to light. In addition, part two of PBS's new four-part television series, *Africans in America*, is available for classroom viewing. Accompanied by a teacher-friendly companion volume by Charles Johnson, Patricia Smith, and the WGBH Research Team, the episode is a surefire way to jumpstart classes in both middle schools and high schools[1]. For teachers with advanced students who want to pursue black involvement in the American Revolution, the third section of Ira Berlin's *Many Thousands Gone* provides a comprehensive view of the revolutionary generation of African Americans, free and slave, in all parts of North America.

The Rise of Free Black Communities

One of the big stories untold in most textbooks even today concerns the rise of free black communities after the American Revolution. Blacks released from slavery, and those who made good their flight from bondage, commonly sought new lives in urban centers. In the North, they gathered especially in the seaports, with Philadelphia and New York attracting the largest black populations. They congregated also in Baltimore, Washington DC, Charleston, and smaller southern towns. In these urban places they constructed the foundations of free black life in the United States.

Especially important was the creation of free black churches, which were originally under white ecclesiastical control, but which became autonomous by 1816. Black leaders such as Absalom Jones and Richard Allen in Philadelphia; Peter Spencer in Wilmington, Delaware; and Peter Williams in New York City became not only apostles to their flocks but political spokespersons, entrepreneurs, and teachers. Many mini-biographies of these black founders are included in Kaplan and Kaplan's *Black Presence in the Era of the American Revolution* and in the five-volume *Encyclopedia of African American Culture and History*, edited by Jack Salzman, et al.

Students need to study how much a generation of blacks accomplished in building free black communities organized around churches and schools. How, one might ask, could those recently emerging from slavery (which taught slaves not to think for themselves and not to think of themselves as capable) find the inner resources and external support to create new names, form families, learn to read and write, find employment, and create neighborhoods and social associations? One of the main themes of this quest for community was the notion that the only secure foundation of free black life was the construction of independent organizations embodying their sense of being a people within a people and relying on their own resources rather than on white benevolence. While coming to grips with this emerging sense of black autonomy and strength, students should recognize that mounting white hostility to free blacks complicated their struggle for family formation, work, education, respectability, civil rights, and justice before the law.

A torrent of scholarship in recent years traces how the Enlightenment ideals of the revolutionary generation crumbled by the early nineteenth century, how discrimination and violence against free blacks increased yet how the free black communities remained vibrant and enterprising. The three largest free black communities—Philadelphia, New York, and Baltimore—were studied respectively by this author in *Forging Freedom*, by Shane White in *Somewhat More Independent*, and by Christopher Phillips in *Freedom's Port*. Although too detailed for most students, they can be mined by teachers interested in explaining community building among free blacks. The surest way to capture the imaginations of students is to view part three of the PBS series *Africans in America* and read the parallel section of the companion book mentioned above.

Early Abolitionism

Most textbooks give only casual references to how the American Revolution fueled a prolonged debate over abolishing slavery. Nonetheless, this was a burning issue for the revolutionary generation and naturally a preoccupation of black American society. More than thirty years ago, Winthrop Jordan wrote, "It was perfectly clear that the principles for which Americans had fought required the complete abolition of slavery; the question was not *if*, but *when* and *how*"[2]. Twenty-four years ago, David Brion Davis wrote brilliantly on the rise of abolitionism—and on the exhaustion of it—in *The Problem of Slavery in the Age of Revolution, 1770-1823*. Both the rise and dissipation of abolitionist fervor ought to be understood in high school American history courses, and selected chapters of these two books can guide classroom discussions.

The North and upper South were the main theaters of abolitionism. Gradual legislated emancipation characterized northern attempts at eradicating chattel bondage while private (and limited) manumission characterized southern discomfort with the peculiar institution. Students need to understand how white economic interest and white abhorrence of the notion of freed slaves mingling on an equal standing with whites dashed revolutionary idealism, thus leaving the issue of slavery to another generation. This lesson of ideology facing off against economic interest and entrenched attitudes provides a weighty lesson for students to consider. The first two essays of this author's *Race and Revolution* discuss this and provide documents for classroom use on the rise and decline of abolitionism.

Two aspects of abolition ought to stick in students' minds. First, the freeing of slaves was not always benevolent, a simple case of morality transcending economic interest. Moreover, freedom came by degrees for emancipated slaves. They did not move from abject slavery to the light of freedom as if moving across the dark side of a river to the bright side. Legal emancipation did not confer full political rights, equal economic opportunity, or social recognition. All of that was denied and contested. Second, abolition was not engineered solely by high-minded whites. It was also produced, especially in the North, by slaves who made it their business to run away and perfect insolence to the point that their masters found slavery more trouble than it was worth.

Every American youngster studies the writing and ratification of the Constitution, but not all consider how the delegates to the 1787 convention in Philadelphia wrestled with the problem of slavery and the slave trade. Sparks will fly in classrooms where the teacher stages a debate pitting those who argue that the convention could—and should—have abolished slavery against those who argue that this was impossible at that point in time. The provocative essays in Paul Finkelman's *Slavery and the Founders* will help teachers construct lively classroom activities. Comparisons of how Washington and Jefferson—both professing to detest slavery and hoping to see it abolished in their own lifetimes—made their own decisions regarding their slave property can also be instructive. Available from the National Center for History in the Schools is a teaching unit utilizing primary documents and lesson plans to allow students to evaluate the positions taken during the congressional debates over slavery in the First Congress [3].

The Spread of Slavery

Many opponents of slavery (and some defenders of it) believed that the slave population would gradually wither after slave importations ceased. But the first state censuses after the Revolution showed that slavery was growing in spite of a wartime hiatus in importations. When Eli Whitney's invention of the cotton gin in 1793 gave a tremendous boost to the production of short-staple cotton, slavery acquired a powerful new lease on life. The cotton gin gave new incentives for reopening the slave trade and insured that slavery would spread rapidly into the deep South where the demand for field hands grew enormously between 1800 and 1830. Berlin's *Many Thou-*

sands Gone provides a fine account of how lawmakers in the lower South defended the expansion of slave society and how large slaveholders consolidated their power as the region's ruling class.

The growth of slavery amidst gradual emancipation needs to be understood. From about 470,000 slaves in 1770, the population grew to about 720,000 in 1790 and 1,200,000 in 1810 (while the population of free blacks grew from about 60,000 in 1790 to 185,000 in 1810). Also notable, the coming of King Cotton led to massive interregional transfers of slaves. The cotton revolution precipitated the widespread sale of slaves from the upper to lower South—a brutal process involving a kind of new Middle Passage that sundered thousands of slave families. Students can learn about this through Toni Morrison's poignant historical novel *Beloved* (which is also available in movie form).

Life under slavery is generally studied during the decades preceding the Civil War, but teachers may have time to delve into this as part of the curriculum that deals with the early republic. Some fine, accessible essays and excellent visual material are available in Edward Campbell's edited volume *Before Freedom Came*.

Black Resistance in the New Nation

If Congress did not listen to petitioners who urged the end of slavery; if hard-nosed economic realities about the profitability of slavery submerged idealistic hopes for a new nation cleansed of its most important cancer; if by the early nineteenth century it became clear that the new nation was to be defined as a white man's republic; then how would slaves and free blacks respond, and how would they carry on their lives? Several rich veins of scholarship have explored this question, and some of the new work ought to make its way into precollegiate classrooms.

One topic well worth discussing is the Haitian Revolution of 1791-1804, the long, slave-centered revolt against the powerful and brutal French slave regime in Saint Domingue. Textbooks hardly mention the prolonged revolution in Haiti, yet it was of signal importance. It was the first racial war to overthrow a European colonial power; the first instance of mass self-emancipation by a populous slave society; the first creation of a black republic in the Americas in the midst of the slaveholding West Indies; and the event that made the Louisiana Territory nearly useless to France, since its main importance was supplying the foodstuffs to feed the hundreds of thousands of French slaves in the Caribbean. Ironically, Jefferson's acquisition of the Louisiana Territory vastly extended the American domain suitable for enslaved labor.

Students can also explore how the Haitian Revolution spread the spark of black rebellion to the United States and how Haiti became a beacon of freedom and an inspiration for all who hoped for the overthrow of slavery. Students can also consider how it produced a morbid fear of black insurrection while dampening white manumitting instincts. Jefferson's personal inner conflict is illuminating. As president, he encouraged the black overthrow of slavery in Saint Domingue and applauded black independence. But he refused to recognize the black government when it came to power in 1804 and worked to quarantine or neutralize Haiti commercially in deference to the interests of southern planters.

Another part of the continuing struggle of African Americans for freedom involved open resistance. Gabriel's Rebellion of 1800 in Virginia and Denmark Vesey's plot in 1822 in South Carolina, both inspired in part by the Haitian Revolution, are well known; but many other smaller insurrections and plots deserve attention, particularly the flight of slaves to the British forces in the War of 1812, paralleling the Revolutionary War attempts by blacks to cash in on British offers of freedom. Much of this resistance is captured in part three of the PBS video series *Africans in America* and in the companion book cited above.

Another aspect of the search for liberty and equality among free and slave, in both the North and South, is the remarkable growth of Afro-Christianity in the early nineteenth century. A transformative process among African Americans living under slavery, it was a resistance movement in its own right, and it had much to do with their ability to endure captivity. Sylvia Frey and Betty Wood's *Come Shouting to Zion* is a rich treatment of this topic. The book pays particular attention to the role of women in fashioning black churches. The northern chapter of this quest for spiritual autonomy and the building of black churches as citadels of social, political, and psychological strength is movingly told by Vincent Harding in chapters three and four of *There is a River*. Many mini-biographies of black church leaders appear in Kaplan and Kaplan's *Black Presence in the Era of the American Revolution* and *The Encyclopedia of African-American Culture and History*.

One final aspect of black resistance that deserves attention involves emigrationist schemes. African Americans, led notably by the mixed-blood merchant and mariner Paul Cuffe, had toyed with immigrating to the African homelands since the 1780s and, after 1804, to Haiti and Canada. But the larger part of the story involves the launching of the American Colonization Society (ACS) in 1816. Historians have argued for many years about the strange mixture of northern clergy, southern slaveowners, and a few free black leaders who came together to promote the voluntary emigration of free blacks to what would become Liberia. The interest of African American leaders was centered in the belief that the rising tide of white hostility to free blacks made repatriation to Africa the only viable option. However, the mass of free blacks correctly understood that the ACS (notwithstanding the fact that some northern clergy who joined the ACS were sincere abolitionists who dwelled on the glory of African Americans return-

ing to their homelands to Christianize black Africa) was for southern leaders a deportation scheme that would remove incendiary free blacks from the United States and provide cover for slavery's expansion.

Most teachers will not have time to explore the mixed motives of the ACS and its limited success. However, at the least they can interest students in how the ACS's emigrationist schemes reflected the crossroads at which the new republic stood. On the one hand, whites who were unwilling to give free blacks real equality and were eager to cleanse the country of them enthusiastically supported the ACS emigrationist efforts. On the other hand, this passion to encourage a back-to-Africa movement galvanized free black leaders who now understood that a new militance and a new inter-city league of black spokespersons were required to keep their revolutionary era hopes alive.

None of the five topics outlined above should be thought of as self-contained *African American* topics. Rather they are *American* history topics. Occupying vastly different social places, white and black Americans were linked together by a common quest for freedom, though freedom had many meanings and required various strategies to achieve. Their lives were intertwined whether on slave plantations, in cities, or on ships at sea. Their productive efforts were part of the development of the expanding nation. Great events outside the United States, such as the French and Haitian Revolutions, left imprints on everybody. While drawing attention to topics vital to the African American experience in the era of the American Revolution and the early republic, this essay is a plea for restoring to memory African American topics that are indispensable elements of the larger American story.

Endnotes

1. Charles Richard Johnson, et al., *Africans in America: America's Journey through Slavery* (New York: Harcourt Brace and Company, 1998); and *Africans in America: America's Journey through Slavery*, produced by WGBH Educational Foundation, 270 min., PBS Video, 1998, videocassette. Teaching kits are also available through WGBH. For more information or to order, write WGBH, 125 Western Avenue, Boston, MA 02134 or call (617) 300-5400.

2. Winthrop Jordan, *White over Black: American Attitudes Toward the Negro, 1550-1812* (Chapel Hill: University of North Carolina Press, 1968), 342.

3. Copies of the teaching unit, *Congress Debates Slavery, 1790-1800*, are available for $12 from The National Center for History in the Schools, 6265 Bunche Hall, UCLA, 405 Hilgard Avenue, Los Angeles, CA 90095.

Sources Cited

Africans in America: America's Journey through Slavery, produced by WGBH Educational Foundation. 270 min. PBS Video, 1998. Videocassette.

Beloved, produced by Harpo Films and Clinica Estetico. Directed by Jonathan Demme. 172 min. Touchstone Home Video, 1998. Videocassette.

Berlin, Ira. *Many Thousands Gone: The First Two Centuries of Slavery in North America*. Cambridge: Harvard University Press, 1998.

Campbell, Edward D. C., Jr., ed. *Before Freedom Came: African-American Life in the Antebellum South.* Richmond, VA: Museum of the Confederacy, 1991.

Davis, David Brion. *The Problem of Slavery in the Age of Revolution, 1770-1823.* Ithaca: Cornell University Press, 1975.

Finkelman, Paul. *Slavery and the Founders: Race and Liberty in the Age of Jefferson.* New York: M. E. Sharpe, 1996.

Frey, Sylvia and Betty Wood. *Come Shouting to Zion: African American Protestantism in the American South and British Caribbean to 1830.* Chapel Hill: University of North Carolina Press, 1998.

Harding, Vincent. *There is a River: The Black Struggle for Freedom in America.* New York: Harcourt Brace Jovanovich, 1981.

Johnson, Charles Richard, et al. *Africans in America: America's Journey through Slavery.* New York: Harcourt Brace and Company, 1998.

Kaplan, Sidney and Emma Nogrady Kaplan. *The Black Presence in the Era of the American Revolution.* Amherst: University of Massachusetts Press, 1989.

Morrison, Toni. *Beloved.* New York: Knopf, 1987.

Nash, Gary B. *Forging Freedom: The Formation of Philadelphia's Black Community, 1720-1840.* Cambridge: Harvard University Press, 1988.

——. *Race and Revolution.* Madison, WI: Madison House, 1990.

Phillips, Christopher. *Freedom's Port: The African American Community of Baltimore, 1790-1860.* Urbana: University of Illinois Press, 1998.

Quarles, Benjamin. *The Negro in the American Revolution.* 1961. Reprint, Chapel Hill: University of North Carolina Press, 1996.

Salzman, Jack, et al., eds. *Encyclopedia of African-American Culture and History.* 5 vols. New York: MacMillan Library Reference, 1996.

White, Shane. *Somewhat More Independent: The End of Slavery in New York City, 1770-1810.* Athens: University of Georgia Press, 1991.

Gary B. Nash is a professor of history at the University of California, Los Angeles, and is the author of many books and articles on race, class, and society in the early republic, including Red, White, and Black: The Peoples of Early America *(1974, 4th ed. 2000). A Guggenheim Fellow, and finalist for the Pulitzer Prize for his book* The Urban Crucible, *Nash is a former president of the Organization of American Historians (1994-1995). He served as co-chair for the National History Standards Project and currendy directs UCLA's National Center for History in the Schools.*

𝔓irates!

On the shores of Tripoli, America becomes a world power

𝕷ewis 𝕷ord

𝔊eorge W. Bush isn't the first president to win cheers for fighting international terrorism. In the early 19th century, Thomas Jefferson and James Madison sent the U.S. Navy into the Mediterranean to combat swarms of state-sponsored cutthroats. Like Bush, the two Founding Fathers drew immense public support, especially after American forces seized the upper hand. The war "is among the most popular that one people ever declared against another," reported the editor of *Niles' Weekly Register,* one of the nation's most influential magazines. "If we may judge the general feeling by what appears in the newspapers, it is almost universally approved."

Americans applauded because their government finally was doing something about the Barbary pirates, the hellhounds from North Africa's northern coast who for centuries preyed on commerce in the Atlantic and the Mediterranean, hijacking ships and cargoes and enslaving the crews. "There is but one language which can be held to these people," one American envoy observed, "and this is *terror.*"

In confronting the scourge, Americans groped with issues not unlike those of today: What is the price of honor? When is the use of force unavoidable? Should more power go to the national government? By the time America's war on piracy finally ended—three decades and four presidents after the young republic's ships were first seized—the United States had done much more than free its commerce from terrorist threats. It had strengthened its sense of nationhood and drawn the respect of much of the world.

There are, to be sure, significant differences between the predators of long ago and the mass murderers of today. The Barbary harpies, from the rogue states of Algiers, Morocco, Tripoli, and Tunis, specialized in what John Adams termed "Avarice and Fear." Preferring plunder to politics, the pirates terrorized people not to satisfy an ideological passion but to collect blackmail and ransom for the deys, beys, and bashaws who ruled what was known as the Barbary Coast.

Still, religion, then as now, was a factor. The pirates were Muslims, their captives Christians. Prisoners who converted to Islam escaped hard labor and landed cushy jobs. Those who dis-

paraged Allah risked being impaled or roasted alive. Jefferson and Adams, as diplomats in Europe, asked Tripoli's ambassador why his government sanctioned such savagery. The Koran established that non-Muslims were "sinners," the envoy replied, and Muslims had a "right and duty to make war upon them wherever they could be found, and to make slaves of all they could take as Prisoners."

In truth, the pirates enslaved only the Christians of countries unable or unwilling to cough up protection money. The major powers with strong navies chose the easy way and paid tribute—a self-serving strategy that reserved the Mediterranean for nations with wealth. Colonial America developed a prosperous Mediterranean trade, thanks to the bribes that its protector, Great Britain, gave the Barbary potentates. But when America won its independence in 1783, it lost its immunity to depredations.

With London looking on approvingly, Algerian pirates in 1785 grabbed two Boston vessels and enslaved their 21 men. The United States—then a loose confederation of 13 squabbling states with no president, no navy, and scant power to raise revenue—was too poor to be shaken down and too impotent to fight. Adams, America's minister in London, agreed that "these nests of Banditti" must be destroyed. But, he added, the "States are so backward that they will do nothing for some years."

Adams was right. The tax-shy Congress, with the states in charge, opted for negotiations, which came to naught. Nor did ratification of the Constitution and the swearing in of George Washington as president in 1789 work wonders. Americans still languished in dungeons and rock quarries, while Algiers tried to extort even more money. Jefferson, as the nation's first secretary of state, told Congress it must choose "between war, tribute and ransom." He favored military action, starting with creation of a navy.

Congress agreed that a navy was the answer—but declined to fund one. In 1792 word arrived that the hostages, in desperation, might abandon Christ and country—a horrid prospect that prompted lawmakers to appropriate $54,000 ransom. But even that abject effort fell short: The money never reached Algiers, and the men remained in captivity.

Subsequent months brought more humiliation. Algerians captured 11 American vessels and took 126 prisoners. "Death," wrote one enslaved captain, "would be a great relief & more welcome than a continuance of our present situation." By now, President Washington and Congress were building a navy, but ransom still seemed the only choice. After the United States pledged to pay $642,500 plus an annual gift of naval equipment, Algiers set the surviving Americans free.

By 1800, the last full year of Adams's presidency, an angry slogan was catching on across the land: "Millions for defense but not one cent for tribute." Still, barrels of blackmail money from America kept pouring into northern Africa. The dey of Algiers added insult to injury by forcing a U.S. warship—the George Washington no less—to replace its American flag with that of Algiers and sail to Constantinople with presents for the Turkish sultan.

In 1801, precisely two centuries before a rookie president began today's war on terrorism, America found itself with a leader ready and willing to curb piracy. Even though the government over 10 years had paid the Muslim states $2 million, the bashaw of Tripoli wanted more. Three months into Jefferson's presidency, the bashaw cut down the flagstaff at the U.S. Consulate and declared war. Jefferson dispatched four warships to patrol the North African coast and bombard Tripoli.

American gunships attack Tripoli in 1804, one of many battles in 30 years of trouble with the Barbary pirates.

Jefferson's campaign, like 1898's Spanish-American conflict, would delight Americans as a splendid little war and spawn tales of daring that thrilled generations of schoolboys. But success did not come quickly. As with Pearl Harbor in 1941 and the September 11 attacks last year, Americans were appalled by word of a calamity: An American frigate, the Philadelphia, ran onto a shoal off Tripoli, and its crew of 309 officers and men was enslaved.

Navy Lt. Stephen Decatur, in the first of several feats that made him the military's first 19th-century hero, turned humiliation into celebration. With 70 volunteers, he sailed into the Bay of Tripoli and slipped onboard the captured ship as it was being refitted for duty against his countrymen. The raiders stabbed the guards, set the ship afire, and rowed away without losing a man.

In another assault, Decatur leaped aboard an enemy gunboat with a sword in one hand and a pistol in his back pocket. A husky Turk pinned him to the deck, and a second enemy sailor took aim at his head with a scimitar. His life was saved when a wounded comrade, Daniel Fraser, jumped in front of the blade and took the blow. (Fraser survived, too.)

But it was an ex-Army officer who directed the war's most unusual exploit, an adventure that inspired the second line of "The Marines' Hymn." What Tripoli needed, diplomat William Eaton argued, was a new regime. (Eaton also voiced another precocious view for the time: "The Christian slaves among the barbarians of Africa are treated with more humanity than the African slaves among the professing Christians of civilized America.") In 1805 in Egypt, Eaton assembled a ragtag army, including a few hundred Arab mercenaries, three dozen Greeks, and 10 Americans, eight of them marines—plus the bashaw's exiled brother. Since the brother feared the sea, the men crossed 400 miles of desert to reach, in the words of the hymn, "the shores of Tripoli." There the handful of marines led a charge that took the pirate state's second-largest city.

The war soon would end, but not as Eaton envisioned. Jefferson, anxious to cut military spending and get back to erasing the federal debt, let another envoy come to terms with the bashaw on a treaty that Eaton, driven to drink, would assail as ignoble. The two sides swapped prisoners, and Tripoli agreed not to expect any future tribute from America. In return, the bashaw got one final payoff—$60,000 in ransom—and kept his throne.

Jefferson's half-measure didn't bring permanent relief from Barbary outrages. In 1812, during Madison's presidency, Algiers hijacked a U.S. ship and enslaved the crew. Madison, immersed in a new war with Britain, did nothing for nearly three years. Then, shortly after peace with London was signed, Congress granted his request for a war against Algiers. Two squadrons sailed to the Mediterranean and at cannon point brought the dey of Algiers to heel. Tunis and Tripoli also behaved. Piracy against America, as an act of governments, came to an end.

Europe was impressed. Thirty years earlier, Jefferson had urged an international coalition against piracy. Now, at last, it took shape. The British and the Dutch announced an end to their policies of appeasement by bombarding Algiers's fleet and fortresses.

France used the strongest remedy, the outright removal of piracy's potentates. In 1830, the French attacked and conquered Algiers before making it part of France. Tunis and Morocco became French protectorates. Italy chipped in by toppling the ruler of Tripoli and forming Libya. What finally cleansed the region of piracy, British historian Paul Johnson contends, was 19th-century colonialism.

Today, hardly anyone favors a revival of colonial rule. But a key element in America's war on terrorism is a willingness to overthrow regimes that wage covert war. In obliterating Afghanistan's terrorist-harboring government, Bush exercised a power that the Founding Fathers in their dealings with pirates could only dream about. "Would to Heaven we had a navy to reform those enemies to mankind," George Washington lamented in 1786, "or crush them into non-existence."

"Weakness provokes insult & injury."

Thomas Jefferson, *urging creation of a navy*

How American Slavery Led to the Birth of Liberia

In 1820, a private group established Liberia as a colony for freed U.S. slaves. But it was troubled from the start.

SEAN PRICE

On January 25, 1851, Edward Blyden's ship dropped anchor just off the coast of Liberia. For the 19-year-old seminary student, it was the end of a weeks-long sea voyage and a kind of homecoming. To the very continent that Blyden's ancestors had left in chains, he was now returning as a free man. He could hardly contain his excitement as he wrote to a friend:

> You can easily imagine the delight with which I gazed upon the land of my forefathers—of those mysterious races of men. It is really a beautiful country. ... The land is exceedingly prolific—teeming with everything necessary for the subsistence of man.

Along with beautiful scenery, Blyden was looking out over one of America's boldest social experiments. Liberia had been founded in 1820 as a colony for freed American slaves. A group called the American Colonization Society had purchased land on Africa's west coast to establish Liberia. Between 1820 and 1865, the society transported at least 12,000 people there. Shipping free blacks back to Africa seemed a sensible idea to the society's white founders and to some blacks, such as Edward Blyden. But the many controversies and problems that nagged at Liberia kept it from ever becoming the freed slaves' promised land.

quick fact
LIBERIA comes from the Latin phrase meaning "Land of the free"

THE SLAVERY QUESTION

By the early 1800s, slavery had died out in the Northern U.S., but it thrived in the South thanks to the region's labor-hungry plantations. Over time some slaves were set free. Others bought their freedom.

This growing class of society—free blacks—troubled many slavery supporters, who often subscribed to views similar to Thomas Jefferson's. The third U.S. President and author of the Declaration of Independence believed slavery was a necessary evil that would one day die out. Yet he saw no place for free blacks in U.S. society when that day came. He once wrote that blacks were inferior and that, "when freed, [they are] to be removed beyond the reach of mixture."

One answer, for people who agreed with Jefferson, was to send African-Americans to Africa. If the thousands of free blacks already living in the U.S. could be successfully settled there, the thought went, then millions could later follow. Other whites, more sympathetic to the plight of blacks, thought sending them to Africa would allow them to live in freedom and without prejudice.

Against this backdrop, the American Colonization Society, a private group, was founded in 1816. It attracted luminaries including Daniel Webster, Henry Clay, and Francis Scott Key, as well as clergymen and philanthropists. It won support from slaveholders such as Jefferson and the fifth U.S. President, James Monroe- and some antislavery activists.

quick fact
1847 Liberia became the **first Independent black-run country** in modern Africa

WHY LEAVE AMERICA?

Some blacks were indeed eager to leave the U.S., but their main motivation was to flee racial hostility. Black abolitionist Martin R. Delany argued for emigration in 1852, saying:

> In the United States, among the whites, their color is made, by law

and custom, the mark of distinction and superiority, while the color of the blacks is a badge of degradation.

Still, the idea of colonization angered many blacks and some white abolitionists, like William Lloyd Garrison. They saw it as a way to bolster slavery by getting rid of free blacks—among the few political allies of the slaves. They also believed sending blacks back to Africa made no more sense than shipping English-Americans back to England. As black abolitionist David Walker wrote in 1829:

America is more our country than it is the whites'. We have enriched it with our blood and tears ... and they will drive us from our property and homes, which we have earned with our blood?

Nevertheless, the society pushed ahead with its plan. From local tribal chiefs, the group purchased a 36-mile-long strip of land next to present-day Sierra Leone for the equivalent of $300 in trade goods. (Some accounts say the purchase was made through intimidation and threats.) The colony's name was taken from the Latin phrase for "land of the free," and its capital,

Monrovia, was named after President Monroe. Hundreds of well-wishers came to see off the ship *Elizabeth* on January 31, 1820, as it left New York with Liberia's first 86 black colonists and three white agents from the society.

DISEASE AND DISSENT

Disease soon proved to be the colony's most dangerous foe. All three agents and 22 of the original colonists died of malaria, yellow fever, or other tropical illnesses. Between 1820 and 1843, disease killed about 22 percent of all new arrivals. Also, tensions quickly arose between the surviving colonists and their leaders. Liberia's early Governors—all white men—were picked by the society and ruled autocratically.

After several near rebellions, the society finally appointed Joseph J. Roberts, a free black from Virginia, as Govenor in 1841. But the push for self-rule continued, and on July 26, 1847 Liberia proclaimed its independence, becoming the first black-run republic in modern Africa. Roberts was elected its President. Liberia's flag and constitution were modeled on those of the U.S.

Unfortunately, instability persisted. Ironically, Liberia's settlers—many of

whom had once been in bondage—often discriminated against the native Africans, whom they considered uncivilized. The natives were excluded from voting and kept out of government. Even the country's Declaration of Independence asserted that "we the people of Liberia were originally inhabitants of the United States of North America." These practices frequently led to fighting between the settlers—known as "Americo-Liberians"—and the 16 ethnic African tribes that lived in the region.

During the 1800s, this turmoil discouraged prospective immigrants. By the 1890s, even Libera's most fervent boosters could see that the experiment had largely failed.

Edward Blyden, who became a successful writer and speaker, mourned the promise for which his country had once stood. "We are keeping these lands, we say, for our brethren in America," he wrote. "But they are not willing to come...."

The "Americo-Liberians" governed until 1980, when a bloody coup by native Africans helped trigger Liberia's current turmoil. But the seeds had been planted from its founding.

Andrew Jackson Versus the Cherokee Nation

"Old Hickory" had been an Indian fighter, and he continued the struggle as president. His new weapon was the Indian Removal Act, which would force Eastern tribes to relocate west of the Mississippi.

By Robert V. Remini

The great Cherokee Nation that had fought the young Andrew Jackson back in 1788 now faced an even more powerful and determined man who was intent on taking their land. But where in the past they had resorted to guns, tomahawks, and scalping knives, now they chose to challenge him in a court of law. They were not called a "civilized nation" for nothing. Many of their leaders were well educated; many more could read and write; they had their own written language, thanks to Sequoyah, a constitution, schools, and their own newspaper. And they had adopted many skills of the white man to improve their living conditions. Why should they be expelled from their lands when they no longer threatened white settlements and could compete with them on many levels? They intended to fight their ouster, and they figured they had many ways to do it. As a last resort they planned to bring suit before the Supreme Court.

Prior to that action, they sent a delegation to Washington to plead their cause. They petitioned Congress to protect them against the unjust laws of Georgia that had decreed that they were subject to its sovereignty and under its complete jurisdiction. They even approached the President, but he curtly informed them that there was nothing he could do in their quarrel with the state, a statement that shocked and amazed them.

So the Cherokees hired William Wirt to take their case to the Supreme Court. In the celebrated *Cherokee Nation v. Georgia* he instituted suit for an injunction that would permit the Cherokees to remain in Georgia without interference by the state. He argued that they constituted an independent nation and had been so regarded by the United States in its many treaties with them.

Speaking for the majority of the court, Chief Justice John Marshall handed down his decision on March 18, 1831. Not sur-

prisingly, as a great American nationalist, he rejected Wirt's argument that the Cherokees were a sovereign nation, but he also rejected Jackson's claim that they were subject to state law. The Indians were "domestic dependent nations," he ruled, subject to the United States as a ward to a guardian. Indian territory was part of the United States but not subject to action by individual states.

When the Cherokees read Marshall's decision they honestly believed that the Nation had won the case, that Georgia lacked authority to control their lives and property, and that the courts would protect them. The Supreme Court, the Principal Chief told his people, decided "in our favor." So they stayed right where they were, and missionaries encouraged them to stand fast.

But they figured without Andrew Jackson—the man the Cherokees called Sharp Knife—and the authorities of Georgia. In late December 1830, the state passed another law prohibiting white men from entering Indian country after March 1, 1831, without a license from the state. This move was obviously intended to keep interfering clergymen from inciting the Indians to disobey Georgia law. Eleven such missionaries were arrested for violating the recent statute, nine of whom accepted pardons from the governor in return for a promise that they would cease violating Georgia law. But Samuel A. Worcester and Dr. Elizur Butler refused the pardon, and Judge Augustin S. J. Clayton sentenced them to the state penitentiary, "there to endure hard labor for the term of four years." They appealed the verdict and their case came before the Supreme Court.

On March 3, 1832, Marshall again ruled in *Worcester v. Georgia,* declaring all the laws of Georgia dealing with the

Cherokees unconstitutional, null, void, and of no effect. In addition he issued a formal mandate two days later ordering the state's superior court to reverse its decision and free the two men.

Jackson was presently involved in a confrontation with South Carolina over the passage of the Tariffs of 1828 and 1832. The state had nullified the acts and threatened to secede from the Union if force were used to make her comply with them. The last thing Jackson needed was a confrontation with another state, so he quietly nudged Georgia into obeying the court order and freeing Butler and Worcester. A number of well-placed officials in both the state and national governments lent a hand and the governor, Wilson Lumpkin, released the two men on January 14, 1833.

With the annoying problem of the two missionaries out of the way, both Georgia and Jackson continued to lean on the Cherokees to get them to remove. "Some of the most vicious and base characters that the adjoining states can produce" squatted on their land and stole "horses and other property" and formed a link with as many "bad citizens" of the Cherokee Nation "as they can associate into their club." Missionaries decried what was happening to the Cherokees. If only "whites would not molest them," wrote Dr. Elizur Butler in *The Missionary Herald*. They have made remarkable progress in the last dozen years and if left alone they can and will complete the process toward a "civilized life."

Ross resolutely resisted any thought of leading his people from their ancient land into a god-forsaken wilderness.

But allowing eastern Indians full control of their eastern lands was virtually impossible in the 1830s. There was not army enough or will enough by the American people to bring it about. As Jackson constantly warned, squatters would continue to invade and occupy the land they wanted; then, if they were attacked, they would turn to the state government for protection that usually ended in violence. All this under the guise of bringing "civilization" to the wilderness.

Even so, the Cherokees had a strong leader who had not yet given up the fight. They were led by the wily, tough, and determined John Ross, a blue-eyed, brown-haired mixed-blood who was only one-eighth Cherokee. Nonetheless he was the Principal Chief, and a most powerful force within the Nation. He was rich, lived in a fine house attended by black slaves, and had influence over the annuities the United States paid to the tribal government for former land cessions. His appearance and lifestyle were distinctly white; in all other respects he was Indian.

From the beginning of Jackson's administration Ross urged his people to stand their ground and remain united. "Friends," he told his people, "I have great hopes in your firmness and that you will hold fast to the place where you were raised. Friends if you all unite together and be of one mind there is no danger."

And the Cherokees cheered his determination. They approved wholeheartedly of his leadership and they took comfort in what he said. So, with the Nation solidly behind him, Ross resolutely resisted any thought of leading his people from their ancient land into a god-forsaken wilderness.

LIBRARY OF CONGRESS

John Ridge, a leader of the Treaty Party, was assassinated by opponents in 1839.

Still the Cherokees held out, even though even they had begun to feel the unrelenting pressure. A so-called Treaty Party emerged within the Nation, made up of chiefs and headmen who understood Jackson's inflexible will and had decided to bow to his wishes and try to get the best treaty possible. They were led by very capable, hard-headed, and pragmatic men, including the Speaker of the Cherokee National Council, Major Ridge; his son, the educated and politically ambitious John Ridge; and the editor of the Cherokee *Phoenix*, Elias Boudinot.

John Ridge took a leading role in the emergence of the Treaty Party, for when the *Worcester* decision was first handed down he instantly recognized that Chief Justice Marshall had rendered an opinion that abandoned the Cherokees to their inevitable fate. So he went to Jackson and asked him point-blank whether the power of the United States would be exerted to force Georgia into respecting Indian rights and property. The President assured him that the government would do nothing. He then advised Ridge "most earnestly" to go home and urge his people to remove. Dejected, the chief left the President "with the melancholy conviction that he had been told the truth.

From that moment he was convinced that the only alternative to save his people from moral and physical death, was to make the best terms they could with the government and remove out of the limits of the states. This conviction he did not fail to make known to his friends, and hence rose the *'Treaty Party.'"*

The members of this Treaty Party certainly risked their lives in pressing for removal, and indeed all of them were subsequently marked for assassination. Not too many years later, Elias Boudinot and John Ridge were slain with knives and tomahawks in the midst of their families, while Major Ridge was ambushed and shot to death.

John Ross, on the other hand, would not yield. As head of the National Party that opposed removal he was shrewd enough to recognize immediately that the President would attempt to play one party off against the other. "The object of the President is unfolded & made too plain to be misunderstood," he told the Nation. "It is to create divisions among ourselves, break down our government, our press & our treasury, that our cries may not be heard abroad; that we may be deprived of the means of sending delegations to Washington City to make known our grievances before Congress…and break down the government which you [Cherokees] have, by your own free will & choice, established for the security of your freedom & common welfare."

Under the circumstance, Ross decided to go to Washington and request a meeting with the President in order to try again to arrange some accommodation that would prevent the mass relocation of his people to what was now the new Indian Territory, which Congress had created in 1834 and which eventually became the state of Oklahoma. He was tormented by the knowledge that his people would be condemned to a "prairie badly watered and only skirted on the margin of water courses and poor ridges with copes of wood." Worse, districts would be laid out for some "fifteen or twenty different tribes, and all speaking different languages, and cherishing a variety of habits and customs, a portion civilized, another half civilized and others uncivilized, and these congregated tribes of Indians to be regulated under the General Government, by no doubt white rulers." The very thought of it sent shivers through Ross's entire body.

Since he had fought with Jackson at the Battle of Horseshoe Bend during the Creek War he reckoned that his service during that battle would provide him with a degree of leverage in speaking with the President. And, as Principal Chief, he could speak with the duly constituted authority of the Cherokee Nation as established under the Cherokee Constitution of 1827.

He had another reason for requesting the interview. He had heard a rumor that Jackson had commissioned the Reverend John F. Schermerhorn, an ambitious cleric who had assisted in the removal of the Seminoles from Florida, to negotiate with Ridge and his associates and see if a deal could be worked out that would result in a treaty. Definitely alarmed, Ross asked to speak with the President at which time he said he would submit his own proposal for a treaty.

Jackson never liked Ross. He called him "a great villain." Unlike Ridge and Boudinot, said Jackson, the Principal Chief headed a mixed-blood elite, and was intent on centralizing power in his own hands and diverting the annuities to those who

LIBRARY OF CONGRESS

Major Ridge, John Ridge's father, was also a member of the Treaty Party. He was killed in an ambush on the same day his son died.

would advance his authority and their economic self-interests. Real Indians were full-blooded Indians, not half-breeds, he declared. They were hunters, they were true warriors who, like Ridge and Boudinot, understood the President's concern for his red children and wished to prevent the calamity of certain annihilation that would ensue if they did not heed his pleas to move west. As for Ross's authority under the Cherokee Constitution, Jackson denied that it existed. He said that this so-called Constitution provided for an election in 1832 and it had not been held. Instead the Principal Chief had simply filled the National Council with his henchmen—another indication, claimed Jackson, of an elitist clique who ruled the Nation and disregarded the interests of the majority of the people.

Despite his feelings about the chief, Jackson decided to grant Ross's request for a meeting. Above all else he wanted Cherokee removal and if that meant seeing this "great villain" and hearing about his proposal for relocating the tribe then he would do it. As a consummate politician, Jackson understood the value of playing one party off against another, so when he granted the interview he directed that Schermerhorn suspend his negotiations with the Treaty Party and wait for the outcome of his interview with the Principal Chief.

Actually Jackson and Ross were much alike. They were both wily, tough, determined, obsessed with protecting the interests of their respective peoples, and markedly dignified and polite when they came together in the White House on Wednesday,

February 5, 1834. It was exactly noon when the Principal Chief arrived, and the Great Father greeted him with the respect due Ross's position. The chief returned the compliment. For a few minutes their conversation touched on pleasantries, then they got down to the question at hand and began playing a political game that involved the lives of thousands, both Native Americans and white settlers.

Unfortunately, despite his many talents and keen intelligence, Ross was no match for the President. He simply lacked the resources of his adversary.

The Principal Chief opened with an impassioned plea. "Your Cherokee children are in deep distress," he said, "... because they are left at the mercy of the white robber and assassin" and receive no redress from the Georgia courts. That state, he declared, has not only "surveyed and lotteried off" Cherokee land to her citizens but legislated as though Cherokees were intruders in their own country.

Jackson just listened. Then the Principal Chief acted imprudently and made impossible demands on the President. To start, he insisted that in any treaty the Nation must retain some of their land along the borders of Tennessee, Alabama, and Georgia, land that had already been occupied by white settlers. He even included a small tract in North Carolina. He then required assurances that the United States government would protect the Cherokees with federal troops in the new and old settlements for a period of five years.

Jackson could scarcely believe what was being demanded of him. Under other circumstances he would have acted up a storm in an attempt to frighten and cower the chief. But, on this occasion he decided against it. Instead, in a calm and quiet but determined voice, he told Ross that nothing short of an entire removal of the Cherokee Nation from all their land east of the Mississippi would be acceptable.

Having run into a stone wall, Ross headed in another direction. In view of the gold that had recently been discovered in Georgia and North Carolina, he wanted $20 million for all their eastern land plus reimbursement for losses sustained by the Nation for violations of former treaties by the United States. He also asked for indemnities for claims under the 1817 and 1819 Cherokee treaties. The total amount almost equaled the national debt.

On hearing this, Jackson also changed direction. His voice hardened, his intense blue eyes flared, and the muscles in his face tightened and registered his growing displeasure. Obviously the Principal Chief had not caught the President's meaning when he rejected the first demand. Jackson snapped at Ross, rejected the proposal as "preposterous" and warned him that the Great Father was not to be trifled with. If these demands were the best the chief could offer then there was no point in continuing the discussion.

That brought Ross up short. Completely surprised by Jackson's reaction he protested his sincerity, and to prove it he offered to accept any award the Senate of the United States might recommend. Apparently the chief was attempting to set up a bidding contest between the upper house and the chief executive. Surprisingly, Jackson accepted the offer and assured Ross that he would "go as far" as the Senate in any award that

might be proposed. And on that conciliatory note the interview ended.

In less than a week Ross received his answer about what the Senate would offer. John P. King of Georgia chaired the Committee on Indian Affairs that considered the question. That was bad enough. Then the committee came up with an offer of $5 million. The figure shocked the Principal Chief. Jackson probably knew beforehand what would happen and therefore agreed to Ross's suggestion. Now the Indian was faced with rejecting the money outright or accepting this paltry sum and thereby losing credibility with his people. Naturally he chose the former course. He claimed he had been misunderstood, that he could not possibly agree to such an amount, and that his reputation among the Cherokees would be shattered if he consented to it. He left Washington an angry and bitter man.

Having disposed of Ross, Jackson turned back to Schermerhorn and instructed him to renew the negotiations with the Treaty Party. With little difficulty the cleric managed to arrange a draft removal treaty signed on March 14, 1835, by Schermerhorn, John Ridge, Elias Boudinot, and a small delegation of Cherokees. After due notice the treaty was submitted to the Cherokee National Council at New Echota, Georgia, for approval and sent to the President for submission to the Senate. The draft stipulated that the Cherokees surrender to the United States all its land east of the Mississippi River for a sum of $5 million, an amount that one modern historian has called "unprecedented generosity." This cession comprised nearly 8 million acres of land in western North Carolina, northern Georgia, northeastern Alabama, and eastern Tennessee. A schedule of removal provided that the Cherokees would be resettled in the west and receive regular payments for subsistence, claims, and spoliations, and would be issued blankets, kettles, and rifles.

At approximately the same time this draft treaty was drawn up and considered at New Echota, a large delegation of Cherokee chiefs—in the desperate hope that their assembled presence would make a difference and prevent the treaty from going forward to the Senate—went to Washington and asked to speak to their Great Father. In contrast to his grudging granting of Ross's request, Jackson was anxious to meet the delegation and give the chiefs one of his celebrated "talks."

The Indians arrived at the White House at the designated hour, and Jackson treated them with marked respect, as though they really were dignitaries of a foreign nation. Yet he did not remotely say or do anything that would indicate an acceptance of their independence or sovereignty. Once the Indians had assembled they faced the President as he began his talk.

"Brothers, I have long viewed your condition with great interest. For many years I have been acquainted with your people, and under all variety of circumstances, in peace and war. Your fathers are well known to me.... Listen to me, therefore, as your fathers have listened...."

Jackson paused. He turned from side to side to look at and take in all the Cherokees standing around him. After a few moments he began again.

"You are now placed in the midst of a white population.... You are now subject to the same laws which govern the citizens of Georgia and Alabama. You are liable to prosecutions for offenses, and to civil actions for a breach of any of your contracts. Most of your people are uneducated, and are liable to be brought into collision at all times with your white neighbors. Your young men are acquiring habits of intoxication. With strong passions... they are frequently driven to excesses which must eventually terminate in their ruin. The game has disappeared among you, and you must depend upon agriculture and the mechanic arts for support. And yet, a large portion of your people have acquired little or no property in the soil itself.... How, under these circumstances, can you live in the country you now occupy? Your condition must become worse and worse, and you will ultimately disappear, as so many tribes have done before you."

They had two years—that is, until May 23, 1838—to cross over the Mississippi and take up their new residence in the Indian Territory.

These were his usual arguments, but he judged them essential for success.

You have not listened to me, he scolded. You went to the courts for relief. You turned away from your Great Father. And what happened? After years of litigation you received little satisfaction from the Supreme Court and succeeded in earning the enmity of many whites. "I have no motive, Brothers, to deceive you," he said. "I am sincerely desirous to promote your welfare. Listen to me, therefore, while I tell you that you cannot remain where you are now.... It [is] impossible that you can flourish in the midst of a civilized community. You have but one remedy within your reach. And that is to remove to the West and join your countrymen, who are already established there." The choice is yours. "May the great spirit teach you how to choose."

Jackson then concluded by reminding them of the fate of the Creeks, that once great and proud Nation. How broken and reduced in circumstances their lives had now become because they resisted. It was a not-so-subtle threat that also struck home. "Think then of these things," he concluded. "Shut your ears to bad counsels. Look at your condition as it now is, and then consider what it will be if you follow the advice I give you."

That ended the talk, and the Indians filed from the room more disappointed and depressed than ever. Jackson would not budge, and they knew their kinsmen were dead set against removal. It was a stalemate that could end only in tragedy.

Meanwhile Schermerhorn called "a council of all the people" to meet him at New Echota in Georgia during the third week of December 1835 to approve the draft treaty, making sure that a large contingent of Treaty Party members attended. Like Jackson, he had the temerity to warn other Cherokees that if they stayed away their absence would be considered a vote of consent for the draft.

Despite the threat and the warning, practically the entire Nation stayed away. As a consequence the treaty was approved on December 28 by the unbelievably low number of 79 to 7. The numbers represented only the merest fraction of the Nation. A vast majority—perhaps fifteen-sixteenths of the entire population—presumably opposed it and showed their opposition by staying away. The entire process was fraudulent, but that hardly mattered. Jackson had the treaty he wanted, and he did not hesitate to so inform the Senate.

The Treaty of New Echota closely, but not completely, resembled the draft treaty in that the Cherokees surrendered all their eastern land and received $4.5 million in return. They would be paid for improvements, removed at government expense, and maintained for two years. Removal was to take place within two years from the date of the treaty's approval by the Senate and President.

A short while later some 12,000 Cherokees signed a resolution denouncing the Treaty of New Echota and forwarded it to the Senate. Even the North Carolina Cherokees, in a separate action, added 3,250 signatures to a petition urging the Senate to reject it. But Jackson was assured by the Treaty Party that "a majority of the people" approved the document "and all are willing peaceable to yield to the treaty and abide by it." Such information convinced the President that the Principal Chief and his "half breed" cohorts had coerced the Cherokees into staying away from New Echota under threat of physical violence.

At New Echota the Treaty Party selected a Committee of Thirteen to carry the treaty to Washington and they were empowered to act on any alteration required by the President or the U. S. Senate. This Committee invited Ross to join the group and either support the treaty or insist on such alterations as to make it acceptable. "But to their appeal [Ross] returned no answer," which further convinced the President that the treaty represented the genuine interests and the will of the majority of Cherokees.

Militiamen charged into the Cherokee country and drove the Cherokees from their cabins and houses.

Although Henry Clay, Daniel Webster, Edward Everett, and other senators spoke fervently against the treaty in the Senate, a two-thirds majority of 31 members voted for it and 15 against. It carried by a single vote on May 18. Jackson added his signature on May 23, 1836, and proclaimed the Treaty of New Echota in force.

And they had two years—that is until May 23, 1838—to cross over the Mississippi and take up their new residence in the Indian Territory. But every day of that two-year period John Ross fought the inevitable. He demanded to see the President and insisted that Jackson recognize the authority of the duly elected National Council, but Sharp Knife would have none of him and turned him away. Back home the Principal Chief advised his people to ignore the treaty and stay put. "We will not recognize the forgery palmed off upon the world as a treaty by a knot of unauthorized individuals," he cried, "nor stir one step with reference to that false paper."

Not everyone listened to him. They knew Andrew Jackson better. Some 2,000 Cherokees resigned themselves to the inevitable, packed their belongings, and headed west. The rest, the vast majority of the tribe, could not bear to leave their homeland and chose to hope that their Principal Chief would somehow work the miracle that would preserve their country to them.

But their fate could not have been worse. When the two-year grace period expired and Jackson had left office, his hand-picked successor, President Martin Van Buren, ordered the removal to begin. Militiamen charged into the Cherokee country and drove the Cherokees from their cabins and houses. With rifles and bayonets they rounded up the Indians and placed them in prison stockades that had been erected "for gathering in and holding the Indians preparatory to removal." These poor, frightened and benighted innocents, while having supper in their homes, "were startled by the sudden gleam of bayonets in the doorway and rose up to be driven with blows and oaths along the weary miles of trail which led to the stockade. Men were seized in the fields, women were taken from their wheels and children from their play." As they turned for one last glimpse of their homes they frequently saw them in flames, set ablaze by the lawless rabble who followed the soldiers, scavenging what they could. These outlaws stole the cattle and other livestock and even desecrated graves in their search for silver pendants and other valuables. They looted and burned. Said one Georgia volunteer who later served in the Confederate army: "I fought through the Civil War and have seen men shot to pieces and slaughtered by thousands, but the Cherokee removal was the cruelest I ever saw."

In a single week some 17,000 Cherokees were rounded up and herded into what was surely a concentration camp. Many sickened and died while they awaited transport to the west. In June the first contingent of about a thousand Indians boarded a steamboat and sailed down the Tennessee River on the first lap of their westward journey. Then they were boxed like animals into railroad cars drawn by two locomotives. Again there were many deaths on account of the oppressive heat and cramped conditions in the cars. For the last leg of the journey the Cherokees walked. Small wonder they came to call this 800-mile nightmare "The Trail of Tears." Of the approximately 18,000 Cherokees who were removed, at least 4,000 died in the stockades along the way, and some say the figure actually reached 8,000. By the middle of June 1838 the general in charge of the Georgia militia proudly reported that not a single Cherokee remained in the state except as prisoners in the stockade.

At every step of their long journey to the Indian Territory the Cherokees were robbed and cheated by contractors, lawyers, agents, speculators, and anyone wielding local police power. Food supplied by the government disappeared or arrived in short supply. The commanding officer, General Winfield Scott, and a few other generals "were concerned about their reputation for humaneness," says one modern historian, "and probably even for the Cherokee. There just wasn't much they could do about it." As a result many died needlessly. "Oh! The misery and wretchedness that presents itself to our view in going among these people," wrote one man. "Sir, I have witnessed entire families prostrated with sickness—not one able to give help to the other, and these poor people were made the instruments of enriching a few unprincipled and wicked contractors."

And this, too, is part of Andrew Jackson's legacy. Although it has been pointed out many times that he was no longer President of the United States when the Trail of Tears occurred and had never intended such a monstrous result of his policy, that hardly excuses him. It was his insistence on the speedy removal of the Cherokees, even after he had left office, that brought about this horror. From his home outside Nashville he regularly badgered Van Buren about enforcing the treaty. He had become obsessed about removal. He warned that Ross would exert every effort and means available to him to get the treaty rescinded or delayed and that, he said, must be blocked. But the new President assured him that nothing would interfere with the exodus of the Cherokees and that no extension of the two-year grace period would be tolerated under any circumstance.

Principal Chief John Ross also shares a portion of blame for this unspeakable tragedy. He continued his defiance even after the deadline for removal had passed. He encouraged his people to keep up their resistance, despite every sign that no appreciable help would be forthcoming from the American people or anyone else; and he watched as they suffered the awful consequences of his intransigence.

Despite the obscene treatment accorded the Cherokees by the government, the tribe not only survived but endured. As Jackson predicted, they escaped the fate of many extinct eastern tribes. Cherokees today have their tribal identity, a living language, and at least three governmental bodies to provide for their needs. Would that the Yemassee, Mohegans, Pequots, Delawares, Narragansetts, and other such tribes could say the same.

Excerpted from *Andrew Jackson and His Indian Wars* by Robert V. Remini. Copyright © Robert V. Remini, 2001. Reprinted by arrangement with Viking Penguin, a division of Penguin Putnam, Inc.

Robert V. Remini is the author of a three-volume biography of Andrew Jackson as well as biographies of Daniel Webster and Henry Clay and many other books about Jacksonian America.

From *American History*, August 2001, pp. 48–53, 55–56. © 2001 by Primedia Consumer Media and Magazines, Inc. All rights reserved. Reprinted with permission.

Storm over Mexico

Godfrey Hodgson tells the colourful story of Jane McManus, political journalist, land speculator, pioneer settler in Texas and propagandist who believed that the United States had a 'manifest destiny' to rule Mexico and the Caribbean.

Godfrey Hodgson

AT THE HEIGHT OF THE FU-RORE over the boundary question in Texas that led to the declaration of war against Mexico on May 11th, 1846, George Bancroft, the famous historian who was President Polk's Secretary of the Navy, received a long letter in Washington telling him how to do his job and claiming,

> I mean to show you that I can call out an expression of public sentiment (and create it too) that Mr Polk would be wise to respect.

The letter was signed 'Storms'.

'Who is Storms?' Bancroft wrote to his colleague William Marcy, the Secretary of War. 'She', Marcy replied, 'is an outrageously smooth and keen writer for the newspapers'.

It was not common for women to write for the newspapers in the mid-nineteenth century, and almost unprecedented for them to do so in as confident and aggressive a tone as did the woman who called herself 'Storms'.

But then she wrote and lived, at a furious pace, under several names. She was born Jane Maria Eliza McManus. She married Allen Storm, and so could claim the vaguely ominous 'Storms'. Sometimes she signed her work plain, unisex 'Montgom-ery', and sometimes she came out as 'Cora Montgomery' or 'Corinne Montgomery'. After her second marriage she could boast the magnificent appellation Jane Eliza McManus Storm Cazneau.

Under any name, she was one of the most formidable women of the antebellum American South, a complete rebuttal of the stereotype of white-skinned Southern ladies at home only in nursery and drawing room. She was Scarlett O'Hara and Rhett Butler in one: a single mother who became one of the first women political journalists, a war correspondent, diplomat, secret agent, explorer, speculator and adventurer.

She was in tune with Young America, an amorphous movement of American nationalists (mostly Democrats) advocating southern expansion, free trade and in sympathy with the European revolutions of 1848. Mostly the Young Americans were Democrats with an interest in slavery. In the 1840s, as the young republic challenged British power in Canada, Oregon and the Caribbean, Spanish rule in Cuba, and Mexican ownership of Texas, New Mexico, Arizona and California, Americans thrilled to the idea of 'manifest destiny'. This brilliant slogan first ap-peared in the *Democratic Review*, organ of the Young America movement, in an anonymous editorial that appeared in the summer of 1845. American destiny, it proclaimed, was to bring the benefits of freedom (an ideal that did not rule out slavery) to the whole of North America, and to Central America and the Caribbean as well. The piece called boldly for 'opposition to the annexation of Texas to cease'. It denounced the behaviour of 'England, our old rival and enemy' for

> ... limiting our greatness and checking the fulfilment of our manifest destiny to overspread the continent allotted by Providence for the free development of our yearly multiplying millions.

The article and phrase, 'manifest destiny' has long been attributed to the Democratic Review's editor John L. O'Sullivan; however, Storms' biographer Professor Linda S. Hudson, has suggested (2001) that Jane was the author. She has used a grammar-checking computer programme, to argue that the style of the 'manifest destiny' article resembles Jane's far more closely than O'Sullivan's. But even if she did not coin the phrase, Jane was certainly one of the chief propagandists for 'manifest destiny', and a vigorous champion of American annexation of Texas, Cuba, the Dominican Republic, Nicaragua and most, if not all, of Mexico.

Jane McManus was born in 1807 near Troy, in the Hudson River valley in upstate New York. Her family had long been settled in North America on both sides. Her father's people came originally from Ireland, but had been living in America since the early eighteenth century, and although Jane later converted to Catholicism she was brought up as a Protestant. Her mother's family, whose name was Kuntz, Americanized as Coons, were German, Protestant refugees from the Catholic Rhineland.

Jane's father, William Telemachus McManus, was briefly a member of Congress. He fought as an officer against the British in the local militia in the War of 1812. Then he returned to Troy to work as a lawyer and businessman. He was also involved in the business affairs of the local Indian tribe, the Mohicans. Jane's 'most striking physical trait', writes Professor Hudson, 'was her dark complexion', and Hudson speculates that she may have been of Native American descent.

She was well-educated at Emma Willard's Troy Female Academy, one of the earliest colleges for women. The coming of the Erie Canal made Troy prosperous, and for a time the McManus family flourished. But Jane's father was hard-hit by the nationwide Panic of 1819, which broke the Farmers' State Bank in Troy, in which the McManus family held both stock and accounts. In 1825, at the age of eighteen, Jane had married Allen Storm, a pupil in her father's law office, and in 1826 she gave birth to a son, William McManus Storm. By 1832, however, the marriage had failed and Jane had resumed her maiden name.

Like other early nineteenth-century Americans on the fringe of the frontier, the McManus family were passionate speculators in land. The dream of a vast fortune in the newly settled south-western frontier, then expanding from Louisiana and Tennessee into Texas, and the Caribbean is one of the keys to Jane's whole career. Her political and business dreams were fused together. All her life she hoped to create a great fortune, and also to bring what she saw as the priceless boon of republican freedom to those not lucky enough to live in the United States.

Jane was first introduced to the potential of Texas, then part of the Mexican state of Coahuila y Texas, when her father became involved with his friend, the spectacular swordsman, rebel and former US vice-president, Aaron Burr, and others in the Galveston Bay and Texas Land Company in 1832. She went to work keeping the books of the Galveston Bay and Texas Land Company in New York and before long was visiting Aaron Burr, fifty years her senior, at his law office in Jersey City, across the Hudson from New York. She was widely said to be Burr's mistress and was cited in his divorce in 1835. Hearsay evidence was given that Burr was seen standing in front of a seated Jane McManus, his trousers lowered.

Late in 1832, Jane and her brother Robert travelled to Texas and acquired rights to two enormous tracts, one on the Gulf of Mexico, and the other near the present site of Waco, Texas. She also tried, without success, to bring several hundred German settlers into Texas.

It was only after these speculative land ventures failed that Jane became a journalist. Her early adventures in Texas left her with two lifelong assets: she learned fluent Spanish and she acquired a set of contacts with many powerful people on the frontier including the founders of the Republic of Texas, among them Sam Houston (who became its first president in October 1836) and his successor, Jane's partner in a lively exchange of letters, the sonorously named Mirabeau Bonaparte Lamar.

Jane's first journalistic assignment came from Horace Greeley, editor of the *New Yorker*, who gave her a choice assignment: to travel to the Mediterranean and the Ottoman empire. She visited Smyrna, Aleppo, Tangier and Cadiz, among other places. One of those she interviewed was the aged Lady Hester Stanhope, an indomitable English aristocrat who had married a Muslim and lived in the Syrian desert.

Back in the US in 1839, Jane wrote for a number of papers, two of them in particular: the *New York Sun*, then owned by Moses Yale Beach, and John O'Sullivan's *Democratic Review*. Both were enthusiastic campaigners for 'manifest destiny' and in particular for its southern form, annexation of Texas—even if that meant war with Mexico.

'Manifest Destiny' supporters were eyeing other parts of the continent as well. Anti-British feeling, focused on British rule in Canada, was stoked by the fact that the Hudson's Bay Company's presence in Oregon blocked American settlement in that promising territory. In 1846 the New York papers got up an agitation under the slogan 'Fifty-four forty or fight!' This meant that the United States should demand a frontier at 54° 40' of latitude, many miles north of the present border at the 49th degree, or make war on British Canada.

Americans insisted that their desire to occupy the whole continent was something quite different to European imperialism. 'What has Belgium, Silesia, Poland or Bengal to do with Texas?', wrote the *New York Morning News* in 1845:

> Acquisitions of territory in America, even if accomplished by force of arms, are not to be viewed in the same light as the invasions and conquests of the states of the old world.

Two philosophical differences were claimed by the leading American historian of the Manifest Destiny movement, Frederick Merk. American expansion would be republican: it would involve no monarch, no aristocracy, no established church. And it would be democratic in an economic, as well as political, sense.

The chief evil of Europe and the blight of England and Ireland, wrote the *Democratic Review*, was that the people did not own the land. This was a doctrine that appealed to would-be pioneers, but also to land speculators such as Jane.

By the 1840s, settlement had poured into the Ohio and Mississippi valleys and was rapidly filling up the cotton lands of the South. The vast, almost empty territory of Mexico—which reached far to the north of modern Mexico—lay ahead. Forward-looking southerners were already conscious that if the slave-holding South lost the battle over free soil in the mid-West and the plains states, the South would lose representation in Congress and therefore political power in Washington. Eventually, the South's 'peculiar institution', slavery itself, might be banned. Ambitious spirits dreamed of creating a great slave empire in central America and the Caribbean to balance what the South might lose in the American West. Jane McManus, New York bred though she was, was one of these.

The *New York Sun*, a penny paper, was the first in America to achieve something like a mass circulation: around 50,000 in the 1840s. Its publisher, Moses Yale Beach, was a businessman and banker as well as a newspaper man. He was a strong supporter of President Polk's war against Mexico. War broke out in 1846 after an American force moved into disputed territory between the Nueces river and the Rio Grande. The Polk administration was keen to annex at least Texas and other Mexican territory if it could.

In November 1846 Beach and the Roman Catholic bishop of New York John Hughes, received word from contacts in Texas and from the Mexican clergy that a negotiated peace might be possible. Jane McManus played a key part in setting up the secret mission, and Beach asked her to travel with him as interpreter and adviser, chaperoned by his daughter Drusilla. Beach had authority from the President to negotiate a peace

settlement. His 'fee' was to be a grant of transit rights across the Isthmus of Tehuantepec, in the southern 'waist' of Mexico. Beach saw the mission essentially as a business opportunity. He wanted the concession to build a canal across the isthmus of Tehuantepec, and also banking concessions in Mexico. For Jane it was a superb journalistic break, and at the same time a chance to forward her dream of spreading American ideals to as much of Mexico and the Caribbean as possible.

Beach, Jane and Drusilla travelled via Havana, to conceal the purpose of their journey. The Havana correspondent of the New Orleans *Picayune* newspaper reported that Beach was on his way to Mexico with 'his wife and daughter'. The party reached Mexico City in late January 1847.

While General Zachary Taylor, (who later succeeded Polk as 12th President in 1849), was fighting one Mexican army in the north where he earned a hard-won victory against the Mexicans in the Battle of Buena Vista of February 22nd-23rd. General Winfield Scott, in turn, was besieging the highly fortified city of Vera Cruz on the east coast of Mexico. Moses Beach was trying to persuade the Mexicans to allow the United States to annex their entire country. Beach met bankers and politicians in Mexico, and also prelates of the Mexican church. He also laid out $40,000 of his own money in vain to back one side in what was becoming a Mexican civil war.

Storms, meanwhile, was filing stories for the *Sun* that argued the case for the United States to annex the whole of Mexico. If this could not be achieved, she was prepared to settle for limited annexation of some provinces.

By March 21st, the Mexican dictator, Santa Ana, had returned to Mexico City after the defeat at Buena Vista, where he assumed the presidency. The Beaches and Jane made their way to Vera Cruz, where on March 27th the fortress surrendered to General Scott, a story she was able

to report. This made her America's first woman war correspondent.

By May 1847 Jane had returned to Washington, where she saw President Polk. She was bitterly disappointed that he had already sent out a new mission in place of Beach to negotiate peace with Mexico, under Nicholas P. Trist, chief clerk of the State Department. Trist's negotiations with the former President Herrera at the end of August ended in disappointment for the Americans and an end to the armistice that had facilitated them.

However, on February 2nd, 1848, Trist, with a victorious army at his back but unauthorised by his government, forced on the Mexicans the Treaty of Guadalupe Hidalgo. By this treaty Mexico agreed to sign over one-third of its territory, including California, Arizona and New Mexico, in exchange for $15 million and a further $3,250,000 in claims by its citizens. The treaty came into effect on July 4th.

Congress and the cabinet seriously debated the 'All Mexico' plan, as it was called. It was defeated, not least because neither leaders nor public in the United States was ready to incorporate eight million new citizens, Spanish-speaking, Roman Catholic and mostly non-white.

Jane now turned her attention to Cuba whose potential greatly interested her. Writing as 'Montgomery' in the *Sun*, even before the Mexican War began, she had called for the annexation of Cuba (and also Canada). Unlike Mexico, which had won its independence in a war that began in 1810, Cuba was still a Spanish colony. She wrote fifteen 'tropical sketches' denouncing the poor conditions caused by Spanish exploitation and neglect of Cuba.

In January 1848, she had accepted the position of editor of *La Verdad* (Spanish for 'Truth') a weekly published in New York and financed by wealthy Cuban liberal exiles. But a romantic plan to turn Cuba into an independent republic that could later be annexed like Texas eventually failed. On September 7th, 1849,

President Zachary Taylor sent the US Navy to turn back the exiles as they sailed to liberate Cuba.

For the rest of her life Jane continued to preach America's manifest destiny, not only to expand to the Pacific, but also to acquire a tropical domain. In 1849 at the age of forty-two, she married an old friend, General William Cazneau. They had met in Texas and both shared a romantic vision of American expansion, and an ambition to make a fortune out of land speculation.

As Cazneau travelled ceaselessly in the service of one scheme after another, Jane settled down at Eagle Pass, a rough frontier village three hundred miles up the Rio Grande from the Gulf. In the book she wrote about her life there, she described the life of an Old Testament matriarch with her flocks and herds. She got to know Native American chiefs with names like Crazy Bear, Gopher John and Wild Cat, whose interpreter was an African-American called John Horse. Life on the frontier had its idyllic moments for Jane as she rode her black pony, Chino, and bathed naked in the river. But she recognized the hardships and dangers for frontier women as well.

She got to know and sympathized with the Indians who had escaped across the border from peonage in Mexico, and the runaway American slaves heading in the opposite direction. Her attitude to slavery was complicated. She sympathized with the plight of individual slaves, and with the Indian peons. She hoped slavery would be ended in time by sending American slaves to colonies in the Caribbean. She disapproved of the Southern secession and was hired by William H. Seward, Abraham Lincoln's Secretary of State, to write propaganda against the South, which she did, like everything else, with gusto. No doubt her position was affected by the patronage of Seward. But Seward and she were both expansionists who feared that the war would weaken the United States and prevent further American thrusts into the Caribbean.

However, she was also contemptuous of abolitionists. In 1851 she and her husband travelled to Morocco to buy camels, which she hoped (unsuccessfully) to introduce into the south-west of the United States. There is even a hint that this project may have disguised a slaving expedition. And she was a supporter of the notorious 'filibuster', William Walker, who tried to set up a slave-holding empire in Central America in the 1850s.

The truth is that two things bulked larger in her mind than the abolition of slavery. One was her own and her husband's speculative investments in Texas land, and in real estate and mines in the Dominican Republic, Jamaica and Nicaragua. The other was her passionate belief in the destiny and ideals of the United States, which—as for many in her generation—implied an inveterate suspicion of Britain and a determination to oppose British interests and influence throughout the Caribbean.

From 1855 until their deaths, with one short interval, she and her husband lived on an estate, Esmeralda, in the Dominican Republic. General Cazneau had been appointed as a secret American agent there by President Buchanan. His job was to report events, and he also lobbied for an American coaling station and port at Santana Bay. For a time they moved, in spite of Jane's hostility to all things British, to a beautiful estate in Jamaica, Keith Hall, where she continued, in spite of failing eyesight, to write up-beat accounts of life in the tropics.

Jane's death was as stormy as her life. In 1878 she set out for Santo Domingo on a 'rattletrap' steamer, the *Emily B. Souder*. She was caught in what proved to be the biggest storm ever recorded in the western Atlantic up to that time. She was drowned at the age of almost seventy-two.

Jane McManus Storm Cazneau's two dreams, of making a great fortune while bringing the benefits of American freedom to Mexico and the Caribbean, were both only partly successful. Yet she had a remarkable degree of influence on the mid-nineteenth-century course of American foreign policy. It came from her ability to impress powerful men, from Burr and Houston to Beach, Polk and Seward, with her romantic vision of America's 'manifest destiny' to bring its own version of a 'freedom' (one that permitted slavery) to the Spanish-speaking lands and islands to the South.

Godfrey Hodgson *is an Associate Fellow of the Rothermere American Institute at Oxford University. He is the author of* More Equal Than Others *(Princeton University Press, 2004).*

UNIT 4

The Civil War and Reconstruction

Unit Selections

Key Points to Consider

- What was the "Underground Railroad?" What did it say about slavery that thousands of blacks risked brutal punishment or death seeking freedom? What did it say to white Southerners that so many Northerners were willing to defy existing laws to assist the runaways?

- Black Northern troops performed valiantly in the doomed assault against Fort Wagner. What were they trying to prove to the world?

- Abraham Lincoln's reputation recently has come under attack from both the right and the left. The right stresses his trampling of personal freedoms and states' rights. The left has criticized him for dragging his feet on abolishing slavery. How valid are these complaints in view of the political situation at the time?

- Discuss the article "America's Birth at Appomattox." How could the South's bitter defeat at the end of a long, bloody war provide the basis for reconciliation? How did Lincoln's treatment of surrendering Confederate forces pave the way for this reconciliation?

- How and why did Radical Reconstruction fail to achieve its goals? How can author Eric Foner claim that it nonetheless provided an "animating vision" for the future?

Student Website

www.mhcls.com/online

Internet References

Further information regarding these websites may be found in this book's preface or online.

The American Civil War
   http://sunsite.utk.edu/civil-war/warweb.html

Anacostia Museum/Smithsonian Institution
   http://www.si.edu/archives/historic/anacost.htm

Abraham Lincoln Online
   http://www.netins.net/showcase/creative/lincoln.html

Gilder Lehrman Institute of American History
   http://www.digitalhistory.uh.edu/index.cfm?

Secession Era Editorials Project
   http://history.furman.edu/~benson/docs/dsmenu.htm

Sectionalism plagued the United States from its inception. The Constitutional proviso that slaves would count as three-fifths of a person for representational purposes, for instance, or that treaties had to be passed in the senate by two-thirds majorities grew out of sectional compromises. Manufacturing and commercial interests were strong in the North. Such interests generally supported high tariffs to protect industries, and the construction of turnpikes, canals, and railroads to expand domestic markets. The South, largely rural and agricultural, strongly opposed such measures. Southerners believed that tariffs cost them money that went to line the pockets of Northern manufacturers, and had little interest in what were known as "internal improvements." Such differences could be resolved because there were no moral issues involved, and matters such as tariffs aroused few emotions in the public.

The question of slavery added a different dimension. Part of the quarrel involved economic considerations. Northerners feared that the spread of slavery would discriminate against "free" farming in the west. Southerners just as adamantly believed that the institution should be allowed to exist wherever it proved feasible. Disputes in 1820 and again in 1850 resulted in compromises that papered over these differences, but they satisfied no one. As time wore on, more and more Northerners came to regard slavery as sinful, an abomination that must be stamped out. Southerners, on the other hand, grew more receptive to the idea that slavery actually was beneficial to both blacks and whites and was condoned by the Bible. Now cast in moral terms, the issue could not be resolved in the fashion of tariff disputes by splitting differences. In what became an increasingly emotional atmosphere, John Brown's raid touched off an explosion of feverish charges and countercharges by both sides.

Moderates in the two national parties, the Whigs and Democrats, tried to keep the slavery question from tearing the country in two. Though suffering some defections, the Democrats managed to stay together until the elections of 1860. The Whigs, however, fell apart during the 1850s. The emergence of the Republican Party, with its strength almost exclusively based in the North, signalled the beginning of the end. Southerners came to regard the Republicans as the party of abolitionism. Abraham Lincoln, Republican presidential candidate in 1860, tried to assure Southerners that although he opposed the spread of slavery he had no intentions of seeking to abolish the institution where it already existed. He was not widely believed in the South. Republican victory in 1860 seemed to them, or at least to the hotheads among them, to threaten not just slavery but the entire Southern society. One by one Southern states began seceding, and Lincoln's unwillingness to let them destroy the union led to the Civil War.

"Free at Last" describes the operations of what became known as the "underground railroad." White Southerners detested and feared its existence for two reasons beyond the sheer number of escapees. First, it revealed the fallacy of Southern arguments that slavery was a benevolent institution and that slaves were a happy, contented lot. Second, it seemed clear that despite what politicians might say, large numbers of Northerners were willing to break the law in order to destroy slavery where it existed. "The Volume of History: Listening to 19th Century America" takes a novel approach to the deepening sectional conflict. Author Mark Smith argues that we must pay attention to aural as well as visual senses. Northerners "heard" the sounds of slavery: the crack of the overseer's lash, the shrieks of slaves being beaten. Southerners "listening" to the North heard the roar of factories and the discordant sounds of crowded city streets.

Once the war got underway, many on both sides believed it would be over quickly. They were wrong. What began as a limited conflict turned into total war against resources and morale. In addition to offensive military operations, the North with its superior navy sought to cripple the South through blockading its ports. "Richmond's Bread Riots" shows how effective such efforts were. In 1863, thousands of women marched in the streets of Richmond demanding food. Confederate President Jefferson Davis had to threaten to open fire on the protestors to get them to disperse.

There are two essays on the actual conduct of the war. "Night and Death on Little Round Top" describes a bloody encounter during the Battle of Gettysburg. What is noteworthy about this article is that it is based to a great extent on letters written by participants after the battle was over. "A Gallant Rush for Glory," provides an account of a courageous assault by a black regiment against a Southern stronghold in South Carolina.

Most scholars regard Abraham Lincoln as one of our greatest presidents. In recent years, as Dinesh D'Souza points out in "Lincoln as Statesman," attacks on him have come from both the political right and left. Right-wingers denounce him as a self-serving tyrant who ran roughshod over civil liberties and who greatly expanded the size of the federal government. Left-wingers criticize him as a racist who really did not care about abolishing slavery.

Lincoln's goal was to achieve reconciliation between the North and South at war's end. When Confederate General Robert E. Lee surrendered his troops at Appomattox Courthouse in Virginia, on April 7, 1865, the president ordered Northern General U. S. Grant to offer the Southerners most lenient terms. "America's Birth at Appomattox" makes the case that what might have caused lasting bitterness on the part of the vanquished actually formed the basis for uniting the nation. How far Lincoln might have carried out his plans to reintegrate the South without vindictiveness will never be known for he was assassinated one week after Appomattox. "Death of John Wilkes Booth" provides an eyewitness account of the assassin's capture and demise.

A struggle took place after the war ended over how the South should be reintegrated into the Union. The most important issue was what status blacks would have in the postwar society. Moderates such as Lincoln wished to make Reconstruction as painless as possible even though this meant continued white domination of the Southern states. "Radical" or "advanced" Republicans wished to guarantee freed people the full rights of citizenship, using force if necessary to achieve this goal. Southern whites resisted "Radical Reconstruction" any way they could, and ultimately prevailed when Northern will eroded. Eric Foner's "The New View of Reconstruction" argues that even though Radical Reconstruction failed in the short run, it provided an "animating vision" for the future.

FREE
AT LAST

A NEW MUSEUM CELEBRATES THE **Underground Railroad**
THE SECRET NETWORK OF PEOPLE WHO BRAVELY LED SLAVES TO LIBERTY BEFORE THE CIVIL WAR.

Fergus M. Bordewich

THE PHONE RANG one drizzly morning in Carl Westmoreland's office overlooking the gray ribbon of the Ohio River and downtown Cincinnati. It was February 1998. Westmoreland, a descendant of slaves, scholar of African-American history and former community organizer, had recently joined the staff of the National Underground Railroad Freedom Center. Then still in the planning stages, the center, which opened this past August in Cincinnati, is the nation's first institution dedicated to the clandestine pre-Civil War network that helped tens of thousands of fugitive slaves gain their freedom.

The caller, who identified himself as Raymond Evers, claimed that a 19th-century "slave jail" was located on his property in northern Kentucky; he wanted someone to come out to look at it. As word of the center had gotten around, Westmoreland had begun to receive a lot of calls like this one, from individuals who said their house contained secret hiding places or who reported mysterious tunnels on their property. He had investigated many of these sites. Virtually none turned out to have any connection with the Underground Railroad.

"I'll call you back tomorrow," Westmoreland said.

The next day, his phone rang again. It was Evers. "So when are you coming out?" he asked. Westmoreland sighed. "I'm on my way," he said.

An hour later, Westmoreland, a wiry man then in his early 60s, was slogging across a sodden alfalfa pasture in Mason County, Kentucky, eight miles south of the Ohio River, accompanied by Evers, 67, a retired businessman. The two made their way to a dilapidated tobacco barn at the top of a low hill.

"Where is it?" Westmoreland asked.

"Just open the door!" Evers replied.

In the darkened interior, Westmoreland made out a smaller structure built of rough-hewn logs and fitted with

barred windows. Fastened to a joist inside the log hut were iron rings: fetters to which manacled slaves had once been chained. "I felt the way I did when I went to Auschwitz," Westmoreland later recalled. "I felt the power of the place—it was dark, ominous. When I saw the rings, I thought, it's like a slave-ship hold."

At first, Westmoreland had difficulty tracking down the history of the structure, where tobacco, corn and farm machinery had been stored for decades. But eventually Westmoreland located a Mason County resident who had heard from his father, who had heard from his grandfather, what had gone on in the little enclosure. "They chained 'em up over there, and sold 'em off like cattle," the Mason County man told Westmoreland.

At Westmoreland's urging, the Freedom Center accepted Evers' offer to donate the 32- by 27-foot structure. It was dismantled and transported to Cincinnati; the total cost for archaeological excavation and preservation was $2 million. When the Freedom Center opened its doors on August 23, the stark symbol of brutality was the first thing that visitors encountered in the lofty atrium facing the Ohio River. Says Westmoreland: "This institution represents the first time that there has been an honest effort to honor and preserve our collective memory, not in a basement or a slum somewhere, but at the front door of a major metropolitan community."

By its own definition a "museum of conscience," the 158,000-square-foot copper-roofed structure hopes to engage visitors in a visceral way. "This is not a slavery museum," says executive director Spencer Crew, who moved to Cincinnati from Washington, D.C., where he was director of the Smithsonian Institution's National Museum of American History. "Rather, it is a place to engage people on the subject of slavery and race without finger-pointing. Yes, the center shows that slavery was terrible. But it also shows that there were people who stood up against it."

Visitors will find, in addition to the slave jail, artifacts including abolitionists' diaries, wanted posters, ads for runaways, documents granting individual slaves their freedom and newspapers such as William Lloyd Garrison's militant *Liberator*, the first in the United States to call for immediate abolition. And they will encounter one of the most powerful symbols of slavery: shackles. "Shackles exert an almost mystical fascination," says Rita C. Organ, the center's director of exhibits and collections. "There were even small-sized shackles for children. By looking at them, you get a feeling of what our ancestors must have felt—suddenly you begin to imagine what it was like being huddled in a coffle of chained slaves on the march."

Additional galleries relate stories of the central figures in the Underground Railroad. Some, like Frederick Douglass and Harriet Tubman, are renowned. Many others, such as John P. Parker, a former slave who became a key activist in the Ohio underground, and his collaborator, abolitionist John Rankin, are little known.

Other galleries document the experiences of present-day Americans, people like Laquetta Shepard, a 24-year-old black West Virginia woman who in 2002 walked into the middle of a Ku Klux Klan rally and shamed the crowd into dispersing, and Syed Ali, a Middle Eastern gas station owner in New York City who prevented members of a radical Islamic group from setting fire to a neighborhood synagogue in 2003. Says Crew, "Ideally, we would like to create modern-day equivalents of the Underground Railroad conductors, who have the internal fortitude to buck society's norms and to stand up for the things they really believe in."

The center's concept grew out of a tumultuous period in the mid-1990s when Cincinnati was reeling from confrontations between the police and the African-American community and when Marge Schott, then the owner of the Cincinnati Reds, made comments widely regarded as racist. At a 1994 meeting of the Cincinnati chapter of the National Conference of Christians and Jews, its then-director, Robert "Chip" Harrod, proposed the idea of a museum devoted to the Underground Railroad. Since then, the center has raised some $60 million from private donations and another $50 million from public sources, including the Department of Education.

THE TERM UNDERGROUND RAILROAD is said to derive from the story of a frustrated slave hunter who, having failed to apprehend a runaway, exclaimed, "He must have gone off on an underground road!" In an age when smoke-belching locomotives and shining steel rails were novelties, activists from New York to Illinois, many of whom had never seen an actual railroad, readily adopted its terminology, describing guides as "conductors," safe houses as "stations," horse-drawn wagons as "cars," and fugitives as "passengers."

Says Ira Berlin, author of *Many Thousands Gone: The First Two Centuries of Slavery in North America:* "The Underground Railroad played a critical role, by making the nature of slavery clear to Northerners who had been indifferent to it, by showing that slaves who were running away were neither happy nor well-treated, as apologists for slavery claimed. And morally, it demonstrated the enormous resiliency of the human spirit in the collaboration of blacks and whites to help people gain their freedom."

Thanks to the clandestine network, as many as 150,000 slaves may have found their way to safe havens in the North and Canada. "We don't know the total number and we will probably never know," says James O. Horton, a professor of American studies and history at George Washington University in Washington, D.C. "Part of the reason is that the underground was so successful: it kept its secrets well."

> By the 1850s, activists from Delaware to Kansas had joined the underground to help fugitives elude capture. Wrote abolitionist Gerrit Smith in 1836: "If there be human enactments against our opening our door to our colored brother. . . .We must obey God."

As the nation's second great civil disobedience movement—the first being the actions, including the Boston Tea Party, leading to the American Revolution—the Underground Railroad engaged thousands of citizens in the subversion of federal law. The movement provoked fear and anger in the South and prompted the enactment of draconian legislation, including the 1850 Fugitive Slave Law, which required Northerners to cooperate in the capture of escaped slaves. And at a time when proslavery advocates insisted that blacks were better off in bondage because they lacked the intelligence or ability to take care of themselves, it also gave many African-Americans experience in political organizing and resistance.

"The Underground Railroad symbolized the intensifying struggle over slavery," says Berlin. "It was the result of the ratcheting up of the earlier antislavery movement, which in the years after the American Revolution, had begun to call for compensated emancipation and gradualist solutions to slavery." In the North, it brought African-Americans, often for the first time, into white communities where they could be seen as real people, with real families and real feelings. Ultimately, Berlin says, "the Underground Railroad forced whites to confront the reality of race in American society and to begin to wrestle with the reality in which black people lived all the time. It was a transforming experience."

FOR BLACKS AND WHITES alike the stakes were high. Underground agents faced a constant threat of punitive litigation, violent reprisal and possible death. "White participants in the underground found in themselves a depth of humanity that they hadn't realized they had," says Horton. "And for many of them, humanity won out over legality." As New York philanthropist Gerrit Smith, one of the most important financiers of the Underground Railroad, put it in 1836, "If there be human enactments against our entertaining the stricken stranger—against our opening our door to our poor, guiltless, and unaccused colored brother pursued by blood-thirsty kidnappers—we must, nevertheless, say with the apostle: 'We must obey God rather than man.'"

From the earliest years of American bondage—the Spanish held slaves in Florida in the late 1500s; Africans were sold to colonists at Jamestown in 1619—slaves had fled their masters. But until British Canada and some Northern states—including Pennsylvania and Massachusetts—began abolishing slavery at the end of the 18th century, there were no permanent havens for fugitives. A handful of slaves found sanctuary among several Native American tribes deep in the swamps and forests of Florida. The first coordinated Underground Railroad activity can be traced to the early 19th century, perhaps when free blacks and white Quakers began to provide refuge for runaways in and around Philadelphia, or perhaps when activists organized in Ohio.

The process accelerated throughout the 1830s. "The whole country was like a huge pot in a furious state of boiling over," recalled Addison Coffin in 1897. Coffin served as an underground conductor in North Carolina and Indiana. "It was almost universal for ministers of the gospel to run into the subject in all their sermons; neighbors would stop and argue pro and con across the fence; people traveling along the road would stop and argue the point." Although abolitionists initially faced the contempt of a society that largely took the existence of slavery for granted, the underground would eventually count among its members Rutherford B. Hayes, the future president, who as a young lawyer in the 1850s defended fugitive slaves; William Seward, the future governor of New York and secretary of state, who provided financial support to Harriet Tubman and other underground activists; and Allan Pinkerton, founder of the Pinkerton Detective Agency, who in 1859 helped John Brown lead a band of fugitive slaves out of Chicago and on to Detroit, bound for Canada. By the 1850s, the underground ranged from the northern borders of states including Maryland, Virginia and Kentucky to Canada and numbered thousands among its ranks from Delaware to Kansas.

But its center was the Ohio River Valley, where scores of river crossings served as gateways from slave states to free and where, once across the Ohio, fugitives could hope to be passed from farm to farm all the way to the Great Lakes in a matter of days.

In practice, the underground functioned with a minimum of central direction and a maximum of grass-roots involvement, particularly among family members and church congregations. "The method of operating was not uniform but adapted to the requirements of each case," Isaac Beck, a veteran of Underground Railroad activity in southern Ohio, would recall in 1892. "There was no regular organization, no constitution, no officers, no laws or agreement or rule except the 'Golden Rule,' and every man did what seemed right in his own eyes." Travel was by foot, horseback or wagon. One stationmaster, Levi Coffin, an Indiana Quaker and Addison's uncle, kept a team of horses harnessed and a wagon ready to go at his farm in Newport (now Fountain City), Indiana. When additional teams were needed, Coffin wrote in his memoir, posthumously published in 1877, "the people at the livery stable seemed to understand what the teams were wanted for, and they asked no questions."

On occasion, fugitives might be transported in hearses or false-bottomed wagons, men might be disguised as women, women as men, blacks powdered white with talc. The volume of underground traffic varied widely. Levi Coffin estimated that during his lifetime he assisted 3,300 fugitives—some 100 or so annually—while others, who lived along more lightly traveled routes, took in perhaps two or three a month, or only a handful over several years.

> The underground clarified the nature of slavery (fugitives brought ashore in Philadelphia in 1856) to Northerners. As the railroad accelerated, "the whole country," wrote conductor Addison Coffin in 1897, "was like a huge pot in a state of boiling over."

ONE OF THE MOST ACTIVE underground centers—and the subject of a 15-minute docudrama, *Brothers of the Borderland*, produced for the Freedom Center and introduced by Oprah Winfrey—was Ripley, Ohio, about 50 miles east of Cincinnati. Today, Ripley is a sleepy village of two- and three-story 19th-century houses nestled at the foot of low bluffs, facing south toward the Ohio River and the cornfields of Kentucky beyond. But in the decades preceding the Civil War, it was one of the busiest ports between Pittsburgh and Cincinnati, its economy fueled by river traffic, shipbuilding and pork butchering. To slave owners, it was known as "a black, dirty Abolition hole"—and with good reason. Since the 1820s, a network of radical white Presbyterians, led by the Rev. John Rankin, a flinty Tennessean who had moved north to escape the atmosphere of slavery, collaborated with local blacks on both sides of the river in one of the most successful underground operations.

The Rankins' simple brick farmhouse still stands on a hilltop. It was visible for miles along the river and well into Kentucky. Arnold Gragston, who as a slave in Kentucky ferried scores of fugitives across the then 500- to 1,500-foot-wide Ohio River, later recalled that Rankin had a "lighthouse in his yard, about thirty feet high."

Recently, local preservationist Betty Campbell led the way into the austere parlor of the Rankin house, now a museum open to the public. She pointed out the fireplace where hundreds of runaways warmed themselves on winter nights, as well as the upstairs crawl space where, on occasion, they hid. Because the Rankins lived so close to the river and within easy reach of slave hunters, they generally sheltered fugitives only briefly before leading them on horseback along an overgrown streambed through a forest to a neighboring farmhouse a few miles north.

"The river divided the two worlds by law, the North and the South, but the cultures were porous," Campbell said, gazing across the river's gray trough toward the bluffs of Kentucky, a landscape not much altered since the mid-19th century. "There were antislavery men in Kentucky, and also proslavery men here in Ohio, where a lot of people had Southern origins and took slavery for granted. Frequently, trusted slaves were sent from Kentucky to the market at Ripley."

For families like the Rankins, the clandestine work became a full-time vocation. Jean Rankin, John's wife, was responsible for seeing that a fire was burning in the hearth and food kept on the table. At least one of the couple's nine sons remained on call, prepared to saddle up and hasten his charges to the next way station. "It was the custom with us not to talk among ourselves about the fugitives lest inadvertently a clue should be obtained of our modus operandi," the Rankins' eldest son, Adam, wrote years later in an unpublished memoir. "'Another runaway went through at night' was all that would be said."

One Rankin collaborator, Methodist minister John B. Mahan, was arrested at his home and taken back to Kentucky, where after 16 months in jail he was made to pay a ruinous fine that impoverished his family and likely contributed to his early death. In the summer of 1841, Kentucky slaveholders assaulted the Rankins' hilltop stronghold. They were repulsed only after a gun battle that left one of the attackers dead. Not even the Rankins would cross the river into Kentucky, where the penalty for "slave stealing" was up to 21 years' imprisonment. One Ripley man who did so repeatedly was John P. Parker, a former slave who had bought his freedom in Mobile, Alabama; by day, he operated an iron foundry. By night, he ferried slaves from Kentucky plantations across the river to Ohio. Although no photograph of Parker has survived, his saga has been preserved in a series of interviews recorded in the 1880s and published in 1996 as *His Promised Land: The Autobiography of John P. Parker*.

On one occasion, Parker learned that a party of fugitives, stranded after the capture of their leader, was hiding about 20 miles south of the river. "Being new and zealous in this work, I volunteered to go to the rescue," Parker recalled. Armed with a pair of pistols and a knife, and guided by another slave, Parker reached the runaways at about dawn. He found them hidden in deep woods, paralyzed with fear and "so badly demoralized that some of them wanted to give themselves up rather than face the unknown." Parker led the ten men and women for miles through dense thickets.

> As many as 150,000 slaves may have gained freedom. "We will probably never know [the total]," says historian James O. Horton. "Part of the reason is that the underground was so successful: it kept its secrets well."

With slave hunters closing in, one of the fugitives insisted on setting off in search of water. He had gone only a short way before he came hurtling through the brush, pursued by two white men. Parker turned to the slaves still in hiding. "Drawing my pistol," he recalled, "I quietly told them that I would shoot the first one that dared make a noise, which had a quieting effect." Through thickets, Parker saw the captured slave being led away, his arms tied behind his back. The group proceeded to the river, where a patroller spotted them.

Though the lights of Ripley were visible across the water, "they might as well have been [on] the moon so far as being a relief to me," Parker recalled. Bloodhounds baying in their ears, the runaways located a rowboat quickly enough, but it had room for only eight people. Two would have to be left behind. When the wife of one of the men picked to stay behind began to wail, Parker would recall, "I witnessed an example of heroism that made me proud of my race." One of the men in the boat gave up his seat to the woman's husband. As Parker rowed toward Ohio and freedom, he saw slave hunters converge on the spot where the two men had been left behind. "I knew," he wrote later, "the poor fellow had been captured in sight of the promised land."

Parker carried a $2,500 price on his head. More than once, his house was searched and he was assaulted in the streets of Ripley. Yet he estimated that he managed to help some 440 fugitives to freedom. In 2002, Parker's house on the Ripley waterfront—restored by a local citizens' group headed by Campbell—opened to the public.

ON A CLEAR DAY last spring, Carl Westmoreland returned to the Evers farm. Since his first visit, he had learned that the slave jail had been built in the 1830s by a prosperous slave trader, John Anderson, who used it to hold slaves en route by flatboat to the huge slave market at Natchez, Mississippi, where auctions were held several times a year. Anderson's manor house is gone now, as are the cabins of the slaves who served in his household, tended his land and probably even operated the jail itself.

"The jail is a perfect symbol of forgetting," Westmoreland said at the time, not far from the slave trader's overgrown grave. "For their own reasons, whites and blacks both tried to forget about that jail, just as the rest of America tried to forget about slavery. But that building has already begun to teach, by causing people to go back and look at the local historical record. It's doing its job." Anderson died in 1834 at the age of 42. Westmoreland continued: "They say that he tripped over a grapevine and fell onto the sharp stump of a cornstalk, which penetrated his eye and entered his brain. He was chasing a runaway slave."

FERGUS M. BORDEWICH is the author of Bound for Canaan: The Underground Railroad and the War for the Soul of America, *to be published in April by Amistad/HarperCollins.*

The Volume of History:
LISTENING TO 19TH-CENTURY AMERICA

Mark M. Smith

IN SIMPLE QUAKER DRESS, determined face framed by dark curls, the 33-year-old South Carolinian stood before a packed Massachusetts legislature in Boston on February 21, 1838. Nervous and apprehensive, she prepared to convince her audience why Southern slavery should be abolished and to explain women's role in the process. Her jitters were understandable. While sympathetic ears filled the hall, scoffers doubting whether a woman should speak so publicly and politically abounded. Angelina Grimké was not the first American woman to denounce slavery, but until that day none had spoken to an American legislative body.

A hush fell. "Mr. Chairman," she began. Her words punched the stillness with the force of novelty. She hit stride, regaling listeners with thoughts on the religious and political enormities of bondage. Her voice rang with the authenticity of someone who had witnessed slavery firsthand. In her choice of images, Grimké conveyed the wretchedness of the peculiar institution in a way that touched hearts and hardened resolves: "I stand before you as a Southerner, exiled from the land of my birth, by the sound of the lash, and the piteous cry of the slave."

What she said was heard in more than one sense. Enabling and urging her audience to hear not just her words but also the sounds of bondage was a way to tease at her listeners' guts and hearts. For many in the hall who had never actually heard slavery, they could now imagine how it sounded. Of course, there were many Northerners who could not or did not have the inclination to hear Grimké's aural representation of slavery. But actual hearing was not necessary, because her speech was reprinted in the antislavery newspaper the *Liberator* a few days later, on March 2. Her aural depiction and its authenticity were replayed via print, and readers, too, could now hear, imagine, and reimagine what she had heard and wanted them to hear.

> Because sound was so embedded in antebellum life and consciousness, we must listen as much to the economic and the political as to the cultural.

Angelina Grimké was neither the first nor the last to represent slavery aurally. Abolitionist travelers to the Old South and, especially, escaped slaves who recounted their experiences to Northerners did the same.

While there was doubtless some recognition that they exaggerated the frequency of screams, lashes, and clanking chains, their characterizations of Southern sounds gained widespread acceptance among abolitionists of all stripes and, later, among supporters of free soil and free labor. For many Northerners, the South became a place alien and threatening because of how it sounded.

IN FOLLOWING YEARS, other speakers added their voices and constructed the South as at once resounding with the noises of bondage and the silence of Southern political tyranny and economic backwardness. Increasingly, abolitionists, free soilers, and Republicans constructed the South as aurally distinct and depraved. Northern advocates of progress also increasingly applauded the virtues of their own soundscape, in contrast to the noises of slavery, for in the hum of industry and the buzz of freedom they heard a society that not only was different from the South but also reaffirmed their belief in the superiority of industrial, urban, free-labor modernity.

William M. Bobo liked to travel. In the early 1850s, the genteel South Carolinian jaunted north to New York City, and in 1852 he published his impressions of the place in a brief travelogue, *Glimpses of New-York City, by a South Carolinian (Who Had Nothing Else to Do)*. "A stranger to New-York City," he began, "has many things to see and hear, most of which he does not really understand." Part of his job was to explain. Resounding with rush and crowd, Gotham was a place where emphatically large and fashionable hotels suffered from too much noise and confusion. The city echoed with the excesses of wage labor and Northern capitalism, and its dissonance became more grating the farther he ventured. Bobo prepared his readers' senses: "Any one who walks the streets of New-York with his eyes and ears open, sees and hears many strange and horrid things." Poverty, sickness, filth, crime, and wretchedness echoed in one ear while, in stark aural contrast, silk rustles of the sashaying skirts of bourgeois women sounded in the other. Islands of tranquility could be found, of course, but they only accentuated city noise.

Just outside the city, in Yonkers, he found residences "free from the musquitoes, dust and noise of the city." But time was not on the side of such quietude: "New-York will be out here one of these days." The expansive tendencies of Northern capitalism would introduce "the noisy and vexatious walks of the living" to Yonkers and places even farther removed. The future sounded bleak to this man of the South.

Back in the city—this time at Five Points—Bobo ventured into one of several drinking and dance houses. "There lies a drunken female, screaming and yelling" while men were "cursing and swearing in the most blasphemous manner, a sort of medley which is indescribable." Overwhelmed, he abandoned his narrative: "Let us get out, my senses refuse to behold longer such scenes." Massive immigration, the exploitation of young factory women, and the general misery and wretchedness of wage-labor society only "sickens the senses." Northern capitalism, urbanization, and industrialization had introduced more "poverty, prostitution, wretchedness, drunkenness, and all the attending vices, in this city, than in the whole South." Minimizing the extent to which similar sounds could be heard in the urban South, Bobo remarked, "This is a comment upon Northern institutions."

William Bobo's aural representations of New York City and Northern modernity were hardly new, and similar examples can be found beginning principally in the 1830s, when Southern defenders of slavery began to hear the rise of what they perceived as an aggressive and threatening Northern society. Often in response to abolitionists' critiques of slavery's evil strains, Southern elites and politicians countered with the kind of aural critique of Northern society offered by Bobo. Southern representations of the Northern soundscape and all that it stood for were expressed in print, communicating the failings of the North to many Southerners who had never actually heard it.

The pro-slavery thinker George Fitzhugh, for example, did not visit, see, hear, or experience the North firsthand until 1855, but he, like Grimké's audiences, had read enough to learn how to listen and what to hear. In all likelihood, Fitzhugh had at some point in his life heard sounds of slavery similar to those that assaulted Grimké's ears, but he, like Bobo and other elite white Southerners, rarely commented on those aspects of the Southern soundscape. Instead, Fitzhugh listened for what he and others believed were the keynotes of Southern society—tranquility and quietude, punctuated by a healthy dose of humming industriousness and the melodies of singing slaves—and contrasted them with what they believed was the destructiveness of Northern modernity. In his 1850 *Slavery Justified*, Fitzhugh argued that the social arrangement of slavery and its harmonizing of labor and capital meant that "we have no mobs, no trades unions, no strikes for higher wages," and "but few in our jails, and fewer in our poorhouses." The consequence was heard as much as seen: "At the slaveholding South all is peace, quiet, plenty and contentment."

Following his visit North, in 1857 Fitzhugh published *Cannibals All!*, a scathing critique of the dangerous tendencies of wage labor. What he had previously read about how Northern society sounded was confirmed by the cultural bias of his hearing and selective listening. The competition between labor and capital, he maintained, led to revolution, and its beginnings could be heard in the noises of poverty, wretchedness, and strife that would reach a crescendo in a destructive cacophony of social dislocation. When capitalists' efforts to tame workers' demands had failed ("We must use violence to keep you quiet," Fitzhugh imagined them saying), "the maddening cry of hunger for employment and bread" would culminate in "the grumbling noise of the heaving volcano that threatens and precedes a social eruption greater than the world has yet witnessed." The rumblings of class conflict and social revolution could be heard in the noises of industrialism, capitalism, and unfettered exploitation.

While exceptional in several respects, Grimké, Bobo, and Fitzhugh were typical in how they understood, imagined, and projected their abstract and actual environments and sectional identities. Most 19th-century Americans experienced their worlds through their senses. At times they understood by using—deliberately and unwittingly—all five senses at once (if they had them); at other times one sense took primacy, but rarely to the exclusion of the others.

It seems almost audacious to point out that in the past, people sensed their worlds, their environments, and their places. Obvious though that fact is, however, it warrants stating, not least because we are prone to examine the past through the eyes of those who experienced it. While people interpreted their worlds visually, it is also worth iterating that seeing was but one way in which they experienced. Yet, for reasons that have to do with the 19th-century preoccupation with visuality, the rise of print culture, and the long shadows cast by those developments, it seems fair to say that a good deal of historical work interprets the past principally, if unwittingly and implicitly, through historical actors' eyes.

Historians rarely consider in any explicit or systematic way the other four senses, and so a good deal of what we know about most historical experience is really a history of what people saw. In this sense (literally), we understand the past in one-fifth of its texture and scope, and historical analyses of how people sensed—heard, tasted, smelled, and touched—are staggeringly few and far between.

Without listening to what and how 19th-century Americans heard, we will remain only partially aware of the depth, texture, and nature of sectional identity and deny ourselves access to a fuller explanation of how that identity came into being with such

terrible resolve. Sectional consciousness was sensed, and hearing and listening as much as looking and seeing were important to its creation.

SOUNDS AND THEIR MEANINGS are shaped by the cultural, economic, and political contexts in which they are produced and heard. Because sound was so embedded in the various fabrics of antebellum American life and consciousness, we must listen as much to the economic and the political as to the cultural if we are to begin to recover the principal meanings that lay in their articulation. Treating aural history as simply a cultural, political, or economic project denudes the past of its interrelated texture and contributes to our deafness by denying us an understanding of how political sounds were shaped by, and in turn influenced, cultural whispers, economic booms, and social screams. Heard worlds, like the seen, were so intimately connected that to reveal their full complexity, we should listen to them in their entirety as best we can.

Contemporaries' insertion of aural imagery into the medium of published discourse effectively gave lasting voice to what is sometimes wrongly considered the silent medium of print. Printed aural projections of sectional identity and a variety of other matters were powerful and palpable because the printed words used to convey the various sounds and their meanings rendered aurality permanent and rescued them from the ephemerality of voice. In this way, what would have remained temporary, elusive sound (many arguments were offered in the form of public speeches) gained permanence in the world. Unlike the modern ability to record and thereby reproduce sounds precisely, the

antebellum aural metaphor and projection that were communicated through print (and actual hearing) allowed contemporaries to have access to a permanent image of how each section (and other things) supposedly sounded. Hearing the sounds did nothing to contradict those printed images and, in fact, largely confirmed and heightened them. Time and again the imagery of how each section of the country sounded was recorded first in the ear, then in a print version that stripped the sounds of their nuance and replaced them with a clumsy written representation, thus giving readers access to a captured record of sectional aurality that they, in turn, could repeat with their voices to other ears.

ELITE CLASSES within each section varied enormously, and the term "elite" captures a general but evolving worldview broadly shared by men and women who articulated the principal ideas of their class and section. Whatever their specific differences, Northern patricians and the new bourgeoisie shared much not only in their assessments of the Northern laboring classes, but, critically, in their understanding and depiction of Southern slaveholding society. The Northern elite—ranging from aristocratic Boston Brahmins to reform-minded abolitionists and capitalists—believed in the virtues of gentility and highbrow culture and, for the most part, the desirability of free labor and virtuous political democracy. On some important matters, Northern elites disagreed, and their differences were manifest in their formal political-party loyalties. But their general preoccupation with gentility and, beginning in the 1830s, the question of slavery muted a good deal of their differences, so that in the 30 or so years before 1860, particularly in the 1850s, many Northerners of all political persuasions united in a broad agreement that slavery was dangerous to the future of the United States and debilitating to aspects of the American present.

Southern elites were similarly variegated and diverse. Southern industrialists, merchants, and the urban middle class sometimes locked horns with the numerically smaller but far more influential planter class. Nor were planters in agreement on all matters (few ruling classes ever are). Again, though, the ways in which merchants, industrialists, and planters were linked through interest, kinship, and their broad support of Southern slavery ensured that major disagreements began to evaporate in the closing decades of the antebellum period. In the face of the Northern critique of slaveholding society, Southern elites, with the planter class at the helm, coalesced around a simple but powerful credo: Southern slavery and all that it stood for were not only desirable but deserving of protection. Whatever nationalist sentiment united Northern and Southern elites, whatever they shared in common, slavery proved the fundamental issue on which they could not agree.

Sectional awareness was shaped by what elites heard at the everyday level of social, economic, and political interaction. Neither Southern nor Northern antebellum patricians considered their heard world utterly harmonious—strains of discord were everywhere. North and South, antebellum workers used the transgressive nature of noise and the disturbing power of silence to limit and sometimes end their exploitation. In doing so, they initiated strategies and tactics of resistance that threatened to rupture the ideal soundscape and the social, economic, and political security that it represented to elites. For the most part, though, respec-tive elites took considerable comfort in how their societies sounded. Northern elites reveled in the hum of industrialism and the satisfying sounds of free and wage labor. When they listened to class relations in the North, they heard discord and noise but also the tremendous productive capacity of capitalism, and they considered the accompanying strains generated by lower orders as sounds necessary for the successful prosecution of their great experiment.

Alternatively, Southern masters cultivated the hum of slavery and emphasized the serenity of Southern social relations. They, too, saw and heard discord within the South, but they prided themselves on their ability to levy quietude on their society. Slaveholders did not reject modernity in toto. They cultivated economic productivity and embraced its sounds. Railroads chuffed happily in their ears, and the sounds of timed labor anchored them to an idealized past and a prosperous future. Even limited urbanization and industrialization were acceptable. But the quietude of plantation life and all the conservatism that masters invested in that serenity were sacrosanct. In other words, while Northern elites often considered noise a necessary component of modernism, Southern slaveholders wanted modernity with quietude, a notion that differed from the image (and, increasingly, the reality) of the ideal soundscape peddled by Northern abolitionists and capitalists.

While ruling classes in the two sections agreed on much, they argued vehemently over the preferred form of social and economic relations. In that debate, sounds took on profound meaning. A rapidly modernizing North listened to the South and heard the shrieks of slavery, the awful silence of oppression, and the unmistakable tones of moral, economic, and po-litical premodernity. Southern masters listened to the North and heard, with increasing volume, so it seemed, the disquieting throb of a mob made reckless by industrialism, urbanism, wage labor, and passionate democracy. Elites both North and South constructed one another aurally; they attempted to change how one another sounded, and they used aural descriptions and representations to try to effect that change. Abolitionists shouted southward, exercising the throat of democracy to critique their perception of silent tyranny and cacophonous slavery. They wanted the masters to hear the benefits of Northern democracy, the productive capacity of free-wage labor, and the undesirability of slavery. A variety of ostensibly competing Northern voices joined the refrain in the mid-1850s, with Republicans and some Northern Democrats applauding the satisfying melody of free labor and castigating the economic and political sounds and silences of slavery.

FOR THEIR PART, Southern masters shouted back and then applied tools of silencing that they had sharpened in their own society. Indeed, as parts of the masters' world came to sound vaguely Northern, they pushed hard to block out those sounds and deafen their population to the evil strains being flung southward. Both sectional ruling classes played on the ear to define themselves as legitimate and cast the "other" as reprehensible.

Given that elites invested so much of their identity in how their society sounded, and given that they heard their pasts and their futures, it is hardly surprising that they acted with a degree of emotional commitment to the preservation of the aural integrity of their society that might strike modern observers as excessive and irresponsible. But precisely because they invested such authority in the heard world, their behavior is perfectly understandable. Sounds of social and economic relations, slavery, and freedom were so meaningful that they helped shape the psycho-acoustical perception of a region. Sounds, noises, and silences took on tactile qualities that proved real, substantive, and palpable for political elites from both sections. Northern and Southern ruling classes did not go to war solely because they listened to one another and disliked what they heard (just as the Civil War was not solely a product of what they saw of one another). Aural representations joined visual ones, and once we begin to understand how sectional con-sciousness was channeled, fed, and articulated through more than one sense, it becomes far more understandable how sectionalism assumed such concrete dimensions and ferocity. A reliance on visuality alone is likely to understate the emotional, visceral quality of the coming of the Civil War, but by adding acoustemological considerations we approach a fuller understanding of how sectional identities assumed such terrible force.

Sounds of war, noises of loss, shrieks of death, and chortles of success and victory followed this aural sectionalism. In a way, the Civil War was an aural victory for a modern North, not least because it cleansed the Southern soundscape of the wretched noise of slavery and paved the way for capitalism's expansion south and west. Yet the noises associated with the Civil War, the boom of battlefields, and the increasing volume of dissatisfied labor on the Northern home front only encouraged Northern elites to turn eagerly to a quiet, tamed South once the thunder of cannon and tumult of war had ended.

> Both Northern and Southern elites acted to preserve the aural integrity of their society to a degree that might strike us now as excessive and irresponsible

Mark M. Smith is a professor of history at the University of South Carolina. This article is adapted from Listening to Nineteenth-Century America, *being published this month by the University of North Carolina Press Copyright © 2001 by the University of North Carolina Press..*

Richmond's Bread Riot

The women who marched through the streets of Richmond, Virginia, in April 1863 demanded food. Facing them, Confederate President Jefferson Davis was equally adamant: If the protesters did not disperse, they would be shot.

By Alan Pell Crawford

ON THE PLEASANT SPRING MORNING of April 2, 1863, a pretty young woman sat down on a bench at Capitol Square in Richmond, Virginia. Another woman on the bench later recalled that the girl had "delicate features" and "large eyes" and wore a clean, skillfully stitched calico gown that indicated she might have been a dressmaker's apprentice. When the girl reached up to remove her sunbonnet, her sleeve slipped, revealing "the mere skeleton of an arm."

As the two women sat together, several hundred people gathered on the grounds of the Confederate Capitol. The older woman, the wife of a former U.S. congressman who was then serving in the Confederate Army, wondered what was happening. "Is there some celebration?" she asked.

"There is," the girl said with great dignity. "We celebrate our right to live. We are starving. As soon as enough of us get together, we are going to the bakeries and each of us will take a loaf of bread. That is little enough for the government to give us after it has taken all our men."

The girl then made her way to the Capitol, where she disappeared into the crowd and from history. Within minutes, the crowd she had joined became a mob and moved noisily down Ninth Street toward the shops on Main Street. No one is sure of everything that happened during the next few hours, but the so-called Bread Riot resulted in dozens of arrests and numerous convictions, further demoralizing an already suffering city.

That conditions had become so dire in the Confederate capital was somewhat ironic. Ever since agricultural Virginia had been a state, and for many years before that, Richmond had been its commercial, if not industrial, center. Many Richmonders were lawyers, merchants, and tradesmen who tended to be Federalists and then Whigs, and therefore Unionists. Governor John Letcher, who took office in 1860, was a Unionist. Richmonders even organized a failed February 1861 "peace conference" at the Willard Hotel in Washington, D.C., and Virginia did not leave the Union until April 17, 1861, four months after South Carolina seceded and two days after President Abraham Lincoln called for 75,000 volunteers to put down the "insurrection" in the Southern states.

When General Robert E. Lee came to the city to accept command of the state's forces a week after Virginia joined the Confederacy, recruits from all over the South followed. With them, as Virginius Dabney wrote in *Richmond: The Story of a City*, came "adventurers, speculators, gamblers, prostitutes and every other type of person" who gravitates to the center of activity in wartime. After the engagement at First Manassas in July 1861, when Southern troops drove Union General Irvin McDowell's Yankees back to Washington, Richmond's population—38,000 before the war—doubled, then tripled. It would reach 128,000 in 1864. Food that otherwise would be feeding the city's residents was by then being commandeered by the military. Almost constant warfare on Virginia's once-fertile farmland soon disrupted agricultural production. Before long, the military took over the railroads, further interrupting the transport of goods.

The momentum of early Southern victories at Manassas and at Ball's Bluff could not be sustained. In the late spring of 1862, Federal forces took Yorktown and Williamsburg in the Peninsular Campaign and then advanced to the outskirts of Richmond. There, spirits were sinking—and prices were rising. As soldiers on leave took advantage of the availability of alcohol and prostitutes, clogging the streets and dining in the gambling "hells" that cropped up near Capitol Square, the nature of the once-genteel city changed. Brawls had to be broken up, and in March, the Confederate Congress imposed martial law on Richmond and for an area 10 miles around the city. The new laws suspended habeas corpus, required passports for anyone leaving town, banned liquor sales without a physician's prescription, and ordered the closing of saloons and distilleries, although many continued to operate. The value of Confederate money declined, and corruption ran rampant.

In June 1862, after the Battle of Seven Pines, nearly 5,000 wounded soldiers came into Richmond, further straining the city's meager resources. A month later Lee's Army of Northern Virginia had driven the Federals away from Richmond and back to Washington, and at least 10,000 more bloodied men, plus thousands of Federal prisoners, poured into the city. And with them came still more prostitutes, who took over an entire block near Capitol Square, "promenading up and down the shady walks," Mayor Joseph Mayo complained, "jostling respectable ladies in the gutter." Venereal disease swept through the city. An outbreak of smallpox, from late 1862 to February 1863, contributed to anxieties against which even the staunchest of residents struggled.

At least 10,000 more bloodied men, plus thousands of Federal prisoners, poured into the city.

"We are in a half-starving condition," John B. Jones, a clerk in the Confederate War Department, wrote in his diary. "I lost twenty pounds and my wife and children are emaciated to some extent. Still I hear no murmuring." Rats ran amok. "Epicures sometimes manage to entrap them and secure a nice broil for supper, declaring that their flesh was superior to squirrel meat," reported Phoebe Yates Pember, a diarist who was the chief matron at one of the city's hospitals.

Food speculators, meanwhile, hoarded vast stores of flour, sugar, bacon, and salt, withholding them from market while prices soared. These speculators, President Jefferson Davis declared, were "worse enemies of the Confederacy than if found in arms among the invading forces." Governor Letcher said such profiteering "embraces to a greater or less extent all interests—agricultural, mercantile and professional." Military officials were also said to be hoarding food or, viewed in the most favorable light, making a botch of their commissary duties.

To make matters worse, nearly a foot of snow—rare in Richmond in any quantity—fell on the city in March 1863. Temperatures then rose quickly, melting the snow and turning roads into mud holes. These near-impassable roads made it difficult for farmers who had produce to sell to get their goods into town.

It was late in the month, apparently, that Mary Jackson, a "tall, daring, Amazonian-looking woman" who was married to a local house-painter, began to talk with her hungry neighbors in Oregon Hill about the need for them to take matters into their own hands. Oregon Hill was a working-class neighborhood where laborers from the Tredegar Iron Works, the largest cannon foundry in the South, made their homes.

Word quickly spread, and on the evening of April 1, Jackson and her female cohorts gathered at the nearby Belvidere Hill Baptist Church, where they decided they would demand food from the governor. The following morning, the women, led by Jackson, "who had a white feather standing erect from her hat," and Minerva Meredith, who carried a pistol, trooped over to the governor's office. Governor Letcher listened to their complaints, expressed his sympathy, and asked them to come back later. Then he might be able to help.

Unimpressed with the governor's response, the crowd moved on, gathering strength. Men and boys and more women—some carrying knives, hatchets, and guns—soon joined their ranks and made their way down Capitol Hill toward Main Street and the shops and the government commissary there. One black maid, seeing the rowdy procession, snatched her young charge away, fearing the child might "catch something from them poor white folks."

Governor Letcher ordered the bell rung in Capitol Square to call out the Public Guard (a state security force that protected the Capitol and other government buildings), as Richmond's small police force was no match for the advancing mob. When the rioters reached Main Street—shouting "Bread"—they broke into the commissary, smashed store windows, and grabbed food and anything else they could get their hands on. Some of them loaded their booty into carts and wagons they had seized for the occasion.

"Women were seen bending under loads of sole-leather, or dragging after them heavy cavalry boots, brandishing their huge knives, and swearing, though apparently well fed, that they were dying from starvation—yet it was difficult to imagine how they could masticate or digest the edibles under the weight of which they were bending," an author identifying herself only as "A Richmond Lady," wrote in *Richmond During the War: Four Years of Personal Observation*, published in 1867. "Men carried immense loads of cotton cloth, woolen goods, and other articles [but] few were seen to attack the stores where flour, groceries, and other provisions were kept."

"We do not desire to injure anyone," President Davis told the crowd, "but this lawlessness must stop."

Hurrying to Main Street, Mayor Mayo and Governor Letcher made fruitless appeals to the swelling crowd. When these attempts at persuasion failed, firemen turned their hoses on the mob. That too had little effect. Then the troops from the Public Guard arrived. They marched up Main Street, driving the looters before them, and then halted before a horseless wagon that had been turned sideways, blocking traffic in the street. The troops noticed some of their own wives among the rioters.

As the mayor and governor attempted to restore order, President Davis made his way from the Executive Mansion and through the crowd. The women hissed as he climbed onto a wagon and shouted for the crowd's attention. The president's widow, Varina, later wrote in her memoirs that he reached into his pocket and flung money into the crowd. The president told the mob that rioting was not the way to redress their grievances. Such disorder, Davis explained, would only make matters worse. It would discourage farmers from trying to bring their produce to town, further restricting access to food.

"We do not desire to injure anyone," he told the crowd, "but this lawlessness must stop."

Then, to back up his words, he announced: "I will give you five minutes to disperse, otherwise you will be fired upon."

No one budged. Davis pulled out his pocket watch. He glanced at the troops. Still none of the rioters moved. The commander of the Public Guard, Lieutenant Edward Scott Gay, Jr., ordered his troops to load their weapons and, when five minutes had elapsed, to shoot to kill. Again no one moved. The soldiers prepared their weapons, and Davis—steadying his hand—studied his watch. The seconds ticked away. Finally, the crowd began to disperse. Before long, the president, the mayor, the governor, and the soldiers were alone. The riot had ended.

Some contemporary versions of the peaceful end to the bread riot dif-fer from Varina Davis's. Included in a series of newspaper articles were accounts that credit Letcher with quashing the riots, while others say Mayor Mayo played the prominent role. Some of the witnesses who gave their accounts to newspaper reporters were not familiar with one or more of the leaders and may have been mistaken when identifying them.

THE RICHMOND CITY COUNCIL met later that day. Members acknowledged that the residents faced hardships, but disputed their severity. Some of the council expressed anger that apparently well-fed residents had stolen dry goods. Some said Richmonders had not taken advantage of existing relief efforts. The council declared the riot to have been "in reality instigated by devilish and selfish motives" and that the city's "honor, dignity and safety" would be maintained, come what may. There was some discussion of requiring anyone who had lived in the city for less than a year to post bond for good behavior, but members dropped the idea.

Eager to contain the damage, President Davis told Secretary of War James A. Seddon to order telegraph operators to send "nothing of the unfortunate disturbance of today over the wires for any purpose," fearing the enemy would use the news to further demoralize the South. Seddon's subordinates also instructed Richmond newspapers to report nothing that would "embarrass our cause and encourage our enemies."

The editors complied. The next day's Richmond *Whig*, for example, reported nothing of the incident but noted that violence, even in response to "artificial wants" caused by "profligate commissaries" and "hoarding speculators," would "not be tolerated." These speculators, contemporary accounts indicate, were often assumed to be Jewish, though Jews had been solid citizens of the city for almost a century. Foreign-born Richmonders also came in for abuse. The *Southern Punch* blamed "the Jew-Yankee, the Dutch-Yankee, French, Irish—in fact all breeds, who like the wild locust of Egypt, are devouring the substance of the land."

Authorities made as many as 47 arrests—accounts vary—and trials appear to have taken several weeks, during which "young men of the veriest rowdy class" as well as female defendants filled city hall. A woman from Oregon Hill said that Mary Jackson had threatened her if she did not participate in the riot, and a market clerk said Mrs. Jackson warned him before April 2 to stay off the street that day. Anybody who got in her way, she supposedly told the man, would be shot.

The city hospital reported the loss of 310 pounds of beef. One merchant lost more than $13,000 in stolen goods. The defendants' arguments did not impress Mayor Mayo. "Boots are not bread," he argued. "Brooms are not bread, men's hats are not bread, and I never heard of anybody's eating them."

> **President Davis told Secretary of War James A. Seddon to order telegraph operators to send "nothing of the unfortunate disturbance of today over the wires."**

Rioters received sentences of up to five years, but details about the incident have been lost to history. Many court records—including those of the circuit court where the bread-riot defendants were tried—were destroyed two years later, when the Yankees broke the defensive lines at Petersburg and headed toward Richmond. The Confederate government fled the city, and Southern troops, eager to prevent anything of value from falling into enemy hands, put much of the town to the torch—destroying, in the process, four-fifths of the city's remaining food supply.

No one knows exactly what happened to ringleader Mary Jackson. Michael Chesson, in *Richmond After the War*, reports that she refused bail and was held for felony trial, though her fate is "unknown." Richmond judge Douglas Tice, who researched the incident for several years, says felony charges against her were reduced to misdemeanors, but then the trail goes cold.

Richmonders' attention soon turned to new dangers. Shortly after Jefferson Davis urged Southern farmers to plant their fields "not in cotton and tobacco but exclusively in crops to feed man and beast," springtime military engagements resumed. At Chancellorsville in May, Lee's army defeated the Federals, but at great cost. The Army of Northern Virginia suffered more than 10,000 casualties at Chancellorsville, but one death hit the South particularly hard. That was the loss on May 10 of General Thomas J. "Stonewall" Jackson, mistakenly shot by his own troops. Jackson had become a hero not only in Virginia but throughout the Confederacy. Two months later, Lee again took his army north across the Potomac River into Maryland and then Pennsylvania, partly to find crops for his hungry troops. The Confederate defeat at Gettysburg in July, and the almost-simultaneous fall of Vicksburg, Mississippi, killed all rational hope for a Southern victory.

The 1863 Bread Riot had been one of the earlier signs that social stability was breaking down in the South. The riot dramatized how desperate matters had become in Virginia a full two years before General Lee surrendered to Union General Ulysses S. Grant at Appomattox and how unrealistic it was for the ill-prepared South to hope it could triumph in its rebellion.

Alan Pell Crawford is the author of Unwise Passions: A True Story of a Remarkable Woman and the First Great Scandal of Eighteenth-Century America *(Simon & Schuster).*

Jefferson Davis and the Jews

Who Was to Blame for the South's Hard Times and High Prices?
Jews in the Government, Said One Confederate Senator—'Davis's Jews.'

By Peggy Robbins

THE SETTING WAS THE CONFEDER-ATE House of Representatives in 1863, but from the tone of the rhetoric, it could have been 1930s Berlin. A slight, bespectacled man was twisting the stomachs of his fellow legislators with hateful words that seemed incongruous with his grandfatherly appearance. Jews, he snarled, had seized control of the South's economy and of Confederate President Jefferson Davis, and were destroying everything. These Jews— "Davis's Jews"—had to be removed from power. And the first to go should be Davis's right-hand man, Secretary of State Judah Benjamin.

The poison words of Congressman Henry S. Foote appealed to people who wanted to believe there was a conspiracy behind the South's military and economic downturns. But no matter what Foote said, and no matter who believed it, Davis was not about to cave in—especially not on the issue of Benjamin, the Confederacy's highest-placed Jewish citizen and Davis's most trusted cabinet member. Instead, for the first three years of his presidency, Davis would take a merciless verbal thrashing

from Foote over Benjamin and the Jewish "conspiracy" he supposedly represented.

Fighting with Henry Foote was nothing new for Davis. Sixteen years before he became the Confederate president, Davis served with Foote in Washington, D.C., where the two men represented Mississippi in the U.S. Senate. They disagreed at every turn, chiefly over the issue of where federal authority stopped and state authority began. Davis's insistence on greater state authority infuriated Foote, and he exercised no restraint in voicing his opposition. The bad blood between the two men quickly exploded into hatred, then smoldered for years through restraint and separation, only to burst back into flames in the early days of the Confederate nation.

Foote had been making enemies all his life. Leaving his native Virginia for Tuscumbia, Alabama, at the age of 22, he had started a family and begun practicing law. For a lawyer, though, Foote was remarkably prone to getting into trouble. In 1826, Alabama barred him from practicing law for three years after he fought a duel with future governor

John A. Winston. Foote moved on to Mississippi, where he worked as a lawyer or editor in Jackson, Natchez, and several other towns. Foote's real love, though, was politics. Easy to dislike, he was nonetheless a talented, fiery speaker, a wily politician, and a stalwart defender of the Union. He was elected to Mississippi's legislature in 1837 and became one of the state's leading Democrats. Ten years later, he was elected to the U.S. Senate.

DAVIS WAS THREE YEARS YOUNGER than Foote. Tall and austere, he was widely regarded as cold and withdrawn; one reporter said "you mistake him for an icicle." An 1828 graduate of West Point, Davis had fought Indians in the West. In 1835, when his wife Sarah died, he resigned from the army to concentrate on managing his Mississippi plantation, Brierfield. In 1845, he married again, this time to a woman nearly 20 years his junior, Varina Howell. When the Mexican war broke out the following year, Davis rejoined the army and fought in several major battles. Hailed as a hero when he returned home in 1847, he was chosen by the Mississippi legislature to fill the unexpired Senate seat of Jesse Spreight, who had just died.

Foote found the seeming arrogance of his reserved new Senate colleague unbearable. In turn, Foote's abrasive manner made Davis's blood boil. The tension between the two men came to a head on Christmas Day, 1847. Davis was having a drink and talking with several other politicians in Gadsby's Hotel, not far from the White House. Across the room, Foote, was antagonizing him. Finally, Davis had had enough. Pushing through the crowed, he charged Foote and tore into him with his fists. Shocked onlookers separated the two. Davis turned away, and Foote struck him from behind. Davis whirled, knocked his foe to the floor and resumed beating him. Hotel patrons struggled to rescue Foote from the bigger Davis, who was out of control with rage. Cooler heads finally prevailed, and it was decided that "the matter should be dropped as a Christmas frolic."

The senators agreed to keep the matter of the brawl quiet. Both men were new to the Senate, and with the nation's sectional crisis heating up there was much work to be done. Still, they continued to butt heads. A Union Democrat, Foote helped draft the Compromise of 1850, an act designed to appease both North and South on the slavery issue and prevent the threat of civil war. The bill passed, despite bitter opposition from Davis and other Southern Democrats.

In 1851, Mississippi Governor John A. Quitman dropped his bid for reelection, and Davis's supporters convinced the senator to seek the post. Davis resigned his Senate seat to square off against Foote, who represented the state's Union Democrats. Foote wanted the position badly and campaigned all over the state. Meanwhile, a severe fever and inflamed left eye kept Davis at home. Rumors circulated that Davis was dead. He managed to get out and stump during the last two weeks of the campaign, but on November 4, 1851, Foote edged him by just 999 votes.

Davis returned to Brierfield, where he contemplated his humiliating loss at the hands of his old enemy. Through the

newspapers, he and Foote blasted each other over the results of their recent campaign. Foote maligned Davis's military record; Davis labeled Foote a slanderer and a liar. Eventually even the newspaper publishers got tired of the whole affair. One editor for the *Natchez Mississippi Free Trader* insisted the men put an end to their squabbling, otherwise, "we will select others under whose guidance we can secure more harmony and good feeling."

In defeat, ironically, Davis had gained legions of new supporters. Reuben Davis (no relation), a Union Democrat who later served in both the U.S. and Confederate congresses, thought Davis's defeat had left him "the head and front of the Democracy in this State and the whole South." Conversely, Foote, alienated by the growing anti-Federal, states' rights sentiment in Mississippi, resigned the governorship in 1853 and moved to California.

Davis was content to live the life of a private citizen for a while. When Governor James Whitfield, Forte's replacement, offered to reappoint Davis to his still-vacant Senate seat, he declined. But Davis's break from public life did not last long. Old friend Franklin Pierce was elected president in 1852, and wanted Davis to join his cabinet. With some reluctance, Davis accepted and was sworn in as secretary of war on March 7, 1853.

Davis did his job exceptionally well. The U.S. Army of 1853 was something of a mess, with roughly 10,000 men scattered across the continent. During his four years as secretary, Davis slowly expanded the ranks by one-third. He upgraded the soldiers' weapons from outmoded flintlocks to rifled percussion models. He tested new gun carriages, pressed for a new pension system for soldiers' widows, and authorized the construction of new Federal arsenals. He even sent a delegation of officers, including future Union general George B. McClellan, overseas to study military advances being implemented in the Crimean War.

DAVIS FOLLOWED PIERCE OUT OF OFfice in March 1857, but Mississippi had

elected him to the U.S. Senate the previous November, and he was glad to return to his old post. He remained there until January 21, 1861, when he resigned in the wake of Mississippi's withdrawal from the Union. When the Confederate government was organized in February, Davis was elected president.

The birth of the Confederacy also meant a return to the public eye for Davis's old rival Foote. After moving to California, he had hoped for a cabinet post from Pierce, but Davis's appointment as secretary had thwarted that possibility. Returning to Mississippi to seek a seat in Congress in 1859, he had received little support. Frustrated, Foote had then moved to Nashville, Tennessee, to resume practicing law. There, the coming of war revived his political fortunes. In the fall of 1861, Tennessee elected him to the Confederate States Congress.

Foote was a political chameleon, changing his views to suit his own agenda. Arthur S. Colyar, who practiced law with Foote after the war, acknowledged his associates's skill as a lawyer, but called him "the most changeable of men." He was consistent only in his hatred for Davis. In the new Confederate government, Foote quickly established himself as the president's primary adversary. He consistently voted against all war measures that Davis backed, including conscription and a defensive military strategy. In some of his hottest speeches, he railed against "the continuance of Davis's war"—yet he also criticized Davis for failing to pursue a vigorous war in the Western theater. Meanwhile, he made as many enemies in Richmond as he had made in Washington. When he called Alabama Congressman E. S. Dargan a "damned rascal," Dargan threatened him with a Bowie knife. On another occasion, Foote provoked congressman William G. Swan into stabbing him with an umbrella.

Foote soon found a new target in Davis's administration—Judah P. Benjamin. The 49-year-old Benjamin was a native of the British West Indies whose family had moved to the United States early in his life. Benjamin was Jewish, and his family eventually settled in New Orleans, then home to one of the largest Jewish communities in America. Highly intelligent and an outstanding orator, Benjamin had great success as a lawyer, planter, and politician. In 1852, he became the first Jew to be elected to the U.S. Senate; he was reelected in 1858.

Davis and Benjamin had been acquainted since 1853, but they had become friends in 1858—strangely enough, through an altercation. During a brief exchange on the Senate floor, Davis, who was ill at the time, snapped at a question Benjamin had posed and dismissed it as "the arguments of a paid attorney." Insulted, Benjamin sent Davis a formal challenge to a duel that very afternoon. Davis knew he had been "wholly wrong," and apologized to Benjamin in the Senate the next morning. From this rough beginning came mutual respect and an enduring friendship.

When Davis assumed the Confederate presidency, Benjamin quickly became his most trusted advisor. Tactful and diplomatic, he deftly handled office-seekers and other petitioners—a task for which the stern Davis was poorly suited. After Davis's first cabinet meeting, Secretary of War Leroy P. Walker noted that "there was only one man there who had any sense, and that man was Benjamin."

To Foote, Judah Benjamin was "the unprincipled minister of an unprincipled tyrant!"

Outside the government, Benjamin had his share of critics. In September 1861, when poor health forced Walker to resign, Davis replaced him with Benjamin. The new secretary of war was not a military man, and quickly ran into problems with Confederate generals such as P. G. T. Beauregard and Thomas J. "Stonewall" Jackson. In February 1862, Roanoke Island, North Carolina, fell to Union forces after Benjamin declined to send reinforcements and more guns to the garrison. In reality, Benjamin had not sent the support because there was none to send. But rather than reveal the new nation's desperate position pub-

licly, Benjamin stoically accepted the public's censures. Davis, who had been behind virtually all of Benjamin's moves as secretary of war, heeded calls for his friend's replacement. He then confounded Foote and other critics by immediately making Benjamin his new secretary of state.

The irascible Foote assailed what he called the "tight and terrible President Davis–Jew Benjamin alliance" at every opportunity. He hurled repeated slurs at "Judas Iscariot Benjamin," who, hand-in-hand with "the President who retains the Jew at his table despite the protest of the Southern people," was leading the South to certain destruction. Foote declared that he would "never consent to the establishment of a Supreme Court of the Confederate States so long as Judah P. Benjamin shall continue to pollute the ears of majestic Davis with his insidious councils." To Foote, Benjamin was "the unprincipled minister of an unprincipled tyrant!"

Benjamin was no stranger to religious intolerance. He usually endured it with the strange smile that seemed a permanent feature of his face. Foote's invective was often designed simply to irk Davis, and Benjamin saw no need to make things harder for the president by caving in to it. Still, Foote took his unending abuse to new heights. Varina Davis wrote of her husband's "personal and aggrieved sense" of the unjust criticism Benjamin received from Davis's enemy.

Davis stood by his "right hand" throughout the war. This maddened Foote. Lamenting his inability to discredit Benjamin and force a wedge "between President Davis and the descendant of those who crucified the Saviour," Foote extended his attacks to include all Jews. During heated congressional debate on January 14, 1863, he declared that Jews had flooded the country, that they traded illegally with the enemy, and that they already controlled nine-tenths of the business in the South. "If the present state of things were to continue," he stated, "the end of the war would probably find nearly *all* the property of the Confederacy in the hands of Jewish Shylocks!" Leveling another shot at Davis, he concluded that Jews had gained their

position because top government officials had "invited" them into the Confederacy.

According to Foote, "Davis's Jews" were gaining control of the cotton and tobacco industries and putting the South's economy at risk of collapse. He repeatedly threatened to expose "the Jewish conspiracy," but never produced evidence to back up his accusations. On January 7, 1864, the Richmond *Examiner* reported that a Confederate congressman had accepted a bribe of $3,000 to obtain passports for three Jews, allowing them to leave the Confederacy and enter Union territory. Foote was outraged and insisted on an investigation of the matter. After a thorough probe, a congressional committee reported that "nothing to sustain the charge" had been found.

By January 1865, Foote believed the Confederacy was doomed. His ceaseless abuse of Davis's administration had accomplished little, and many of his colleagues had tired of him. Still a Unionist at heart, he proposed peace talks between the Confederate and Union governments. Davis and his generals had no such inclination.

Foote decided to contact President Abraham Lincoln himself. On January 10, 1863, he and his wife hurried toward the Potomac River and Federal lines, only to be captured by Confederate troops. Foote was sent back to Richmond. Two weeks later, as the Confederate Congress debated his fate, he fled again, and this time he reached Union territory. Imprisoned in New York, he wrote letters to Lincoln, Northern newspapers, and other Federal politicians, trying to gain an audience. He got nowhere. Foote remained in confinement until after Lincoln's assassination in mid-April, when new President Andrew Johnson banished him from the country.

From Canada, Foote pleaded with Johnson to let him return to the United States. He took the Federal oath of allegiance, and in August Johnson relented. An opportunist to the last, Foote later supported the Republican administrations of Ulysses S. Grant and Rutherford B. Hayes. In 1878, Hayes appointed the aging Virginian superintendent of the U.S. Mint in—of all places—New Orleans, where Benjamin had grown up and where many Jews lived. Foote died two years later in Nashville; at the time, noted a reporter, he was "a decrepit old gentleman with a fiery red head, almost entirely bald." Foote never expressed any regret for his abuse of Davis, Benjamin, or Jews in general.

When the Confederacy crumbled in April 1865, Benjamin burned his private papers and fled the country. He never returned. He established himself in England, where he became a prominent and wealthy lawyer and, later, a Queen's counsel. Davis, who had retired to Mississippi, occasionally visited him, but Foote wasted no time dwelling on the past. He refused to discuss the war. In his last years Benjamin rejoined his long-estranged family in Paris, France, where he died in May 1884. "He was," Davis said, "a master of law, and the most accomplished statesman I have ever known." He was also a friend, whom Davis had been more than willing to defend from a bitter and unrelenting anti-Semite.

PEGGY ROBBINS *is a long-time contributor to* Civil War Times.

A Gallant Rush for Glory

For the men of the 54th Massachusetts, the assault on a Confederate fort outside Charleston was much more than just another battle. It was their chance to show the world that black troops could fight—and die—for the Union.

by William C. Kashatus

BEFORE UNION FORCES could capture Charleston, South Carolina, they first had to take Fort Wagner, a Confederate stronghold guarding the harbor's entrance. So shortly after 6:30 p.m. on July 18, 1863, Union Colonel Robert Gould Shaw readied 600 men of the 54th Massachusetts Regiment for an assault on the fort. Shaw, the 25-year-old son of Boston abolitionists, was white, as were all his officers. The regiment's men were black.

The 54 would spearhead a three-pronged attack aimed at capturing the necklace of heavily fortified islands that dotted Charleston harbor. If they could take Fort Wagner, the Federals would launch a major assault on nearby Fort Sumter. From there, it would only be a matter of time before Charleston fell. But capturing Fort Wagner would be no easy task.

At first glance, the fort appeared to be little more than a series of irregular, low sand hills. In fact, it was much more formidable than that. A timber and sandbag foundation beneath the sand-covered hills allowed the structure to absorb artillery fire without any significant damage. The fort had 11 heavy guns mounted in fixed positions behind the parapets, while smaller wheeled cannon could be quickly repositioned where needed. Defending it were 1,300 men from the 51st and 31st North Carolina Regiments as well as several companies of South Carolina artillerymen.

Fort Wagner sat in the middle of Morris Island's northern sandy peninsula. Four batteries at the island's northern tip

guarded the entrance to Charleston harbor. The largest of these batteries was Battery Gregg, whose guns faced the ocean and covered the harbor mouth. South of the batteries, a deep moat with a sluice gate and three guns bounded Fort Wagner along its northern sea face. To the east lay the Atlantic Ocean, and on its western boundary were the impassable marshes of Vincent's Creek. On its southern side the fort had guns and mortars for direct and flanking fire on any advancing troops. The only possible assault approach was east of the fort, along a slim stretch of sand, narrow even at low tide. Shaw and his troops would have to launch their attack on the seemingly impregnable fort from there.

Colonel Shaw readied his men on the beach. Tightly wedged together, elbow to elbow, the soldiers of the 54th began their gallant rush, determined to disprove the popular belief among whites that Negroes were an inferior race, lacking the courage and intelligence of combat-ready soldiers.

THE ONSET OF THE Civil War set off a rush by free black men to enlist in the U.S. military, but a 1792 law barred "persons of color from serving in the militia." Also, strong opposition in the North as well as a widespread prejudice that blacks were intellectually and socially inferior limited their involvement in the war to driving supply wagons, burying the battle dead, and building railroads.

Shaw came from a prominent New England anti-slavery family, but he was initially hesitant about accepting command of the 54th. Once in command of the black regiment, he encountered considerable scorn from other white officers.

Yet public opinion slowly began changing. Northern morale faltered after Union forces suffered a series of military defeats, and fewer white men were willing to join the army. Pressured by this turn of events, on July 17, 1862, Congress passed a Confiscation Act that declared all slaves of rebel masters free as soon as they came into Union lines, and a Militia Act that empowered the president to "employ as many persons of African descent" in "any military or naval service for which they may be found competent." Congress also repealed the 1792 law.

On August 25, 1862, the War Department authorized Brigadier General Rufus Saxton, military governor of the Union-controlled South Carolina Sea Islands, to raise five regiments of black troops for Federal service, with white men as officers. Volunteers came forward slowly at first, but by November 7 the regiment had reached its quota and was mustered in as the 1st South Carolina Volunteer Regiment under the command of Massachusetts abolitionist Colonel Thomas Wentworth Higginson. A second regiment followed, led by Colonel James Montgomery.

Still, President Abraham Lincoln refused to raise a large black army on political grounds. "To arm the Negroes would turn 50,000 bayonets from the loyal Border States against us that were for us," he told his abolitionist critics. Black leaders continued to urge the necessity of enlisting black troops, realizing that if the black man proved his patriotism and courage on the battlefield, the nation would be morally obligated to grant him first-class citizenship. No one expressed those sentiments more eloquently than Frederick Douglass, a former slave and the nation's most prominent black abolitionist. He insisted that "once the black man gets upon his person the brass letters 'U.S.', a musket on his shoulder and bullets in his pocket, there is no power on earth which can deny that he has earned the right to citizenship in the United States."

Debate continued within the Union command until January 1, 1863, when President Lincoln signed the Emancipation Proclamation. Having freed, by executive order, those slaves in the South, Lincoln could no longer deny the black man the opportunity to fight. Now the Civil War was being fought not only to preserve the Union, but for the freedom of all the American people, white and

black. The success of the 1st and 2nd Carolina Colored Troops only reinforced that position. Higginson and Montgomery had already led their black troops on several successful raids into the interior of Georgia and Florida, and in March 1863 they captured and occupied Jacksonville.

On February 13, 1863, Senator Charles Sumner of Massachusetts introduced a bill proposing the "enlistment of 300,000 colored troops." Although the bill was defeated, abolitionist governor John A. Andrew of Massachusetts requested and received authorization from Secretary of War Edwin M. Stanton to organize a colored regiment of volunteers to serve for three years.

Massachusetts had a small black population, and only 100 men volunteered during the first six weeks of recruitment. Disillusioned by the turnout, Andrew organized a committee of prominent citizens and Negro leaders to supervise the recruitment effort. Within two months the committee collected $5,000 and established a line of recruiting posts from Boston to St. Louis, resulting in the recruitment of 1,000 black men from throughout the Union who became part of the 54th Regiment Massachusetts Volunteer Infantry, Colored, the first black regiment raised in the free states. Toward the end of the second recruiting month, volunteers arrived at the rate of 30 to 40 each day, and Andrew soon had enough men to form a second black regiment, the 55th Massachusetts.

For the 54th's commander, Governor Andrew turned to Robert Gould Shaw, captain of the Massachusetts 2nd Infantry. Charming and handsome, Shaw came from a wealthy and socially prominent Boston abolitionist family. His parents Francis and Sarah had joined the American Anti-Slavery Society in 1838, and by 1842 Francis was working with the Boston Vigilance Committee to help runaway slaves gain their freedom. Robert entered Harvard University in 1856 but abandoned his studies during his third year and moved to New York to work in his uncle's mercantile office. Shaw joined an exclusive militia regiment, the 7th New York National Guard, where he talked about what he would do if the South made trouble. Shaw did not

possess the strong anti-slavery calling of his parents, but he was fiercely patriotic. When the Civil War began, he was primed to take revenge on the South. To Shaw, the South was the transgressor, and if it took the end of slavery to redeem the honor of America, then he was willing to fight for that. When the 7th disbanded, Shaw accepted a commission in the 2nd Massachusetts Infantry. During his 20 months there, Captain Shaw received a minor wound at Antietam, during the single bloodiest day of the war.

When Governor Andrew asked the young captain to lead a black volunteer infantry, Shaw was hesitant. The prospect of heading a regiment of armed blacks would not be popular among the white ranks. Nor did he want to abandon the men of the 2nd Infantry. Shaw initially refused the position but changed his mind after much discussion with his parents. In a February 1863 letter to his future wife, Annie Haggerty, Shaw wrote, "You know how many eminent men consider a negro army of the greatest importance to our country at this time. If it turns out to be so, how fully repaid the pioneers in the movement will be, for what they may have to go through…. I feel convinced I shall never regret having taken this step, as far as I myself am concerned; for while I was undecided I felt ashamed of myself, as if I were cowardly." Shaw received a promotion to major on April 11, 1863, and attained the rank of colonel the following month. Colonel Shaw would now have to navigate the turbulent forces of discrimination that existed within the Union Army.

The men of the 54th trained near Boston at Readville, under the constant scrutiny of white soldiers, many of whom believed black soldiers lacked the stomach for combat. Yet the negative perceptions seemed only to inspire a sense of unity within the ranks of the regiment and their white officers.

Contrary to recruitment promises, the soldiers of the 54th were paid only $10.00 per month, $3.00 less than the white troops. Shaw had become so committed to his men that he wrote to Governor Andrew, insisting that his entire regiment, including white officers, would refuse pay until his soldiers were "given the same payment as all the other

Massachusetts troops." Yet Congress did not enact legislation granting equal pay to black soldiers until June 15, 1864.

Shortly after the 54th was mustered into service, the Confederate Congress passed an act stating its intention to "put to death" if captured, "any Negro" as well as "white commissioned officer [who] shall command, prepare or aid Negroes in arms against the Confederate States." The directive only served to strengthen the resolve of the black soldiers.

On May 18 Governor Andrew traveled to the camp to present Shaw with the regimental flags. He made the trip with 3,000 other visitors, including such prominent abolitionists as Frederick Douglass, William Lloyd Garrison, and Wendell Phillips. Douglass had a strong personal link with the 54th—two of his sons, Lewis and Charles, had joined the unit. Andrew presented the flags to Shaw. "I know not, Mr. Commander, in all human history, to any given thousand men in arms, has there been committed a work at once so proud, so precious, so full of hope and glory as the work committed to you," the governor said.

Massachusetts Governor John A. Andrew advocated the enlistment of black men into the Union Army. After President Lincoln issued the Emancipation Proclamation on January 1, 1863, Andrew approached Secretary of War Edwin Stanton and obtained authorization to raise a black Massachusetts regiment.

Ten days later the 54th Regiment of Massachusetts Volunteer Infantry marched through the streets of downtown Boston, greeted by the cheers of thousands who assembled to see them off at Battery Wharf. It was an impressive spectacle. Shaw, atop his chestnut brown horse, led the way. Close behind marched the color bearers, followed by young black soldiers, handsomely clad in their sharp, new uniforms.

The dress parade gradually made its way to the wharf and boarded the *De Molay* bound for Port Royal Island, South Carolina. There the regiment reported to the Department of the South. Once the men arrived, however, reality set in when they were relegated to manual labor. Not until June 8, when Shaw and his men joined Colonel James Montgomery and the black troops of his 2nd South Carolina Colored Volunteers on an "expedition" to Georgia, did they see any action, and that was during a pointless raid on the small town of Darien. After plundering the 100 or so residences, three churches, the market-house, courthouse, and an academy, Montgomery ordered Darien set afire. Begrudgingly, Shaw directed one of his companies to torch the town. Fanned by a high wind, the flames eventually destroyed everything but a church and a few houses.

Afterward, Shaw wrote to lieutenant Colonel Charles G. Halpine, the acting adjutant general of the department, to condemn this "barbarous sort of warfare." Shaw knew his complaint could result in his arrest or even court-martial, but he felt compelled to express his feelings. He later learned that Montgomery had acted in accordance with the orders of his superior officer, General David Hunter. Soon after the Darien raid, President Lincoln relieved Hunter of his command.

The sacking of Darien and the manual labor his troops were compelled to do disheartened Shaw. "Our whole experience, so far, has been in loading and discharging vessels," he wrote to Brigadier General George C. Strong, commander of Montgomery's brigade. "Colored soldiers should be associated as much as possible with the white troops, in order that they may have other witnesses beside their own officers to what they are

capable of doing." That opportunity finally arrived on the morning of July 16, 1863. Fighting alongside white troops on James Island, Shaw's men acquitted themselves well in a sharp skirmish. That same night they ferried to Morris Island, where battle lines had already been drawn for the anticipated attack on Fort Wagner. Despite their exhaustion, hunger, and wet clothes, the men of the 54th were determined to fight on.

WHEN GENERAL STRONG, now Shaw's brigade commander, heard of the of the 54th on James Island, he asked the colonel if he and his regiment would lead the attack on Fort Wagner. Shaw and his men readily agreed and prepared to lead the charge across a narrow beach obstructed by felled branches, crisscrossed wire, and a deep moat—all of which were constructed to slow the attackers, making them vulnerable to enemy fire. Eight all-white units were to follow. All day long, Union artillery bombarded Fort Wagner in an effort to soften the Confederate defense and minimize the bloodshed that would inevitably follow. Late in the day Shaw arranged the 600 able-bodied men of his regiment into two wings of five companies each and moved them slowly up the beach. He assigned Company B to the right flank, using the surf as its guide. The other companies lined up on its left.

At dusk, General Strong addressed Shaw and his men. Pointing to the flag bearer, he said: "If this man should fall, who will pick up the flag?" Shaw stepped forward. "I will," he said. Addressing his troops with final words of inspiration, Shaw reminded them: "The eyes of thousands will look on what you do tonight." Then, drawing his sword, the young Boston Brahmin barked: "Move in quick time until within a hundred yards of the fort, then, double-quick and charge!" Quickstep became double-quick, and then a full run, as Confederate riflemen on the ramparts of the fort let loose a torrent of fire upon the Union soldiers. Men fell on all sides, but those who were able continued the charge with Shaw in the lead.

Company B passed through the moat to the base of the fort where canister, grenades, and small arms fire rained down

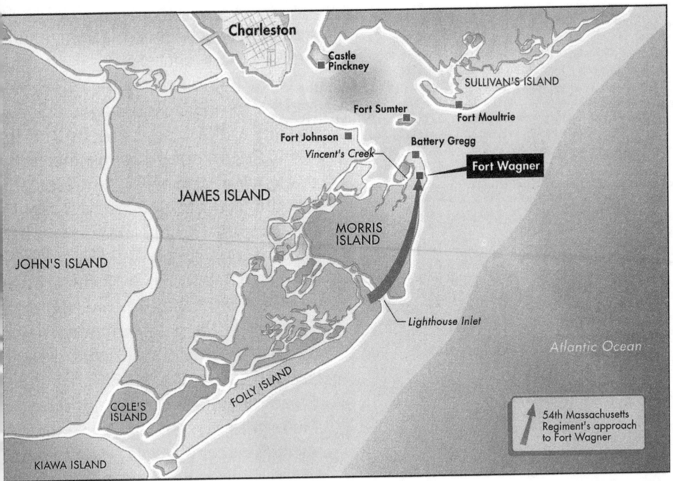

MAP BY RICK BROWNLEE

The 54th Regiment approached Fort Wagner along a narrow stretch of beach by the Atlantic Ocean.

on them. Surrounded by bloodshed, the 54th commander realized that he could not retreat, and he ordered the final assault on the fort. Shaw somehow managed to reach the parapet before a Confederate bullet pierced his heart.

"Men fell all around me," Lewis Douglass later wrote. "A shell would explode and clear a space of twenty feet, our men would close up again, but it was no use we had to retreat, which was a very hazardous undertaking. How I got out of that fight alive I cannot tell, but I am here."

The intense fire mowed down the color bearers. Sergeant William Carney, a barrel-chested 23-year-old, seized the national flag and planted it upon the fort's parapet. The men of the 54th fought gallantly for about an hour until Confederate guns forced them to abandon their position. Before retreating, Carney once again grasped the flag, and

despite bullets in the head, chest, right arm, and leg, he returned it to Union lines. His heroism earned him the distinction of being the first of 21 black men during the war to earn the Medal of Honor.

Subsequent waves of Federal troops tried for two hours to take the fort but failed, and casualties mounted by the hundreds. At the end of the assault, the Union had lost 1,515 killed, wounded or missing. Of that number, 256 were black soldiers from the 54th Massachusetts.

The following morning revealed a grisly scene. The dead lay in contorted positions along the beach, their fingers and legs stiffened from rigor mortis. The soft but painful cries and moans of the dying could be heard, begging for help.

A few days after the siege, a Union party under a flag of truce requested the return of Shaw's body. Brigadier General Johnson Hagood, Fort Wagner's

new commander, reportedly answered, "We buried him in the trench with his niggers." Learning of Hagood's reply, Colonel Shaw's father declared, "I can imagine no holier place than that in which he is, among his brave and devoted followers, nor wish for him better company."

From a military standpoint, the assault on Fort Wagner proved to be a costly failure. The blame rested on the shoulders of commanding general Quincy A. Gillmore and his commander in the field, Brigadier General Truman Seymour, who had not ordered the usual preparations for such an assault—no one sent out guides to check the terrain in advance or dispatched lines of skirmishers to soften the enemy. Nor had the 54th ever practiced storming a fort. Nevertheless, the assault proved to be a turning point for black soldiers, serving to dismiss any lingering skepticism among whites about the combat readiness of African Americans. "I have given the subject of arming the Negro my hearty support," General Ulysses S. Grant wrote to President Lincoln in August. "They will make good soldiers and taking them from the enemy weakens him in the same proportion they strengthen us."

When other Union generals remained recalcitrant, Lincoln responded swiftly.

"You say you will not fight to free Negroes," he said. "Some of them seem to be willing to fight for you. When victory is won, there will be some black men who can remember that, with silent tongue and clenched teeth, and steady eye and well-poised bayonet, they have helped mankind on to this great consummation. I fear, however, that there will also be some white ones, unable to forget that with malignant heart and deceitful speech, they strove to hinder it."

William C. Kashatus is a professional historian at Chester County Historical Society, West Chester, Pennsylvania.

Lincoln as Statesman

THE KEY TO UNDERSTANDING LINCOLN'S PHILOSOPHY OF STATESMANSHIP IS THAT HE ALWAYS SOUGHT THE MEETING POINT BETWEEN WHAT WAS RIGHT IN THEORY AND WHAT COULD BE ACHIEVED IN PRACTICE.

Dinesh D'Souza

MOST AMERICANS—INCLUDING MOST historians—regard Abraham Lincoln as the nation's greatest president. But in recent years powerful movements have gathered, both on the political right and the left, to condemn Lincoln as a flawed and even wicked man.

For both camps, the debunking of Lincoln usually begins with an exposé of the "Lincoln myth," which is well described in William Lee Miller's 2002 book *Lincoln's Virtues: An Ethical Biography.* How odd it is, Miller writes, that an "unschooled" politician "from the raw frontier villages of Illinois and Indiana" could become such a great president. "He was the myth made real," Miller writes, "rising from an actual Kentucky cabin made of actual Kentucky logs all the way to the actual White House."

Lincoln's critics have done us all a service by showing that the actual author of the myth is Abraham Lincoln himself. It was Lincoln who, over the years, carefully crafted the public image of himself as Log Cabin Lincoln, Honest Abe and the rest of it. Asked to describe his early life, Lincoln answered, "the short and simple annals of the poor," referring to Thomas Gray's poem "Elegy Written in a Country Churchyard." Lincoln disclaimed great aspirations for himself, noting that if people did not vote for him, he would return to obscurity, for he was, after all, used to disappointments.

These pieties, however, are inconsistent with what Lincoln's law partner, William Herndon, said about him: "His ambition was a little engine that knew no rest." Admittedly in the ancient world ambition was often viewed as a great vice. In Shakespeare's Julius Caesar, Brutus submits his reason for joining the conspiracy against Caesar: his fear that Caesar had grown too ambitious. But as founding father and future president James Madison noted in *The Federalist*, the American system was consciously designed to attract ambitious men. Such ambition

was presumed natural to a politician and favorable to democracy as long as it sought personal distinction by promoting the public good through constitutional means.

WHAT UNITES THE RIGHT-WING and left-wing attacks on Lincoln, of course, is that they deny that Lincoln respected the law and that he was concerned with the welfare of all. The right-wing school—made up largely of Southerners and some libertarians—holds that Lincoln was a self-serving tyrant who rode roughshod over civil liberties, such as the right to habeas corpus. Lincoln is also accused of greatly expanding the size of the federal government. Some libertarians even charge—and this is not intended as a compliment—that Lincoln was the true founder of the welfare state. His right-wing critics say that despite his show of humility, Lincoln was a megalomanical man who was willing to destroy half the country to serve his Caesarian ambitions. In an influential essay, the late Melvin E. Bradford, an outspoken conservative, excoriated Lincoln as a moral fanatic who, determined to enforce his Manichaean vision—one that sees a cosmic struggle between good and evil—on the country as a whole, ended up corrupting American politics and thus left a "lasting and terrible impact on the nation's destiny."

Although Bradford viewed Lincoln as a kind of manic abolitionist, many in the right-wing camp deny that the slavery issue was central to the Civil War. Rather, they insist, the war was driven primarily by economic motives. Essentially, the industrial North wanted to destroy the economic base of the South. Historian Charles Adams, in *When in the Course of Human Events: Arguing the Case for Southern Secession,* published in 2000, contends that the causes leading up to the Civil War had virtually nothing to do with slavery.

THIS APPROACH TO REWRITING history has been going on for more than a century. Alexander Stephens, former vice president of the Confederacy, published a two-volume history of the Civil War between 1868 and 1870 in which he hardly mentioned slavery, insisting that the war was an attempt to preserve constitutional government from the tyranny of the majority. But this is not what Stephens said in the great debates leading up to the war. In his "Cornerstone" speech, delivered in Savannah, Ga., on March 21, 1861, at the same time that the South was in the process of seceding, Stephens said that the American Revolution had been based on a premise that was "fundamentally wrong." That premise was, as Stephens defined it, "the assumption of equality of the races." Stephens insisted that instead: "Our new [Confederate] government is founded upon exactly the opposite idea. Its foundations are laid, its cornerstone rests upon the great truth that the Negro is not equal to the white man. Slavery—subordination to the superior race—is his natural and normal condition. This, our new government, is the first, in the history of the world, based upon this great and moral truth."

This speech is conspicuously absent from the right's revisionist history. And so are the countless affirmations of black inferiority and the "positive good" of slavery—from John C. Calhoun's attacks on the Declaration of Independence to South Carolina Senator James H. Hammond's insistence that "the rock of Gibraltar does not stand so firm on its basis as our slave system." It is true, of course, that many whites who fought on the Southern side in the Civil War did not own slaves. But, as Calhoun himself pointed out in one speech, they too derived an important benefit from slavery: "With us the two great divisions of society are not the rich and the poor, but white and black; and

all the former, the poor as well as the rich, belong to the upper class, and are respected and treated as equals." Calhoun's point is that the South had conferred on all whites a kind of aristocracy of birth, so that even the most wretched and degenerate white man was determined in advance to be better and more socially elevated than the most intelligent and capable black man. That's why the poor whites fought—to protect that privilege.

Contrary to Bradford's high-pitched accusations, Lincoln approached the issue of slavery with prudence and moderation. This is not to say that he waffled on the morality of slavery. "You think slavery is right, and ought to be extended," Lincoln wrote Stephens on the eve of the war, "while we think it is wrong, and ought to be restricted." As Lincoln clearly asserts, it was not his intention to get rid of slavery in the Southern states. Lincoln conceded that the American founders had agreed to tolerate slavery in the Southern states, and he confessed that he had no wish and no power to interfere with it there. The only issue—and it was an issue on which Lincoln would not bend—was whether the federal government could restrict slavery in the new territories. This was the issue of the presidential campaign of 1860; this was the issue that determined secession and war.

Lincoln argued that the South had no right to secede—that the Southern states had entered the Union as the result of a permanent compact with the Northern states. That Union was based on the principle of majority rule, with constitutional rights carefully delineated for the minority. Lincoln insisted that since he had been legitimately elected, and since the power to regulate slavery in the territories was nowhere proscribed in the Constitution, Southern secession amounted to nothing more than one group's decision to leave the country because it did not like the results of a presidential election, and no constitutional democracy could function under such an absurd rule. Of course the Southerners objected that they should not be forced to live under a regime that they considered tyrannical, but Lincoln countered that any decision to dissolve the original compact could only occur with the consent of all the parties involved. Once again, it makes no sense to have such agreements when any group can unilaterally withdraw from them and go its own way.

IF THE RIGHT-WINGERS DISDAIN LINCOLN FOR BEING TOO AGGRESSIVELY ANTISLAVERY, THE LEFT-WINGERS SCORN HIM FOR NOT BEING ANTI-SLAVERY ENOUGH.

The rest of the libertarian and right-wing case against Lincoln is equally without merit. Yes, Lincoln suspended habeas corpus and arrested Southern sympathizers, but let us not forget that the nation was in a desperate war in which its very survival was at stake. Discussing habeas corpus, Lincoln insisted that it made no sense for him to protect this one constitutional right and allow the very Union established by the Constitution, the very framework for the protection of all rights, to be obliterated. Of course the federal government expanded during the Civil War, as it expanded during the Revolutionary War, and during World War II. Governments need to be strong to fight wars. The evidence for the right-wing insistence that Lincoln was the founder of the modern welfare state stems from the establishment, begun during his administration, of a pension program for Union veterans and support for their widows and orphans. Those were, however, programs aimed at a specific, albeit large, part of the population. The welfare state came to America in the 20th century. Franklin Roosevelt should be credited, or blamed, for that. He institutionalized it, and Lyndon Johnson and Richard Nixon expanded it.

THE LEFT-WING GROUP of Lincoln critics, composed of liberal scholars and social activists, is harshly critical of Lincoln on the grounds that he was a racist who did not really care about ending slavery. Their indictment of Lincoln is that he did not oppose slavery outright, only the extension of it, that he opposed laws permitting intermarriage and even opposed social and political equality between the races. If the right-wingers disdain Lincoln for being too aggressively antislavery, the left-wingers scorn him for not being antislavery enough. Both groups, however, agree that Lincoln was a self-promoting hypocrite who said one thing while doing another.

Some of Lincoln's defenders have sought to vindicate him from these attacks by contending that he was a "man of his time." This will not do, because there were several persons of that time, notably the social-reformer Grimké sisters, Angelina and Sarah, and Senator Charles Sumner of Massachusetts, who forthrightly and unambiguously attacked slavery and called for immediate and complete abolition. In one of his speeches, Sumner said that while there are many issues on which political men can and should compromise, slavery is not such an issue: "This will not admit of compromise. To be wrong on this is to be wholly wrong. It is our duty to defend freedom, unreservedly, and careless of the consequences."

Lincoln's modern liberal critics are, whether they know it or not, the philosophical descendants of Sumner. One cannot understand Lincoln without understanding why he agreed with Sumner's goals while consistently opposing the strategy of the abolitionists. The abolitionists, Lincoln thought, approached the restricting or ending of slavery with self-righteous moral display. They wanted to be in the right and—as Sumner himself says—damn the consequences. In Lincoln's view, abolition was a noble sentiment, but abolitionist tactics, such as burning the Constitution and advocating violence, were not the way to reach their goal.

We can answer the liberal critics by showing them why Lincoln's understanding of slavery, and his strategy for defeating it, was superior to that of Sumner and his modern-day followers. Lincoln knew that the statesman, unlike the moralist, cannot be content with making the case against slavery. He must find a way to implement his principles to the degree that circumstances permit. The key to understanding Lincoln is that he always sought the meeting point between what was right in theory and what could be achieved in practice. He always sought the common denominator between what was good to do and what the people would go along with. In a democratic society this is the only legitimate way to advance a moral agenda.

Consider the consummate skill with which Lincoln deflected the prejudices of his supporters without yielding to them. In the Lincoln-Douglas debates during the race for the Illinois Senate, Stephen Douglas repeatedly accused Lincoln of believing that blacks and whites were intellectually equal, of endorsing full political rights for blacks, and of supporting "amalgamation" or intermarriage between the races. If these charges could be sustained, or if large numbers of people believed them to be true, then Lincoln's career was over. Even in the free state of Illinois—as throughout the North—there was widespread opposition to full political and social equality for blacks.

Lincoln handled this difficult situation by using a series of artfully conditional responses. "Certainly the Negro is not our equal in color—perhaps not in many other respects; still, in the right to put into his mouth the bread that his own hands have earned, he is the equal of every other man. In pointing out that more has been given to you, you cannot be justified in taking away the little which has been given to him. If God gave him but little, that little let him enjoy." Notice that Lincoln only barely recognizes the prevailing prejudice. He never acknowledges black inferiority; he merely concedes the possibility. And the thrust of his argument is that even if blacks were inferior, that is not a warrant for taking away their rights.

Facing the charge of racial amalgamation, Lincoln said, "I protest against that counterfeit logic which concludes that because I do not want a black woman for a slave, I must necessarily want her for a wife." Lincoln is not saying that he wants, or does not want, a black woman for his wife. He is neither supporting nor opposing racial intermarriage. He is simply saying that from his antislavery position it does not follow that he endorses racial amalgamation. Elsewhere Lincoln turned antiblack prejudices against Douglas by saying that slavery was the institution that had produced the greatest racial intermixing and the largest number of mulattoes.

LINCOLN WAS EXERCISING the same prudent statesmanship when he wrote to New York newspaper publisher Horace Greeley asserting: "My paramount object in this struggle is to save the Union, and is not either to save or to destroy slavery. If I could save the Union without freeing any slave, I would do it; and if I could save it by freeing all the slaves, I would do it; and if I could do it by freeing some and leaving others alone, I would also do that." The letter was written on August 22, 1862, almost a year and a half after the Civil War broke out, when the South was gaining momentum and the outcome was far from certain. From the time of secession, Lincoln was desperately eager to prevent border states such as Maryland, Delaware, Kentucky and Missouri from seceding. These states had slavery, and Lincoln knew that if the issue of the war was cast openly as the issue of slavery, his chances of keeping the border states in the Union were slim. And if all the border states seceded, Lincoln was convinced, and rightly so, that the cause of the Union was gravely imperiled.

Moreover, Lincoln was acutely aware that many people in the North were vehemently antiblack and saw themselves as fighting to save their country rather than to free slaves. Lincoln framed the case against the Confederacy in terms of saving the Union in order to maintain his coalition—a coalition whose victory was essential to the antislavery cause. And ultimately it was because of Lincoln that slavery came to an end. That is why the right wing can never forgive him.

In my view, Lincoln was the true "philosophical statesman," one who was truly good and truly wise. Standing in front of his critics, Lincoln is a colossus, and all of the Lilliputian arrows hurled at him bounce harmlessly to the ground. It is hard to put any other president—not even George Washington—in the same category as Abraham Lincoln. He is simply the greatest practitioner of democratic statesmanship that America and the world have yet produced.

America's Birth At Appomattox

Anne Wortham

It would of course be easy to make too much of the general air of reconciliation.... And yet by any standard this was an almost unbelievable way to end a civil war, which by all tradition is the worst kind of war there is.[1]
—Bruce Catton

On April 9, 1865, eighty-nine years after the Continental Congress declared the independence of "thirteen united States of America," the United States of America was born at the residence of farmer Wilmer McLean in the hamlet of Appomattox Courthouse, Virginia. Civil War historian James Robertson has said, "Lee signed not so much terms of surrender as he did the birth certificate of a nation—the United States—and the country was born in that moment."[2] An American nationality in the sense of a general feeling of being American above all else did not yet exist when Grant and Lee put their names to the surrender document. But there were at work nineteenth-century values, ideas, and attitudes that transcended sectional loyalties, that remained intact throughout the war, and made possible the birth of the United States as a nation.

I will look at the function of friendship, battlefield comradeship and courtesy, and shared nationality in that process; and argue that these qualities of association—as well as the high value the combatants placed on courage, duty, honor, and discipline—enabled the Federals and Confederates to achieve what Robert Penn Warren called "reconciliation by human recognition." I intend to show how reconciliation was played out in numerous meetings between Union and Confederate officers and soldiers at Appomattox between April 9, 1865, when Lee surrendered, and April 12, when the Confederates stacked their arms, folded their flags, and were paroled.

LINCOLN'S ATTITUDE

We are not enemies, but friends.... Though passion may have strained, it must not break our bonds of affection. The mystic chords of memory, stretching from every battlefield, and patriot grave, to every living heart, and hearthstone, all over this broad land, will yet swell the chorus of the Union, when again touched, as surely they will be, by the better angels of our nature. —*Abraham Lincoln*

Reconciliation was an explicit policy goal of Abraham Lincoln's, which he made clear to Generals Grant and Sherman and Adm. David Dixon Porter in a conference aboard the *River Queen* at City Point, Virginia, after his visit to the front on March 27, 1865. Lincoln knew that unless "the better angels of our nature" could be asserted by unambiguous action at war's end, there was no hope for the new birth of freedom and the national community he believed was possible. The problem for Lincoln was how to simultaneously end the war and win the peace. As Bruce Catton puts it, he argued that the Union's aim should be not so much to subdue the Confederacy as to checkmate those forces of malice and rancor that could jeopardize peace. For if the North won the war and lost the peace, there would be no way to realize his hope that "the whole country, North and South together, [would] ultimately find in reunion and freedom the values that would justify four terrible years of war."[3]

In the only existing documentation of the meeting, Admiral Porter wrote:

My opinion is that Mr. Lincoln came down to City Point with the most liberal views toward the rebels. He felt confident that we would be successful, and was willing that the enemy should capitulate on the most favorable terms.... He wanted peace on almost any terms.... His heart was tenderness throughout, and, as long as the rebels laid down their arms, he did not care how it was done.[4]

Lincoln knew that the peace and reconciliation he envisioned would not stand a chance without generous surrender terms. He expected Grant, "the remorseless killer," and Sherman, "destruction's own self," to "fight without mercy as long as there must be fighting, but when the fighting stopped they [must] try to turn old enemies into friends."

Lincoln knew his fellow citizens, and he was confident that while they were politically disunited, the raw material of reconciliation resided in their hearts.

But could reconciliation be coaxed out of defeat? There were reasons to think it possible. Lincoln knew his fellow citizens, and he was confident that while they were politically disunited, the raw material of reconciliation resided in their hearts. Indeed, friendliness and respect were present within the armies, and there was now less bitterness between them than when the war began. Yet another resource was the extraordinary resilience of the friendships between the former West Pointers leading those armies. Finally, whether he knew it or not, but must have sensed, Lincoln had a most reliable resource in the antisecessionist gray commander himself, Robert E. Lee—but not until he was defeated.

WEST POINT 1: A CHEERFUL COLLOQUY

If one would have a friend, one must be willing to wage war for him: and in order to wage war, one must be capable of being an enemy.... In one's friend, one shall find one's best enemy.   —*Frederich Nietzsche*

"The soldiers did not need to be told that it would be well to make peace mean comradeship. All they needed was to see somebody try it," writes Catton. [5] Well, on Palm Sunday, April 9, 1865, there were plenty of occasions to see the vanquished and the victorious extend the hand of friendship. On the morning of that dramatic day, white flags of truce were held aloft as messengers rode between the lines, and a cease-fire was in place until the anticipated surrender meeting between Grant and Lee. By late morning the contending armies stood on either side of the town, with their picket lines out, their guns silent, nervously contemplating the meaning of surrender and ever alert for the resumption of hostile fire. But gathered on the steps of the Appomattox Courthouse, awaiting the arrival of the two commanding generals, was a curious group of Union and Confederate generals, most of them West Point graduates, and many of them from the same graduating classes.

As historian Frank Cauble points out, because of the more significant surrender meeting that everyone was anticipating, this earlier conference of officers has been largely overlooked and seldom mentioned in Civil War histories. However, the sight of these former combatants was "a singular spectacle," wrote New York reporter L.A. Hendrick.

There were mutual introductions and shaking of hands, and soon was passed about some whiskey (General [Romeyn] Ayres furnished the whiskey and he alleges it was a first class article) and mutual healths were drank and altogether it was a strange grouping. The rebel officers were all elegantly dressed in full uniform. Gradually the area of the conference widened. From the steps the conferring party got into the street, and before it closed some were seated on the steps, and others, for lack of more comfortable accommodations, chatted cosily, seated on a contiguous fence. [6]

Gen. Joshua Chamberlain overheard two West Point classmates who had been combatants for four years renewing an old acquaintance. "Well Billy, old boy, how goes it?" the Union officer said. "Bad, bad, Charlie, bad I can tell you; but have you got any whiskey?" [7]

When we consider the pain, suffering, and death these men had inflicted upon one another and their comrades, how are we to explain their apparent lack of resentment and bitterness?

When we consider the pain, suffering, and death these men had inflicted upon one another and their comrades, how are we to explain their apparent lack of resentment and bitterness? How could one so easily drink of the cup of fraternity with someone who has been shooting at him and his comrades—and sometimes hitting the mark—for four years? Can vanquished and victor really be friends?

Well, yes—if the fellow who had been shooting at you was a friend before he was your enemy, and if he was bound to you by that precious ethos called the "spirit of West Point." Vindictiveness was not the order of the day for these men. They just wanted it over. Indeed, two months before, on February 25, Union Gen. Edward Ord met under a flag of truce with his former classmate, Confederate Gen. James Longstreet, and discussed the possibility of Lee and Grant declaring peace on the field. Now, as the officers waited for Grant and Lee, John Gibbon, a North Carolinian whose three brothers fought for the Confederacy, proposed that if Grant and Lee couldn't come to terms and stop the fighting, they should order their soldiers to fire only blank cartridges to prevent further bloodshed. By noon, when Grant still had not appeared, the West Pointers rode back to their respective lines, all hoping, as Gibbon said, "that there would be no further necessity for bloodshed."

CONDITIONAL SURRENDER

Another year would go by before President Andrew Johnson, on April 2, 1866, proclaimed "that the insurrection... is at an end and is henceforth to be so regarded." But Grant and Lee's task of reconciliation could not wait for the U.S. government's official certification of the end of the war. They knew it had to begin with the surrender terms themselves. Grant finally arrived from the field between 1:30 and 2:00 and entered the McLean house where Lee was waiting. By 3:00 the surrender documents were signed, the two commanders had shaken hands, and Lee had mounted Traveller and returned to his lines. At 4:30 Grant telegraphed Washington, informing the secretary of war that Lee had surrendered "on terms proposed by myself."

Gen. Ulysses S. Grant standing at Cold Harbor, Virginia, in June 1864 (National Archives).

They agreed that all officers and men of the Army of Northern Virginia should be paroled and disqualified from taking up arms against the government of the United States until properly exchanged; that they should turn over all arms, artillery, and public property to the Union army; but that officers should not be deprived of their sidearms, horses, and baggage. In stating that "each officer and man will be allowed to return to their homes not to be disturbed by United States authority so long as they observe their paroles and the laws in force where they may reside," Grant effectively made it impossible for Lee to be tried for treason.

Lee asked that those of the enlisted men who owned their horses be permitted to keep them. At first Grant rejected this request, but then he changed his mind. Since this was the last battle of the war, the men needed their horses to put in their spring crops, and since the United States did not want the horses, he said he would instruct the parole officers to "let every man of the Confederate army who claimed to own a horse or mule to take the animal to his home." It was ironic that for four years Grant had tried to kill these men, and now he didn't want to stand in the way of their planting their crops so they could live. But Grant now saw himself as an instrument for a lasting peace. He extended his generosity further by ordering his army to share its rations with the hungry rebels.

The surrender terms were entirely consistent with the policy of reconciliation that Lincoln had articulated back in March. According to Admiral Porter, when Lincoln learned of the surrender terms, he was "delighted" and exclaimed "a dozen times, 'Good!' 'All right!' 'Exactly the thing!' and other similar expressions." Confederate Porter Alexander was also moved by Grant's generosity at Appomattox and wrote later: "Gen. Grant's conduct toward us in the whole matter is worthy of the very highest praise & indicates a great & broad & generous mind. *For all time it will be a good thing for the whole United States, that of all the Federal generals it fell to Grant to receive the surrender of Lee*" (emphasis in the original).[8]

Union soldiers like Maj. Holman Melcher of the 20th Maine were also impressed by Grant's magnanimity and resolved to follow his example. In a letter to his brother, Melcher noted that "the good feeling between the officers and men of the two armies followed General Grant [who] set us the example by his conduct at the surrender." He went on to "confess" what no doubt many Union officers and soldiers felt—that "a feeling of indignation would rise within me when I would think of all the bloodshed and mourning these same men had caused. But it is honorable to be magnanimous to a conquered foe. And as civilized men and gentlemen, we strive to keep such feelings of hatred in subjection."[9]

Melcher's attitude confirmed Lincoln's insight that, as Catton puts it, "if the terms expressed simple human decency and friendship, it might be that a peace of reconciliation could get just enough of a lead so that the haters could never quite catch up with it." But it would require just the level of self-control that Melcher imposed on himself.

Having signed the certificate of birth, Grant and Lee still had to attend to the business of delivering a deathblow to the idea of secession while simultaneously injecting some vitality into the promise of this new beginning. They did so by word and deed. When news of the surrender reached the Union lines, the men began to fire a salute and cheer, but Grant issued orders forbidding any demonstrations. He wrote later that "the Confederates were now our prisoners, and we did not want to exult over their downfall." While Grant taught his men to resist acts of humiliation, Lee's assignment was to instill stoic dignity.

The Confederates could not believe what had transpired. Orderly Sgt. James Whitehorne of the 12th Virginia, wrote in his diary, "I was thunderstruck.... What would Jackson, Stuart, or—any of [those who had been killed fighting under Lee] say about us?... It is humiliating in the extreme. I never expected to see men cry as they did this morning. All the officers cried and most of the privates broke down and wept like children and Oh, Lord! I cried too."

The emotions of the weary and humiliated men in Lee's tattered army ranged from bitterness and anger to sadness and acceptance. But they were relieved when they learned that they would be paroled and free to go home rather than sent to Northern prisons. They were also grateful for the much-needed rations. But men need more than rations; they need meaning. And only Robert E. Lee, their beloved Marse Robert, could satisfy that most pressing of human needs by reinforcing their sense of honor, legitimating their pride, and redirecting their tired fury.

Having signed the certificate of birth, Grant and Lee still had to attend to the business of delivering a deathblow to the idea of secession while simultaneously injecting some vitality into the promise of this new beginning.

In his farewell order to the army, Lee praised their "four years of arduous service, marked by unsurpassed courage and fortitude," told them that they were brave and had "remained steadfast to the last," and urged them to peacefully return to their homes, taking with them "the satisfaction that proceeds from the consciousness of duty faithfully performed." He ended by honoring them: "With an increasing admiration of your constancy and devotion to your country, and a grateful remembrance of your kind and generous consideration for myself, I bid you all an affectionate farewell."[11]

What Lee accomplished in his address, says Bruce Catton, was to set the pattern, to give these men the right words to take with them into the future. "Pride in what they had done would grow with the years, but it would turn them into a romantic army of legend and not into a sullen battalion of death."

There were Federals, like General Chamberlain, who would not begrudge the Confederates the sentiments that Lee tried to instill in them. Although he believed they were wrong in their beliefs, "they fought as they were taught, true to such ideals as they saw, and put into their cause their best." Reflecting on the parade of Confederates stacking their arms and flags, Chamberlain, who was appointed to command the formal surrender of arms, said: "For us they were fellow-soldiers as well, suffering the fate of arms. We could not look into those brave, bronzed faces, and those battered flags we had met on so many fields where glorious manhood lent a glory to the earth that bore it, and think of personal hate and revenge."[12]

WEST POINT 2: SAM GRANT'S COMRADES

The next day, April 10, some of Grant's generals asked for permission to enter the Confederate lines to meet old friends. As he sat on the porch of the McLean house waiting for his officers to prepare his army to leave Appomattox, they began arriving with many of Grant's old comrades. Along with Phil Sheridan, John Gibbon, and Rufus Ingalls came the beloved Confederate Cadmus Wilcox, who had been best man at Grant's wedding. Confederate Henry Heth, who had been a subaltern with Grant in Mexico, was joined by his cousin George Pickett, who also knew Grant from Mexico. Pickett and Heth were friends of Gibbon, whose Union division bore the brunt of Pickett's charge at Gettysburg. Federal George Gordon and a number of others also came along.

Grant talked with them until it was time to leave. He later wrote that the officers "seemed to enjoy the meeting as much as though they had been friends separated for a long time while fighting battles under the same flag. For the time being it looked very much as if all thought of the war had escaped their minds."[13] No doubt somewhere deep in their hearts were the sentiments of the West Point hymn traditionally sung at the last chapel service before graduation:

> When shall we meet again?
> Meet ne'er to sever?
> When will Peace wreath her chain
> Round us forever?
> Our hearts will ne'er repose
> Safe from each blast that blows
> In this dark vale of woes,—
> Never—no, never.[14]

These friends were a band of brothers whom historian James McPherson describes as "more tightly bonded by hardship and danger in war than biological brothers." Now, on this spring day in April, the guns were quiet, and, as historian John Waugh points out, they "yearned to know that they would never hear their thunder or be ordered to take up arms against one another again."

By the time Longstreet arrived to join other Confederate and Union commissioners appointed to formulate the details of the surrender ceremony, Grant had apparently moved inside to a room that served as his temporary headquarters. When Longstreet walked by on the way to the room where the commissioners were meeting, Grant looked up and recognized him. He rose from his chair and, as Longstreet recalled, "with his old-time cheerful greeting gave me his hand, and after passing a few remarks offered a cigar, which was gratefully received."[15] Grant, addressing Longstreet by his nickname, said jokingly, "Pete, let us have another game of brag, to recall the days which were so pleasant to us all."[16] The two men had been best friends since West Point. They had served together for a time in the same regiment at Jefferson's Barracks, Missouri. Longstreet introduced Julia Dent, his distant cousin, to Grant and was present at their marriage vows. Three years after Appommatox, in 1868, Longstreet endorsed Grant's presidential candidacy and attended his inauguration.

Three years after Appommatox, in 1868, Longstreet endorsed Grant's presidential candidacy and attended his inauguration.

"The mere presence of conflict, envy, aggression, or any number of other contaminants does not doom or invalidate a friendship," says professor of English Ronald Sharp.[17] Much of the behavior of the West Pointers can be explained by the enormous strength of their friendships to withstand the horror of war. As Waugh points out, "It had never been in their hearts to hate the classmates they were fighting. Their lives and affections for one another had been indelibly framed and inextricably intertwined in their academy days. No adversity, war, killing, or political estrangement could undo that."[18] In his poem, "Meditation," Herman Melville, who visited the Virginia battlefront in the spring of 1864, celebrated their comradeship in the following verse:

> Mark the great Captains on both sides.
> The soldiers with the broad renown—
> They all were messmates on the Hudson's marge,
> Beneath one roof they laid them down;
> And, free from hate in many an after pass,
> Strove as in school-boy rivalry of the class.[19]

With some exaggeration, former West Pointer Morris Schaff wrote some forty years later that when "the graduates of both armies met as brothers" they symbolically "planted then and there the tree that has grown, blooming for the Confederate and blooming for the Federal, and under those whose shade we now gather in peace."[20] Our knowledge of the hatred and vengeance that Northerners and Southerners, including many West Pointers, felt toward each other and of the political conflicts attending Reconstruction might lead us to argue with the vision of West Pointers planting the tree of peace at Appomattox. But we cannot deny that, as their various diaries, letters, and memoirs document, that is what they thought they were doing.

EMBATTLED CIVILITY

A well-known paradox of the Civil War, writes Alan Nolan, was that "although fighting against each other with a devastating ferocity, the enlisted men and officers of the two sides tended to trust each other and did not see themselves in the manner of soldiers in most wars."[21] By the time Grant took command of the troubled Army of the Potomac in 1864, as Catton put it, "a fantastic sort of kinship"—"a queer combination of antagonism and understanding"—had grown up in regard to the Army of Northern Virginia. "There was no soft sentimentality about it, and the men would shoot to kill when the time for shooting came. Yet there was a familiarity and an understanding, at times something that verged almost on liking, based on solid respect." Now, on April 9, despite the fact that it was officially forbidden to prevent unpleasant contacts between members of the two armies, as soon as the surrender was announced there was quite a bit of visiting back and forth between the lines among Union and Confederate troops. Pvt. Charles Dunn of the 20th Maine reported that there was considerable trading that night.

> The two picket lines were within speaking distance, and we were on speaking terms with the "Johnnies" at once. There was nothing that resembled guard duty that night.

It resembled a picnic rather than a picket line. They like ourselves were glad the war was over. We exchanged knicknacks with them, and were reminded of the days when at school we swapped jews-harps for old wooden toothed combs. The articles we exchanged that night were about the same value.[22]

Chamberlain wrote of receiving Confederate visitors all the next day. "Our camp was full of callers before we were up," he recalled. "The inundation of visitors grew so that it looked like a country fair, including the cattle-show."

J. Tracy Power notes that Confederates

were impressed by Federal soldiers who shared rations or money with them and carried on pleasant, and sometimes friendly, conversations about the end of the war. Maj. Richard Watson Jones of the 12th Virginia was visited by a Federal officer he had known before the war when they attended the same college. Sgt. James Whitehorne described the scene when the Federal entered the Confederate camp. "We saw him come up and hold out his hand—the Major did nothing for so long it was painful. Then he took the offered hand and I had a feeling the war was really over."[23]

It was in just such conduct that Bell Wiley, in his study of the common soldier, saw "undeveloped resources of strength and character that spelled hope for the country's future."[24] For his own part, Whitehorne declared, "After all, I never hated any one Yankee. I hated the spirit that was sending them to invade the south."

TWO SIDES BUT ONE IDENTITY

In his moving tribute to the men in gray, Chamberlain asserted that "whoever had misled these men, we had not. We had led them back home." While it is true that Confederates had seceded from the Union politically, they had not left the Union culturally. A significant overarching factor in the reconciliation of the former combatants was the fact that the soldiers "were not alien foes but men of similar origin." The Civil War was not a conflict between Southern Cavaliers and New England Puritans, between a nation of warriors and a nation of shopkeepers, or, as abolitionist Wendell Phillips insisted, between a civilization based on democracy and one based on an aristocracy founded on slavery. Rather, it was, in the words of Walt Whitman, "a struggle going on within one identity." Robert Penn Warren concurs in his argument that the nation that went to war "share[d] deep and significant convictions and [was] not a mere handbasket of factions huddled arbitrarily together by historical happen-so."[25]

While it is true that Confederates had seceded from the Union politically, they had not left the Union culturally.

Whether consciously acknowledged by them or not, Northerners and Southerners shared significant elements of national identity that the war could not annihilate. By national identity I do not mean nationalism, to quote Merle Curti, "in the sense of both confidence in the strength of the federal government and devotion to the nation as a whole," which in the nineteenth century was only a hope, an aspiration. Rather, I mean shared nationality in the sense that, again, quoting Curti, rank-and-file Americans "[cherish] the Union as a precious symbol of a revered past and a bright future, identifying it with abundance, opportunity and ultimate peace."[26]

The social, cultural, philosophical, and ideological differences between the combatants have been fully documented. But, as Wiley concluded, "the similarities of Billy Yank and Johnny Reb far outweighed their differences. They were both Americans, by birth or by adoption, and they both had the weaknesses and the virtues of the people of their nation and time." Alan Nolan concurs: "They shared the same revolutionary experience, the same heroes, the same Founding Fathers; and, despite the south's departure from the Bill of Rights in the effort to protect slavery, they shared, at bottom, a sense of political values."[27]

> *America was becoming American. Johnny Reb and Billy Yank were creating a new kind of American and a new awareness of America.*

A key element of the national identity that Northerners and Southerners shared was a vision of the nation as the promised land to which God had led his people to establish a new social order that was to be, as John Winthrop said in 1630, "a city upon a hill, the eyes of all people are upon us, so that if we shall deal falsely with our God in this work we have undertaken and so cause him to withdraw his present help from us, we shall be made a story and a by-word through the world."[28]

The sense of being on show and tested before God and the world was no less true of Civil War combatants than it was for the Puritans. And just as persistent was the corollary concern of Americans that they would fall short of the vision. Because of this "fear of falling away," as historian Rupert Wilkinson calls it, Northerners and Southerners alike were faced with two basic philosophical questions: Are we worthy of our revolutionary forebears? Are we undoing, by our divisiveness, all that they worked so hard to obtain? Both sides compared America with its past and found themselves wanting. Both invoked the Revolutionary-Constitution era in seeking redemption of the Republic.

Civil War combatants were also bound by their perception of the changes swirling around them in the wider society as well as within their armies. "Always the army reflected the nation," writes Catton. And the nation itself was changing. Increased immigration, factory production, and urbanization eroded and destroyed old unities— "unities of blood, of race, of language, of shared ideals and common memories and experiences, the very

things which had always seemed essential beneath the word 'American.' In some mysterious way that nobody quite understood, the army not only mirrored the change but represented the effort to find a new synthesis."[29]

America was becoming American. Johnny Reb and Billy Yank were creating a new kind of American and a new awareness of America. As Warren points out,

> The War meant that Americans saw America. The farm boy of Ohio, the trapper in Minnesota, and the pimp of the Mackerelville section of New York City saw Richmond and Mobile. They not only saw America, they saw each other, and together shot it out with some Scot of the Valley of Virginia or ducked hardware hurled by a Louisiana Jew who might be a lieutenant of artillery, CSA.[30]

Out of the cauldron of hell into which were thrown Billy Yank, Johnny Reb, their immigrant comrades, as well as the black soldiers they all despised, came a pluralistic national community.

THE NATIONALIZATION OF LEE

In the decades following the war, as Americans became more American, so too did Robert E. Lee's image. By the turn of the century he was nationally elevated to a hero status shared by only a handful of individuals, such as Washington, Lincoln, and Jefferson. In their study of the transformation of Lee's image, Thomas Connelly and Barbara Bellows report: "A writer in *Harper's Weekly* proclaimed him 'the pride of a whole country.'... The *New York Times* praised Lee's 'grandeur of soul,' and the *Nation* called Lee 'great in gentleness and goodness.' "[31]

> The Americanization of Lee began long before he surrendered. When Brig. Gen. Samuel Crawford, in the 5th Corps of the Army of the Potomac, visited briefly with Lee the day after his surrender to Grant, he told Lee that, should he go North, he would find that he had "hosts of warm friends there." With tears in his eyes, Lee said, "I suppose all the people of the North looked upon me as a rebel traitor." Far from it. An unlikely contributor to his elevation was Julia Ward Howe, the abolitionist who wrote "Battle Hymn of the Republic":

A gallant foeman in the fight,
A brother when the fight was o'er,
The hand that led the host with might
The blessed torch of learning bore.
No shriek of shells nor roll of drums,
No challenge fierce, resounding far,
When reconciling Wisdom comes
To heal the cruel wounds of war.
Thought may the minds of men divide,
Love makes the heart of nations one,
And so, the soldier grave beside,
We honor thee, Virginia's son.[32]

The nationalization of Lee is a very American cultural practice: the elevation of worthy "native sons"—beyond the soil of their birth, beyond the privileges or lack of privileges of their class, beyond the dogma of their creed—to the position of national icon. In 1900 Virginia's son was inducted into the newly established Hall of Fame for Great Americans along with Washington, Jefferson, John Adams, and Benjamin Franklin. In 1934, Virginia presented statues of Lee and Washington to Congress to be placed in Statuary Hall in the U.S. Capitol, which houses statues of outstanding citizens from each of the states. The Lee so honored—the Lee that won over the nation and was praised by every American president—was, as Connelly and Bellows describe him, "the man of basic American values of decency, duty, and honor, the devotee of unionism trapped in 1861 by conflicting loyalties." Lee was the postwar nationalist, driven by an unswerving determination to help restore the old Union.

In truth, America had never been united, but now it was on the road toward becoming American.

But Lee is the supreme paradoxical American hero. As McPherson insightfully points out, Lee's heroism has to be seen in terms of his gigantic role in prolonging the war longer than it might have been. When Lee took command of the Army of Northern Virginia in June 1862, the Confederacy was on the verge of collapse. In the previous four months, it had lost its largest city, New Orleans; much of the Mississippi Valley; and most of Tennessee; and Maj. Gen. George McClellan's Army of the Potomac had moved to within five miles of Richmond, the Confederate capital. McPherson cites the irony of Lee's command as follows:

> Within three months Lee's offensives had taken the Confederacy off the floor at the count of nine and had driven Union forces onto the ropes. Without Lee the Confederacy might have died in 1862. But slavery would have survived; the South would have suffered only limited death and destruction. Lee's victories prolonged the war until it destroyed slavery, the plantation economy, the wealth and infrastructure of the region, and everything else the confederacy stood for. That was the profound irony of Lee's military genius.[33]

THE SIGNIFICANCE OF APPOMATTOX

In an April 12 telegram to Grant, who had departed for Washington two days earlier, General Gibbon informed him that "the surrender of General Lee's army was finally completed today," then went on to comment on the meaning of Appomattox: "I have conversed with many of the surrendered officers, and am satisfied that by announcing at once terms and a liberal, merciful policy on the part of the Government we can once more have a happy, united country."[34]

This is what Lincoln wanted. In truth, America had never been united, but now it was on the road toward becoming American. And this is how it sounded: A Confederate officer at the head of his surrendering corps told Chamberlain, "General, this is deeply humiliating; but I console myself with the thought that the whole country will rejoice at this day." Another told him, "I went into that cause and I meant it. We had our choice of weapons and of ground, and we have lost. Now that is my flag (pointing to the flag of the Union), and I will prove myself as worthy as any of you."[35]

References

1. Bruce Catton, *The Centennial History of the Civil War: Never Call Retreat*, vol. 3 (New York: Doubleday and Co., 1965), 455–56.
2. James Robertson Jr., *Civil War Journal: Robert E. Lee: A History TV Network Presentation*, Time-Life Video (Alexandria, Va.: Time, 1994).
3. Bruce Catton, *A Stillness at Appomattox* (New York: Doubleday and Co., 1957, 340.
4. David Dixon Porter, quoted in Philip Van Doren Stern, *An End to Valor: The Last Days of the Civil War* (Boston: Houghton Mifflin Co., 1858), 103–104.
5. Catton, *Stillness at Appomattox*, 341.
6. L.A. Hendrick, "Conferences of Commanding Officers," *Freeman's Journal and Catholic Register*, 22 April 1865. Quoted in Frank Cauble, *The Surrender Proceedings: April Ninth, 1865, Appomattox Court House* (Lynchburg, Va.: H.E. Howard, 1987), 43–44.
7. Joshua Lawrence Chamberlain, *The Passing of the Armies: The Last Campaign of the Armies* (Gettysburg, Pa.: Stan Clark Military Books, 1995 reprint ed.), 244.
8. Gary Gallagher, ed., *Fighting for the Confederacy: The Personal Recollections of General Edward Porter Alexander* (Chapel Hill, N.C.: University of North Carolina Press, 1989), 540.
9. William Styple, ed., *With a Flash of His Sword: The Writings of Maj. Holman S. Melcher, 20th Maine Infantry* (Kearny, N.J.: Belle Grove Publishing Co., 1994), 219.
10. J. Tracy Power, *Lee's Miserables: Life in the Army of Northern Virginia From the Wilderness to Appomattox* (Chapel Hill, N.C.: University of North Carolina Press, 1998), 282.
11. Thomas Connelly, *Marble Man: Robert E. Lee and His Image in American Society* (Baton Rouge, La.: Louisiana State University Press, 1978), 367.
12. Chamberlain, *Passing of the Armies*, 270.
13. Ulysses S. Grant, *Memoirs and Selected Letters: Personal Memoirs of U.S. Grant: Selected Letters 1839–1865* (New York: Library of America, 1990), 744.
14. Quoted in George Pappas, *To the Point: The United States Military Academy, 1802–1902* (Westport, Conn.: Praeger, 1993), 322.
15. James Longstreet, *From Manassas to Appomattox* [1896] (New York: Konecky and Konecky, 1992), 630.
16. Jeffrey Wert, *General James Longstreet: The Confederacy's Most Controversial Soldier* (New York: Simon and Schuster, 1994), 404.
17. Ronald Sharp, *Friendship and Literature: Spirit and Form* (Durham, N.C.: Duke University Press, 1986), 120.
18. John Waugh, *The Class of 1846: From West Point to Appomattox: Stonewall Jackson, George McClellan and Their Brothers* (New York: Warner Books, 1994), 500.
19. Herman Melville, *Battle-Pieces and Aspects of the War* [1866]. Quoted in Richard Dilworth Rust, ed., *Glory and Pathos: Responses of Nineteenth-Century American Authors to the Civil War* (Boston: Holbrook Press, 1970), 177.
20. Morris Schaff, *The Spirit of Old West Point, 1858–1862* (Boston: Houghton-Mifflin, 1907), 140, 251–53
21. Alan Nolan, *Lee Considered: General Robert E. Lee and Civil War History* (Chapel Hill, N.C.: University of North Carolina Press, 1991), 158.

22. Quoted in J.J. Pullen, *The Twentieth Maine* (Philadelphia: J.B. Lippincott Co., 1957), 270.

23. Quoted in Power, *Lee's Miserables*, 283.

24. Bell Wiley, *The Life of Johnny Reb and the Life of Billy Yank* [1943, 1952], reprint, Essential Classics of the Civil War (New York: Book-of-the-Month Club/Louisiana State University Press, 1994), 361.

25. Robert Penn Warren, *The Legacy of the Civil War* (New York: Random House, 1961), 83.

26. Merle Curti, *The Growth of American Thought* (New Brunswick, N.J.: Transaction Publishers, 1991), 423–24.

27. Nolan, *Lee Considered*, 157.

28. John Winthrop, "A Modell of Christian Charity," (1630), reprinted in Daniel Boorstin, ed., *An American Primer,* vol. 1 (Chicago: Chicago University Press, 1966), 22.

29. Catton, *Stillness at Appomattox*, 216.

30. Warren, *Legacy of the Civil War*, 13.

31. Thomas Connelly and Barbara Bellows, *God and General Longstreet: The Lost Cause and the Southern Mind* (Baton Rouge: Louisiana State University Press, 1982), 83.

32. Julia Ward Howe, "Robert E. Lee," in Lois Hill, ed., *Poems and Songs of the Civil War* (New York: Gramercy Books, 1990).

33. James McPherson, *Drawn With the Sword: Reflections on the American Civil War* (New York: Oxford University Press, 1996), 158.

34. Quoted in Bruce Catton, *Grant Takes Command* [1968] (New York: Book-of-the-Month Club, 1994), 473.

35. Chamberlain, *Passing of the Armies*, 266.

Anne Wortham is associate professor of sociology at Illinois State University.

From *The World & I,* May 1999, pages 295–305, 307–309. Copyright © 1999 by The World & I Magazine. Reprinted with permission.

Death of John Wilkes Booth

Within minutes of shooting President Abraham Lincoln, assassin John Wilkes Booth was mounted and making his escape. Crossing the Navy Yard Bridge over the Anacostia River into Maryland, Booth and his accomplice David Herold headed south. Seeking treatment for the actor's leg, which he had broken in the jump from Lincoln's theater box to the stage, they spent that night and part of the next day in the house of Dr Samuel Mudd, who splinted the fracture. Continuing on, the two passed the next five days and five frigid nights holed up in a thicket awaiting a chance to cross the Potomac River into Virginia. The night of April 20, with Booth aboard, Herold began rowing a small boat acquired from a sympathizer toward the Virginia side of the river. Carried upstream by the incoming tide, they were forced to hide, still on the Maryland shore, for two more days before successfully crossing the river the night of April 22. Once across, they were passed from house to house inland, eventually crossing the Rappahanock River at Port Conway and continuing about two miles to the farm of Richard Garrett. Meanwhile, following a series of leads and with some blind luck, detectives and a detachment of the 16th New York Cavalry tracked Booth and Herold to the Garrett farm. This account of their capture and Booth's death on the morning of April 26 is from the report of the cavalry unit's commander, Lieutenant Edward P. Doherty.

I dismounted, and knocked loudly at the front door. Old Mr Garrett came out. I seized him, and asked him where the men were who had gone to the woods when the cavalry passed the previous afternoon. While I was speaking with him some of the men had entered the house to search it. Soon one of the soldiers sang out, "O Lieutenant! I have a man here I found in the corncrib." It was young Garrett, and I demanded the whereabouts of the fugitives. He replied, "In the barn." Leaving a few men around the house, we proceeded in the direction of the barn, which we surrounded. I kicked on the door of the barn several rimes without receiving a reply. Meantime another son of the Garrett's had been captured. The barn was secured with a padlock, and young Garrett carried the key. I unlocked the door, and again summoned the inmates of the building to surrender.

After some delay Booth said, "For whom do you take me?"

I replied, "It doesn't make any difference. Come out."

He said, "I am a cripple and alone."

I said, "I know who is with you, and you had better surrender."

He replied, "I may be taken by my friends, but not by my foes."

I said, "If you don't come out, I'll burn the building." I directed a corporal to pile up some hay in a crack in the wall of the barn and set the building on fire.

As the corporal was picking up the hay and brush Booth said, "If you come back here I will put a bullet through you."

I then motioned to the corporal to desist, and decided to wait for daylight and then to enter the barn by both doors and overpower the assassins.

Booth then said in a drawling voice, "Oh Captain! There is a man here who wants to surrender awful bad."

I replied, "You had better follow his example and come out."

His answer was, "No, I have not made up my mind; but draw your men up fifty paces off and give me a chance for my life."

I told him I had not come to fight; that I had fifty men, and could take him.

Then he said, "Well, my brave boys, prepare me a stretcher, and place another stain on our glorious banner."

At this moment Herold reached the door. I asked him to hand out his arms; he replied that he had none. I told him I knew exactly what weapons he had. Booth replied, "I own all the arms, and may have to use them on you, gentlemen."

I then said to Herold, "Let me see your hands." He put them through the partly opened door and I seized him by the wrists. I handed him over to a non-commissioned officer. Just at this moment I heard a shot, and thought Booth had shot himself. Throwing open the door, I saw that the straw and hay behind Booth were on fire. He was half-turning towards it.

He had a crutch, and he held a carbine in his hand. I rushed into the burning barn, followed by my men, and as he was falling caught him under the arms and pulled him out of the barn. The burning building becoming too hot, I had him carried to the veranda of Garrett's house.

Booth received his death-shot in this manner. While I was taking Herold out of the barn one of the detectives went to the rear, and pulling out some protruding straw set fire to it. I had placed Sergeant Boston Corbett at a large crack in the side of the barn, and he, seeing by the igniting hay that Booth was leveling his carbine at either Herold or myself, fired, to disable him in the arm; but Booth making a sudden move, the aim erred, and the bullet struck Booth in the back of the head, about an inch below the spot where his shot had entered the head of Mr Lincoln. Booth asked me by signs to raise his hands. I lifted them up and he gasped, "Useless, useless!" We gave him brandy and water, but he could not swallow it. I sent to Port Royal for a physician, who could do nothing when he came, and at seven o'clock Booth breathed his last. He had on his person a diary, a large bowie knife, two pistols, a compass and a draft on Canada for 60 pounds.

The New View of Reconstruction

Whatever you were taught or thought you knew about the post-Civil War
era is probably wrong in the light of recent study

Eric Foner

In the past twenty years, no period of American history has been the subject of a more thoroughgoing reevaluation than Reconstruction—the violent, dramatic, and still controversial era following the Civil War. Race relations, politics, social life, and economic change during Reconstruction have all been reinterpreted in the light of changed attitudes toward the place of blacks within American society. If historians have not yet forged a fully satisfying portrait of Reconstruction as a whole, the traditional interpretation that dominated historical writing for much of this century has irrevocably been laid to rest.

Anyone who attended high school before 1960 learned that Reconstruction was a era of unrelieved sordidness in American political and social life. The martyred Lincoln, according to this view, had planned a quick and painless readmission of the Southern states as equal members of the national family. President Andrew Johnson, his successor, attempted to carry out Lincoln's policies but was foiled by the Radical Republicans (also known as Vindictives or Jacobins). Motivated by an irrational hatred of Rebels or by ties with Northern capitalists out to plunder the South, the Radicals swept aside Johnson's lenient program and fastened black supremacy upon the defeated Confederacy. An orgy of corruption followed, presided over by unscrupulous carpetbaggers (Northerners who ventured south to reap the spoils of office), traitorous scalawags (Southern whites who cooperated with the new gov-

ernments for personal gain), and the ignorant and childlike freedmen, who were incapable of properly exercising the political power that had been thrust upon them. After much needless suffering, the white community of the South banded together to overthrow these "black" governments and restore home rule (their euphemism for white supremacy). All told, Reconstruction was just about the darkest page in the American saga.

Originating in anti-Reconstruction propaganda of Southern Democrats during the 1870s, this traditional interpretation achieved scholarly legitimacy around the turn of the century through the work of William Dunning and his students at Columbia University. It reached the larger public through films like *Birth of a Nation* and *Gone With the Wind* and that best-selling work of myth-making masquerading as history, *The Tragic Era* by Claude G. Bowers. In language as exaggerated as it was colorful, Bowers told how Andrew Johnson "fought the bravest battle for constitutional liberty and for the preservation of our institutions ever waged by an Executive" but was overwhelmed by the "poisonous propaganda" of the Radicals. Southern whites, as a result, "literally were put to the torture" by "emissaries of hate" who manipulated the "simple-minded" freedmen, inflaming the negroes' "egotism" and even inspiring "lustful assaults" by blacks upon white womanhood.

In a discipline that sometimes seems to pride itself on the rapid rise and fall of his-

torical interpretations, this traditional portrait of Reconstruction enjoyed remarkable staying power. The long reign of the old interpretation is not difficult to explain. It presented a set of easily identifiable heroes and villains. It enjoyed the imprimatur of the nation's leading scholars. And it accorded with the political and social realities of the first half of this century. This image of Reconstruction helped freeze the mind of the white South in unalterable opposition to any movement for breaching the ascendancy of the Democratic party, eliminating segregation, or readmitting disfranchised blacks to the vote.

Nevertheless, the demise of the traditional interpretation was inevitable, for it ignored the testimony of the central participant in the drama of Reconstruction—the black freedman. Furthermore, it was grounded in the conviction that blacks were unfit to share in political power. As Dunning's Columbia colleague John W. Burgess put it, "A black skin means membership in a race of men which has never of itself succeeded in subjecting passion to reason, has never, therefore, created any civilization of any kind." Once objective scholarship and modern experience rendered that assumption untenable, the entire edifice was bound to fall.

The work of "revising" the history of Reconstruction began with the writings of a handful of survivors of the era, such as John R. Lynch, who had served as a black congressman from Mississippi after the Civil War. In the 1930s white scholars like Francis Simkins and Robert Woody carried the task forward. Then, in 1935, the black historian and activist W. E. B. Du Bois produced *Black Reconstruction in America,* a monumental revaluation that closed with an irrefutable indictment of a historical profession that had sacrificed scholarly objectivity on the altar of racial bias. "One fact and one alone," he wrote, "explains the attitude of most recent writers toward Reconstruction; they cannot conceive of Negroes as men." Du Bois's work, however, was ignored by most historians.

Black initiative established as many schools as did Northern religious societies and the Freedmen's Bureau. The right to vote was not simply thrust upon them by meddling outsiders, since blacks began agitating for the suffrage as soon as they were freed.

It was not until the 1960s that the full force of the revisionist wave broke over the field. Then, in rapid succession, virtually every assumption of the traditional viewpoint was systematically dismantled. A drastically different portrait emerged to take its place. President Lincoln did not have a coherent "plan" for Reconstruction, but at the time of his assassination he had been cautiously contemplating black suffrage. Andrew Johnson was a stubborn, racist politician who lacked the ability to compromise. By isolating himself from the broad currents of public opinion that had nourished Lincoln's career, Johnson created an impasse with Congress that Lincoln would certainly have avoided, thus throwing away his political power and destroying his own plans for reconstructing the South.

The Radicals in Congress were acquitted of both vindictive motives and the charge of serving as the stalking-horses of Northern capitalism. They emerged instead as idealists in the best nineteenth-century reform tradition. Radical leaders like Charles Sumner and Thaddeus Stevens had worked for the rights of blacks long before any conceivable political advantage flowed from such a commitment. Stevens refused to sign the Pennsylvania Constitution of 1838 because it disfranchised the state's black citizens; Sumner led a fight in the 1850s to integrate Boston's public schools. Their Reconstruction policies were based on principle, not petty political advantage, for the central issue dividing Johnson and these Radical Republicans was the civil rights of freedmen. Studies of congressional policy-making, such as Eric L. McKitrick's *Andrew Johnson and Reconstruction,* also revealed that Reconstruction legislation, ranging from the Civil Rights Act of 1866 to the Fourteenth and Fifteenth Amendments, enjoyed broad support from moderate and conservative Republicans. It was not simply the work of a narrow radical faction.

Even more startling was the revised portrait of Reconstruction in the South itself. Imbued with the spirit of the civil rights movement and rejecting entirely the racial assumptions that had underpinned the traditional interpretation, these historians evaluated Reconstruction from the black point of view. Works like Joel Williamson's *After Slavery* portrayed the period as a time of extraordinary political, social, and economic progress for blacks. The establishment of public school systems, the granting of equal citizenship to blacks, the effort to restore the devastated Southern economy, the attempt to construct an interracial political democracy from the ashes of slavery, all these were commendable achievements, not the elements of Bowers's "tragic era."

Unlike earlier writers, the revisionists stressed the active role of the freedmen in shaping Reconstruction. Black initiative established as many schools as did Northern religious societies and the Freedmen's Bureau. The right to vote was not simply thrust upon them by meddling outsiders, since blacks began agitating for the suffrage as soon as they were freed. In 1865 black conventions throughout the South issued eloquent, though unheeded, appeals for equal civil and political rights.

With the advent of Radical Reconstruction in 1867, the freedmen did enjoy a real measure of political power. But black supremacy never existed. In most states blacks held only a small fraction of political offices, and even in South Carolina, where they comprised a majority of the state legislature's lower house, effective power remained in white hands. As for corruption, moral standards in both gov-

ernment and private enterprise were at low ebb throughout the nation in the postwar years—the era of Boss Tweed, the Credit Mobilier scandal, and the Whiskey Ring. Southern corruption could hardly be blamed on former slaves.

Other actors in the Reconstruction drama also came in for reevaluation. Most carpetbaggers were former Union soldiers seeking economic opportunity in the postwar South, not unscrupulous adventurers. Their motives, a typically American amalgam of humanitarianism and the pursuit of profit, were no more insidious than those of Western pioneers. Scalawags, previously seen as traitors to the white race, now emerged as "Old Line" Whig Unionists who had opposed secession in the first place or as poor whites who had long resented planters' domination of Southern life and who saw in Reconstruction a chance to recast Southern society along more democratic lines. Strongholds of Southern white Republicanism like east Tennessee and western North Carolina had been the scene of resistance to Confederate rule throughout the Civil War; now, as one scalawag newspaper put it, the choice was "between salvation at the hand of the Negro or destruction at the hand of the rebels."

At the same time, the Ku Klux Klan and kindred groups, whose campaign of violence against black and white Republicans had been minimized or excused in older writings, were portrayed as they really were. Earlier scholars had conveyed the impression that the Klan intimidated blacks mainly by dressing as ghosts and playing on the freedmen's superstitions. In fact, black fears were all too real: the Klan was a terrorist organization that beat and killed its political opponents to deprive blacks of their newly won rights. The complicity of the Democratic party and the silence of prominent whites in the face of such outrages stood as an indictment of the moral code the South had inherited from the days of slavery.

By the end of the 1960s, then, the old interpretation had been completely reversed. Southern freedmen were the heroes, the "Redeemers" who overthrew Reconstruction were the villains, and if the era was "tragic," it was because change did not go far enough. Reconstruction had been a time of real progress and its failure a lost opportunity for the South and the nation. But the legacy of Reconstruction— the Fourteenth and Fifteenth Amendments—endured to inspire future efforts for civil rights. As Kenneth Stampp wrote in *The Era of Reconstruction,* a superb summary of revisionist findings published in 1965, "if it was worth four years of civil war to save the Union, it was worth a few years of radical reconstruction to give the American Negro the ultimate promise of equal civil and political rights."

> *Under slavery most blacks had lived in nuclear family units, although they faced the constant threat of separation from loved ones by sale. Reconstruction provided the opportunity for blacks to solidify their preexisting family ties.*

As Stampp's statement suggests, the reevaluation of the first Reconstruction was inspired in large measure by the impact of the second—the modern civil rights movement. And with the waning of that movement in recent years, writing on Reconstruction has undergone still another transformation. Instead of seeing the Civil War and its aftermath as a second American Revolution (as Charles Beard had), a regression into barbarism (as Bowers argued), or a golden opportunity squandered (as the revisionists saw it), recent writers argue that Radical Reconstruction was not really very radical. Since land was not distributed to the former slaves, the remained economically dependent upon their former owners. The planter class survived both the war and Reconstruction with its property (apart from slaves) and prestige more or less intact.

Not only changing times but also the changing concerns of historians have contributed to this latest reassessment of Reconstruction. The hallmark of the past decade's historical writing has been an emphasis upon "social history"—the evocation of the past lives of ordinary Americans—and the downplaying of strictly political events. When applied to Reconstruction, this concern with the "social" suggested that black suffrage and officeholding, once seen as the most radical departures of the Reconstruction era, were relatively insignificant.

Recent historians have focused their investigations not upon the politics of Reconstruction but upon the social and economic aspects of the transition from slavery to freedom. Herbert Gutman's influential study of the black family during and after slavery found little change in family structure or relations between men and women resulting from emancipation. Under slavery most blacks had lived in nuclear family units, although they faced the constant threat of separation from loved ones by sale. Reconstruction provided the opportunity for blacks to solidify their preexisting family ties. Conflicts over whether black women should work in the cotton fields (planters said yes, many black families said no) and over white attempts to "apprentice" black children revealed that the autonomy of family life was a major preoccupation of the freedmen. Indeed, whether manifested in their withdrawal from churches controlled by whites, in the blossoming of black fraternal, benevolent, and self-improvement organizations, or in the demise of the slave quarters and their replacement by small tenant farms occupied by individual families, the quest for independence from white authority and control over their own day-to-day lives shaped the black response to emancipation.

> *The Civil War raised the decisive questions of American's national existence: the relations between local and national authority, the definition of citizenship, the balance between force and consent in generating obedience to authority.*

In the post–Civil War South the surest guarantee of economic autonomy, blacks believed, was land. To the freedmen the justice of a claim to land based on their years of unrequited labor appeared self-evident. As an Alabama black convention put it, "The property which they [the planters] hold was nearly all earned by the sweat of *our* brows." As Leon Litwack showed in *Been in the Storm So Long,* a Pulitzer Prize–winning account of the black response to emancipation, many freedmen in 1865 and 1866 refused to sign labor contracts, expecting the federal government to give them land. In some localities, as one Alabama overseer reported, they "set up claims to the plantation and all on it."

In the end, of course, the vast majority of Southern blacks remained propertyless and poor. But exactly why the South, and especially its black population, suffered from dire poverty and economic retardation in the decades following the Civil War is a matter of much dispute. In *One Kind of Freedom* economists Roger Ransom and Richard Sutch indicted country merchants for monopolizing credit and charging usurious interest rates, forcing black tenants into debt and locking the South into a dependence on cotton production that impoverished the entire region. But Jonathan Wiener, in his study of postwar Alabama, argued that planters used their political power to compel blacks to remain on the plantations. Planters succeeded in stabilizing the plantation system, but only by blocking the growth of alternative enterprises, like factories, that might draw off black laborers, thus locking the region into a pattern of economic backwardness.

If the thrust of recent writing has emphasized the social and economic aspects of Reconstruction, politics has not been entirely neglected. But political studies have also reflected the postrevisionist mood summarized by C. Vann Woodward when he observed "how essentially nonrevolutionary and conservative Reconstruction really was." Recent writers, unlike their revisionist predecessors, have found little to praise in federal policy toward the emancipated blacks.

A new sensitivity to the strength of prejudice and laissez-faire ideas in the nineteenth-century North has led many historians to doubt whether the Republican party ever made a genuine commitment to racial justice in the South. The granting of black suffrage was an alternative to a long-term federal responsibility for protecting the rights of the former slaves. Once enfranchised, blacks could be left to fend for themselves. With the exception of a few Radicals like Thaddeus Stevens, nearly all Northern policy-makers and educators are criticized today for assuming that, so long as the unfettered operations of the marketplace afforded blacks the opportunity to advance through diligent labor, federal efforts to assist them in acquiring land were unnecessary.

Probably the most innovative recent writing on Reconstruction politics has centered on a broad reassessment of black Republicanism, largely undertaken by a new generation of black historians. Scholars like Thomas Holt and Nell Painter insist that Reconstruction was not simply a matter of black and white. Conflicts within the black community, no less than divisions among whites, shaped Reconstruction politics. Where revisionist scholars, both black and white, had celebrated the accomplishments of black political leaders, Holt, Painter, and others charge that they failed to address the economic plight of the black masses. Painter criticized "representative colored men," as national black leaders were called, for failing to provide ordinary freedmen with effective political leadership. Holt found that black officeholders in South Carolina most emerged from the old free mulatto class of Charleston, which shared many assumptions with prominent whites. "Basically bourgeois in their origins and orientation," he wrote, they "failed to act in the interest of black peasants."

In emphasizing the persistence from slavery of divisions between free blacks and slaves, these writers reflect the increasing concern with continuity and conservatism in Reconstruction. Their work reflects a startling extension of revisionist premises. If, as has been argued for the past twenty years, blacks were active agents rather than mere victims of manipulation, then they could not be absolved of blame for the ultimate failure of Reconstruction.

Despite the excellence of recent writings and the continual expansion of our knowledge of the period, historians of Reconstruction today face a unique dilemma. An old interpretation has been overthrown, but a coherent new synthesis has yet to take its place. The revisionists of the 1960s effectively established a series of negative points: the Reconstruction governments were not as bad as had been portrayed, black supremacy was a myth, the Radicals were not cynical manipulators of the freedmen. Yet no convincing overall portrait of the quality of political and social life emerged from their writings. More recent historians have rightly pointed to elements of continuity that spanned the nineteenth-century Southern experience, especially the survival, in modified form, of the plantation system. Nevertheless, by denying the real changes that did occur, they have failed to provide a convincing portrait of an era characterized above all by drama, turmoil, and social change.

Building upon the findings of the past twenty years of scholarship, a new portrait of Reconstruction ought to begin by viewing it not as a specific time period, bounded by the years 1865 and 1877, but as an epi-sode in a prolonged historical process—American society's adjustment to the consequences of the Civil War and emancipation. The Civil War, of course, raised the decisive questions of America's national existence: the relations between local and national authority, the definition of citizenship, the balance between force and consent in generating obedience to authority. The war and Reconstruction, as Allan Nevins observed over fifty years ago, marked the "emergence of modern America." This was the era of the completion of the national railroad network, the creation of the modern steel industry, the conquest of the West and final subduing of the Indians, and the expansion of the mining frontier. Lincoln's America—the world of the small farm and artisan shop—gave way to a rapidly industrializing economy. The issues that galvanized postwar Northern politics—from the question of the greenback currency to the mode of paying holders of the national debt—arose from the economic changes unleased by the Civil War.

Above all, the war irrevocably abolished slavery. Since 1619, when "twenty negars" disembarked from a Dutch ship in Virginia, racial injustice had haunted American life, mocking its professed ideals even as tobacco and cotton, the products of slave labor, helped finance the nation's economic development. Now the implications of the black presence could no longer be ignored. The Civil War resolved the problem of slavery but, as the Philadelphia diarist Sydney George Fisher observed in June 1865, it opened an even more intractable problem: "What shall we do with the Negro?" Indeed, he went on, this was a problem *incapable* of any solution that will satisfy both North and South."

As Fisher realized, the focal point of Reconstruction was the social revolution known as emancipation. Plantation slavery was simultaneously a system of labor, a form of racial domination, and the foundation upon which arose a distinctive ruling class within the South. Its demise threw open the most fundamental questions of economy, society, and politics. A new system of labor, social, racial, and political relations had to be created to replace slavery.

The United States was not the only nation to experience emancipation in the nineteenth century. Neither plantation slavery nor abolition were unique to the United States. But Reconstruction was. In a comparative perspective Radical Reconstruction stands as a remarkable experiment, the only effort of a society experiencing abolition to bring the former slaves within the umbrella of equal citizenship. Because the Radicals did not achieve everything they wanted, historians have lately tended to play down the stunning departure represented by black suffrage and officeholding. Former slaves, most fewer than two years removed from bondage, debated the fundamental questions of the polity: what is a republican form of government? Should the state provide equal education for all? How could political equality be reconciled with a society in which property was so unequally distributed? There was something inspiring in the way such men met the challenge of Reconstruction. "I knew nothing more than to obey my master," James K. Greene, an Alabama black politician later recalled. "But the tocsin of freedom sounded and knocked at the door and we walked out like free men and we met the exigencies as they grew up, and shouldered the responsibilities."

Y ou never saw a people more excited on the subject of politics than are the negroes of the south," one planter observed in 1867. And there were more than a few Southern whites as well who in these years shook off the prejudices of the past to embrace the revision of a new South dedicated to the principles of equal citizenship and social justice. One ordinary South Carolinian expressed the new sense of possibility in 1868 to the Republican governor of the state: "I am sorry that I cannot write an elegant stiled letter to your excellency. But I rejoice to think that God almighty has given to the poor of S.C. a Gov. to hear to feel to protect the humble poor without distinction to race or color.... I am a native borned S.C. a poor man never owned a Negro in my life nor my father before me.... Remember the true and loyal are the poor of the whites and blacks, outside of these you can find none loyal."

Few modern scholars believe the Reconstruction governments established in the South in 1867 and 1868 fulfilled the aspirations of their humble constituents. While their achievements in such realms as education, civil rights, and the economic rebuilding of the South are now widely appreciated, historians today believe they failed to affect either the economic plight of the emancipated slave or the ongoing transformation of independent white farmers into cotton tenants. Yet their opponents did perceive the Reconstruction governments in precisely this way—as representatives of a revolution that had put the bottom rail, both racial and economic, on top. This perception helps explain the ferocity of the attacks leveled against them and the pervasiveness of violence in the post-emancipation South.

In the end neither the abolition of slavery nor Reconstruction succeeded in resolving the debate over the meaning of freedom in American life.

The spectacle of black men voting and holding office was anathema to large numbers of Southern whites. Even more disturbing, at least in the view of those who still controlled the plantation regions of the South, was the emergence of local officials, black and white, who sympathized with the plight of the black laborer. Alabama's vagrancy law was a "dead letter" in 1870, "because those who are charged with its enforcement are indebted to the vagrant vote for their offices and emoluments." Political debates over the level and incidence of taxation, the control of crops, and the resolution of contract disputes revealed that a primary issue of Reconstruction was the role of government in a plantation society. During presidential Reconstruction, and after "Redemption," with planters and their allies in control of politics, the law emerged as a means of stabilizing and promoting the plantation system. If Radical Reconstruction failed to redistribute the land of the South, the ouster of the planter class from control of politics at least ensured that the sanctions of the criminal law would not be employed to discipline the black labor force.

An understanding of this fundamental conflict over the relation between government and society helps explain the pervasive complaints concerning corruption and "extravagance" during Radical Reconstruction. Corruption there was aplenty; tax rates did rise sharply. More significant

than the rate of taxation, however, was the change in its incidence. For the first time, planters and white farmers had to pay a significant portion of their income to the government, while propertyless blacks often escaped scot-free. Several states, moreover, enacted heavy taxes on uncultivated land to discourage land speculation and force land onto the market, benefiting, it was hoped, the freedmen.

As time passed, complaints about the "extravagance" and corruption of Southern governments found a sympathetic audience among influential Northerners. The Democratic charge that universal suffrage in the South was responsible for high taxes and governmental extravagance coincided with a rising conviction among the urban middle classes of the North that city government had to be taken out of the hands of the immigrant poor and returned to the "best men"—the educated, professional, financially independent citizens unable to exert much political influence at a time of mass parties and machine politics. Increasingly the "respectable" middle classes began to retreat from the very notion of universal suffrage. The poor were not longer perceived as honest producers, the backbone of the social order; now they became the "dangerous classes," the "mob." As the historian Francis Parkman put it, too much power rested with "masses of imported ignorance and hereditary ineptitude." To Parkman the Irish of the Northern cities and the blacks of the South were equally incapable of utilizing the ballot: "Witness the municipal corruptions of New York, and the monstrosities of negro rule in South Carolina." Such attitudes helped to justify Northern inaction as, one by one, the Reconstruction regimes of the South were overthrown by political violence.

In the end, then, neither the abolition of slavery nor Reconstruction succeeded in resolving the debate over the meaning of freedom in American life. Twenty years before the American Civil War, writing about the prospect of abolition in France's colonies, Alexis de Tocqueville had written, "If the Negroes have the right to become free, the [planters] have the incontestable right not to be ruined by the

Negroes' freedom." And in the United States, as in nearly every plantation society that experienced the end of slavery, a rigid social and political dichotomy between former master and former slave, an ideology of racism, and a dependent labor force with limited economic opportunities all survived abolition. Unless one means by freedom the simple fact of not being a slave, emancipation thrust blacks into a kind of no-man's land, a partial freedom that made a mockery of the American ideal of equal citizenship.

Yet by the same token the ultimate outcome underscores the uniqueness of Reconstruction itself. Alone among the societies that abolished slavery in the nineteenth century, the United States, for a moment, offered the freedmen a measure of political control over their own destinies. However brief its sway, Reconstruction allowed scope for a remarkable political and social mobilization of the black community. It opened doors of opportunity that could never be completely closed. Reconstruction transformed the lives of Southern blacks in ways unmeasurable by statistics and unreachable by law. It raised their expectations and aspirations, redefined their status in relation to the larger society, and allowed space for the creation of institutions that enabled them to survive the repression that followed. And it established constitutional principles of civil and political equality that, while flagrantly violated after Redemption, planted the seeds of future struggle.

Certainly, in terms of the sense of possibility with which it opened, Reconstruction failed. But as Du Bois observed, it was a "splendid failure." For its animating vision—a society in which social advancement would be open to all on the basis of individual merit, not inherited caste distinctions—is as old as America itself and remains relevant to a nation still grappling with the unresolved legacy of emancipation.

Eric Foner is Professor of History at Columbia University and author of Nothing but Freedom: Emancipation and Its Legacy.

From *American Heritage*, October/November 1983, pp. 10–15. Reprinted by permission of American Heritage, Inc., a division of Forbes, Inc.

Index

Test Your Knowledge Form

We encourage you to photocopy and use this page as a tool to assess how the articles in *Annual Editions* expand on the information in your textbook. By reflecting on the articles you will gain enhanced text information. You can also access this useful form on a product's book support Web site at *http://www.mhcls.com/online/*.

NAME: _____ DATE: _____

TITLE AND NUMBER OF ARTICLE: _____

BRIEFLY STATE THE MAIN IDEA OF THIS ARTICLE:

LIST THREE IMPORTANT FACTS THAT THE AUTHOR USES TO SUPPORT THE MAIN IDEA:

WHAT INFORMATION OR IDEAS DISCUSSED IN THIS ARTICLE ARE ALSO DISCUSSED IN YOUR TEXTBOOK OR OTHER READINGS THAT YOU HAVE DONE? LIST THE TEXTBOOK CHAPTERS AND PAGE NUMBERS:

LIST ANY EXAMPLES OF BIAS OR FAULTY REASONING THAT YOU FOUND IN THE ARTICLE:

LIST ANY NEW TERMS/CONCEPTS THAT WERE DISCUSSED IN THE ARTICLE, AND WRITE A SHORT DEFINITION:

We Want Your Advice

ANNUAL EDITIONS revisions depend on two major opinion sources: one is our Advisory Board, listed in the front of this volume, which works with us in scanning the thousands of articles published in the public press each year; the other is you—the person actually using the book. Please help us and the users of the next edition by completing the prepaid article rating form on this page and returning it to us. Thank you for your help!

ANNUAL EDITIONS: American History, Volume 1

ARTICLE RATING FORM

Here is an opportunity for you to have direct input into the next revision of this volume.
We would like you to rate each of the articles listed below, using the following scale:

1. **Excellent: should definitely be retained**
2. **Above average: should probably be retained**
3. **Below average: should probably be deleted**
4. **Poor: should definitely be deleted**

Your ratings will play a vital part in the next revision.
Please mail this prepaid form to us as soon as possible.
Thanks for your help!

RATING	ARTICLE	RATING	ARTICLE
	1. America's First Immigrants		19. The Revolution of 1803
	2. 1491		20. Paddle a Mile in Their Canoes
	3. Mystery Tribe		21. African Americans in the Early Republic
	4. Before New England		22. Pirates!
	5. Instruments of Seduction: A Tale of Two Women		23. How American Slavery Led to the Birth of Liberia
	6. Penning a Legacy		24. Andrew Jackson Versus the Cherokee Nation
	7. Blessed and Bedeviled: Tales of Remarkable Providences in Puritan New England		25. Storm Over Mexico
	8. Were American Indians the Victims of Genocide?		26. Free at Last
	9. Flora MacDonald		27. The Volume of History: Listening to 19th Century America
	10. Info Highwayman		28. Richmond's Bread Riot
	11. Midnight Riders		29. Jefferson Davis and the Jews
	12. The Rocky Road to Revolution		30. A Gallant Rush for Glory
	13. Making Sense of the Fourth of July		31. Lincoln as Statesman
	14. Hamilton Takes Command		32. America's Birth at Appomattox
	15. Winter of Discontent		33. Death of John Wilkes Booth
	16. Your Constitution Is Killing You		34. The New View of Reconstruction
	17. The Best of Enemies		
	18. Cliffhanger		

(Continued on next page)

BUSINESS REPLY MAIL
FIRST CLASS MAIL PERMIT NO. 551 DUBUQUE IA

POSTAGE WILL BE PAID BY ADDRESEE

McGraw-Hill Contemporary Learning Series
2460 KERPER BLVD
DUBUQUE, IA 52001-9902

ABOUT YOU

Name   Date
_____

Are you a teacher? ☐   A student? ☐
Your school's name
_____

Department
_____

Address   City   State   Zip
_____

School telephone #
_____

YOUR COMMENTS ARE IMPORTANT TO US!

Please fill in the following information:
For which course did you use this book?
_____

Did you use a text with this ANNUAL EDITION?   ☐ yes ☐ no
What was the title of the text?
_____

What are your general reactions to the *Annual Editions* concept?
_____

Have you read any pertinent articles recently that you think should be included in the next edition? Explain.
_____

Are there any articles that you feel should be replaced in the next edition? Why?
_____

Are there any World Wide Web sites that you feel should be included in the next edition? Please annotate.
_____

May we contact you for editorial input?   ☐ yes ☐ no
May we quote your comments?   ☐ yes ☐ no